THIS TIME
NO
MISTAKES

WILL HUTTON is a British journalist and author. He currently writes a regular column for the *Observer*, is the President of the Academy of Social Sciences, hosts *The We Society* podcast and is Co-Chair of The Purposeful Company. He was formerly Economics Editor of the *Guardian*, Editor-in-Chief of the *Observer* and Principal of Hertford College, Oxford. Hutton's books include the bestselling *The State We're In, How Good We Can Be, The World We're In* and *The Writing on the Wall*.

WILL HUTTON

THIS TIME NO MISTAKES

HOW TO REMAKE BRITAIN

HEAD of ZEUS

An Apollo Book

First published in the United Kingdom in 2024 by Head of Zeus Ltd,
part of Bloomsbury Publishing Plc

9 7 5 3 2 4 6 8

A catalogue record for this book is available from the British Library.

ISBN (HB): 9781804549377
ISBN (E): 9781804549407

Printed and bound in Great Britain by
CPI Group (UK) Ltd, Croydon CR0 4YY

MIX
Paper | Supporting
responsible forestry
FSC® C171272

Head of Zeus Ltd
First Floor East
5–8 Hardwick Street
London EC1R 4RG

WWW.HEADOFZEUS.COM

To my grandchildren

Contents

Preface

This book was born during the summer of 2022. That Britain was suffering acutely from the most incompetent, negligent government in modern times was obvious – but it was the mixture of arrogance, entitlement and moral vacuity with which it was all being done that completed my sense of outrage. The resignation of sixty-one members of Boris Johnson's government in July 2022 over his noxious lie-too-far, his graceless departure, Liz Truss's vacuous campaign to succeed him and then her resignation, induced by the collapse of market confidence in her plainly half-baked economics, forced a decision on me. British conservatism had lost its ethical and intellectual anchorage, and was now embracing the far shores of libertarianism and right-wing populism. Over thirteen years it had led the country into singular economic and social failure, profoundly degrading our public realm in the process; worse could only lie ahead. A tendency begun by Mrs Thatcher in 1979 had transmuted into the grotesque spectacle of a cartoon figure with laughable ideological views, backed by fewer than 100,000 Tory activists, becoming one of our shortest-lived prime ministers – but she was unrepentant and still had support in her party. Writing is a solitary and obsessive business – at least for me – but it was time to summon my energies, brave those challenges and write.

The book I had in mind would of course be angry about why a country with so much potential had been so misgoverned and fallen so far. It would set out proposals to turn matters around. But, reflecting my long-standing view that ideas are central in political and economic affairs, it would foreground the role of good and bad ideas in Britain's unravelling. It would examine the roots of the bad right-wing ideas of the last forty-five years – monetarism, austerity, Brexit, 'light-touch' regulation, shareholder value-maximisation and vast unfunded tax cuts – that should never have been taken seriously, let alone carried out as government policy.

But the book would also have to examine why Britain's liberal left had failed to develop better and more electorally convincing alternatives, and so partly contributed to the disaster by giving the right so much free political and economic space. Britain has a rich progressive tradition, of which a socialism with powerful ethical foundations but often weak policies is only one part. Could not a better synthesis be created out of the varying strands of progressive thought, some of it drawn from the liberal tradition of Hobson, Keynes and Beveridge, to deliver a viable, appealing liberal left philosophy and resulting policy programme for today? I might not pull it off, but a book that could combine these elements would at the very least begin a much-needed process. So here is the result. You, the reader, will judge if it makes any sense.

The State We're In, which I wrote nearly thirty years ago, had similar roots; however, looking back on it, Britain seemed less far-gone than it is now. The country retained great assets, and it was becoming obvious to the majority that Thatcherism was obviously and transparently wrong and that if it was replaced by a better government with better ideas Britain might quickly turn a corner. That book became a bestseller, but too many of its main arguments, despite its success, were largely neglected until the financial crisis of 2008 forced a reappraisal – but by then it was too late.

Hence the title of this book. Until the better angels of the right regain control of their party, it is unfit to govern. Britain's renaissance perforce has to be led by the Labour Party, the only realistic progressive governing party, and it behoves all those on the liberal left and in the centre who are well disposed towards it to help it succeed. It is a national imperative. A new government not only needs a feasible economic and social programme; it needs a broad, progressive intellectual and philosophic base on which such a programme can rest.

So part of this book is about mining ideas within the British progressive tradition – looking abroad where necessary – in search of an alchemy that can attract and hold the majority together and keep the sectarianism to which the left is so susceptible at bay. Writing is, as I've said, a lonely task, but I never felt lonely. I was keeping company with some of the great political minds of the last 250 years – the surprising progressive Adam Smith, the remarkable Robert Owen, whose New Lanark Mill I visited, the great New Liberal thinkers like Thomas Green, Leonard Hobhouse, John Hobson and of course John Maynard Keynes, Richard Tawney, Harold MacMillan (whose Middle Way uncannily prefigured some of my own thinking), the too-little-known Evan Durbin, Hannah Arendt, the passionate Nye Bevan and a few more to whom I will introduce you. And, of course, on the other political wing it was necessary to encounter Ayn Rand, Friedrich Hayek, Milton Friedman, Grover Norquist, Newt Gingrich and William Buckley, who have been so influential on the US right, and thus on our own.

I argue that a British progressive fusion is available – and that it would blend an ethic of socialism with the best of progressive liberalism. Interestingly, the Clause 4 that Tony Blair bequeathed the Labour Party goes nearest to capturing that fusion, and may be his best contribution to progressive politics. But I anticipate what lies ahead.

This is a book, then, of political economy in the tradition of writers on whose shoulders I stand. From a marriage of ethical socialism and progressive liberalism – the 'We' and the 'I' – I try to develop a progressive economic, social and political programme that has a place both for individual agency, just deserts, personal ambition and responsibility married to the demands of fellowship, solidarity, fairness and mutuality – and point to some of the policies and institutions that should result from such a combination. Fellowship and individual agency are not exclusive concepts, but interdependent. I hope I persuade you; if not something like this, then what?

1

ON THE EDGE

This is a book about a society and an economy in crisis, and how they can be changed for the better. It is also a book about capitalism and democracy, and how the degraded forms they have taken in one European country have diminished the lives of its citizens. There is a way out of this. Nothing is immutable.

The sweet spot for any prosperous, well-run economy and society is the marriage of capitalist dynamism – which can deliver jobs, innovation and prosperity – with social cohesion, freedom and tolerance. But capitalism is neither stable nor fair; it has exuberant booms and terrible busts; it has no innate propensity to moderation; it causes inequality and gross imbalances of power and wealth; it seeks profit in the soft option of monopoly. Chance and undeserved good and bad luck are everywhere in the system. Capitalism's excuse is its vibrancy, its ability to innovate, to offer individuals agency and the chance to prosper, and in so doing to be the sponsor of growth and rising living standards. By these criteria no system has yet surpassed it. But to deliver on its promise capitalism needs constant vigilance, umpires and guiderails.

Some capitalist risk needs to be shared with public institutions. Social risk has to be underwritten by a powerful social contract to protect against individuals and their families not being able to meet basic human needs. The gains from productivity-enhancing innovation must be widely shared or else a pall of injustice will settle over society. Capitalism's rollercoaster rhythms need to be managed and counteracted, and its tendency to monopoly and racketeering constantly challenged. Nor can capitalism be relied upon by itself to organise best how firms are governed and ownership responsibilities discharged; to organise how workers are best trained and paid; or to ensure that fair dealing is the norm between firms and their customers.

We live on a tightrope – too much surrender to capitalism and society is harmed; too much constraint on capitalism and it cannot do its work. Creative public philosophies are needed to achieve the right balance. It is the job of vibrant democratic institutions to throw up the right philosophy that can inform the right public response to economic instability. Capitalism needs democracy – and a pluralist, vibrant democracy can grow out of capitalism. How well that democracy and state function is of paramount importance.

Britain today cannot be described as hitting any of these sweet spots. The country has its back against the wall to a degree unparalleled in its peacetime history. The dank mist of failure has penetrated virtually every fibre of our national life. And there is no easy way out. Our economy is seriously underperforming, and even the mighty City of London is struggling. Our society is fractured, ill at ease with itself and disfigured by enormous gaps between rich and poor. Our public services – from the NHS to the courts – are starved of resources and impose on our people avoidable illness, needless anxiety and too often unconscionable delays. They fail to deliver.

That failure is matched in the sphere of politics. The barrel was scraped, it was possible to imagine, when Prime Minister Boris Johnson was ignominiously forced out of office with an unprecedented twenty-eight ministers and twenty-five personal private secretaries resigning over his false claim that he did not know about the errant sexual behaviour of his deputy chief whip.* This was merely the last straw after months of similar lies and evasions. A second low was reached by the forty-nine-day prime ministership of Liz Truss, who went on a libertarian, unfunded tax-cutting crusade, only to succeed in losing the confidence of both the financial markets and a majority of her MPs. She too was

---

* In addition, five prime ministerial envoys and three vice/deputy-chairs resigned, while Michael Gove was sacked – bringing the entire tally to 62.

forced to resign in disgrace, the author of a 'moron' premium on British government debt. Even more dismal and shameful records were set later in 2023, when Boris Johnson was found guilty by a committee of his peers for lying to Parliament over drunken parties that had taken place under his nose at 10 Downing Street, while the rest of the population was living under strict lockdown during the Covid pandemic. He resigned as an MP rather than suffer the humiliation of being expelled for a period from the House of Commons. In the space of a few months, the British state and its Parliament were exposed not as exemplars of good government and democracy but as test cases in how institutions can be abused and captured by the populist, the hyper-ideological fanatic and the serial liar.

Britain has faced other peacetime crises – notably the currency panics of 1931, 1949, 1976 and 1992 – but what is happening today is qualitatively more threatening. In the past the country could fight its way out of its economic crises by belt-tightening and by devaluing the pound within a structure of secure trading relationships, anchored by the empire and later the European Union. Our international assets far exceeded our liabilities. Our national debt was well structured and built on long-term bonds whose servicing requirements were manageable. We retained great industrial strengths. We were fundamentally credit-worthy. Even when the financial crisis broke in 2007 the low level of national debt meant that the country could bail out its dissolute banks.

None of that is true today. The UK has been living beyond its means in every area. We are no longer a creditor nation. We depend on the kindness of strangers, in the famous words of former Bank of England Governor Mark Carney, to support our currency. Our liabilities to foreigners exceed our assets by 30 per cent of GDP and that figure is growing. Our fading industrial base produces permanent current account deficits; since 2000, they cumulatively exceed £1.5 trillion. Rather than tighten our belts, we have run up debt and sold vast quantities of our assets to foreigners in order to maintain our living standards.[1] We no longer have the empire or the EU anchoring our trade. We are alone.

Our national debt has trebled in twenty years – its fastest

growth since the war – to over 100 per cent of GDP. A few other countries carry even more national debt, but ours has become very vulnerable to rising interest rates and inflation because a quarter of it is held in inflation-linked bonds. Debt service now occupies nearly 10 per cent of all tax revenues, the highest in the G7. If a second financial crisis as significant as that of 2007/8 occurred, we could not put the public balance sheet behind our banking system without expecting a run on the pound.

We have in the past had major constitutional, foreign policy and industrial relations crises in peacetime. The monarch abdicated in 1936, an invasion twenty years later to seize the Suez canal ended in abject failure, there was a general strike in 1926 and what became known as the 'Winter of Discontent' brought chaos in 1978–9; however, all these storms were weathered and the caravan moved on. George VI succeeded Edward VIII with the constitutional monarchy intact; Suez may have marked the end of Britain's ability to act autonomously as a great power, but we remained a Permanent Member of the UN Security Council; however excessive trade union power may have seemed at the time, both the Winter of Discontent and the earlier general strike marked fever peaks rather than revolutionary challenges to the economic and social order.

What Britain now confronts is something much more profound and deep-rooted, and its resolution demands much more extensive economic, social and political reform than the national conversation currently admits. We have dropped so far down the international league tables of productivity, real incomes and wealth that we can no longer consider ourselves a rich country. Our productivity is wretched. Our average incomes per head are lower than most other Western nations. In fact, if you strip out super-rich London, the poverty in the rest of the country is even more marked. The *Financial Times*' John Burn-Murdoch has calculated that excluding the richest city in calculations of average income in a variety of rich countries has a more dramatic impact in Britain than in the Netherlands, Germany or the USA. London is so disproportionately rich that if it is not included in the figures, the average income per head in the rest of the UK falls below that of the poorest US state, Mississippi.[2]

For those at the bottom of our society, these low incomes translate into near destitution. Two million people report that they go without food for at least a day a month. Our five-year-olds are among the shortest in Europe.* One in three children live in poverty. The distress goes far up the income scale. The National Institute of Economic and Social Research forecasts that between 2019 and 2024, household incomes for those in the entire lower half of the population will have fallen by 17 per cent.[3]

It is time to stop talking and thinking of Britain as a rich and broadly fair country. We are poor, our society is deeply unfair and we are living on the edge.

The campaign to leave the EU in 2016 presented an easy solution to our problems, and those suffering economic and social distress were ready to hear that message. The austerity policies of 2010–16 had accentuated Britain's inequalities. The status quo did not seem worth preserving. But after forty-seven years of membership, leaving the EU was never going to be easy; the economic, social, political and cultural ties ran deep. The EU had conferred strong advantages on Britain, as the country beyond those who voted Remain is now discovering. If we were to make a success of leaving, it required sensitivity, respect for those who had wanted to stay and careful preservation of what worked in the interests of both the UK and EU. That did not happen. The

---

* In 1985 British boys and girls ranked 69 out of 200 countries for average height aged five. At the time they were on average 111.4cm and 111cm tall respectively. British boys are now 102nd, and girls 96th, according to data collated by the Non-Communicable Diseases Risk Factor Collaboration and reported in June 2023. It finds that British five year olds are on average up to 7cm shorter than other wealthy European countries. An exploration of the regional effects in short stature in England between 2006 and 2019 published by the National Library of Medicine in September 2021 reports that height differences were most closely associated with areas of deprivation – the more deprived the area the greater the height difference. Although other factors may be in play, the increasingly poor diets of five year olds are widely agreed to be the most important cause of their reduced height.

Brexiters gave no quarter and insisted that they and only they had the right to interpret what the vote for Brexit meant. Prime Minister Johnson, who had won the referendum promising only sunlit uplands and no sloughs of despond, negotiated the most radical severance possible in the name of British sovereignty. He made all Tory parliamentary candidates give a commitment to his form of Brexit for the 2019 election, and afterwards he and his government signalled their readiness to abrogate the treaty commitments they themselves had signed that Northern Ireland should stay in the EU customs union and single market. This was essential to preserve the Good Friday Agreement and avoid the very damaging reintroduction of a hard, controlled border between the two parts of Ireland.

Law for Johnson was always contingent on circumstances. This perfidy added to the poison in British public life, and lost the trust of our friends and allies. It fell to his successor Rishi Sunak to retreat and sign the Windsor accords that respected both Brexit and the terms of the Good Friday Agreement – but not to relinquish a euroscepticism that presumes everything 'European' should be opposed on principle.

The Tory Party and its army of media cheerleaders are rightly despondent about the whole baleful picture; they have been in power for fourteen years and this is the result. Part of the attraction of first Brexit and then the Liz Truss pitch for the Tory leadership was that they seemed to offer a fast route out of trouble that remained true to the Thatcherite faith. *The Daily Telegraph* columnist Allister Heath swooning over Truss ally Kwasi Kwarteng's budget as 'the best I have ever heard a Chancellor deliver' was not only displaying epic bad judgement and a commitment to ideological economics; it reflected his and many of the other faithful's desire to break out of what Chancellor Jeremy Hunt acknowledges is a 'low-growth trap'.

At least Hunt genuflects towards the truth, even if he is unable to acknowledge its causes. The refusal to accept that Brexit has failed, with a plethora of damaging costs and virtually no benefits, the blame-shifting and the invective, the misdirected insistence that the solution is to double down on what we know has failed

– the cocktail of tax cuts, efforts to shrink the state, deregulation – gives contemporary British discourse a particular vindictiveness. A once-tolerant and easy-going public culture is disappearing.

On the great challenges of our lifetimes – the environment, managing the rise of awesome new technologies, the need for higher taxation as our population ages, the urgent requirement to narrow inequality, recognition that some form of reassociation with the EU is a national necessity – there is merely point-scoring and a lack of honesty. Those who might frame answers are in retreat, their values mocked and under assault. It is the right-wing zealots that frame our national conversation. This clinging to myths stifles the debate we need. We have to recognise that Britain in 2024 has as much in common with a middle-income developing economy as with other developed countries.

What we need is a readiness to make common cause. This is what characterises truly successful economic development. And we need a strong social contract to support such development. The public philosophy that will help achieve these reforms will necessitate a repudiation of the faith in individualism alone that has been the hallmark of the Conservative years – that what matters is tax cuts, deregulation, a minimal social safety net and, above all, self-reliance and the pursuit of self-interest. Deifying the unfettered 'I', the selfish first-person singular, has been at the centre of ideas and policy, and it has had disastrous consequences. Objectives like lowering dependence on fossil fuels, reducing grievous regional inequalities or ensuring that everyone has access to the essentials of life can easily be side-lined if they threaten the primacy of individual choice.

Instead, Britain must revive the solidarities of the 'We', the first-person plural of fellowship, solidarity and concern for others. This not only recognises that economic strength has social foundations, but that the quality of a country's private and public institutions are central to the creation of the different capitals – from human capital to innovative investment capital – that drive an economy and society forward. Britain needs to create a new fusion of the 'We' and the 'I'. All societies should celebrate individual agency as an essential freedom, but agency is different from placing the pursuit of individual self-interest at the centre of our moral universe.

The great task is to bring Britain's social liberal tradition together with its social democratic, reformist Labour tradition, as Attlee did so effectively in the government he led between 1945 and 1951. On this foundation, Britain could successfully relaunch itself to become Europe's best-regarded economic and social model – and in the process take its place again in the front rank of European nations. We owe it to ourselves to bring this off, but also to Europe and the world. In the battle of economic, social and political models, Britain can be a winner and an exemplar. It is a far cry from where we are now.

A Perfect Storm of Policy Mistakes

Our economic distress is symbolised first and foremost by our negligible growth in productivity, and in the very low growth of capital per worker which in turn has meant that real wages – that is, wages adjusted for inflation – have not risen since 2008. In no fifteen-year period since the Industrial Revolution has this trio of indicators been so weak. This reality could hardly be more serious or damaging. In the 700 years until the middle of the eighteenth century most peoples' living standards hardly rose. The life of an early-eighteenth-century rural villager was not greatly different to that of their eleventh-century counterpart – clothes, levels of nutrition, modes of transport, housing, yield from the fields were all broadly similar. Around the middle of the eighteenth century, first an agricultural and then an industrial revolution transformed society; science, cross-fertilisation and crop rotation in newly enclosed fields began to improve strains of seed and yields alike, prompting an agricultural revolution, and then science and specialisation did the same for industry. The cleverer the process and smarter the machine, the more workers could produce – slowly at first, but gradually the pace accelerated over the nineteenth century.

The process has continued. Pay and living standards have

increased more than fifteen-fold since 1750 largely due to productivity growth as workers have more and smarter machines at their disposal. British labour productivity was overtaken in the twentieth century by the Americans and Europeans, but in the twelve years up to the 2007 financial crisis the UK's productivity did grow at roughly the same 2 per cent as other advanced countries. But over the twelve years since the crisis, the UK's has fared much worse. UK productivity grew by only 0.4 per cent per year, less than half the 0.9 per cent achieved by the rest of the pack.[4]

A lot of Western businesses after the 2007/8 financial crisis found they had over-borrowed in the expectation that growth would continue, holding assets that had fallen in value as the weakened financial system pulled in its horns. The financial system could no longer stimulate growth by over-plentiful credit, thus forcing over-indebted Western business to stabilise its collective balance sheet by cutting back investment and focusing on paying back its debts – 'deleveraging', in the jargon.

Influential Japanese economist Professor Richard Koo explained that the rest of the world was now experiencing the recession induced by overstretched balance sheets that Japan had endured during the 1990s and early 2000s.[5] Western governments should have compensated for such a private-sector 'balance sheet recession', he has argued consistently, by expanding their public balance sheets – boosting demand by lowering taxes or increasing public spending. But they did not do this. They were wary of assuming more public debt, given the fragility of their banking systems and the extent to which they had underwritten them; better to keep their fiscal powder dry until a stronger banking system was created in case there were further financial shocks.

As an alternative that was second best, governments required their central banks to print money to flood their financial systems with cash, both to encourage them to resume lending and to stave off any further liquidity crisis. At the same time companies were reluctant to lose workers as well as capital investment in case demand returned. Workforces are an increasing source of competitive advantage in economies where knowledge, both formal and informal, is of growing importance. Too little capital plus swollen workforces produced a fall in productivity growth. The collapse in productivity growth, if you like, is a hangover from which all of us suffered after the bankers had indulged in an inebriated binge.

But if this was a trend apparent in many of the developed economies, it was most acute in the UK, made worse by a series of ideologically driven policy mistakes and a continuing failure to address fundamental structural economic weaknesses. Although productivity growth matched other Western countries in the run-up to the financial crisis, British growth and investment had been uniquely dependent on reckless credit growth, an unsustainable asset price boom and the British financial system towering over the rest of the economy like a malignant triffid. When the crisis broke in 2007, British bank assets were nearly five times British GDP, relatively higher than in any other country.[6] One bank alone, Royal Bank of Scotland (RBS), had assets exceeding British GDP and only survived the combination of a run on its deposits and write-downs of its assets by being taken into public ownership. The balance sheet recession in the UK would inevitably be more acute as bank lending froze and companies paid back as much debt as possible – deleveraging. The government should have moved only slowly and carefully to lower the large budget deficit – some 11 per cent of GDP – that had emerged, given a recession deeper than that of 1930–2.

That did not happen. The financial crisis and the menace a broken banking system presented to British capitalism, and the immediate deep recession it spawned, should have provoked a fundamental rethink of the neoliberal policies of the previous thirty years. The free-market dogma of dismantling regulation and leaving the bankers to their own devices, on the grounds that private business in free markets never made mistakes, had given the financial system too much licence. The financiers abused their freedoms, inventing financial instruments that allegedly guarded against risk while lending extravagantly with too little capital to support the heightened risks.

The scale of personal reward for banking executives, with bonuses linked to profits and share prices, reached new heights of decadent opulence – unlinked to any real-world merit before the crisis and palpably undeserved after it. Yet almost no one was held to account and the bonuses continued to be paid. Rather than rethink the whole economic paradigm, the Tory leadership opted to blame extravagant Labour public spending as the main cause of the crisis, doubling down on Thatcherite deregulation and 'sound money' as the right way forward. New Labour had also indulged the City, continuing the 'light-touch' regulation it had inherited from the Conservatives up to the crisis and contemplating only minor reforms afterwards. Critique and proposals for structural change were not seriously entertained by either of the two main political parties.

There were two inter-related consequences. After narrowly winning the 2010 general election, the Tory-led coalition government launched a savage programme of austerity, with the aim of balancing the books and securing a fall in the national debt by the end of the Parliament in 2015. The threat of a recession that the state should offset was simply ignored; it did not fit Chancellor George Osborne's ideological assumptions, nor his political agenda of shrinking the state to please the Thatcherite right, and to create a wedge issue with Labour. It is true that under pressure from the Liberal Democrats in coalition, commercial and investment banking would be required in future to operate as separate entities to insulate commercial, day-to-day banking from losses incurred in high-risk investment banking (so-called ring-fencing) – but that slow-burn reform was quickly relegated to a side show. There were to be no serious inquests into the causes and impact of the financial crisis, and no effort was made to hold bank boards and leading executives to account.

Instead, the economic focus was entirely on austerity, with swingeing cuts in public spending, halving some departmental budgets in real terms over the decade, while cutting capital investment by a third. As business deleveraged, the overall effect was to stifle what economic recovery there was, and certainly the 'animal spirits' that enliven a capitalist economy, already dimmed by the seizing-up of credit after the financial crisis, were further smothered. The quest for the small state and the reliance on laissez-faire to resuscitate British capitalism turned out to be the pursuit of a mirage. Growth stubbornly refused to fulfil forecasts, as did tax revenues, and by 2015 the deficit was still 4 per cent of GDP. The economic impasse had a disastrous impact on British society.

It was also a lost opportunity. What was really needed was a reassertion of the values of solidarity, fellowship and the wider public good. Financial and corporate governance reform, industrial policy and moves to lower inequality should have been put centre stage. By carrying on as if nothing had happened, with bankers' pay hardly dented, the public discovered that not only did the elite not know what they were doing, but that they faced no consequences when it all blew up. The scene was set for the rise of populism, the distrust of experts and the rise of anti-system parties and personalities like Boris Johnson and Nigel Farage. British democracy's weak guardrails were exposed. An unwritten constitution conferring an exceptional degree of executive power implicitly depends on a sense of fair play and the acceptance of unwritten rules of the game to work effectively. Johnson, when he came to power, showed that he possessed neither attribute. And part and parcel of this attitude has been a lack of honesty about costs and trade-offs – taking refuge in belief and faith rather than reason. The scene was set for Brexit.

The election of 2015, conferring a Commons majority on a Conservative Party in thrall to ideology and with no viable economic policy, took bad policy a decisive step further. Membership of the European Union had been an unsung source of growth since the mid-1980s, even though no front-rank politician dared risk the opprobrium of the right-wing press by saying so openly. Joining the single market in 1986 was the most important of the measures taken by Mrs Thatcher to promote increased competition and trade. Together with a surge of inward investment to take advantage of exporting from low-tax Britain, the country's national output was lifted more than it would otherwise have grown over the two decades up to the financial crisis.[7] But that cut no ice with the dominant faction in contemporary Conservatism.

Mrs Thatcher's legend was invoked to support the wilder claims of anti-expert, anti-immigrant, take-back-control populism, succoured by the still-forceful jingoist belief that Britain was and is exceptional and should go it alone. This is nineteenth-century 'splendid isolation' in contemporary guise, only without an empire, a vast fleet or industrial pre-eminence. Yet the groundswell grew, skilfully captured by Nigel Farage's anti-immigrant UKIP. Terrified of being outflanked on the right, Prime Minister David Cameron conceded the case for an EU referendum in 2016.

The Leave vote's narrow majority in the 2016 Brexit referendum was driven by Britain's economically, socially and culturally marginalised citizens, rejecting in their millions the prevailing status quo. Every deprived town or region, their plight made worse by austerity, voted for Brexit. But the activists and politicians behind the Leave campaign, good as they were at harnessing protest, had never decided positively what Brexit really means. The version that Boris Johnson negotiated, after three years of bitter parliamentary and intra-party wrangling, made no effort to preserve our vital trade in services and knowledge goods with the EU. An idea – a fantasy, really, of absolute national sovereignty – trumped the needs of the economy.

Northern Ireland, which remains in the EU customs union, the EU single market and the UK single market, is now the UK's top-performing region outside London. Had the rest of the UK grown similarly, aggregate output would have been £100 billion higher – with £35 billion of much-needed tax receipts.[8]

Business, with such uncertain demand prospects, has gone on an investment strike, trapping the economy in a vicious circle, made even worse by Brexit. The choking-off of trade with the EU meant that exports to the EU were still 9 per cent below pre-pandemic levels in 2022, with a parallel decline in inward investment. Brexit alone has induced a fall in investment of between 9 and 11 per cent, on one estimate.

The London Stock Exchange, third in the world in 2000 based on the aggregate value of shares traded, ranked tenth in 2022. UK car production in 2016 stood at 1.75 million; by 2022, it had fallen to 775,000. The UK ranks twenty-fourth in the world in the use of robots, the only G7 economy outside the top twenty. Britain's robot stock is 10 per cent that of Germany's.[9] And only 4 per cent of the value of the London Stock Exchange is represented by tech companies.

The Balance Sheet Today

There is no serious effort at addressing the issues, and certainly no industrial strategy. One such strategy was launched by Prime Minister Theresa May, then abandoned under Boris Johnson, and then resurrected by Chancellor Jeremy Hunt – but it is not a strategy at all. Economic policy is focused on deficit and inflation reduction, trusting in the market to deliver, aided and abetted with ad hoc subsidies for particular projects – a battery factory here, help for semi-conductors there – but with no consistency. Typical of the numerous random lurches was the lowering of corporation tax, from 28 per cent in 2010 to 19 per cent in 2017, only to discover that the reduction had no impact on investment, and then putting it back up to 25 per cent. A Green Bank was initiated, developed and sold off, and then an Infrastructure Bank was created to fill the gap. Policy is made up on the hoof, with one depressing certainty: friends of the Conservative Party will be first in line for handouts and grants.

A duty of care to the *governed* is entirely lacking, sometimes resulting in not just outrageous indifference and neglect, but actual loss of life. Trivial savings on cladding in the construction of London's Grenfell Tower, exploiting weak building regulations, led to Britain's biggest residential fire since the Second World War and killed seventy-two people. On current estimates, remedial spending on one tower block alone has already exceeded £1.2 billion – enough to build 10,000 social houses.[10] A parallel abdication of duty of care, albeit with origins preceding 2010 but intensifying over the period of Conservative government, was evident in the false prosecution of some 900 sub-postmasters for theft and then foot-dragging over compensation – an injustice that scandalised the nation in the first weeks of 2024. Meanwhile, one in ten workers are in insecure employment, and enforcement of even the UK's lax employment laws is feeble.

Yet the lens through which all these issues have been framed is heavily skewed to the right. Our print media on the political right – the Murdoch press from *The Sun to The Times*, the Harmsworth empire of the *Daily Mail* and *The Mail on Sunday*, *The Telegraph* – decided decades ago that its mission was to be an unrelenting propagandist rather than a source of unslanted reporting and fair argument. Take, for example, the 2023 Immigration Act which, limiting asylum seekers to those arriving by a government-approved channel, effectively killed off asylum-seeking, however legitimate or humane. The House of Commons Library finds that the UK is ranked sixteenth among European countries for asylum seekers per head of population, and that asylum seekers eke out miserable lives pending a ruling on their application.[11] Britain, in other words, takes very few asylum applicants compared to Germany, France or other countries. Yet the right-wing media ecosystem portrays Britain as being swamped by illicit immigration. Similarly, a proposal to abolish inheritance tax is billed as promoting aspiration – despite the overwhelming body of evidence that it will further entrench the inequality created by inherited wealth.

Our unwritten constitution, in the face of all this, has never looked so threadbare. The 2019–24 Parliament will enter the record books not only for the extraordinary turnover of prime ministers, chancellors and cabinet ministers, but for the record number of ninety-seven MPs from all parties who resigned, were suspended or apologised to Parliament over sexual misconduct, ethical lapses or bullying and harassment charges – fifty-eight of them Conservative. No other organisation could survive nearly 15 per cent of its members falling below acceptable standards of behaviour without major questions over whether it remained fit for purpose, and significant proposals for reform.[12] Yet little or nothing is proposed to remedy the situation. Two prime ministerial ethics advisers – Sir Alex Allan and Lord Geidt – resigned over Boris Johnson's failures to act on their advice. He appointed at least one peer – Peter Cruddas – by overriding the advice of the

House of Lords Appointments Commission, and another, Michael Spencer, who had been refused at least three times. The going rate to buy a Tory peerage, reports *The Sunday Times*, is £3 million.

This moral decline has been in the making for decades. It is true that until 2010 the wider system stayed afloat. It functioned well enough to deliver reasonable public services, the social contract was just about intact and the economy grew, however flawed the roots of growth. Constitutional checks, balances and proprieties worked after a fashion. But underneath the surface the structural weaknesses in the economy, the social contract and the constitution were intensifying. Events today force us to look them in the eye.

Geopolitics Makes the World More Threatening

All this would have been serious enough at any time. But the world is moving into an era of exceptional turbulence, when such weaknesses will have more profound consequences. There are new threats – environmental, technological and geopolitical – against which Britain must guard and to which, as matters stand, the country is cruelly exposed.

It is clear that the thirty-year-long 'age of markets' – of neoliberalism and globalisation – that took off after the Cold War has come to an end. The advocates for Brexit assumed that this world would continue, and an 'independent' Britain outside the EU could manoeuvre in it more adroitly. Instead, that world is disappearing. The USA is no longer an undisputed global hegemon, and in any case it no longer believes that globalisation as practised over the last thirty years serves its best interests. President Joe Biden has shifted radically away from the neoliberal policies of his recent Democrat predecessors in a way that is analogous to Franklin Roosevelt's New Deal in the 1930s. The USA is spending many trillions of dollars on infrastructure, research and development and supporting hi-tech strategic industries like semi-conductors and green technologies on a scale not seen since the Second World War. There is an overt bias towards supporting manufacturing in the USA. Supply chains are to be 'on-shored' in an effort to recapture industries that have moved overseas. No longer will there be a blanket disposition in favour of free trade; instead, trade deals with friendly EU and Pacific countries will be carefully structured and US industrial interests protected. The priority is no longer tax cuts and business deregulation. Reindustrialisation serves the twin aims of creating middle-class jobs and advancing US security interests. The aim is less to confront China than to become less dependent on it.[13]

China, for its part, is feeling its way to a new geopolitical order, which in its view more fairly represents its new global standing. President Xi's move to abolish term limits for Chinese presidents, ratified by the Party Congress in March 2023, gives him an unprecedented third five-year term in office and signals that the country is reverting formally into dictatorship. There will be a fourth term, until finally there will be a vicious succession battle as he ages. In the meantime, Xi has made it clear that he regards the current world order as asymmetrically biased towards the USA, and he has launched a new programme of ultra-patriotism, promoting 'Xi Jinping' thought, enforced by rigorous social control. In reintegrating Hong Kong into the mainland's political system – the end of the much-vaunted 'one country, two systems' promised when Britain withdrew from the territory – Xi has signalled that the same fate awaits Taiwan. China's growth is levelling off, as the model that served it until now – a Leninist capitalism in which a state-controlled banking system finances vast and increasingly uneconomic job-creating infrastructure projects – is delivering fewer and fewer returns. In its wake, there is a spectacular military build-up, and an aggressive patriotism. Nobody can say whether the USA and China can manage peaceful coexistence, or what the US response would be if China were to invade Taiwan. What is there for all to see is a combination of growing tension and toxic interdependence; China holds over $3 trillion of foreign exchange reserves, but in 2021 it exported some $540 billion to the USA, with a trade surplus of $383 billion.

The globalising, peaceful world presupposed by the Brexiters, in which a 'global Britain' would strike favourable trade deals with the two superpowers, deals unavailable to the EU, looks not only absurd but dangerous. There is no prospect of a trade deal with either of them, nor, given the tough, one-sided bargain they would seek, is such a deal very desirable. Instead, the new world is multipolar with three playmaker blocs – the USA, China and the EU. Britain is now outside all three. The notion that Britain will be a global standards-setter in such a context is risible. We have been turned into a rule-taker. The great blocs will create and follow their own standards – whether in finance, artificial intelligence (AI) or in the new transversal technologies that bridge AI and life sciences. If we are correctly wary of China's long-run intentions, and if America First mercantilism continues, the only realistic option is aligning ourselves with the EU.

Here, too, the outlook is changing fast. Russia's invasion of Ukraine, starting a major war in Europe for the first time since 1945, together with the risk that a Republican US president might withdraw the USA from NATO, further dramatises a reality that did not exist on referendum day, 23 June 2016. For the UK to be outside the system of EU ministerial meetings where security is discussed and sanctions decided and enforced is self-defeating. Ukraine's admission to or even association with the EU will not be easy; the size of Ukraine's agricultural sector alone will pose huge challenges to the Common Agricultural Policy. Yet Britain will be a bystander in future negotiations as the geopolitics and security of Europe is decided. Churchill, Disraeli and Gladstone would have all agreed that at such a dangerous juncture, Britain should be inside the Congress of Europe – in effect what today's EU represents. The barbarous attacks by Hamas in Israel in October 2023, murdering some 1,200 civilians, and the scale of Israel's response, which threatens the stability of the Middle East because there is no obvious durable peace settlement in sight, only underlines the geopolitical reality. Britain has no essential foreign policy interests that are different from the rest of Europe; we are menaced by the same threats and our best response is to be part of a powerful collective – not voices off struggling to make ourselves heard.

Yet the political complexion of the EU is also changing; its liberal character is under profound threat, in a way that is intensely against our interests. Before he invaded Ukraine, Russia's Vladimir Putin was not the pariah he is now, even in right-wing circles. His brand of ultranationalism and his disdain for all aspects of Western liberalism endeared him to a resurgent European far right – and to Donald Trump. France's xenophobic nationalist leader Marine Le Pen openly admired him, as did Italy's neofascist leader, now prime minister, Giorgia Meloni.

Putin's exposure as a neofascist dictator has made these politicians beat a retreat. Meloni has supported Ukraine, NATO, the EU and sanctions against Russia. Both she and Marine Le Pen recognise that their electorates will not vote for overt fascism or indulge Putin's invasion. Yet this is only a tactical retreat. Across the EU, liberals and the left are falling back before parties that celebrate the primacy of family and faith, oppose same-sex marriage, want a crackdown on immigration and multiculturalism, do not believe in climate change and, above all, believe that their nation is more special than any other. Culture wars have come to Europe. There are parties in almost every country in Europe who repeat the same refrain and are climbing in the polls, and they are either taking part in national or regional government (Finland, Denmark, Austria, Sweden, Italy, Hungary) or soon could be (Germany, France, the Netherlands). Holding the line is possible – witness national election results in Spain and Poland in 2023, where the extreme right suffered setbacks – but the pressures incubating it remain. Mr Putin looks on smugly.

More ominously, if they could lift the constraints, Europe's varying ultra-right parties would follow the lead of Hungary's Viktor Orbán (a self-declared ally of Putin) and reinvent their democracy, eliminating an independent judiciary and a free press. But as witnesses to what has happened to the UK after Brexit, none of these parties argue for leaving the EU – its cash and the trade links it offers are too important. Their strategy instead is to change the EU from within, to accommodate their attacks on the basic pillars of a liberal democratic order. Sixteen right-wing EU parties came together to sign a joint declaration in July 2021, echoing the old refrain of UKIP and the Tory right, objecting to Europe becoming a super-state and arguing that it should instead be a confederation of 'homelands'. In particular, they declared the following:

> European nations should be based on tradition, respect for the culture and history of European states, respect for Europe's Judeo-Christian heritage and the common values that unite our nations.
> We reaffirm our belief that family is the basic unit of our nations. In a time when Europe is facing a serious demographic crisis with low birth rates and ageing population, pro-family policy making should be an answer instead of mass immigration.[14]

In Brexitland, 'Global Britain' is indifferent to what is happening in Europe; what matters is the Americas, Africa and Asia, not developments in our own back yard. But the political currents in Europe cannot be a matter of indifference to the UK. A battle for European liberal democracy and values has begun – for the separation of powers, freedom of the press, rule of law, an independent judiciary, respect for human rights and a rules-based international order. The American Republican Party has rediscovered its historic attachment to isolationism, as the strength of support for Trump's presidential candidacy is witness; leading Republican senators and congressmen want to wind down support for Ukraine. Nor are they any more keen on liberal democracy than the European right. If we want to resist the rise of fascist despots worldwide, we have to live our values, and show that liberal democracy works. The European Commission tries to enforce the view embodied in the EU founding treaties, but when the governments of the two principal states – France and Germany – risk falling into the hands of the neofascist right, the stench of retreat is in the air. Britain should have been in the EU, building alliances and holding the line. It is not only our economy that is under siege. The EU with Britain has a better chance than an EU without Britain.

Economic and Societal Threats

There are other perils. The world needs rules on the use of artificial intelligence (AI) and the way it will jump across scientific and technological boundaries. Already its potential power for good – radically improving education, mapping the human body and enhancing wider human capacities – and for bad – developing an ability to be super-intelligent that could threaten civilisation – are evident. Ian Hogarth, tech investor and chair of the UK government's newly created AI task force, recently warned against the commercial race towards artificial generative intelligence (AGI) or, as he calls it, 'God-like AI'.[15] This new generation of AI will be able to think autonomously in ways computer scientists barely understand; it could, independent of human surveillance, develop viruses or weapons that bring life on earth to an end. There are understandable calls to pause research pending better understanding of the risks. Again, only three global blocs have the power, resources and enforcement capacity to organise the necessary regulation. Britain is not a member of any of them.

If AGI threatens our civilisation, so does global warming, which menaces our planet 'and looms over our future like a Colossus', in the words of William Nordhaus, co-recipient of the 2018 Nobel Prize in Economic Sciences. Even optimistic projections show global emissions continuing to rise over the next decade before falling only gradually. CO_2 remains in the atmosphere for centuries, so even with reduced emissions today, the atmospheric CO_2 concentration will continue to rise. The hope of containing the temperature rise to 1.5°C above pre-industrial levels by emissions peaking in 2025 looks increasingly forlorn. July 2023 was officially the hottest month ever recorded, surpassing the previous record, set in 2019, by 0.3°C, while global warming is supercharging weather events such as wildfires and floods. The planet is fast approaching a number of 'tipping points', threatening a global cascade of irreversible harm. Scientists warn that the ocean circulation in the North Atlantic could change radically, that the Amazon rainforest could shrink beyond recall and that large parts of the Antarctic ice cap could melt.

The socioeconomic costs of climate change are potentially vast. The World Economic Forum estimates that approximately half of global GDP ($44 trillion) is moderately or highly dependent on nature and is therefore exposed to nature loss.[16] Faced with this threat, and the enormous costs of mitigation, international collaboration on a scale never seen before is needed. It will be the big blocs that negotiate with each other and have the necessary leverage to enforce compliance with treaties. Britain has relegated itself to the second tier.

There will be more pandemics after Covid. Viruses do not acknowledge borders. Although true believers like to claim that Brexit freedoms allowed a speedier response to Covid than in the EU, excess mortality in the UK during the pandemic in fact exceeded that of most comparable Western European countries. The UK had the highest excess mortality rate among people under sixty-five in Western European countries such as France, Belgium and Sweden. Only Eastern European countries, with weaker health systems, had higher death tolls.[17] Rather than losing, Britain would have benefited from joint-buying of vaccines, preventive equipment and all the cross-learning that comes with being in a community of twenty-eight nations. In the EU we would have had the option of opting out of joint vaccine procurement had we chosen to do so. Splendid isolation is not so splendid in the twenty-first century.

The same holds for energy and raw material security. The big blocs can buy and invest in bulk, and they are best able to secure cheap long-term deals with producers – of cereals, of liquified natural gas, of hydroelectric and wind power, of lithium – in a world where suppliers are prepared to leverage their position for political advantage. Where Russia has led, using oil and gas to extort political favours, Iran and Saudi Arabia will surely follow – at least until the West has adequate alternative supplies of renewable energy. Following the Russian suspension of oil and gas supplies in the early months of the Ukraine war, the new geopolitical realities were brutally exposed as the USA and EU scrambled to look after themselves. The USA, for example, required all US refineries exporting petrol, diesel and distillates to build up their reserves first rather than honouring export contracts.

Little Britain by itself suddenly felt very exposed – with even supplementary electricity supplies through the European interconnector system potentially threatened. A neurotically anti-EU British government had devised a bureaucratic and expensive auction system, instead of the previous automatic supply through the interconnectors, raising the price of electricity and making Britain vulnerable to European suppliers simply turning off the tap at periodic auctions. Those whom the Gods would destroy, they first make mad.

The shame of it is that Britain never needed to be in this vulnerable position. We had manoeuvred ourselves into a pole position in the EU, with opt-outs for what did not suit us, a budgetary rebate and the ability to use EU membership to leverage our diplomatic, economic, financial and regulatory power. We were a lead member of one of the blocs that will dominate the multipolar world of the twenty-first century. All this has been torched by the British right, for whom dogma and personal and factional party interest have been put before the national interest.

We have arrived at a decisive moment in our history. A further extension of Conservative governments, repeating the terrible errors of the last fourteen years, will sink us. Britain is backing off the worst stupidities of Brexit – dropping the idea of introducing its own expensive safety standards kitemark and continuing with the cheaper and more effective EU one, abandoning the revocation of any law or regulation that might have emanated from Brussels, reaching an accommodation over Northern Ireland and rejoining the Horizon programme of scientific collaboration. We even meet with other European leaders! But it is all done within a larger pattern of sullen, suspicious disengagement and of doing the least possible, so as not to damage the purity of Brexit – and in the process damaging our trade, security and wider interests. In the West's wider councils our voice is becoming marginalised. We are seen as the sick country of the West. Britain needs the self-confidence to reassociate with the continent of which it is part – but that will only come from economic and social success, so that not only will we feel good in our collective skins, but the EU will actively welcome us. It will require a monumental national effort.

The Argument of This Book in Brief

The task is to find a philosophy and programme that will allow British capitalism to be managed successfully, to create a paradigm shift in investment and productivity, while simultaneously promoting fairness and social cohesion in ever-more-turbulent times. Our public services can be made to work. We can lift the pall of despair that has settled over the country. It is difficult to achieve, but British conservatism has run out of road and ideas. The baton necessarily passes to the liberal left.

America's New Deal in the 1930s (explored in Chapter 2) is an exemplar of what can be done with self-confidence and the right philosophy. Non-conservatives can combine imaginative government activism and institution-building to provide capitalism its necessary guiderails, unleash its creativity and dynamism to serve the common good and build a viable social contract so that ordinary men and women know that society has their backs. It is that inspiration that Britain needs to reproduce.

There is now the chance of creating a British progressive consensus that is first cousin to Roosevelt's New Deal Democrats, and which could replicate that success in the very particular circumstances in which Britain finds itself in the 2020s. Chapters 4 to 7 recount our economic, political and intellectual history since the Industrial Revolution to explain the roots of that possibility. We have two progressive traditions that overlap and now need to discard their mutual distrust – New Liberalism (or social liberalism) and social democratic labourism, at whose core is the ethic of socialism. New Liberalism was born at the end of the nineteenth century among thinkers and writers who saw the horrors of early industrialisation and urbanisation at first hand and acknowledged that the state must correct gross social deformations. We are all part of the social whole, it argued, and we have obligations to make it work in all our interests so that it enfranchises and liberates rather than oppresses us. Social democratic labourism was born from the lived experience of such deformations, in particular through trade unionism. Workers had to fight collectively to transform their working lives; capitalism would not deliver this improvement on its own. For both traditions, the important values were fellowship, mutuality, fairness, the primacy of the social and the imperative to look out for one another. New Liberals might stress individual agency and individual responsibilities to the whole as much as entitlements, while ethical socialists might stress solidarity, but much more united than divided them.

Opportunities to build alliances and make common cause between the two traditions were attempted; however, after initial experimentation with LibLab MPs in the decades up to the First World War, they were lost. Nonetheless, it was the secret Gladstone–MacDonald Pact of 1903 (as I will show in Chapter 5), after all, that contributed to the Liberal victory in 1906 (the greatest ever defeat of the Tory party) and launched the breakthrough parliamentary presence of the Labour Party. The Liberal government went on to create a Royal Commission that examined and made the case for proportional representation as fairest for a multiparty democracy, which reported in 1910. This did not happen. Instead, the Conservative Party, an electoral minority for almost all of the 139 years since the 1885 Reform Act, has exploited the first-past-the-post voting system and the divisions in the progressive vote to be in government for nearly two-thirds of that time. This stark fact should prompt much heart-searching on the left.

Progressivism emerged from the social horrors of early industrialisation. Being the first to industrialise was advantageous for Britain, but it has left a hangover of belief in the bad concept of laissez-faire, a lack of economic institutions dedicated to economic development and acute tensions between the classes. As long ago as 1924, the great economist and embodiment of new liberal thinking John Maynard Keynes delivered his superb lecture on 'The Death of Laissez-Faire'. It could not be allowed to continue, he argued; if capitalism operated according to its precepts, only instability, inequality and unemployment would result – undermining its legitimacy. However, if correctly managed, it could work well, better than socialist economies. In fact, the death agonies of laissez-faire were much more prolonged. It was not until Britain was forced off the gold standard, and endured the depression – while looking on at the activism of Roosevelt's New Deal but with no impulse to follow suit – that Britain devised its own version of a New Deal under the 1945–51 Labour government. In many ways, it was a brilliant administration, putting in place a social contract that in its essence has survived until today, pioneering the practice of Keynesian economics and experimenting with planning. It was the much-needed rupture with laissez-faire. But although it had many great achievements, British finance was not reshaped. There was no great programme of reconstruction. Industrial relations were not hauled out of the nineteenth century. The newly nationalised corporations operated as surrogate bureaucratic government departments rather than public *enterprises*. Protection from competition behind high tariffs and indulgence of monopoly weakened economic dynamism. The dysfunctions of British capitalism were not addressed.

The decades since have seen that social contract eroded, with no systematic attempts to make up for what Labour failed to do at its peak. New Liberals and social democratic Labour were good at social contract-building, much less good at revitalising British capitalism. As I argue in Chapter 7, they left the door open to Thatcherism. Mrs Thatcher's ideological success was her ability to combine the British tradition of laissez-faire and nineteenth-century 'Manchester liberalism' with the new energy and tropes emanating from the USA with the rise of American conservatism. And although her record in office has been much lauded, in fact its achievements were more modest, amid many great mistakes. Indeed so great were the cumulative mistakes that far from the saviour, she should rather be seen as the prime architect of Britain's accelerated economic and social decline. Yet the short-term results were good enough for the right to believe that she represented an effective marriage of right-wing ideology and good real-world results. In reality, its imperfections have made it impossible to build on, and in the process Conservativism has split into libertarian, Thatcherite, populist and one-nation wings – explored in Chapters 2 and 3.

With the collapse of the post-war settlement, in the 1980s a disoriented Labour Party rehearsed the internecine battles of the 1930s and 1950s over the nature of socialism, which had been left deliberately ambiguous by its founding fathers. A reshaped Labour Party under Tony Blair emerged, accepting Mrs Thatcher's economic settlement when it won power in 1997, but it aimed to spend the expected growth dividend on greatly improved public services. This was its attempt to hit the sweet spot, and it was partly successful until the financial crisis exposed the fault lines in the Thatcherite British economic model which was so dependent on credit growth and asset price inflation and so neglectful of the industrial base. Then the mantle of a socialist challenge – repeating the cycle of Labour's history – eventually fell to Jeremy Corbyn, with the same electoral consequences in 2017 and 2019 as there had been in 1935, 1955, 1959 and 1983.

The British progressive tradition now has a second chance. Around the alchemy of fusing the 'We' and the 'I', of social democracy and new liberalism described in Chapter 8, Britain can rejuvenate itself. In Chapters 9 to 13 the book sets out my analysis of today's Britain and how by deploying this philosophy we can take control of our destiny and reshape our economy, society and democracy for the better. Above all, we must learn to invest in ourselves and build the public and private institutions to do that. Strategically the task is to use much increased public investment within a credible fiscal framework supported by the reshaping of our savings and investment landscape in order to mobilise the hundreds of billions that are necessary to invest in a new generation of great companies and great infrastructure. Our institutional 'plumbing' must be organised to get the maximum multiplier impact on private investment from every pound of public investment. Work, housing, health, education, the criminal justice system and transport do not need to be as bad as they are. Nor need we allow so many of our citizens and children to live in poverty. Economic growth can be reignited, the money can be found, our social fissures and fractures healed.

As I argue in more detail in later chapters of this book, achieving net zero and levelling up must become national strategies from which we create new industries. There must be serious spending on research and development. The tax system must be reformed so that taxation of wealth is fairer and the yield higher. Partnership with trade unions must be achieved in a new economy-wide system of collective bargaining and worker participation in company decision-making. We must reassociate with the institutions, regulations and policies of the continent of which we are part. Last but not least, Britain's democracy must be reformed and renewed around a fairer voting system, wholesale decentralisation and effective checks and balances. The British Parliament must become again what it once was – a beacon of democracy.

There is a brighter future ahead. But to reach it, we cannot live with yet more years of disastrous or even timidly reformist policies. Britain can make itself less vulnerable to any mishap, whether another pandemic or an energy crisis. Our country does not need to be the invalid of the West. We can pioneer a twenty-first-century civilisation in which everyone flourishes. It is more than possible, as this book will show. We just have to want it enough.

2

THE USA AS WARNING
AND INSPIRATION

The United States of America is the most undiluted capitalist economy on earth. It displays all of capitalism's strengths and all of its weaknesses. It is where laissez-faire ideology is at its most developed, but where its full-blooded application has produced the most obviously faulty results. It is also, paradoxically, a living example of how to corral capitalism so it gives of its best, and an awesome warning of the damage to a society and an economy if capital is left to its own devices. The two great economic disasters of the last hundred years – the stock market crash of 1929, leading to the Great Depression of the 1930s, and the Great Financial Crisis of 2008 and its aftermath – have their origins in the dogmatic pursuit of free-market economics. And the recovery from the Depression, spearheaded by Franklin Roosevelt's New Deal, is perhaps the greatest example the world has witnessed of determined, innovative, experimental and successful government turning round a capitalist economy and relaunching it on a better course.

Roosevelt not only reconfigured and re-legitimised American capitalism, but in the process he greatly strengthened an American society grievously wounded by inequality, destitution and insecurity. His economic and social settlement became the framework for American economic success and its capacity to shape the world for the rest of the twentieth century. Energised businesses responded to a reformed financial system and huge federal research spending; scientific and technological dynamism were one part of his legacy. Another was the creation of a vast

American middle class of which a crucial element was wide-spread home ownership through the new federal agencies that promoted and backstopped mortgage lending. The success of the programme and its core philosophy – that government activism is necessary and that it works – framed American politics for half a century.

The counter-revolution launched by the American right took fifty years to incubate, and for all its political success since Ronald Reagan's election in 1980 it has been ever more obviously mistaken and has induced a social disaster. But that has not prevented the misplaced energy of American conservative ideas from having a profound impact on the British right, beginning with Mrs Thatcher and continuing today with both Liz Truss and Rishi Sunak, and almost all Britain's many right-wing think tanks.

In the mid-2020s, the tide is going out on the American right's revolution – although not without resistance – because its ideas have proved so deeply dysfunctional in practice. The American left has begun to shape a viable philosophy of action – a second New Deal. President Joe Biden is proving, especially if, despite his age, he succeeds in winning a second term against a Republican party in thrall to right-wing populism and losing its democratic bearings, to be the most consequential Democrat president since Lyndon Johnson and arguably since Roosevelt himself. The effect of this will surely be felt in Britain. It is time that we had a first New Deal, let alone a second one. So our story starts here, with events nearly a hundred years ago.

The Fallout from 1929

The crash of 1929 shook the USA to its core. Up until then, the American public and its leaders self-confidently thought that the new world to which so many millions had migrated offered such bounty that the best economic and social model was one in which everyone looked after themselves. Capitalism would deliver the goods – output had quadrupled between 1870 and 1930, at the fastest pace in world history, and the USA was the home of a bewildering array of transformatory inventions ranging from the mass-produced motor car to the telephone. Living standards rose in tandem. The idea that capitalism needed very little governance had been qualified in the three decades before the First World War, in the so-called Progressive Era, by the partial breakup of the great steel, tobacco and oil trusts (which were de facto monopolies) as well as measures to regulate banking, drugs and food safety. But these measures were to help capitalism function better, by not abusing its market power and wealth. After the First World War, the USA boomed; the mass production of cars and other consumer goods was so prolific that even semi-skilled and unskilled workers could find a place in the huge factories and long production lines. Prosperity was shared. There seemed no reason to believe that growth and living standards would not rise at the same pace in the years ahead.

The Great Depression shattered those beliefs. The need to find a response to the catastrophe that hit American society produced Franklin Delano Roosevelt's New Deal, with a new political consensus; an interventionist Democrat president, backed by a Democrat-controlled House of Representatives and Senate, elected to save America from unfettered capitalism. Roosevelt had no thought-out plan, beyond using government to address the obviously malfunctioning banking system and the labour market – and to continue to innovate and act wherever necessary. Half-hearted tinkering would not do. Government would be used actively to reshape American capitalism, and to reconfigure American society – all to ensure that the common good was delivered. The exigencies of the Second World War sealed the new bargain, with a massive state direction of the economy that allowed the USA vastly to outproduce its enemies, and the investment in science and research paid huge economic and military dividends. This approach became the foundation for a post-war world order of managed capitalism which, with the Bretton Woods system of internationally agreed exchange rates and controlled capital flows alongside free trade in a rules-based international system, was created in the same image of the New Deal. Over the next thirty years, this world of managed capitalism and strong safety nets would see global and US output trebling, living standards rising and inequality falling to new lows by the mid-1970s. It was a liberal social democratic order that worked so well it seemed permanent.

The political consensus underpinning these ideas held up, too; Democrats only lost control – briefly – of the House twice in the sixty-two years between 1932 and 1994, and of the Senate twice in the forty-eight years up to 1980. And by the 1960s, the New Deal inspired further initiatives, symbolised by the New Frontier and Great Society of Presidents Kennedy and Johnson. Even when Republican presidents were elected, like Eisenhower and Nixon, they governed within the social democratic order, accepting its core principles of regulated capitalism and a strong safety net. American conservatives seemed to be marginalised; the new order challenged everything in which they believed – the small state, free-market capitalism and standing on your own two feet without help from the state.

The comprehensiveness and audacity of the New Deal in breaking with the past still astonishes, and its scope is worth briefly setting out. Roosevelt had three watchwords: relief, recovery and reform – in particular, a wholesale recasting of the US financial system, creating a new set of institutions to replace what had been brutally short-term finance.

The way the free market had hardwired speculative losses in the stock market into the core of the banking system (so causing its implosion and a credit crunch – the immediate reason for the slump) was never to be repeated. The Federal Deposit Insurance Corporation was created, to protect bank depositors from collapsing banks. The US Banking Act, with its Glass-Steagall provisions, forbade commercial banks from lending to finance the purchase of financial securities as collateral, separating commercial and investment banking. The transmission mechanism from losses on falling share prices to the destruction of banks' capital positions and their capacity to lend would be broken. The Securities and Exchange Commission was created to ensure probity and integrity in the capital markets. In a few short years, via the Home Owners' Loan Corporation and the Farm Mortgage Corporation, the Roosevelt administration invented affordable twenty-five-year mortgages. Earlier in my career, I spent hours in the underground stacks of the Library of Congress, reading the personal letters from farmers and homeowners thanking Roosevelt personally for the miracle of being able to pay back mortgages over twenty-five years instead of the previous five (and sometimes less) – it lifted the financial monkey off middle America's back.

Roosevelt did not stop there. He beefed up the Reconstruction Finance Corporation to refinance short-term business lending with more long-term, engaged lending. Fannie Mae (the Federal National Mortgage Association) and Freddie Mac (the Federal Home Loan Mortgage Corp) were instituted to offer a steady flow of long-term credit to savings and loans institutions. Central banking was formalised with the creation of the Federal Reserve system. This was innovative public institution-building and regulation – and it worked.

The ambition, energy and experimentation of these reforms is impressive even after nearly a century. To accelerate economic recovery, the federal government directly employed millions of unemployed men in vast public works programmes, via the Civilian Conservation Corporation, Public Works Administration and Work Progress Administration set in train by the 1933 National Industrial Recovery Act. The Tennessee Valley Authority was created to offer relief to that hard-hit river valley, building dams and hydroelectricity capacity – and it is still the USA's single largest provider of electricity. Road and highway building, strengthening the postal service, and building dams, levees and canals across the country left an indelible mark on the USA. The 1935 National Labor Relations Act recognised the right of workers collectively to organise (without the threat of dismissal from employers) and introduced various arbitration procedures to resolve disputes, while the Fair Standards Act provided for a minimum wage. The labour and financial markets were transformed. The economy stabilised and recovered.

The main vehicle for Roosevelt's third aim, relief, was provided by the Social Security Administration, established to provide a national system of pensions, unemployment insurance and aid to mothers and children. American capitalism was turned on its head. Its job was to serve the people.

Philosophically, Roosevelt was blending the best of social democracy – using the state to assert the 'We' – with recognition that there must be scope for individual and business autonomy – a liberal respect for the 'I'. Reciprocity of obligation was built into these interventions; the state wanted to provide work, not unconditional handouts. Professor J. Bradford DeLong, in his *Slouching Towards Utopia*, dubs the New Deal a fusion of the ideas of the famous free-marketeer-cum-classical-liberal Friedrich Hayek with the call of Karl Polanyi for markets to serve society, a fusion blessed by liberal helpings of John Maynard Keynes. I see in the New Deal very little of Hayek, who entertained the state only guaranteeing the minimal wherewithal to live (Roosevelt was not remotely Hayekian). To the extent that there was a classic liberal element, it was more Bentham's liberal determination to achieve the greatest good for the greatest number, along with a recognition that there should no inhibitions on those who worked and contributed earning proportionally what they deserved, although they should contribute proportionally more to the whole through progressive taxation. However, with DeLong, I believe that we need to create the same fusion of liberal and social democratic traditions as the best public philosophy for governing liberal democratic capitalism.

One ugly blot disfigured the New Deal: its concessions to racism and segregation in the American South. Roosevelt owed his nomination in 1932 to Southern Democrats who were determined that white supremacy should continue; the New Deal programmes respected that Faustian bargain. Black Americans were paid less than whites in relief programmes, and were assigned to separate work projects. As Robert Kuttner describes in *Going Big*, the racism extended poisonously to housing; to win the support of Southern Democrats who chaired key legislative committees, federal public housing had to be segregated – even in the North, where casually integrated working-class neighbourhoods were replaced by colour-coded public housing complexes. The rules extended to mortgages; the Federal Housing Administration's

1935 housing manual disallowed mortgages that allowed Black homeowners into white neighbourhoods – an approach that continued in the secondary mortgage market. The great Home Owners' Loan Corporation even had colour-coded maps to ensure its mortgage guarantees did not extend to Black Americans.[1]

As the civil rights movement got underway in the 1950s and 1960s, it would be the American South that would peel away from the great Roosevelt coalition, but the breadth and depth of that coalition was still extraordinary. The working class, homeowners, farmers, small business, media, academics, teachers, doctors and professionals formed a base for congressional majorities that survived for at least half a century. Appeals to racism would be an important contribution to destroying that coalition. Yet, at the time, the momentum seemed unstoppable; tomorrow would continue to get better than today, even extending to civil rights.

But the world was about to become much darker.

First Stirrings

America's first non-Democrat president in twenty years was Dwight Eisenhower, a respected general and the commander of the liberation forces in Europe in 1944–5. He was a political moderate, who cut a non-partisan figure; before his nomination, both Republicans and Democrats alike approached him to be a candidate. He understood that the Republican Party – like the Conservatives in Britain under Churchill accepting the Labour Party reforms after 1945 – had to accept the terms of the post-war settlement. He had to live within the rules of the liberal social democratic order, with its commitment to high marginal tax rates, strong social security and regulated markets – an order that was already in competition with the communism of the Soviet Union and China. 'If any party messed with the New Deal', he told his brother, 'you would not hear of that party again in our political history.'

There could be no risking another crisis of capitalism by abandoning the New Deal or Bretton Woods, which would disarm the West in its existential fight. In Europe, the USA had been actively combating the spread of communism, first with the Marshall Plan and then the Mutual Security Act promoting liberal capitalism and rapid post-war reconstruction, and in Asia it went to war against North Korea as a surrogate for China. Where the American political divisions ran deeper was in the paranoia about communism's seductive appeal within the USA, though in fact the Communist Party of the USA was a tiny sect.

Eisenhower assumed the presidency just as the extraordinary hearings launched by Senator Joseph McCarthy into alleged infiltration by communists into US government and politics were reaching a crescendo. McCarthy would overreach himself and be ostracised by his party for his excesses and cruelties. But strident anti-communism remained a powerful force in American conservatism and politics more generally, and while McCarthy may have been discredited, anti-communist sentiment remained ferocious. It would remain an important buttressing plank – the defining characteristic of so-called neoconservatives – in an otherwise defensive Republican Party for decades.

Another prop was the growing dismay among Southern white Americans at the successes of the campaign to treat Black Americans equally under the law. The Supreme Court's *Brown v. Board of Education* ruling in 1954, declaring that segregation was unconstitutional, was a decisive moment. The USA, after all, had permitted and benefited from the enslavement of Black Americans until the end of the Civil War in 1865, and for the next century it had tolerated racial segregation, discrimination and the 'Jim Crow' laws in Southern states that codified racial exclusion. Racist attitudes were always going to die hard – even sharing a water fountain was seen as the thin edge of the wedge – but by the 1950s, the Supreme Court was willing to intervene against racial discrimination. Conservatives were consumed by a nightmare; it seemed as if their opponents had history on their side, that liberal-left thinking now dominated the national discourse across party lines, that the New Deal order was now establishment orthodoxy and that the USA was heading inexorably towards interventionist government, social welfare and racial equality. Worse, many mainstream Republicans were colluding in this Democrat-driven, unconservative dystopia.

The nightmare would increasingly bring conservatives and 'true' classical liberals together in the 1960s and 1970s. Socialism, or its softer cousin social democracy, threatened to have an irresistible appeal, as a 'middle way' between fascism and communism, menacing their vision of free-market capitalism, with its attendant freedoms. Friedrich Hayek, then a professor at the London School of Economics, in 1947 gathered an extraordinary collection of free-market intellectuals from Europe and the USA in the Swiss village of Mont Pelerin, including a young Milton Friedman, to discuss how to reanimate 'classical' liberalism. The cornerstones of Western civilisation, they agreed, were the pluralism of the free market, the primacy of private property rights and freedom of speech; all were now menaced, as they saw it, not only by communism, but also by the increasing reliance of post-war Western states on planning, public spending (especially on welfare) and public ownership.

It was a hysterical response to vital post-war reconstruction in Western Europe that in fact took care to respect the capitalist order, the rule of law and the Universal Declaration of Human Rights – and did a better job of protecting essential freedoms at the time than the attendees at Mont Pelerin. The group also had a curious lack of intellectual interest in capitalism's dysfunctions, why they might be inherent to the system and why they threw up social forces so firmly pledged to its reform or overthrow. These lacunae disabled Mont Pelerin thinkers as a credible force throughout the 1950s and 1960s, but by the 1970s and 1980s, when the social democratic alternatives seemed spent, with entrenched stagflation and waves of industrial conflict, the group produced nine Nobel Prize-winning economists, including Friedman. Their moment had come – although contact with the complex realities of capitalism was to discredit most of their theories.[2]

Hayek and Friedman were the foremost intellectual representatives of this counter-establishment movement – both sharing the belief that markets always worked better than the state, with Friedman particularly attacking governments for the inflationary impact of printing money. In *The Road to Serfdom*, written during the war and published in 1944, Hayek had set out how the state could be captured by the collectivism of right or left – the communist Soviet Union or National Socialist Germany – and either could snuff out the pluralism and experimentation which he saw as essential to capitalism, a superior system to any form of collectivism. The essence of a market was that it enabled individuals to exercise liberty as they experimented and tried ideas out, especially as capitalist entrepreneurs – hence the importance of the price mechanism as a means of discovery and a way of coordinating economic activity. The basic building block of the good society is thus the individual and their interests: the unfettered 'I'. Admittedly, Hayek was not blind to individuals' or markets' failings, or to the role of undeserved good and bad luck in determining people's fortunes – but a comprehensive social contract to compensate for this was decisively ruled out as a step on the 'road to serfdom'. Only the most minimal social provision could be entertained. However, Hayek still accepted that the exercise of individual freedom should be qualified by the necessity to do no harm – which would need publicly created guiderails. This was part of his wider acceptance that there are some public goods that require state involvement – the defence of the realm, the administration of justice via the courts, the building of roads and even the protection of private property. To a degree, markets, he accepted, have to be created by public action. Thus a realm does exist beyond the individual, he acknowledged – a public realm. But it was an unfortunate necessity, rather than an essential actor in the economic and social drama. It was imperative that its coercive proclivities and narrowing of liberties were actively kept in check; there must be strict limits on the circumstances in which the state could act.

Reading Hayek today, the clarity of his anti-state passion is obviously driven – understandably, in the context of war – by his ferocious Germanophobia. The intellectual fathers of statism were German thinkers like Marx, and thus bad. Extreme accusations could be made about any advocacy of public action, confident that his reading public would nod their head in agreement if he linked such advocacy to Nazism; anything German was bad. It was a persuasive way of discrediting statist thinkers of all kinds. An impressed Mrs Thatcher, who in her early years as Tory leader collected quotes and ideas from right-wing thinkers in a personalised ideas folder for speeches and policy proposals, would circulate *The Road to Serfdom* to all her shadow cabinet.

But if Hayek offered a high-level attack on collectivism in principle, the greater challenge was turning this worldview into the basis of an order that would displace the liberal social democratic consensus of the 1940s and 1950s, which at the time seemed a fantastical dream. How to find sufficient common ground to make the right cohere around a language of anti-collectivism that spoke to the 'real-world' issues of the average voter? After all, the post-war settlement had delivered jobs, housing, social security, pensions, paid holiday, doctors and hospitals. Trying to build a politics challenging those achievements would not be an easy task anywhere, but in the USA, the differences between the varying strands of right-wing thought made getting the project off the ground particularly difficult.

On the ultra-right, attached to the University of Chicago from 1950, were libertarians influenced by the Russian exile Ayn Rand, who took classic liberal concerns about the monopolistic state to another level of detestation. Any human being has a moral obligation to pursue only his or her self-interest, she argued, rather than to any group, and especially not to the state, with its monopoly of coercive power. Selfishness, instead of a reprehensible sin, was transmuted into the highest moral obligation. The authoritarian state of fascism or communism was obviously coercive, but so was any appeal to the 'We' as a basis for action. The case for state power even in the limited terms Hayek accepted was morally dubious, but also unnecessary. The man, she wrote, is an 'ass, with no conception of a free society at all'.[3] He had surrendered too much ground to statists. Individuals could be relied upon spontaneously to create their own order, and to respect accumulated laws which their own interactions had created; no external intervention was necessary, certainly not the state, nor an appeal to religion or God as a basis for morality. She was a convinced atheist. Taxation was on the same continuum of coercion as prison or forced detention; even to get into personal debt was to accept an inadmissible claim of the other on oneself, to be accepted as a last resort, and only on clear terms. Order would emerge naturally from the interaction of self-interested individuals, who would create and observe law. It did not need the apparatus of the state. 'Altruism is a great evil [...] while selfishness is a virtue', she famously declared.[4]

Thus Rand became the author of the idea that 'Greed is good', inspiring Barry Goldwater, Paul Ryan, Rand Paul and Donald Trump, central banker Alan Greenspan, the billionaire Koch brothers, who have funded so many right-wing causes, and even media moguls like Rupert Murdoch. Unsurprisingly, she was a passionate opponent of the New Deal. Randism remains a live force in US politics. In the 1990s, a survey by the Library of Congress named *Atlas Shrugged* – her near-1,200-page novel whose central hero is the arch-individualist John Galt – as the most influential book in the USA after the Bible. Donald Trump claims (credibly, for once) that it is one of the few novels he has read. In Britain, former Tory cabinet minister Sajid Javid is a self-declared Randian, and a number of her ideas informed the ill-fated government of Liz Truss, an ardent libertarian. The ruinous trajectory of right-wing politics in both the USA and Britain would have been impossible without Rand.

It is the Hayekian willingness to accept some public action, however constrained, that differentiates the two traditions. Hayekians value the role of some public institutions – chiefly the Central Bank, whose vital importance in their eyes is to ensure the integrity of the currency, guarantee price stability and encourage vital financial freedoms. Price stability is seen as the fundamental precondition for economic order, and central banks had better do their job well; Hayek remembered the ruinous way German hyperinflation had created Hitler's political opportunity.

Beyond central banks, Hayekians are curiously mute on the institutions that might encourage a dynamic capitalism. Their view of economic growth is disarmingly simple – trust in markets, private property and pluralist competition – and on questions such as from where our preferences and values come, or what institutions best foster opportunity, they have little to say. It is a doctrine grounded in a utopian vision of how a society of minimally governed individuals might spontaneously develop and operate.[5] It has its feet a little more on the ground than the Randians, but only just.

First Efforts at Right-Wing Populism

The Mont Pelerin Society's worldview did not make much progress during the 1950s and early 1960s – the arguments between Hayek and Rand were noises off. Over the decade, output increased by more than a third, unemployment and inflation stayed low and the USA began to develop its extensive suburban middle class. Traditional conservatives, like Senator Robert Taft, failed again and again to get the Republican Party's presidential nomination. The grip of the New Deal settlement seemed secure.

Enter Republican Senator Barry Goldwater, the party's presidential nominee who lost the election of 1964 by a landslide, but who sowed the seeds of the conservative rebirth. His trenchant criticism of the New Deal as a Trojan horse for communism was informed by his reading of Ayn Rand, and it signalled a profound change in right-wing thinking that began to gain a grip on the broader, inchoate conservative movement. Indeed, it was while campaigning for Goldwater in 1964 that Ronald Reagan first delivered 'The Speech' (otherwise known as 'A Time for Choosing') setting out his own credo of self-reliance, hostility to government and advocacy of the free market. Sensing the same change in the right-wing political weather, the suave journalist William F. Buckley Jr. emerged as a leading provocateur and what we would now call an influencer. He had launched the *National Review* in 1955 with the explicit aim of bringing together anti-communist, libertarian, conservative and orthodox liberal views into a more or less seamless coalition that would turn the preoccupations of the Mont Pelerin attendees into political reality, and, after uniting them, to then make them popular. As political commentator and former aide to President Bill Clinton, Sidney Blumenthal argues in *The Rise of the Counter-Establishment*, his success was crucial.[6]

Other intellectuals were arguing in the same vein. Professor Leo Strauss, another refugee from Nazism, had published *Natural Rights and History* in 1953, arguing that what was needed to defend civilisation from the utopian evils of communism and fascism were men and women of moral virtue and courage. Strauss evolved an argument for a Platonic republican elite that would stand against the demands of mass democracy, and he believed that it was self-reliance and free markets that bred such virtues. Strauss was one of the early supporters of Buckley's *National Review* – other enthusiasts included Milton Friedman – and he would become crucially influential on a generation of what later came to be called neoconservatives, who played key roles in the administration of George W. Bush. Buckley's capacity to corral such disparate figures into one movement, along with his relaxed television style that won millions of viewers, would be pivotal in paving the way for Ronald Reagan and later Newt Gingrich. Buckley was one of the most significant figures on the American right in the last half of the twentieth century.

Buckley saw clearly that if the post-war Keynesian, interventionist New Deal order, which promised jobs, security and pensions, was to be rolled back, the right's divisions had to be bridged. A battle of ideas would have to be fought within a movement that included classical liberals, libertarians, fundamentalist Christians and cultural conservatives, a new consensus forged and charismatic political leaders enlisted to popularise the cause. It was no use being at the margins, or being dismissed as 'nuts' (as popular bumper stickers described Goldwater in 1964), or, even worse, quasi-racist. From the get-go, Buckley's aim was to create a neoliberal paradigm around which the right could unite and to couch it in language that would ensure the Republican party could become electorally competitive again.

The new right had enormous assets on which to build, which were not available to its British counterparts. The USA possesses a class of ideologically motivated rich people – non-existent on the same scale in Britain – who are prepared to finance ideas, think tanks and politicians to serve a passionate belief in the freedom of business that is, in their view, part of the USA's foundational essence. This class likes to invoke the legend of the Founding Fathers, whose original oligarchical constitution has become a totem for conservatives. Persistent racial tensions animate white America, especially the South, to a still-extraordinary degree. Many Southern whites still resent the outcome of the Civil War. It is part of a skein of cultural issues – gun control, abortion, religion – which act as wedges between right and left which do not work in Britain. And the USA is a rich continental economy with vast resources, dynamic entrepreneurs and universities that are innovation-factories and whose research is deftly and aggressively supported by the Pentagon. The dollar was – and is – the world's reserve currency, giving scope for economic policy extravagance and an avoidance of budgetary constraints unavailable to Britain. Yet the two countries did have one thing in common: as the 1960s gave way to the 1970s, deindustrialisation began to create a disillusioned working class. It was a heady cocktail, and one that was extremely potent given the right circumstances. In this epic story the British right were the junior – if willing – partner, picking up ideas and useful money and becoming animated by what they would witness across the Atlantic.

The Rise of Neoliberalism

For nearly thirty-three years, Buckley hosted *Firing Line*, a chat show on US public television, in which his courteous and forensic questioning of guests injected right-wing thinking into the mainstream. It remains the longest-running TV series of its type in American history. To win over conservatives, Buckley would take stances like defending the Vietnam War and the necessity of winning the war against communism. To appeal to Hayekian liberals, he launched broadsides against the scale of taxation and the perverse unintended consequences of government intervention, and stressed the danger that welfare absolved recipients from taking responsibility for their lives. His depiction of welfare as a 'lifestyle choice' – separating it from genuine need – was a particularly useful ploy. It was a disguised way of being racist without being racist. His audience understood that it was 'lazy Blacks' receiving welfare cheques from 'hard-working American whites'. By pitching the criticism in the moral framework of dependency, the charge of racism could be sidestepped.

All of this might have come to nothing, but broader events were playing into the hands of Buckley and his collaborators. The 1964 Civil Rights Act may have seemed seismic – 'we may have lost the South for a generation', Johnson is said to have remarked as he signed it into law – but it stopped short of securing the right to vote or ending segregation in housing. Those would be delivered by the 1965 Voting Rights Act and 1968 Fair Housing Act. Meanwhile, the war in Vietnam saw mounting student protest, and rioting convulsed cities. In 1968, both Martin Luther King and Robert Kennedy were assassinated. This would be a seminal year for the fraying of the New Deal coalition; while the Democrats would continue to control the House and Senate, the presidency was won by Nixon, after crucial Electoral College votes in the South went not to Democrats but to the segregationist George Wallace. The vast deficits necessary to finance war abroad and the Great Society at home were beginning to trigger inflation; if the dollar was to continue anchoring the Bretton Woods system, that would require sacrifices in US economic policy.

Nixon stopped pegging the US dollar to gold in 1971 and effectively collapsed the Bretton Woods-managed exchange rate regime, and in doing so freed the USA from all such constraints. The curtain was coming down. The oil price quadrupled in 1973 in reaction to Israel's victory in the Yom Kippur War and the USA scuttled out of South Vietnam two years later, which provoked national soul-searching. American economic and military power seemed to be ebbing; inflation soared and the economy stagnated. 'Stagflation' took hold, a deadly combination of economic paralysis and rising prices. New Deal thinking seemed beside the point and a prosperous middle class did not feel the need for New Deal activism, as it had done in the 1930s. William Buckley's efforts were now making an impact on mainstream politics and culture. Persistent inflation could not be controlled by tripartite deals with unions, government and business, as the UK also seemed to demonstrate in these years.

The opportunity had come for a new approach. The right and its remedies would move centre stage. When Buckley died in 2008, tributes to his impact came from across the Republican Party establishment. The Republican whip in the House of Representatives, Roy Blunt, declared, 'He was the undisputed leader of the conservative movement and laid the groundwork of the Reagan Revolution.'[7]

The 1970s as the Pivot Decade

Milton Friedman, thirty years on from the launch of the Mont Pelerin Society, seized the moment. It was not the Viet Cong or the Arab-led consortium of oil-producing exporters (OPEC) that had caused the USA's problems. It was the overmighty New Deal state, he argued, empowering trade unions, running budget deficits and recklessly expanding the money supply that had degraded the dollar and undermined the vitality of American capitalism. The answer was for the federal government to be reined in, the Federal Reserve to print less money, the New Deal to be abandoned and trade unions to be curbed, and the American economy would once again take flight. A bevy of newly established, richly funded right-wing think tanks – notably the Manhattan Institute and the Heritage Foundation, joined by a rejuvenated American Enterprise Institute – made the case for 'supply-side' economics in which individual freedoms were the central priority.

This was the era when a right-wing counter-establishment fully emerged, and it would offer powerful political and intellectual support to Reagan. It was the age of the 'Laffer Curve', which claimed to show that lower taxes paid for themselves through higher growth; of George Gilda at the Manhattan Institute insisting that the poor were poor because they were work-shy; of

Charles Murray and his infamous 'Bell Curve' suggesting that the distribution of intelligence was partly genetic in origin, so that welfare programmes trying to promote opportunities for ethnic minorities were doomed. It was open season on the New Deal.

At Harvard Business School, Professor Michael Jensen developed the theory – building on Milton Friedman's ideas – that the prime objective of a company was to maximise shareholder value. He was also part of a school of market-fundamentalist economists who argued that financial markets were inherently efficient and could not make systemic mistakes. Yale's Robert Bork argued in 1978 that competition's only purpose was to promote consumer welfare, but that cartels and monopolies could do the same or better, so breaking up concentrations of market power was counterproductive. It lowered consumer welfare. This was the heyday of 'supply-side economics'.

Faced with stagflation, the New Deal recipe of managed capitalism seemed obsolete; being 'free to choose' chimed not only with the liberal right but with the freedom-loving ex-hippies. Even the campaigning liberal Ralph Nader would make common cause with Jimmy Carter over deregulation. American business began ever more aggressively to proselytise the cause against New Deal thinking, stepping up the case for 'free' enterprise as opposed to capitalism within guiderails and given licence by a 1976 Supreme Court judgement that corporations had the same right as individuals to donate to political parties. American elections were about to be flooded with money.

President Carter, elected in 1976, genuflected to the new times by positioning himself as a social liberal but fiscal conservative. His January 1978 State of the Union address summed up his retreat from his Democratic predecessors: 'Government cannot solve our problems', he intoned. 'It can't set the goals. It cannot define our vision, eliminate poverty, provide a bountiful economy, or reduce inflation, or save our cities, or cure illiteracy or provide energy.'[8] By contrast, Eisenhower had mentioned government forty times in his 1953 State of the Union address, almost always to praise what it could do. Now the language was of tax cuts, restraining the state and deregulating. Great Society or New Deal programmes were off the table. American progressives had run up the white flag eighteen months before Margaret Thatcher was elected. Far from being an original politician, she was riding a wave of right-wing energy from across the Atlantic. When she was elected leader of the Tory Party in 1975, her ideas folder began to fill up with missives, reports and books from the USA. Her task would be to unite this brightly optimistic American propaganda with the historic elements in British conservative thought that meshed with it. Free markets, free trade and balanced budgets had, after all, been Tory mantras for generations. Now the old verities could be rebranded and resold as supply-side economics.

From the Counter-Revolution to the Financial Crisis

The stage was set for Republican victory – and in 1980 Ronald Reagan duly delivered, carrying all but six states and winning Republican control of the Senate for only the third time since 1932. After all, if a Democrat president proclaimed the uselessness of government, the American public could hardly be blamed for turning to a charismatic politician who had been saying the same for more than a decade. Ronald Reagan had the political charisma to turn the ideas of Buckley, Friedman and their co-thinkers into an ambitious 'supply-side' political programme while deftly masking its incoherencies. Libertarian and free-market economists might praise markets in terms of their alleged efficiency, powers of coordination and experimentation, but Reagan, as Sidney Blumenthal writes, had the genius instead to frame the argument in terms of returning to the certainties of small-town America, the virtues of volunteering and neighbourliness and the demonic obstruction of government to those virtues.[9] Government would now get out of the way. There had once been room for all on the American frontier, so there was now room for all in a free market. There was a new moral majority, Reagan proclaimed, who had found their voice, and now wanted to put God and individualism back at the heart of America. Abroad, the USA would contest the tyranny of the godless Soviet Union. Buckley had achieved what he had set out to achieve in 1955: united the right and found his charismatic leader.

The right to choose had become the new mantra. This new conservatism burned with moral righteousness, championing a feasible political programme anchored in tax cuts for the rich, weakening trade unions, privatisation of public assets and as little regulation as possible for business and finance – who now began to spend on donations to the Republicans on a stupendous scale. Ominously, this new creed had a messianic character; it claimed to be true to an idea of America that progressive New Dealers had betrayed. There could be no compromise with a political philosophy that had dominated the USA for more than half a century and, as they characterised it, brought the country so low. A functioning democracy depends on accepting the legitimacy of political opponents, but this principle was about to disappear. The polarisation that now transfixes the USA was taking shape.

Reagan's programme appealed both to his intellectual backers and his electoral base. Under the 'supply-side' banner, he launched a programme of unfunded tax cuts and deregulation that would please Hayekian liberals and conservatives alike – with rewards dressed up as incentives for business and middle-class America. His massive boost in military spending, culminating in the 'Star Wars' programme, was meat and drink to the anti-communist neoconservatives. Reagan would cut the top rate of income tax from 70 per cent at the beginning of his tenure to 50 per cent and then to 28 per cent in 1986 (moving years before Britain's celebrated tax-cutting chancellor Nigel Lawson). It was all cloaked in the language of freedom; the wealth would inevitably trickle down. If there were huge budget deficits, so be it; the USA felt no fiscal constraints, bullying its partners to sell or support the dollar as circumstances required. The requirement to make a large deposit to secure a mortgage was scrapped in 1982; a housing boom followed and consumption and property price inflation drove a strong economic recovery. Reagan cut back social programmes, claiming that he was ending the dependency culture and weaning folk off welfare cheques; as cited earlier, it was a well-understood code for ending big income transfers from white to Black America. Race is never far from the surface in US life, particularly in the South. Lyndon Johnson's prediction that Democratic championing of civil rights would lose them the South proved all too prescient. In the 1984 presidential election, Reagan would win all but one state. Well could he boast it was 'morning again in America'.

As the recovery took hold and US interest rates were raised to drive out inflation, in line with Friedman's recommendations, the dollar soared, hollowing out manufacturing jobs in the USA's industrial heartlands. High-paying male jobs in manufacturing began to disappear – the growing sectors were in low-paid services or in the non-unionised South.

From the Republicans' point of view, the key task was to ensure that these structural changes did not allow the national conversation to be captured again by liberals, so one of the most important and baleful acts of deregulation came at the end of Reagan's tenure: ending the Fairness Doctrine, which had required American broadcasters to balance their coverage of controversial issues. The way was now open for an avalanche of right-wing talk shows. The era of Rush Limbaugh had arrived, and the launch of Fox News was another plank in the polarisation of the American public square. Republican media dominance was assured. Over the next generation, Limbaugh and Fox were to treat politics less as a competition of ideas than a contest between their definition of an overweening liberal elite and the great American public, salting their commentary with irreverence, scandal, their sense of victimhood and tonally defamatory argument. Radio, television and later social media privileged sheer volume, anger and rhetoric. Trump, thirty years later, would understand this toxic brew very well. Republicans now trust their own outlets but not 'mainstream' news; by 2016, only 14 per cent of Republicans said they generally trusted the media. To seal the deal, campaign money flowed in escalating billions towards Republicans. Hostility to New Deal liberalism was now a staple of popular culture, and the disintegration of the Roosevelt coalition accelerated.

A Republican could hardly fail to win in 1988, and George H. W. Bush took office as the Soviet Union began to withdraw from its Cold War empire, a process that would lead to German reunification in November 1989 and ultimately the dissolution of the Soviet Union itself in 1991. Francis Fukuyama captured the moment in his 1989 essay 'The End of History', later to be turned into a famous book of the same title; if history was a long process of experimenting with varying forms of governance, he argued, it was now over. Liberal democracy had emerged as the undisputed, the only, form of viable government. If that judgement was infected by political triumphalism as the Soviet Union collapsed, there was a parallel triumphalism in economics, expressed by the economist John Williamson: the new worldwide orthodoxy was aiming for balanced budgets, the privatisation of public assets, the promotion of markets and embrace of free trade. It was, he declared, 'the Washington consensus'.

Others took a darker view. In 1993, Samuel Huntington's *Clash of Civilizations* warned that the end of the Cold War meant the revival of ethnic, national and religious conflict, enacted primarily between 'civilisations' based on ancient cultural divides, above all the contest between Islamic extremism and Western values. The USA would be compelled to resist as its own Anglo-Protestant cultural base, shared history and common language came under attack – setting in train a dangerous internal dynamic, to which an out-of-touch financial, business and political elite tied into a globalised world would be indifferent. Republicans, who were now well versed in weaponising culture wars, took note; this would be another profitable line of attack.

In the face of all of this, Democrats regrouped; given neoliberalism's remarkable renaissance, they would have to accept some of the tenets of the new orthodoxy. It would fall to Bill Clinton to mount a successful challenge in the 1992 presidential election under the banner of being a 'New Democrat'. (Tony Blair would echo Clinton by rebranding his party as 'New Labour' in his first party conference as leader in 1994.) Like Carter in 1976, Clinton would openly accept the Republican free-market, deregulatory, anti-trade-union orthodoxies. Independent Ross Perot, running as a popular third candidate championing balanced budgets and reflecting the new consensus, sealed off any temptation to do otherwise. Clinton's inaugural speech in

THE USA AS WARNING AND INSPIRATION

1993 mentioned government half as many times as Eisenhower had done forty years earlier, and not in anything like as warm terms; taxes were a problem, as was organised labour, again in contrast to the veteran Republican. Yet Clinton was still enough of a Democrat not to give up attempts to sustain a social contract; he championed a national healthcare system and 'active labour market' policies to lower unemployment – extending training, but making welfare conditional on searching for a job. It was a 'third way' triangulation that Tony Blair would also imitate, keeping alive the social elements of a New Deal approach. But the free-to-choose neoliberal tide was running too strongly in the other direction.

In 1994, Republican Congressman Newt Gingrich capitalised on the anti-government rage of the conservative base. He had already made a name for himself by taking political partisanship to new levels. As Republican whip in 1990, he had famously advised candidates with a manual of 'optimistic positive governing words' to describe themselves (change, courage, family, hard work), with derogatory 'contrasting words' to describe political opponents (cheat, corrupt, traitors, steal).[10] In his 'Contract with America', he inaugurated politics as combat with enemies giving no quarter, rather than democratic argument; he promised Republicans would aggressively scrutinise all public spending and require Congressional super-majorities to raise taxes. There would be no more George Bush-style compromises. It was a crystallisation of the right-wing fundamentalist position, encompassing everything from opposition to gun control to a commitment to balanced budgets as the American way. Democrats lost both the House and Senate for the first time in forty years. Any hopes of progress towards universal healthcare died.

Clinton's second-term presidential victory was converted into a political stalemate, dominated by impeachment proceedings over his sleazy sexual escapades and pushing the Democrat on to the defensive. There was no Rooseveltian programme of public investment, even though the budget deficit moved from the 3.7 per cent of GDP he had inherited to a mere 0.3 per cent in 1997. What Clinton had to do was to keep the US economy cooking with more financial deregulation, more credit flows, more consumption and more property price inflation. The New Deal Glass–Steagall legislation was repealed in 1999, a measure pushed for aggressively by the Federal Reserve chair Alan Greenspan, a fervent disciple of Ayn Rand, on the basis that markets and profit-seeking firms never knowingly make mistakes – an absurd philosophy which he later acknowledged to be wrong, but it was symptomatic of the times. And in one of Clinton's last acts in office, he allowed over-the-counter derivatives not to be categorised as either 'securities' or 'futures' – what legendary investor Warren Buffet would a few years later describe as 'financial weapons of mass destruction' – thus permitting the vast bulk to be traded without being regulated, again at Greenspan's urging.[11] Dancing to market-fundamentalist tunes, the seeds of the later financial crisis had been sown. It was the final repudiation of the New Deal's mission to constrain the destructive tendencies of unfettered American finance. But only a few years later, the ghost of FDR would have the last laugh.

Yet for all that, Democrats remained electorally competitive – popular with ethnic minorities and some (if not all) of the hard-pressed working class. The 2000 presidential election saw George W. Bush successfully appeal to just enough blue-collar workers with his Reaganite promise of 'compassionate conservatism' – respecting remnants of New Deal liberalism, laced with tax cuts – to snatch an election victory without winning the popular vote. As it was, the Senate broke 50/50, and Republican control of the House was wafer-thin. But Osama bin Laden would hand another winning card to the Republicans with his atrocious attack on the Twin Towers. The War on Terror was born.

President George W. Bush seized the opportunity to pursue the neoconservative agenda of reasserting US power overseas, with Islamic terror substituting for the communist threat, and in the process he would suck Britain into compromising and unwinnable wars in Iraq and Afghanistan. Both were first-order strategic disasters. The USA would scuttle out of Afghanistan twenty years later in scenes reminiscent of the last days in Saigon in 1974, while the unilateral attack on Iraq has turned the country into a failed state, undermined the international rule of law and partially disarmed the West as it tries to marshal non-aligned countries to support Ukraine against the 2022 Russian invasion. But at the time, both these wars served Republican interests. The War on Terror fed a national paranoia that the country could be overrun by terrorists, which Republicans claimed they alone had the moral backbone to resist. New Deal liberals were soft on terror.

It was a slur, but a minority party faced with demographics that will diminish its electoral base still more has to fight with what it can. Reagan had been adept at aligning neoliberalism with 'authentic' American values, but now Republicans became ever more adept at fighting fully fledged culture wars. In the 2004 presidential election, Bush strategist Karl Rove promoted propositions against gay marriage in eleven Republican battleground states. The aim was to remind voters of the Republican Party's moral values, and encourage turnout among the religious right. He argued afterwards that these propositions helped win Bush a second term. Culture wars seemed to work.

All around the country, New Deal concerns to improve working-class lives receded in importance and were played down by Democrats even as globalisation and technology undermined blue-collar work and wages. Working-class voters responded to the appeal of cultural rallying calls on gun control, on abortion, on immigration and, more recently, 'the war on woke'. These issues certainly fuel the polarisation, populism, democratic gerrymandering and post-truth politics which now characterise the American public realm. They are a crucial mechanism to keep the Republican Party electorally competitive – especially as its underlying policies, particularly on tax, have become ever more skewed to the interests of the plutocratic rich. In this respect, it has much in common with other right-of-centre parties in democracies with high levels of inequality or ethnic divisions; stoking up atavistic fears is effective in rallying working-class voters to the right. American politics, as Jacob Hacker and Paul Pierson argue in *Let Them Eat Tweets*, has become locked in a 'doom loop of tax cutting and fearmongering' to sustain Republican power.

Even the Financial Crisis Does Not Stem the Tide

The financial crisis that struck in 2007 and persisted through 2008 was a direct result of nearly thirty years of financial deregulation, indulging the growth of an absurdly large financial sector, while imagining that markets could anticipate, and insure against, risk by themselves alone. The 'efficient markets' hypothesis peddled by the supply-side economists – that markets never make mistakes – was blown sky-high. It was obvious that only the state could protect the system against the kind of risks that Big Finance had been running. The backdrop to the last weeks of the 2008 presidential election was the massive bailout of the US and Western financial systems. First-term Senator Barack Obama managed to look more statesmanlike than veteran Republican John McCain, and echoes of the need to resurrect the New Deal approach to American finance reverberated with the electorate. The folk memory of Roosevelt's vital activism still lingered.

But, unfortunately, the newly inaugurated President Obama did not fully seize the moment to revitalise the New Deal settlement. His focus instead was on achieving just one dimension, more universal healthcare, a goal that had eluded his Democrat predecessors, and where – in fairness – he succeeded. He might tell bankers that his administration was all that stood between them and the pitchforks, but he sued for no substantive change in the way the economy and financial system were run, even as he saved the bankers. Professor Lawrence 'Larry' Summers had been US Treasury secretary under Clinton and was now Obama's director of the National Economic Council. He had written two years earlier that Democrats had to be as honest as Nixon had been in 1971, when he had said he was now a Keynesian in economics. Democrats should now acknowledge they were now all Friedmanites; the veteran of Mont Pelerin had won all the arguments. Even though the financial crisis proved just the opposite, Obama could not turn it into a political opportunity and remained shackled to Summers' version of the new orthodoxy.

Folly would succeed folly. Obama had managed to formulate a big extension in healthcare and pass it into law, a gain, even if it fell short of universal coverage. But even this was fiercely resisted by many in business and on the right. The US Chamber of Commerce launched a lavish lobbying campaign – cumulatively costing $270 million – against Obama's plans both on healthcare and on beefing up consumer protection against banks; the very free-enterprise system, the campaign intoned hysterically, was at stake. Business and finance were not going to allow another New Deal. Their spending and ideological aggression helped the Democrats lose control of the House of Representatives in 2010 – with the Republicans returning to their anti-state, cut-taxes-at-all-costs roots.

Rather than Obama's moment, this was Grover Norquist's. Norquist, a ferocious anti-communist in his youth, had now transmuted into a leading conservative activist with a monomaniacal focus on the evils of taxation as oppressive and coercive. He had founded Americans for Tax Reform back in 1985, which had become ever more powerful as the neoliberal tide had surged. His Wednesday-morning meetings in his Washington office had become almost mandatory for all ambitious Republicans, who were enlisted to fight any tax increase to the last ditch. But in the run-up to the 2010 congressional elections, he had become a prime architect of a nationwide, grassroots 'Tea Party' movement, dedicated to halting the growth of Big Government and cutting taxes, with rallies and town hall meetings across the USA. It was not bankers who were to feel the people's pitchforks but Democrats, who had used the state to save the financial system. More than fifty Republicans owed their House seats to Tea Party support, and in 2011 they resolved they would only vote to lift the US national debt in return for swingeing spending cuts. It was the kind of uncompromising political combat Newt Gingrich had pioneered twenty years earlier. And, with a big majority in the House, the Republicans meant it. Obama caved in and delivered the cuts.

Then, in 2012, Norquist insisted that every Republican running for Congress should sign a pledge to resist any tax increase for any purpose whatsoever. Some 95 per cent of them complied. Republicans were now engaged in an intransigent political war, giving no quarter to what they depicted as an out-of-touch, immoral and un-American Democrat elite. Obama's presidency, like Clinton's, disintegrated into a stalemate. Republicans resisted the case for acting on climate change or any measure to limit the sale and use of guns, of which there are now 393 million in private hands in the USA, many of them military-grade automatic rifles. 'Real men' burned fossil fuels and cherished their weapons. It was rarely admitted, and almost never in public, but white conservative Americans recoiled from a Black President. His willingness to sing 'Amazing Grace' in public only confirmed their worst prejudices: for all his intelligence, charm and evident moderation, he was Black and revelled in Black culture. A scurrilous story was promoted that Obama had not even been born in the United States but in Kenya, and was therefore not entitled to his office – a convenient way of suggesting that the first Black President was not a real American without saying anything explicitly racist. Donald Trump, long before he ran for president, was an ardent proponent of this transparently false claim.

The Broken Social Contract and the Menace of Trump

Neoliberalism may have been a political success for the American right, but its real-world results had truly baleful effects on US society. The US economy, straddling a continent and possessing a creative academic-cum-research ecosystem that fosters great innovations, backed by a venture capital system with the muscle to take risks in support of start-ups, had become the leader of the new high-tech digital economy. Silicon Valley was admired worldwide. American public culture rarely admits it, but the foundation for this success was laid by unprecedented federal government spending – mainly by the Pentagon – on scientific research and development. The 'entrepreneurial flywheel', declares Margaret O'Mara in *The Code: Silicon Valley and the Remaking of America*, 'started spinning during the Cold War' – aided and abetted by the space race. The money was dispensed cleverly, through private contractors and universities, with the Pentagon's research arm DARPA taking the lead and prepared to back the apparently impossible. Great names like Google, Intel, Oracle, Microsoft and Apple can all trace their success to this extraordinary ecosystem.

But this was an economy that had to deal with the fallout from a bankrupt financial system, caused by the wilful dismantling of the New Deal settlement. And while the new knowledge economy might have been booming, and productivity rising, real wages were stagnating. The undermining of trade unions had interacted with more atomised, fragmented economic structures to weaken labour's bargaining power. The public education and training system was and is inadequate to deliver the skills necessary for twenty-first-century requirements. Tax cuts that focused on the rich, attacks on welfare, the dilapidation of the public infrastructure and phenomenal indulgence of the growth of the financial sector had all proven to be a social cancer. Inequality had mushroomed; life expectancy had fallen in the face of opioid addiction and an epidemic of obesity. Incarceration rates for Black Americans were impossibly high. Loneliness and mental illness were rampant. The USA in 2016 could not boast of being the good society, and its problems cast a shadow over its dynamic capitalism.

Hillary Clinton as the Democratic presidential nominee in 2016 recognised many of these deformations, even if she could not develop a compelling narrative about how to fix them. Donald Trump, billionaire real estate developer, reality show host and epic narcissist, saw the anger and dissatisfaction of Americans as ground ripe for political populism. America's ills should be blamed on illegal migrants, Muslims, New Deal liberals, organised labour and the swamp that was Washington. His programme was a cynical mish-mash of culture wars and degenerate supply-side economics, overtly deployed to serve the rich, a re-run of the Reaganite messages he had been rehearsing since he first touted a presidential run in 1987. He would build a 'big beautiful wall' along the nearly 2,000-mile border with Mexico to keep out immigrants. He would cut deals in a way no one else could. He would save the USA. Ludicrously, given his own sexual mores and free-wheeling attitudes to women and the truth, he would restore virtue in American public life – belief in faith, family and flag.

This was an echo of the conservative political philosopher Leo

Strauss, guru of the original neoconservatives: a great republic has to be ruled by the god-fearing virtuous, one of the themes William F. Buckley Jr. had emphasised. From the National Rifle Association to the pro-life movement, it was a message they were ready to hear. Moises Naim, in *The Revenge of Power*, describes the rise of Trump, and other populists like him, as being based in three 'Ps' – polarisation, populism and post-truth. It is a useful framework, but it only produces electoral results in the fertile soil of economic and social distress. There was enough of that in 2016. Hillary Clinton's failure was that she had neither the charisma, the language nor the campaigning creativity to counter the demagogic appeal of Trump and Trumpism. However crude and bowdlerised, Trumpian 'supply-side' economics had been thirty-five years in the making, and it would need either a crisis or a special politician to drive the alternative home.

Once he was elected president, Trump's 2017 Tax Cuts and Jobs Act went a long way to helping mainstream Republicans forgive him for his antics. It had deliberate echoes of Reagan's 1981 Economic Recovery Tax Act – cuts in social programmes, increases in military spending and, above all, big tax cuts. More than 80 per cent of Trump's tax-cutting largesse went to the top 1 per cent of taxpayers, and the cuts were permanent; almost everyone else's tax cuts were both smaller and time-limited. By 2027, 70 per cent of those in the middle-income brackets would be paying higher taxes than if the law had never been enacted. Corporation tax was lowered to 21 per cent. It was pure plutocratic politics disguised by Trump's boast that it was part of Making America Great Again.

Higher US growth would, he hoped, come to the rescue. But there was no mass support for his attacks on Obamacare. His characterisation of captured US soldiers as losers spoke only of his own moral failure. His racism manifested itself in outspoken attacks on immigrants and immigration. The mantle of sleaze, sexism and lying settled over him, never to be dispelled. He would lose the 2018 mid-terms and in August 2019, the American Business Roundtable of some 200 leading CEOs announced in a famous declaration that business's purpose should be the pursuit of long-term value for *all* its stakeholders – an astonishing repudiation of the doctrines of the previous forty years, in which shareholder maximisation had been put first and foremost. In practice, short-term profit maximisation is counterproductive. This was a recognition that the times were changing. Trump would lose the 2020 presidential election to Joe Biden, refuse to acknowledge the defeat and, like Ayn Rand's bombastic exponent of selfishness John Galt, insist that the world should revolve around him and his views of truth.

Trump had neither promoted virtue in American public life nor bound its society together; Covid and the events after the election, trying to deny the result and indulging the storming of the Capitol, exposed him as the self-obsessed monster he had always been.

A Second New Deal?

Biden won a comfortable majority in the presidential Electoral College, but the Democrats controlled the House and the Senate by the narrowest of margins. Yet Biden astonished both his party and the wider world by reaffirming New Deal liberalism and doing so on a scale unprecedented for over fifty years. The investments in infrastructure, measures to address climate change, commitments to science, research and development and education, and support for early-years education, housing and transport have not been matched since Lyndon B. Johnson's Great Society. Biden saw the pressing case for capital investment and drove the vital budgets and legislation to deliver on them as much as he could. In a key 2022 Executive Order, he aimed to promote competition and attack monopoly more aggressively than any other president since the trust-busting of Theodore Roosevelt before the First World War.

Jake Sullivan, President Biden's national security adviser, voiced the new American doctrine in an important speech in spring 2023. The USA had been wrong to believe the supply-siders' gospel of the previous forty years. The tax cuts directed at the rich, and deregulation of business and finance, had all failed comprehensively to deliver in their own terms. What it meant in practice was 'the privileging of finance over fundamental economic growth, which was a mistake'. The willingness freely to open up US markets to cheap imports had also undermined the industries that delivered middle-class jobs. Instead, they had been hollowed out with supply chains and entire industries moving overseas, creating disillusion, disaffection and undermining democracy – a not-very-veiled reference to Donald Trump. Russia and China had seized the opportunity to subsidise their industries, and were now aggressively challenging the USA.

The Biden approach was to deploy government spending on a vast scale to trigger investment in new and green technologies. This, it was hoped, would bring supply chains and industries back to the USA, along with middle-class jobs, and also enhance security and democracy. It seemed to be working. Large-scale investment in semi-conductors and green technologies had jumped twenty-fold since 2019, Sullivan said, implying a $3.5-trillion boost to investment in the decade ahead. The USA would not collapse into mercantilism; rather, it would seek carefully structured trade deals with the EU and Pacific countries. The aim was not to confront China but to become less dependent on it. In the end, invoking President Kennedy, Sullivan concluded by saying that we all rise or fall together.[12]

Professor Gary Gerstle thinks that this is the fall of neo-liberalism – but that verdict can be justified only if the Democrats win the presidential election in 2024.[13] The stakes could not be higher; in the view of the great liberal commentator Robert Kuttner, what is at stake is American democracy itself – a not unreasonable claim given Trump's apparent plans to consolidate as much executive power as possible in the person of the Presidency to achieve his goals, in which naked revenge plays a large part.[14] Neoliberalism *should* fall; it should never have had the grip that it did. The New Deal had succeeded, and had shown the USA and other liberal capitalist democracies the need for public guiderails, public agencies, public regulation – especially of the financial system and labour markets – in producing a successful capitalism. It had framed American politics for more than fifty years, and the electoral alliance Roosevelt forged was to sustain consistent Democratic majorities. Even now it is largely gerrymandering and aggressive culture wars that keep the Republicans electorally competitive. The great supply-side revolution launched in 1980 has failed, and the American left is growing increasingly self-confident that New Deal ideas should be revisited, can work and can form the basis of a new period of sustained Democrat rule. Despite reeling from four major lawsuits in the wake of his refusal to accept the result of the 2020 election result, at the time of writing, Donald Trump has sufficient support to win the Republican nomination to be the party's presidential candidate in 2024. His appeal does not extend much beyond the Republican base. But Biden's age, political division, social disillusion and the too slow evidence of an improving economy in people's pockets make the electoral outcome closer than it should be. The truth remains: neoliberalism has failed. It is only a rancorous, polarising populism based on Trump's unique capacity to fan blue-collar America's sense of shared victimhood that gives the American right any prospects at all. Democrats need the time for their policies to deliver demonstrably, attacking the causes of blue-collar victimhood with good jobs, allied with talking in American terms much more confidently of fusing the 'We' and the 'I'. It is New-Deal thinking that has made America great – not conservatism's embrace of hyper-individualism and libertarianism.

On our side of the Atlantic, British economics and politics have been dominated by American conservative ideas – the USA's Little Sir Echo. But Britain did not have to reproduce America's mistakes so slavishly – nor does it now. Instead, we should have been learning the lessons of the New Deal and fashioning our own. We must now turn to the reasons why.

3

EPIC MISTAKES AND
THE FATE OF THE TORY PARTY

M rs Thatcher's election in 1979 saw the curtain rise on the neoliberal age. Ronald Reagan joined her as US president eighteen months later and the two leaders began their joint effort to dismantle the post-war settlement in both their countries. Thatcher and Reagan were united in the conviction that the route to free societies, free markets and prosperity was government minimalism, and market and individualist maximalism. This was, for them, not just an economic proposition, but a moral one. The more individuals took responsibility for their own lives and controlled their own destinies as free as possible from regulation, access to welfare and taxation, the more whole and independent they would be. The free marketplace was the centrepiece of this vision. Business and individuals could be relied upon to look after their own interests, and use markets to self-organise into the best outcomes for themselves and the wider society. To achieve this, the New Deal in the USA and the framework bequeathed by the 1945–51 Labour government both had to be disassembled.

But markets and capitalism are much more complex than this. Individual agency and responsibility are of course prime movers in human affairs, as are dynamic markets – but so are cooperation and mutuality. The trick is to get the alchemy right. The great neoliberal experiment that emphasised the first and neglected the latter has palpably failed – even more visibly in Britain than the USA.

Four avoidable disasters informed by the neoliberal economic vision have followed one another. The first was the excess of deindustrialisation and financialisaton of the Thatcher decade; then the financial crisis of 2007/8, and the deregulated euphoria that led up to it; the austerity of the 2010s; and finally the Brexit debacle. Cumulatively, they have laid the country very low. Britain in the 2020s is economically disarmed and socially distressed. A vast and concerted effort is needed to turn round the situation in which the country finds itself. The conviction and sustained energy required to do that will be reinforced if we understand just how disastrous the neoliberal hegemony has been.

Mrs Thatcher as the Architect of Decline

Mrs Thatcher is the undisputed, deified lioness of Tory politics. The hallowed story is that she achieved a quadruple whammy, a radical programme of privatisation, anti-union legislation, tax-cutting (and the top tax rates in particular) and financial deregulation, all satisfying deeply held Tory principles. In the process, she achieved growth with significantly lower inflation and raised productivity. She won three successive general elections. The resolve and bravery on display in taking back the Falkland Islands and confronting the National Union of Mineworkers (NUM) demonstrated her toughness, even if her economic decisions meant that huge parts of the old British manufacturing economy were lost for ever and unemployment climbed to over 3 million. She restored British greatness by sheer force of character, faithful to Tory principles of free markets and sound money, only to be betrayed in the end by fainthearts in a final tragic *denouement*. She was among the first to see how the EU was holding Britain back with its webs of 'socialist' regulation. She is seen by her more ardent admirers as the author of euroscepticism, and allegedly would have been delighted with Brexit – although in office she was notably more pragmatic than in her retirement. Mrs Thatcher did have some achievements, but the story I have outlined is a myth. In reality she was the prime architect of sustained British decline.

Her ideology drew on a blend of the English liberal, laissez-faire tradition, profoundly distrustful of the state, and from thinkers like John Stuart Mill, celebrating the sovereignty of the individual, and a crude understanding of Adam Smith's belief in the self-organising properties of markets; however, in Thatcher this native tradition was turbocharged by the work of European and American right-wing economic intellectuals. If the monetarist economist Milton Friedman and the anti-collectivist thinking of the Austrian-British political philosopher Friedrich Hayek were influential in the USA, they were just as influential on her – in part, as described in the last chapter, because of their growing American success. Especially attractive was that their ideas offered a *moral* cutting edge. Socialism, in her terms, took away responsibility for individuals' decisions; the market economy, offering individual choice and riches for those with drive and initiative, handed back responsibility to the people. She burned with moral fervour. In an election speech at Birmingham City Hall in April 1979, she declared, 'Old Testament prophets didn't go into the highways saying, "Brothers I want consensus." They said, "This is my faith and my vision. This is what I passionately believe."'[1] It was this rejuvenated economic and political liberalism that gave her the intellectual ammunition, which she fused with long-standing Tory suspicions of the crimes of collectivism into an effective programme of political action.

It was almost wholly wrong, but she was lucky in her timing. Ten years earlier or ten years later, the message would have had less resonance, but in the late 1970s the post-war world of incomes policies, industrial strategies and Keynesian demand management was flailing. Inflation seemed endemic after the first oil shock in 1973, peaking at over 20 per cent. Resisting both Labour's attempted reforms in 1969's *In Place of Strife* and Conservative attempts to tame them and outlaw unofficial strikes in the 1971 Industrial Relations Act, the then very confident trade unions wielded too much power, especially in the eyes of Margaret Thatcher and her supporters. British efforts to manage the economy as a partnership between business, government and unions, supported by incomes policies and active demand management, had failed. In desperate times, a new approach had to be adopted; old verities reinvigorated by modern free-market thinkers and a moral crusade seemed the way forward.

In this, she was reflecting ideas that had been incubating in the Conservative Party, especially on the right, for over a decade. In January 1970, Ted Heath, then the leader of the opposition, had gathered his shadow cabinet at the grandiloquent Selsdon Park Hotel in Croydon to devise a manifesto for the forthcoming election based on free-market ideas. This built on the particular conservatism of the influential right-wing MP Enoch Powell, who had from the late 1950s been arguing against the post-war welfare state and social democracy as enemies of freedom and capitalism, but who then disgraced himself by warning in 1968 that the reaction to unchecked immigration would leave, as he put it, 'the river Tiber foaming with much blood'. Yet Powell's critique of incomes policies, and his defence of the free market, 'sound money' and the minimal state, were becoming the new common sense of conservatism.

Ted Heath was elected in 1970 on a free-market, 'sound money', anti-union platform – 'Selsdon Man', in Labour leader Harold Wilson's dismissive phrase – and imposed a legal framework for industrial relations that was fiercely resisted by the trade union movement. Reality soon crowded in. The bailout of Rolls-Royce in 1971 showed that free markets had limits, the Industrial Relations Act seemed unenforceable and, as inflation rose in 1972, Heath established a Price Commission and Pay Board before finally being engulfed by the 1973/4 miners' strike. The Selsdon Man approach had failed, leaving the Tory leadership badly shaken. It would take some chutzpah to mount a second attempt.

The 'Winter of Discontent', capping years of inflation and fading economic progress, provided the opportunity. Prime Minister Callaghan had, in the third year of an incomes policy, set a 5 per cent upper limit on wage settlements in the year from 1978 to 1979. Inflation was running at 8 per cent. It was a stretch too far for the unions, and as 1979 unfolded strike succeeded strike, fatefully including grave-diggers and refuse collectors. Thatcher had the opportunity she had yearned for; it was time, she claimed, to declare war on the minority of trade union 'wreckers' using the power of secondary picketing (the picketing of other employers' staff and customers, who impact on the company but are not involved in the dispute) to hold the country to ransom. Hayek and Friedman had been setting out their arguments for decades, but their thinking now seemed to be validated by events. An emboldened Thatcher could at last reframe a right-wing alternative which had popular traction. Uncollected refuse and unburied corpses vividly supported her message.

One series of congenial propositions flowed from another. Friedman argued that inflation was always a monetary phenomenon, fed by governments printing money to pay their bills. Instead, they should sell bonds to their public to finance their spending, but this had the danger of the state 'crowding out' the potential to borrow by virtuous private business and individuals. To get around the problem, governments typically took the soft option of in effect printing money, thus either not having to sell bonds at all, or selling very short-term bonds that were effectively surrogates for cash. The solution was good 'public housekeeping', keeping public spending and public debt under close control. This would cap the growth of the money supply and – hey presto – lower inflation.

Targeting the growth of the money supply to reduce inflation sounds like a benign technical measure, but in practice it means rolling back public spending and borrowing, providing fewer social services and less investment in public goods. But in 1979, it did mean that the whole paraphernalia of post-war incomes policies was unnecessary. 'Don't try to limit inflation through incomes policies', the new orthodoxy stated; 'Instead, curb public debt and thus the money supply, which, coupled with more flexible labour markets and less union power, will naturally lower inflation.' Moreover, in Friedman's view, the close link between expansionary monetary and fiscal policies and lower unemployment – one of the foundational principles of the post-war economic consensus – was just wrong. Unemployment was determined by labour market realities, namely over-mighty trade unions pricing men and women out of work. Inflation was determined by monetary dynamics. They had to be separately addressed, rather than conceived as two variables that could be traded off against each other. All this chimed with Thatcher.

Another set of propositions, no less congenial, flowed from Hayek. To guarantee economic and political freedom, it was vital to enlarge the private sphere of action enabled by private property. Accordingly, as many people as possible should have a stake in such property. Nationalisation should give way to privatisation. Planning should be abandoned and markets should be freed up or created to undertake what planning had attempted to do. Trade unions were a particular Hayekian *bête noire*; they allegedly coerced their members into overbidding for excessive wages, helped along by Keynesian demand management. To remove their bargaining power they should be offered no legal protection or privileges. Wages should be set in flexible labour markets, rather than being the outcome of 'collective' bargaining agreements between unions and industries.

Thatcherism thus had a moral *and* an economic rationale, and it was gifted with enemies ranging from the militant National Union of Mineworkers to the inefficient nationalised industries. She could turn her fire on them all. It did not matter that the data on which Friedman based his case was manipulated, nor that booms and busts had many more causes than the fluctuation of economies' money supply. Nor did it matter that finding a measure of money that was controllable – even had the theory worked – was in practice impossible. (This was paradoxically a critique which Hayek shared, even while he endorsed Friedman's basic philosophy.) Friedmanite monetarist economics was intellectually flawed and inoperable. But it offered Thatcher a rationale to do what she wanted to do: to insist on the homely analogy that, like any housewife, the state had to balance its books so that it did not risk printing money. Nor did it matter to Thatcher, Hayek and Friedman that any good society necessarily combines elements of individual agency and collective action: the 'I' and the 'We'. That was the despised philosophy of social democrats and, to an extent, of the 'one nation' Tories whose concerns she dismissed as 'wet'.

Excessive collectivism can indeed collapse into authoritarian control, but institutions like social insurance to provide relief for unemployment, the postal service, a licence fee-funded BBC, publicly owned utilities or policies that through higher public investment aim at encouraging higher private investment were hardly the thin end of a 'socialist' wedge. Nor is the market so magical that it will spontaneously produce long-term investment (as opposed to short-term profits) and high levels of training, or stop private business imposing costs on society by polluting the environment or selling faulty products. Even an alleged high priest of the free market like Adam Smith acknowledged the need for government to set guiderails for business behaviour. There is certainly a debate to be had about how to get this vital alchemy right, but the real magic in economic growth and development comes from the interplay of the 'We' and the 'I', the marrying of public stimulus and business entrepreneurialism – as America's New Deal or the rapid European reconstruction after the war had shown. Thatcher was not interested in either, or their message about how to get the best from capitalism. Her absolutist belief in the moral primacy of the individual, the market and private property, and the accompanying distrust of any form of purposeful common enterprise, was always the intellectual demon at the heart of Thatcherism. It was why her project would ultimately fail on so many levels.

She was also self-contradictory in her own terms – the neoliberal statist. Thatcher was more than prepared to reach back into older and more authoritarian conservative traditions. She used the state's powers to suppress the miners' strikes, to force the sale of council houses on reluctant local authorities while forbidding them to replenish the stock, to launch financial deregulation and to make collective bargaining arrangements that had been freely arrived at illegal. She was an arch-liberal who was prepared to use state authority with as much conviction as any pre-democratic oligarch. All the while, she would celebrate the self-organising and incentivising power of free markets, making her blind to the consequences of the credit boom over which she presided, and blind to the unchecked rise of the pound during the 1980s, which so badly damaged manufacturing and exports. Praise was heaped on the private and the individualistic in (almost) all its forms, even though her tearing up of regulations unleashed greed, and a wave of takeovers whose motive was unashamed asset-stripping rather than value creation – risks that Hayek, in his devotion to free markets, never anticipated. Indeed, some of her most outspoken supporters in the business world, like Lord Hanson or Sir James Goldsmith, made their fortunes through predatory takeovers that broke up the victim companies rather than reorganising them to create value. If the market permitted naked asset-stripping, who was to say it was wrong? Meanwhile, as inequality rose and fissures deepened in British society, Thatcher in 1987 would controversially ask the question:

> Who is society? There is no such thing! There are individual men and women and there are families and no government can do anything except through people and people look to themselves first.[2]

It was a foundational statement of her belief in the priority of individuals, individual responsibility and the inevitability of their looking out for themselves first – an echo of Ayn Rand's commitment to selfishness as a prime moral virtue. It was also despairing about the potential of government. It could be mocked – and was mocked – as being clueless about the importance of social institutions and structures in shaping people's lives, but she saw the denial of society as a moral statement. It also gave shape to public policy. The justification for introducing the Right to Buy policy that led to 970,000 council houses being sold off at a discount over her decade in office was that it was a price worth paying in the larger cause of extending private property ownership and enhancing individual responsibility, even though it gave incumbent council house tenants a one-off dowry at the expense of future generations. The tragedy was that only 20,000 new council houses a year were being built by the end of the 1980s, so the rapidly diminishing stock was not replaced.[3] It is one of the principal causes of today's social housing crisis.

The successive privatisations Thatcher organised were designed not only to get public assets off the public balance sheet and into private management, but also to build individual share ownership; in 1979, 3 million people owned shares; by 1990, that figure had grown to 10 million.[4] Again, the aim was as much moral as economic; individual shareholders would have an individual stake in companies, promoting a culture of enterprise and individual responsibility. The pity is that this was not matched by any enlightened reform of company law to make individual share ownership meaningful. Privatisation simply meant the creation of public limited companies on pre-existing corporate governance rules that had failed for decades. That did not diminish the forcefulness of her message. She really believed in the moral value of what she was doing. It cast a spell, despite the futility of where the doctrine led – and it still does.

Unpacking the Thatcher Legend

The centrepiece of Thatcher's economic policy was the Medium Term Financial Strategy (MTFS), published as part of the 1980 budget. It ranks with the return to the gold standard in 1925 and the launch of austerity in 2010 as among the most damaging economic policies in British history. It set out to translate Friedmanite theory into fiscal and monetary policy. The strategic aim was for public spending and borrowing to fall over the four years after 1980, congruent with a trajectory for the growth of the money supply that would automatically deliver a sharply falling rate of inflation. It was monetarism in action. Like austerity thirty years later, it was intellectually wrong and would fail on its own terms with disastrous economic consequences.

The first consequence was that interest rates were driven higher to curb the rate of money supply growth at the same time as North Sea oil was turning sterling into a much-desired petrocurrency. The pound soared, putting intolerable pressure on British exporters. In 1981, the former Bundesbank president Dr Otmar Emminger told a House of Commons Select Committee that the rise in sterling's value was 'by far the most excessive overvaluation which any major currency has experienced in recent monetary history'.[5] The overvaluation – some 30 per cent above its proper value as indicated by British prices relative to overseas prices[6] – would ease a little, but over the decade as a whole it would shackle British exporters and prove a boon to importers. It was also the single most important cause of deindustrialisation. The second consequence was the approach to budget-making, driving the extraordinary 1981 budget that raised taxes and cut spending by 3 per cent of GDP even as unemployment climbed to 2 million. It was a repudiation of the Keynesian approach of the previous twenty-five years, which allowed budget deficits to rise during recessions so as to compensate for the fallaway in demand. It failed, for despite the powerful recessionary impetus, money supply growth continued unabated, so the pound remained high – with the happy result of bearing down on inflation despite the consistent failure to control money supply growth, and the unhappy result of devastating British exporters.

Manufacturing industry, particularly dependent on exports and exposed to competition from imports, bore the brunt of this disastrous policy. Only 46 per cent of manufacturing establishments present in 1979 still survived in 1989 as companies closed increasingly uncompetitive factories; in other words, around half of Britain's industrial workplaces vanished in ten years. Manufacturing employment fell by 28.3 per cent. In those years, the overall share of manufacturing in total employment fell from 24.3 per cent to 17.3 per cent. Yet within the manufacturing rump labour productivity did rise by 51.4 per cent, so that the productivity gap with West Germany fell from 40.3 per cent to 5.9 per cent. But this closing of the gap did not deliver higher output; overall manufacturing output was only 8 per cent higher in 1989.[7]

The social effects on the worst-hit areas can only be described as 'carnage', with industrial districts of the Midlands, Wales, Scotland and the North of England losing the businesses that provided jobs and all the other companies that serviced the shuttered factories. These areas still bear the scars; there has been very little 'regeneration'. A recent Oxford University discussion paper shows that more than forty years later, nearly all the areas knocked into deprivation are still deprived, with male employment and earnings particularly hard-hit. Once a local authority district gets into a vicious circle of decline it is almost impossible to reverse it – either through policy or self-correcting economic forces.[8]

Even in Thatcher's own terms this was counterproductive. The abiding feature of the 1980s was unemployment centred in the traditional industrial areas, climbing to 11 per cent in 1982. Between 1983 and 1986, 3 million people were unemployed, that figure falling only gradually thereafter. These were stunning numbers, on a scale not seen since the 1930s. Aside from the incredible social hardship, it made the much-vaunted control of public spending even harder; by the mid-1980s, social security spending was running at 12 per cent of GDP, up from 8 per cent a decade earlier.[9] This forced spending cuts elsewhere, notably on capital investment, which declined to derisory levels, but it also blocked any hope of tax cuts.

Thatcher and her government were vandalising the economy and wounding society in the name of an unworkable theory, and she should have paid the electoral price. But she was lucky. For all its flaws, Thatcherism offered a solution to the impasse in which British economic management found itself in 1979. Trade union membership had already peaked and unions were hardly popular, and a significant tranche of working-class voters were attracted to Mrs Thatcher's brand of individualism. She had a bedrock of support and, crucially, she enjoyed great prestige from winning the Falklands War, sending a fleet halfway around the world to take on a contemptible dictatorship.

By contrast, the Labour Party could not unite around an alternative prospectus. Could a better-designed incomes policy work? What concessions, if any, should be made to the new wave of neoliberal thinking? Should its economic approach continue to be built on the planning, nationalisation and Keynesian demand management laid out by the 1945–51 government? In 1981, the party split, with the high-profile defections of the 'Gang of Four' heralding the further departure of twenty-seven MPs to the new Social Democratic Party (SDP), while the rump of the party was led by the veteran socialist Michael Foot. Finally, as I argue in Chapter 7, the tensions between a left aiming for socialist transformation and a softer left aiming for reform within the pro-capitalist club of Europe became unbridgeable. Britain's grotesquely unfair first-past-the-post electoral system made the split fatal. In the 1983 general election, the powerful combined anti-Thatcher vote of 52 per cent was divided between Labour, the Liberals and the SDP, so although she commanded only 42 per cent of the vote, that represented a landslide in terms of seats. The pattern would be repeated in 1987. Unable to forge a unifying social democratic philosophy, the left was to an extent the author of its own downfall – the subject of future chapters. But the electoral system settled the matter.

Yet within an overall pattern of failure, gross errors and omissions, there were some positive scores on the ledger. Employee representation and participation in company decision-making is generally associated with greater levels of employee satisfaction, higher levels of productivity, less workplace friction and workplaces more quickly adapting to change. British trade unionism in the 1970s was not delivering such results – and had not done so for decades. The heart of the problem was not so much the closed shop (the insistence that all workers had to belong to the union) or a propensity to strike, although both were problematic, but as Professor Nicholas Crafts describes in *Forging Ahead, Falling Behind and Fighting Back*, Britain had too many unions, all too often on one large site. It was difficult, bordering on impossible, to organise agreements with them all that made overall economic sense. Although the capacity of trade unions to deliver bad outcomes was overstated, governments for the previous decade had wanted to find some way of reducing strikes and to limit workers' capacity to support other workplace disputes, in particular in the form of secondary picketing. The hope was that this would be a route to more workplace rationality, with fewer and less powerful unions on any individual site. Thatcher would abolish the closed shop, outlaw secondary picketing and require ballots for strike action – measures that had eluded the Wilson, Heath and Callaghan governments. During the 1980s, there were spurts in productivity, particularly in sectors where the closed shop had ruled (for example, in printing and parts of the car industry, which had become bywords for restrictive practices). The newly 'flexible labour market' would become an economic asset, especially and paradoxically in attracting inward investment. Employees should not be married to companies, and the UK's reformed labour market structures have driven higher proportions of the workforce to participate in employment.

But there are limits. Thatcher's hostility to trade unions and worker representation in the workplace now looks a lot less clever. The productivity growth of the late 1980s, 1990s and early 2000s has not been sustained. Low pay, poor productivity and job insecurity are all now widespread; new forms of exploitation have emerged, with the zero-hours contract emblematic of the power imbalance between the unrepresented, non-unionised worker and their boss. No account of the emergence of profound inequality in British society is plausible without factoring in the deliberate enfeeblement of organised labour, with the top 10 per cent earning five times more on average than the bottom 10 per cent. That compares to a more normal rate elsewhere in the industrialised world (outside the USA) of the most well-rewarded getting three times more than the lowest-paid.[10] Employees are vital human capital in any enterprise, not notations on a spreadsheet, to be exploited and disposed of at will. The policy objective should not be eviscerating the principle of trade unionism, but rather creating trade unions and bargaining structures that make economic sense.

Another gain of the Thatcher era but which right-wing commentators and analysts downplay was membership of the European Common Market and the creation of a single market in goods and services, a development pushed for by Mrs Thatcher herself and her appointee as the European Commission's internal market commissioner, Lord Cockfield, who together could be reasonably regarded as its joint architects. In 1985, Cockfield had identified 300 barriers to trade that had to be dismantled to create a comprehensive pan-European single market. His white paper was well received in Europe, and led to the treaty establishing the single market in 1992. The system of imperial preference had been only slowly dismantled after the war; average tariffs still stood at 14.5 per cent in 1960. Entry into the tariff-free Common Market and then the progressive elimination of non-tariff barriers in the single market gave a massive and much-needed competitive jolt to British business. In an important paper, Nicholas Crafts demonstrates that the total impact was to raise British GDP by between 8 and 10 per cent – in part by the impact of increased competition and in part by the additional inflows of inward foreign investment.[11]

There the success story ends. Privatisation meant turning over public assets to profit-maximising private companies, within a framework of 'light-touch' regulation. It may have had some initial short-term success in lifting productivity, but now, forty years later, it is clear that the experiment has largely failed. Investment in everything from water pipes and reservoirs to railway lines has been miserly, and too little attention has been paid to public-interest objectives. Electricity and gas remain expensive and vulnerable to supply shocks, as we saw in the autumn of 2022, while too many water companies have disgracefully neglected basic investment. Water wastage and pollution of beaches and rivers are a national scandal. The rail network, privatised by the Major government, has become a byword for inefficiency, waste, expense, cancelled trains and indifference to passengers. First the rail infrastructure was taken back into public ownership and now the operating companies are following the same path. Meanwhile, the executives and shareholders of the privatised companies are paid as if they were running high-risk private companies in highly competitive markets rather than utility monopolies.

Privatisation emerged not as a thought-through strategy, but as a wheeze, triggered by British Telecom's (BT) need to invest in digital switching. In order to get much-needed borrowing for such investment off the public sector's balance sheet and to meet the borrowing targets in the MTFS, the company was sold off. Sell half of BT's shares to the private sector and at a stroke its borrowing would be off the public balance sheet. No thought was given to the corporate governance of the privatised utilities so that they would prioritise their obvious social purpose. No judgement was made about what kind of private owner was preferred – a publicly listed company, say, rather than private equity – nor were regulators empowered as they should have been. No consideration was given to which industrial structures might best suit privatisation. It became an ideological obsession, proudly moving, as Russell Jones writes in *The Tyranny of Nostalgia*, 5 million workers and 5 per cent of GDP from the public to the private sector.[12]

Blindness to all these weaknesses has allowed an orgy of asset-looting, tax avoidance and indifferent service. The water companies, privatised for similar reasons to BT, were sold at a discount to encourage investment, but the regulatory weakness of Ofwat allowed borrowing to be used instead to take cash out of the companies – in Thames Water's case, via complex tax havens. More importantly, short-term private-sector time horizons have proved very difficult to overcome for all but the most determined managements in industries whose assets need sustaining over the long term. Eye-watering sums of money have been paid to executives who have presided over neglect and low investment. In the early 2020s, while some utilities that are publicly listed and pursuing social-purpose objectives are meeting the promise of privatisation, many are weaker than they would have been if privatisation had been better designed and regulated, or if (a heretical thought) those entities had been left in public ownership. If privatisation was briefly popular back in the 1980s, large majorities now favour renationalisation.[13]

An epic error of omission, ranking with the MTFS, austerity and Brexit as policy failures, was the failure to create a sovereign wealth fund with the proceeds of North Sea oil. Instead, Britoil, Britain's national champion in the North Sea, was sold off. Established by the Labour government, Britoil could have been the foundation of a sovereign wealth fund (like Norway's) that would have gathered North Sea oil revenues in a massive endowment for future generations. The Norwegian fund is now worth $1.4 trillion – or $250,000 per head of population – and its dividends fund 4 per cent of all Norwegian government spending. It believes in responsible investment for which it has earned a global reputation.

On one estimate Britain could now have a sovereign wealth fund nearly as large as Norway's, which would have supplied a growing £60 billion per year to the annual government budget.[14] In just one year, for example, Britain would have had the ready-made revenue to create a fund to invest in the start-ups and scale-ups for which I call in Chapter 10, and GDP would already be up to 10 per cent larger than it is. However, the very concept of such a fund was anathema to Thatcher and her allies and dismissed as a statist intrusion; the private sector was the only way forward – and licences were awarded on exceptionally lax terms. Forty years later, that lost opportunity is one of the most damning charges to be levelled against Thatcher and Thatcherism. She squandered a once-in-a-century opportunity.

Last and certainly not least of the failures was the abandonment of controls on mortgage lending and investment banking. First, in the name of laissez-faire economics, controls on mortgage lending were progressively lifted, so that in 1981 banks could become mortgage lenders in a major way. Building societies would later be permitted to demutualise and turn themselves into profit-seeking, publicly listed banks, lending on an even bigger scale, with Abbey National beginning the gold rush in 1989. The result was a two-stage credit, mortgage and property price boom, first building up over the 1980s and then, after the recession at the end of the decade, continuing into the mid-2000s. It was financial deregulation, spawning higher consumer spending and the 1980s property boom that began to make up for the depredations of the MTFS. In effect, it was a privatised reflation.

As the credit and asset price boom took off towards the end of the 1980s, tax revenues were lifted, and Chancellor Nigel Lawson lowered the top rate of income tax from 60 to 40 per cent in his 1988 budget, following the lead from the USA. The idea was that lower tax would stimulate enterprise, risk-taking and innovation. Forty years later, we are still waiting for this miracle to occur. The evidence that tax cuts are any significant spur to economic growth is paltry, but that has not stopped the right in both the UK and the USA from unwavering support for the proposition. What tax cuts do deliver is straitened public services and more inequality.

To alleviate the distress, what was needed was a lower exchange rate, coupled with a determined effort to reshape British capitalism – to reform corporate governance, reframing the very concept of a company – to boost training massively, boost real long-term investors and increase investment spending on infrastructure and research and development. But that represented the kind of proactive state initiative that Thatcher loathed. The so-called Big Bang in 1986 was a policy error to match the Medium Term Financial Strategy. The 'restrictive practice' of separating the market-making function in security markets from the ability to lend money was scrapped. This allowed investment banks from all over the world both to lend commercially and trade in financial securities markets if they were based in London, and was another giant step towards making the economy dangerously subordinate to the volatility of finance and its short-term priorities. This twin capacity to lend and trade had been outlawed by New Deal legislation because it had been the cause of the 1929 stock market crash, but reviving the practice would allow the City of London to once again become the world financial centre it had been under the gold standard. Crucially, the Big Bang would force the USA to follow suit when President Clinton scrapped the Glass–Steagall legislation in 1999; the clincher argument in Washington was that the USA should allow Wall Street banks to do in Wall Street what they could do in London. In the following decade, American and European banks would use the capital that underwrote their commercial lending to also underwrite vast trades in the financial derivatives markets, claiming that, unlike in the 1920s, they could manage and insure against the risks. They could not, as we know. When the financial crisis inevitably broke, Britain was revealed as the economy most acutely exposed, requiring proportionally the largest support package of all the major economies to its stricken banks and building societies. The legacy – ranging from the balance sheet depression of the 2010s to the astonishing level of today's house prices – is there for all to see. The Thatcher financial boom was an unsustainable palliative, distracting voters from the loss of manufacturing and genuine sources of creating long-term economic value.

The Aftermath: New Labour and the Great Financial Crisis

As free-market globalisation took hold after the collapse of the Soviet Union, the open British economy prospered, first at the tail-end of the Conservative years under John Major and then under New Labour. The last vestiges of MTFS thinking were exploded when, in 1992, Britain was forced out of the European Exchange Rate Mechanism of managed exchange rates, with the non-inflationary deutschmark at its heart – membership was meant to anchor the fight against inflation after successive failures to control the money supply. From now on, the Bank of England would be asked to meet an inflation target of 1–4 per cent. But the rest of Thatcher's economic settlement seemed to have been vindicated. It was certainly not disturbed in its essentials by New Labour, even if it took a very different approach to constitutional reform, the promotion of social cohesion and better provision of high-quality public services. It would accept privatisation and the priority of keeping inflation low and stable by making the Bank of England independent with a mandate to hit a 2 per cent inflation target. Thatcher's labour market reforms would not be challenged – a flexible labour market with unemployment benefit contingent on actively searching for a job was seen as the route to full employment. New Labour would resist attempts to build a stakeholder economy, preferring to leave corporate governance, the savings and investment industry and the City to their own free-market devices. A growing financial sector seemed an immutable fact of post-industrial life; financial services would grow from 3.5 per cent of GDP in 1980 to over 9 per cent in 2007, providing both employment and a rich source of tax revenue. The light-touch, indulgent regulatory regime launched by Thatcher would not be endangered; indeed, it would be entrenched. Ed Balls, as economic secretary to the Treasury in 2006, declared the following:

> The Government's interest in the City and financial services is specific and clear: to safeguard the light touch and proportionate regulatory regime that has made London a

magnet for international business [...] [The Labour government] will outlaw the imposition of any rules that might endanger the light touch, risk based regulatory regime that underpins London's success.[15]

So attached was New Labour to giving the City its head that when, in 2007, Northern Rock suffered the worst bank run for more than a century, Prime Minister Gordon Brown refused for months to take it into public ownership. Even after the Great Financial Crisis of 2008, Chancellor Alistair Darling would jointly chair with City nabob Sir Win Bischoff an inquiry not into the *causes* of the crisis, but how to retain City competitiveness by resisting calls for too much regulation in response. In economic and financial matters, New Labour were truly Thatcher's children; she would boast that one of her greatest successes was Tony Blair.

In fairness to Blair and Brown, for a decade it seemed to work, providing the tax base for a notable range of social reforms – asset-based welfare with the child trust fund, Sure Start, academy schools – and serious investment in the NHS. Labour did not have the self-confidence or the intellectual curiosity to put its head under the bonnet and reform the capitalist engine. It was far too respectful of what Thatcher had done, just as post-First World War Labour governments were wrongly respectful of laissez-faire. Of course the regulatory regime in the years before the financial crisis was too lax. Of course the demutualised building societies, now banks, were lending mortgages recklessly and had balance sheets far too large and risky compared to their underlying capital. Of course the large British banks were running trading books of trillions of pounds of dangerous financial derivatives. The whole structure more closely represented a giant Ponzi scheme than an adult financial system aimed at promoting genuine wealth creation. Britain and the Labour Party would pay a heavy price for the indulgence of Thatcherite myth: a vast bailout, the biggest recession since the 1930s and the balance sheet recession that followed. First, excess deindustrialisation; now, reckless financialisaton and a banking crash. But, as if this wasn't enough, two more disasters followed.

Austerity and Brexit

Thatcher's heirs in opposition, William Hague, Iain Duncan Smith and Michael Howard, faced by New Labour's triumphant parliamentary majorities, made due obeisance to Thatcherism. They could not attack New Labour for economic improvidence given its wholesale acceptance of the Thatcherite settlement and evident economic moderation. Their chosen avenue to regain popularity was to give Thatcherism populist appeal by foregrounding her case against the alleged dark designs of the EU.

Thatcherism thus left the Tory Party with two particular neuralgic beliefs: distrust of the EU, along with a belief that taxation is in principle illegitimate and coercive so that lowering it is an economic policy priority above any other. Euroscepticism morphing into europhobia was the most toxic outcome – which was particularly odd because Thatcher had secured a pro-capitalist single market and she had won a custom-made EU budget rebate that became the model for further opt-outs from EU legislation Britain did not like. Moreover EU membership was transforming the UK economy for the better.

But the collapse of the Soviet Union, the rise of globalisation on the West's free-market terms and the conversion of the Labour Party to the European cause changed the right's calculus. 'Europe', as personified by the socialist president of the European Commission from 1985–95, Jacques Delors, was as interested in building a 'social' Europe as it was in promoting the freedom to trade in goods, to move capital and to enjoy private property rights. It would aim, for example, to create common standards on employee entitlements. This was all anathema to Mrs Thatcher, who said she had not deregulated the British labour market to see it re-regulated by 'Brussels'. Her 1988 Bruges speech famously declared that the EU should not interfere with or limit the policy options of Member States. She stopped short of arguing for EU withdrawal, instead inaugurating opt-outs from EU legislation, which successive governments reproduced. But the pound's humiliating ejection from the Exchange Rate Mechanism in 1992 was a turning point. Euroscepticism became the Tory cult.

In opposition it seemed a rich seam to exploit, perhaps the only one the party had. William Hague's so-called 'foreign land' speech in the spring before the 2001 general election, pitting 'the people' against a supposedly elitist, liberal government, could, in a blind test, quite easily have come from the leader of a radical right-wing populist party. Twelve days before the June 2001 general election, Hague would warn in lurid terms that there were just twelve days to save the pound – even to save British democracy.

As an electoral ploy, it failed; British voters were not that fussed about Europe. After the disastrous interregnum of Iain Duncan Smith, Michael Howard as Tory opposition leader took the same tack – this time with the more fruitful case against a treaty proposing an EU constitution that could restrict Member States' power for autonomous action. Now, with the press in full cry, Howard insisted that Britain must hold a referendum on the issue. Indeed, the overall campaign was so effective that Blair felt obliged to match the offer in Labour's 2005 manifesto. So feverish was the atmosphere that dastardly Europeans were portrayed as plotting to remove Britain's constitutional monarchy – a self-evidently absurd proposition. A concerned Prince Philip called a private dinner at Buckingham Palace in early 2006 with so-called experts to discuss the question (I was invited as one of the twelve wise men and women nominated to draft the Constitution Treaty's preamble about common European values). I listened amazed amid the guttering candles and plentiful dishes of game as William Rees-Mogg (Jacob Rees-Mogg's father) told the prince that Britain's existence as an independent state was menaced, with all that implied for the monarchy. But by the dinner's end, the prince, joking that he himself was a 'European mongrel', seemed to accept it was extravagant scaremongering. The EU could not be represented as attacking the principle of constitutional monarchy, entrenched in half a dozen other Member States, nor the concept of the nation-state.

Yet the fact the prince could call such a dinner was emblematic of the unjustified paranoid mood. When David Cameron succeeded as Tory leader, he wanted to strike out in a very different direction. The Tories should stop banging on about

Europe, he said, which was a dead end, and instead emulate Blair's programme of modernisation and party renewal. Cameron would champion the idea of the 'Big Society' as a direct repudiation of Mrs Thatcher's individualistic denial of society; the new mantra was to be socially liberal, concerned about the environment and economically conservative.

Yet the right of the party was unreconciled, clinging to the Hayekian free-market creed laced with europhobia. A standard right-wing trope held that Europe was responsible for uncontrolled immigration, for enterprise-choking regulation and for the squandering of British money. It viewed the EU as ambitious to subsume the UK into a federal superstate, reproducing Nazi ambitions for a German-dominated Europe. Cameron's suspension of Tory hostility to Europe had opened an opportunity for the populist anti-European UK Independence Party (UKIP) to exploit the Tory language of the previous eight years and maintain the phobic momentum. The Home Office's calculation that EU enlargement would only imply between '5000 and 13,000 additional immigrants a year' from the accession countries proved wildly wrong; the actual figure would soon exceed 125,000. Step forward Nigel Farage. He claimed he was the true heir to Thatcherite economics, to Thatcherite objections to Europe and now to out-of-control immigration. It was a powerful cocktail.

In the 2004 and 2009 elections for the European Parliament, Farage's party won 16 per cent of the vote and twelve and then thirteen MEPs – but in national elections, no UKIP candidate ever won a seat. After the 2010 general election, it might have been without a seat, but its million votes were a warning to nervous Conservative Party managers. Europe could not be relegated to the sidelines.

Doubling Down: The Rise of the Populist and Libertarian Right

David Cameron and his chancellor George Osborne knew that to win elections they had to be less socially abrasive, to stop being 'the nasty party', as Theresa May famously told the Conservative

Party conference in 2002.[16] David Cameron as leader and then prime minister could have fashioned a post-Thatcherite Tory Party, in which both liberal conservatives and Thatcherites could hang together. Indeed, this is what he tried to do; his embrace of the 'Big Society', although little tangible came of it, was an open declaration of independence from the Thatcherite claim that there was no such thing as society. He reached for a new and more liberal base.

However, the myths of the Thatcher decade, although twenty years in the past, would be impossible to challenge. To acknowledge openly that the Conservative Party's attachment to financial deregulation made it complicit in the Great Financial Crisis would be political and economic poison. Better, as described in the opening chapter, to turn the crisis into a narrative about Labour's profligate public spending that the Tories in government would correct. The coalition government immediately took on a Thatcherite hue – in which even the Liberal Democrats colluded as their own economic thinking moved steadily to the right. Osborne launched the economics of austerity in his post-election 'emergency' budget speech with the crazed accusation that just as there had been questions about the viability of banks, now there were questions about the bankruptcy of states – Britain among them. The failures of the past had to be escaped by fiscal discipline. It was a variant of the MTFS, thirty years on.

But no lessons had been learned from Thatcher's failures; she occupied too large a place in the Tory pantheon. This time round, a privatised reflation via financial deregulation could not come to the economy's rescue as it had in the 1980s – and even in the 1980s, trying to implement deep spending cuts and tax increases had delivered self-defeatingly high unemployment and enormous social security spending. Osborne was doing the wrong thing with an economy confronted by a balance sheet recession (as set out in Chapter 1). Savings in Britain were running at 6 per cent of GDP since the financial crisis, despite the fact that interest rates were at a 300-year low, as companies and households alike tried to rebuild their shattered financial position. With that degree of saving, to go beyond the perfectly viable programme of balanced public spending restraint and tax increases Osborne had inherited from his predecessor, Chancellor Alistair Darling, was economically dangerous. What was required was the opposite of what he proposed. The record low interest rates in bond markets were telling governments not to *cut* their borrowing, but to expand it, a very different message to that conveyed by Osborne.

Nor had he learned anything about the impact of tax cuts. Twenty-six years earlier, Chancellor Nigel Lawson had reformed corporation tax by eliminating allowances and so dramatically lowering the rate. There had been little or no impact on British investment levels in the 1980s. To suppose that a variant of the same measure in 2010 – a commitment to cut corporation tax steadily over the 2010s – would have any different impact was nonsensical.

But Osborne was not only genuflecting to Thatcherite myth; he was looking across the Atlantic at the success of the Tea Party movement and the Republican threats to close down government over burgeoning US national debt levels. American intellectual influence did not end there. The growing energy in right-wing libertarian British politics was reflected in the bewildering number of right-wing think tanks – the Institute of Economic Affairs, the TaxPayers' Alliance, the Adam Smith Institute, the Global Warming Policy Foundation and a baffling alphabet soup of single-issue campaign groups – housed in a few streets in Westminster, many of them in a single building at 55 Tufton Street, just hundreds of yards from Parliament, and sometimes funded by undeclared rich right-wing American donors. One common expression of this mood was the way in which the EU was cast as the enemy of individualism, enterprise and the valiant nation-state. The fruits of this poison tree would soon be eaten in the Brexit referendum in 2016.

The Influence of the American Right

The energy with which the Republicans had adopted extreme and obstructive politics in Congress, along with voter suppression and gerrymandering, supported by clever slogans to convey very right-wing ideas, had begun to have an impact on British Conservatives. A growing stream of politicians and think tank leaders took time out to learn first-hand about their American counterparts' ideas and slogans and the dark arts of campaigning tactics. The TaxPayers' Alliance, set up in 2004, openly mimicked Americans for Tax Reform; although it claimed to be non-aligned, its campaign for lower taxes was a mirror image of the American right, drank from the same philosophic well and used the same media techniques. Its founder, Matthew Elliot, would go on to become chief executive of Vote Leave.

By the mid-2000s, the flow of ideas from the USA had become a flood. The libertarian Douglas Carswell, then a Tory MP, co-wrote *The Plan* with his friend Daniel Hannan, a member of the European Parliament and a tireless europhobe who would later figure prominently in the Leave campaign. *The Plan* was a book advocating for Britain what Newt Gingrich had achieved with his 'Contract with America' fourteen years earlier, a programme the authors uncritically admired. Invoking Hayek's critique of the dysfunctionality of *any* form of centralised government, the pair argued that in just twelve months, British citizens could take back power from all public power centres – most obviously the EU, but also central and local government, schools and all public agencies administering welfare. The centrepiece of *The Plan* was a libertarian 'Great Repeal Bill' in which all legislation that limited individual freedom and choice would be repealed

The 2010 Conservative general election manifesto – an 'invitation to join the government of Great Britain' – did not go as far as the two radicals wished, but it picked up several of their libertarian themes. The Tories' aim, the manifesto proclaimed, was to empower people in their local communities with more direct democracy and more control over schools and hospitals, and to launch a new wave of voluntary activity in the Big Society – all enabled by lower taxes. 'Our fundamental tenet', it declared, 'is that power should be devolved from politicians to people, from the central to the local. Personal ambition should be set as high as is humanly possible, with no barriers put in its way by the state.'[17]

It was not the pure milk of libertarianism as promised in *The Plan* or by the US right, but it went a good way towards it. The state was the enemy; the central moral actor was the individual. If these zealots had anything to do with it, the American conservative revolution was coming to Britain to resuscitate pure Thatcherism.

Another milestone was passed when the newly elected Tory MP Liz Truss launched the Free Enterprise Group at the 2011 Tory Party conference, with over thirty-five MPs associating themselves with the cause. Working closely with the Institute of Economic Affairs, set up in the 1950s to promulgate radical free-market liberalism, and closely in touch with the leading lights of the American conservative movement, it insisted that only the bracing impact of competition, choice and free markets could halt Britain's decline. The following year, five of its loudest supporters – Liz Truss, Kwasi Kwarteng, Priti Patel, Dominic Raab and Chris Skidmore – published *Britannia Unchained*. Their book, including a diatribe against lazy British workers, would be endlessly quoted in the light of subsequent events. Four of the five authors would go on to become cabinet ministers, and Truss would become a forty-nine-day prime minister. Kwarteng, her blinkered chancellor, and Patel, once a disastrously incompetent home secretary, are both now on the back benches with her. Dominic Raab's political career has ended over charges (which he contests) that he bullied civil servants. Chris Skidmore (of whose environmental advocacy there is more in Chapter 9) has announced his intention to stand down as an MP and forced a by-election in protest against legislation to introduce annual sales of oil and gas drilling licences. They may be in eclipse now; they were the future once.

For there was no doubting by the early 2010s that the intellectual and political energy lay on the right of the Tory Party. Fired up by the rise of radical conservatism in the USA, and believing – entirely erroneously – that it was policies like theirs which lay behind the Asian economic miracle (despite the fact that from China to Singapore, the state was the dominant factor in development), the political centre of gravity in Britain was moving rightwards. Osborne was genuflecting towards them with his commitment to austerity. His fiscal retrenchment matched the scale of the first mad years of the MTFS, growth was subdued, public investment consistently fell below 2 per cent of GDP, the budget deficit remained high while spending on public services and benefits were savagely squeezed.[18] Indeed, in those areas of the country hardest hit, support for UKIP grew the fastest. Without austerity, argues one influential paper, the referendum would have been won by Remain.[19] Britain's left-behind communities were protesting about deindustrialisation, excessive financialisaton and eviscerated public services – but putting their faith in the very authors of the policies whose impact they so resented.

Given the tensions in the Tory Party, the rise of UKIP and the precedent that Michael Howard had called for a referendum on the EU constitution, it was almost inevitable that Cameron would concede the case for a plebiscite on continuing EU membership. Opinion polls at the time of the referendum announcement in January 2013 suggested that the Conservatives were unlikely to win an outright majority in 2015, so it was not a promise that Cameron necessarily intended to keep. But he did win outright – and the starting gun was fired.

But although the Brexiters were jubilant, winning the vote for Brexit still remained a long shot. The way in which it was won would lay the seeds of Brexit's ultimate disintegration.

The Vote Leave campaign – the official campaign – led by Boris Johnson and Michael Gove was from the start a melange of Thatcherism, stressing the liberties that would be won by leaving, and the restoration of control over money and borders. Nigel Farage's Leave.EU was more overtly populist, playing up fears over immigration which appealed to many sections of the hard-pressed working class. The key to winning their vote was to turn their justified dissatisfaction with a status quo made worse by austerity into the hope that Brexit promised a better future. The status quo could hardly be worse. Both campaigns had to dismiss the economic realities laid out by the Remain side as 'project fear', while vastly exaggerating the benefits of gaining greater 'sovereignty' and escaping EU 'burdens'. Voters were told that the new Brexit deal with the EU would allow Britain to keep all that was good while enjoying all the benefits of independence – Boris Johnson's famous claim that he was in favour of both having his cake and eating it. Growing hyperbole had characterised successive British general elections; now the Leave campaign, knowing that to acknowledge the truth would lose the referendum, had to take the culture of hyperbole to a new level. Facts had to be put to one side; as Aaron Banks, one of the founders of Leave.EU, declared after the referendum: 'The Remain campaign featured fact, fact, fact, fact, fact. It doesn't work. You've got to connect with people emotionally. It's the Trump success.'[20]

To connect emotionally meant that all the advocates of leaving necessarily became populisers, polarisers and merchants of post-truth, setting up a dynamic that would shake the foundations of British democracy and shatter the Tory Party. Appealing to emotion meant that Remain had to be depicted as an out-of-touch, self-regarding elite (echoing US Republican attacks on Democrats), who were wedded to 'experts', while Leave represented the real 'healthy popular feeling', as earlier generations of the far right used to put it. Hence Michael Gove's infamous remark about the British having had enough of experts. Leave.EU could make the edgier case about immigration: Britain's national borders had to be made safe – it was obviously far too easy for immigrants to broach them due to elite indifference. It was an open season on facts, with the guardians of the integrity of the public realm – the Electoral Commission and public-service broadcasters – either too weak or too cowed to make strong corrective interventions.

The fateful 52–48 per cent victory on 23 June 2016 meant that populist politics had been vindicated in a referendum that represented the will of the people rather than of the House of Commons. The leadership of the Tory, Labour, LibDem, SNP and Green Parties had all campaigned for Remain, and had been defeated. The practices, protocols and even legitimacy of Parliament were about to be challenged as never before, along with institutions like the Supreme Court, the Electoral Commission, ethics watchdogs and systems ensuring the probity of public appointments. The Tory Party and the country at large were about to be viciously polarised.

But what did Brexit mean? Did it mean having our cake and eating it? Or did it mean a complete severance with the EU so that Britain could complete, as Nigel Lawson claimed a few months after the poll, the Thatcherite revolution? Or should the whole issue be put back to the people for a confirmatory referendum?

With the exit clock ticking, Britain was consumed by two years of parliamentary paralysis over what Brexit meant. Parliamentary majorities for any way forward – halfway-house solutions that would allow the Good Friday Agreement in Northern Ireland to stand, a total break in a 'No Deal' Brexit or even a second referendum – could not be agreed. With no agreement on a potential deal, in March 2019, the prime minister had to apply for a six-month extension of the exit date, which humiliatingly involved participating in elections for the European Parliament in May. The country's polarisation now played itself out in plain sight; the outright winner of the European poll was UKIP, now rebranded as the Brexit Party, followed by the LibDems, who wanted a second referendum. The Conservative Party came fifth, with 8.8 per cent of the popular vote, its lowest ever vote in a national election. It was the final straw. May resigned and her nemesis Boris Johnson succeeded her in July 2019.

Mrs May, who had succeeded Cameron unopposed by any Brexiter, might have saved herself – and the country – had she defined her task from the outset as a national project to find the least-damaging exit while securing enough of the alleged freedoms to say that Brexit had been achieved. This would require cross-party support. After all, the choice between Leave and Remain had cut across party boundaries; the deal would be one everyone had to live with. Ted Heath had needed the support of sixty-nine Labour MPs, led by Roy Jenkins, to win the parliamentary vote to join the then Common Market in 1971; to win parliamentary support for a less self-harming soft Brexit was clearly now going to require some support from Labour to have any chance of success. But in Mrs May's mind only Tories were legitimate players in the game. She was looking for a Brexit settlement with which the

Conservative Party could live and stay together – and that did as little harm to the country as possible. Party was always first, country second. Not until it was obvious that there was implacable opposition among the Brexit ultras in her own party to any deal that involved institutional links with the EU did she turn to the opposition parties in 2019. By then, it was too late.

Brexit as a project might have begun with libertarian and Thatcherite ultras, but the process of beating off UKIP meant that it was now owned by the Conservative Party as a whole. The rise of radical insurgent right-wing thinking put paid to May's hopes. This was a process that had taken forty years to come to fruition. The fusion of Hayekian and libertarian thought that now defined the Tory right had collapsed from a reasoned position confronting contemporary challenges – which could just about be said of free-market economics and monetarism in the 1970s and 1980s – into unthinking memes and slogans rehearsed by the denizens of the right-wing ecosystem that had little relation to business, financial or societal realities. The EU had come to represent all they were philosophically against – regulation, workers' rights, action against climate change, protection of agriculture, states acting in concert. Worse, Britain was paying good money towards a supranational authority to deliver all this. It was a foreign intrusion into the monopoly of power the British political system conferred on Conservatives, who won most elections under the unreformed first-past-the-post system.

The European Union morphed into a demonic enemy. Fanciful trade deals – impossible in practice – with China, India and the USA would be better than any form of trade deal with the EU. Indeed, by 2019, many Brexit ultras touted a No Deal Brexit, with Britain trading with the EU on World Trade Organization terms, as the best way forward. This was not a thought-through strategy. This was public policy devised through the blind lens of europhobia. Forty years of bad ideas were coming home to roost.

Enter Boris Johnson

Johnson had won the referendum. Now his job as successor to May was ruthlessly to cut through the morass of Parliament, institutional and party obstacles to deliver the Brexit that the right wanted, and win a general election. Through a combination of free-trade deals abroad and levelling up at home, together with improved public services, growth would be ignited. It might have been an impossible fusion of Brexit right-wing fundamentalism and the kind of interventionism championed by Michael Heseltine in the 1980s, but it was a winning electoral formula for the moment. Its inconsistencies would wreck Brexit.

The events of the second half of 2019 are well known – the proroguing of Parliament, the suspension of the whip from twenty-one Tory MPs from the centre and left of the old Tory Party, the Supreme Court ruling that prorogation was illegal, the recall of Parliament and the December general election in which the country would back Johnson's 'oven-ready' Brexit. In fact, the deal was a minimalist hard Brexit that ignored the needs of Britain's service-sector exporters and the City, and brushed aside Northern Irish realities.

But, having achieved Brexit, a fissure began to open up and progressively deepened between the free-market heirs to Thatcher (who wanted to create a true Hayekian Britain, scrapping all remnants of EU regulation and contact with the EU) and an electorate who were looking for bread-and-butter improvements – money spent on public services, rising wages and improving economic prospects. Johnson tried to keep everyone on board, but even his capacity to square impossible circles came to an end with the onset of the Covid pandemic, for whose careful management to safeguard public health he was ideologically and temperamentally unsuited. His lies over Partygate, when he and his aides were caught red-handed boozing and singing while the rest of the country huddled at home under lockdown restrictions became habitual, and would finally trigger open revolt.

Johnson's passing exposed the ideological and practical dead end in which Toryism now found itself. Liz Truss succeeded him, elected by the elderly Conservative Party membership as a convinced libertarian pursuing policies that would win the approval of the American Enterprise Institute and the British Institute of Economic Affairs (IEA) – indeed, the IEA had been crucial in their development. Tax burdens were to be lifted from the very rich and from business, and regulation-free and largely tax-free investment zones set up around the country. The overwhelming priority was to grow the pie, she and her chancellor Kwasi Kwarteng declared, and only then worry about its distribution. All that held wealth creation back was the state, inhibiting individual initiative and freedom. Even the commitment to engage in fracking, commercially and geologically unviable in highly urbanised Britain, was borrowed from the US right-wing playbook. A £45-billion programme of unfunded tax cuts was proposed in a fateful 'mini' budget, designed to achieve growth that would otherwise be impossible. The financial markets recoiled, sterling collapsed, yields on bonds and the accompanying mortgage rate soared. Truss was compelled to resign after the shortest premiership in British history.

Libertarian economics could not be made workable. Brexit was being exposed as a failure, its 'opportunities' a chimera. The earlier austerity of Cameron and Osborne had imposed social suffering but not created any platform for growth. Lady Thatcher's policies of the 1980s and 1990s were exposed not as triumphs but as ideological missteps that led to today's travails – the massive revenues from North Sea oil dissipated, public services disintegrating and no compensating economic dynamism. There was not even a national wealth fund. The renewed semi-austerity policies of Truss's successor Rishi Sunak and his chancellor Jeremy Hunt – allied to concessions to nimbyism, climate change-denial and HS2 sceptics – have further exposed the intellectual exhaustion of the right and can only prolong the economic and social crisis. There have been no less than eleven growth plans or industrial strategies since 2010, the latest announced in the 2023 Autumn Statement – all with different priorities and emphases.[21] The problem that the Tory Party cannot overcome is that the vote for Brexit was a vote by Britain's disadvantaged against radical right-wing policies whose effects on the ground are such a disaster, but the dominant right wing of the party wants to deliver more of the same policies that have so emphatically failed. Brexit and the philosophy behind it have no future; the only question is the pace and breadth of their unwinding.

The long right-wing ascendancy is over. All that is left is to charge that its opponents are soft on immigration and in thrall to woke concerns on gender and race. It is a wretched, desperate political position revealing the poverty of current conservative ideology – but worse, dangerously splitting the party as its mainstream insists that the UK must adhere to international law, treaty obligations and basic principles of natural justice, even on immigration, while the right want to disregard all such constraints in the name of a sovereign parliament delivering what it says is the will of the people. A split party, with unappealing leaders for all its multiple right-wing factions, making barely coded appeals to racism and rank prejudice, is unlikely to broaden Conservativism's popularity.

By the end of the current Parliament, even the Tory right has split into five 'families' representing variants on right-wing tropes – ranging from protecting 'levelling up' (the Northern Research Group) to being self-appointed custodians of Brexit (the European Research Group).[22] Three failed ex-prime ministers will have sat on the Tory back benches behind Sunak, representing in their different ways all three failed currents of the modern right – the libertarian Truss, the populist Europhobe Johnson and the weak one-nation Tory Theresa May. None had been able to address the profound institutional failures and dysfunctions of British capitalism; the doctrines in which they all believed, variants of the Thatcherite theme, did not provide any viable remedies. Instead, Britain has suffered a succession of economic debacles. Conservatives themselves are appalled and dismayed by their own record in government, but they are unable to cohere around an electorally attractive and feasible right-wing way forward that addresses the moment, for a very good reason: it does not exist, as the extraordinary turnover of ministers since 2016, ranging from thirteen housing ministers to eight home and business secretaries, testifies.

There are other and better traditions that can be mined for the clues to economic renewal – traditions that combine the 'We' and the 'I', and in so doing get to the heart of the alchemy that makes a successful capitalism and a good society. The open question is why Britain's liberal left has been so poor in putting that counter-argument together, developing policies and winning enough elections to put them into practice. To delve into that, first we must address some history.

4

THE IRON GRIP OF LAISSEZ-FAIRE

The Conservative Party may be in trouble today, but historically it is one of the most successful political operations in the world. It has a keen lust for power, and until recently was ready to travel ideologically light, shifting from one-nation liberal conservatism to an embrace of free-market fundamentalism in one generation. It is also the party drawn from the apex of the social pyramid, led by people whose accents and demeanour seem to make them natural governors. But Conservative rule has been enabled by another crucially important factor: the weakness of its opposition. Non-Tory Britain has never managed to cohere for any sustained period around a shared critique of capitalism, a philosophy that describes how to shape it to serve the common good. Now, circumstances demand that it find one – and quickly.

The problem is that the contours of such a philosophy are intensely contested. The never-ending debate between liberals, social democrats and socialists is about whether the goal is the socialist transformation of the country because capitalism is endemically unreformable, or if the majority of the electorate remains dubious about that proposition, about the extent and means of reform. Should it be from the bottom up around cooperatives, guilds, unions, charities and non-governmental organisations, or from the top down by the state via public ownership and regulation? And, if so, how and by what kind of state?

Progressive Britain certainly shares the belief that flagrant inequalities – of income, wealth, opportunity and life chances – are intolerable and must be ameliorated. That concern draws people to progressive politics. The question is to what extent the liberal left gets beyond programmes of social reform to the necessary reform of capitalism itself, without which little progress is possible – and what that might mean in practice.

What bedevils the argument is the lure of socialism – an ethic, a scientific solution, a promise of utopia, a means of banishing exploitation, injustice and poverty and an abiding belief that capitalism is immutably exploitative and beyond redemption. Yet in the third decade of the twenty-first century, it is time to move beyond what is often a sterile argument. Liberals and socialists have been wrestling with each other for too long, and in so doing have allowed the dominant narrative to be framed by the right, with our current electoral system conferring on it far too much power. Too many lives have been compromised or ruined and opportunities foregone in the 150-year wait for the moment of socialist transformation. This is politics as a form of millenarian salvation, which, of course, never comes. That trait in socialism – 'the theology of the final goal' (of economic and social transformation of capitalism), as German SPD leader Willy Brandt once put it – has to be put to one side.[1] To put it bluntly, capitalism in some form is going to continue because it is endlessly dynamic and permits individual agency, which is a fundamental human trait, and competition allows trial-and-error experimentation with different ideas, some of which end up immensely benefiting humankind. But it also suffers from instability, inequality, a proclivity to create monopoly, economic rent and exploitative workplaces. With those strengths and weaknesses, it will still be here in a hundred years' time. There is an urgent need for progressive Britain to accept that truth, come together, forge a shared critique about how to manage it and then act on it.

The starting point is that we are social animals, creatures of a group, with a powerful urge to belong, help the weakest, collaborate and cooperate. This ethic gives socialism its appeal. It was socialism and socialists, writes Donald Sassoon in his magisterial *One Hundred Years of Socialism*, which, through fealty to these values, performed the vital task over the twentieth century of keeping capitalism honest – ironing out its worst proclivities and addressing unemployment and poverty. Without that pressure, there would be no welfare state, no universal health service and no state-funded universal education. But we are also individuals with agency, who want to take responsibility for our lives and expect to reap the rewards for our success and the penalties for our failure. We are neither wholly individualists nor wholly socialist communitarians. We draw inspiration from both.

The right went too far – and was allowed to do so – in the neoliberal experiment of building capitalism solely around individualism and the supreme 'I'. Now the task is to reassert the 'We', but not to imagine that it is possible to do away with capitalism by building a wholly socialist society. Any successful new progressive political philosophy must entrench the ethic of socialism – the need to stand by one another in the pursuit of the common good, fellowship, fairness and justice – while blending it with the best of liberalism, which, while acknowledging obligations to the whole, still finds room for individual agency and responsibility. Too often, Labour, while in power or aiming for power, has wanted to assure the capitalist masters and those at the top of the social pyramid that it accepts laissez-faire orthodoxies and that it is moderate and can be trusted; in essence, it aims to be a nicer, kinder neoliberal. This gets nowhere, robbing it of any distinctive philosophy of its own, articulating its own moral position and offering an energising policy programme. It may close its annual conference by singing 'The Red Flag', but the socialism it so expresses has become like much Christianity – a faith whose values may be admired but are not practised by a majority who quietly declare themselves to be agnostic or atheist.

The two great traditions that define progressive thought – the ethic of socialism and progressive liberalism – must abandon the notion that they are the sole custodians of virtue and are nobler than the other, and recognise that, like a Venn diagram, there is a vast amount that they share in common. Where they differ is in fact a source of strength. The socialist ethic allows for the necessary confrontation with vested capitalist interests, while liberalism's anxiety not to oppress and regiment individuals deepens its appeal. The socialist tradition, having crowded out other ways to skin the capitalist cat that have no less deep roots in our political culture, must now see the importance of bringing them back in. The ethic of socialism first emerged as a desire to put the collective first during the traumatising, dehumanising years of early industrialisation. Those horrific aspects of capitalism may have receded, at least in most European countries, but the need to assert the primacy of the social remains. Socialism can afford to be more generous and inclusive – liberalism can repay the compliment.

The left needs to stop finding itself in the same trap of jettisoning doctrinal socialism to win elections, faltering in government because it has too little progressive direction and then reverting to a 'socialist' fightback, such as that by Stafford Cripps in the 1930s, Aneurin Bevan in the 1950s, Tony Benn and Michael Foot in the early 1980s or Jeremy Corbyn after 2015. On each occasion, the cycle repeats itself. This must not happen again if there is a Starmer-led government. We can strike out on different and more rewarding paths. But that requires a better understanding of our past, together with the potential roads not taken, what drove the recurrent disputes and the repetition of the same mistakes. We need this in order to help us achieve what our forebears failed to do. The liberal left must cohere around a programme over time, building durable networks of progressive institutions and practices that embody its shared values. Mutuality, fairness and fellowship must be embedded in the DNA of our capitalism. In this way a stronger economy, social justice and creative civilisation can be founded. The twenty-first century can be a progressive one, with foundations laid by a Labour government that is as broad a progressive political coalition as possible, representing a no less broad electoral coalition.

Bear with me. Ideas and policy proposals will follow in later chapters. But first, the task requires us to revisit a little history.

The Industrial Revolution, the Snuffing Out of Mutuality and the Rise of Laissez-Faire

During the Enlightenment period of the mid-eighteenth century onward, Europe transformed intellectually, economically and politically. The ambition of that moment is captured by Immanuel Kant's invocation that the world 'must dare to know' and put aside the superstitions that supported monarchy and the alleged bottomless wisdom of the church. Jean-Jacques Rousseau argued that the legitimacy of government was derived from the will of the people, and insisted that society should be held together by a social contract. Scientists revealed new insights into nature, notably Isaac Newton, with his theory of gravity. Adam Smith would show that the same gravitational laws worked in the world of commerce as long as human beings were able to trade freely in markets – but he insisted that they also had instincts to collaborate and cooperate. Moral beings, Smith declared, must stand outside of themselves and empathise with the impact of their actions on others. Thomas Paine argued that men and women were born with natural rights, one of which was the right to participate in government. These were revolutionary propositions in a world of absolute monarchies and oligarchies.

Nor were these abstract ideas confined to the salon, library and laboratory. They changed the world. Rousseau, Paine and Voltaire helped inspire the American and French Revolutions. They had implications that spilled into the economy. In *The Enlightened Economy*, Professor Joel Mokyr points to the way Britain's constitutional development and comparative political and religious freedoms interacted with the urge to think freely and scientifically which characterised the European Enlightenment. Britain became a gigantic laboratory for European scientific ideas, the European scientists sometimes living and working in Britain themselves, interacting with indigenous British thinkers and makers in a unique fusion of thinking, experimentation and pragmatic doing. It was a marriage of *penseurs* and *fabriquants*, for which Britain was uniquely hospitable, helping to create the new machines, mills and factories that propelled the Industrial Revolution.

But contemporaries did not call the Industrial Revolution a revolution – because at first its transformatory potential was not immediately obvious, but also because, after the 1790s, there was a reluctance to call anything revolutionary, with the French deposing their own monarchy and upsetting the entire European political order. The British political and business establishment was terrified that the forces unleashed would affect Britain. Anything that could succour the rise of British Jacobins or stir the British masses had to be resisted at all costs. The instinct of the elite was not to talk of revolution and ideas of democracy – liberty, equality and fraternity – that might poison men's minds and incite them to revolution. Instead, as the parliamentarian and conservative political philosopher Edmund Burke stressed, there should be an emphasis on order, stability, respect for tried-and-tested institutions – the small platoons of society – and keeping violence and tyranny at bay.

Adam Smith: The Hidden Man of the Left?

Even Adam Smith, as Gareth Stedman Jones writes in *An End to Poverty*, was seen as a dangerous thinker. He wanted to open up long-established monopolies and price-fixing guilds to market forces, was no defender of the landed aristocracy, did not favour primogeniture, did not support the established church and supported ordinary workers' demands to share in capitalist prosperity. The French philosopher the Marquis de Condorcet was even more forthright, condemning the dependence of so many families on the physical health of their single breadwinner, and proposing a rudimentary system of universal welfare and education to eliminate undeserved poverty. Thomas Paine endorsed these proposals, along with the establishment of pensions for the elderly. If Condorcet and Paine were avowed revolutionaries, mixing economic and political radicalism, then Smith, for all his advocacy of commercial freedom, was decidedly among the subversive thinkers who might inflame the ambitions of the masses. Best keep Paine and Condorcet out of sight, and suppress any reading of Smith that might challenge the current order.

These were unsettling times. Life before the Industrial Revolution may have been grindingly tough, as Condorcet acknowledged, with families' wellbeing depending not only on good harvests but also on the physical health of the male breadwinner. Yet society and its values remained the master of the economy. For all pre-Industrial Revolution Britain's cruelties and prejudices, there was an understanding that the bonds between men and women were grounded in reciprocity. When the Industrial Revolution and its bewildering transformation of the economy's capacity to produce arrived, new rules took hold. People left their villages and fields, the physical places that underwrote communal social bonds, for the towns and the factories – where they sold their labour transactionally for a wage. Communal bonds were severed and people were dislocated in every sense from the old ways of life. Yet the rewards of being the first economy to industrialise were awesome, as textiles poured out of the mills, cheap coal was dug out of the mines and steam locomotives later criss-crossed the country. Living standards began to move slowly away from subsistence. The population began to grow. How to explain what was happening?

The great insight of Adam Smith was that the emergence of transactional relationships in markets – for land, labour and capital – offered the opportunity for economic specialisation. He famously showed how, while one craftsman would do well to make one pin a day if he undertook all the manufacturing stages himself, ten specialised workers repeating parts of the eighteen elements which contributed to the manufacture of a pin – the division of labour – would allow for 48,000 pins to be manufactured in any given day: 4,800 per worker.[2] This process was coordinated by the 'invisible hand' of the market. The origin of the wealth of nations was the market economy and commercial society, enabling the division of labour. By allowing prices to rise and fall following the ebb and flow of supply and demand, not only would new wealth be created but also the economy would always arrive at the best possible balance between the appetites of consumers and the capacity of suppliers. There was a natural price for any good or service constituted by the real price of its inputs, which would exert a gravitational pull on market prices so that they reached a kind of harmony. This was Newtonian physics at work in the economy. The public interest would be achieved by private, individual initiative responding to price signals in free markets.

But in his *Theory of Moral Sentiments* – and later in *The Wealth of Nations* – Smith reveals himself to be a far more sophisticated and rounded thinker than today's characterisation as the father of individualistic, free-market capitalism. If Milton Friedman had read Smith properly, it's unlikely that he would have so proudly worn his Adam Smith-embossed tie. Acknowledging the power of markets and the division of labour did not mean that Smith was unaware that capitalism had a tendency to being exploitative, nor did he deny that a good society must be based on mutuality and opportunity for everybody, whatever their rank. As Emma Rothschild writes in *Economic Sentiments: Adam Smith, Condorcet, and the Enlightenment*, he sympathised that the division of labour can 'benumb the understanding' and lead the mind into a 'drowsy stupidity'. The individual 'whose whole life is spent performing a few simple operations' is 'mutilated and deformed' in the 'character of human nature', including in his capacity to enjoy 'rational conversation' and 'to make judgments about private and public life'.[3]

For Smith, the beneficial consequence of the arrival of a commercial society was that it swept aside feudal bonds and created new opportunities. But to embrace the possibilities it offered and give the maximum number of people the chance to benefit, he championed a system of national education. This would involve taxation, which he saw not as oppressive but as a badge of liberty – a necessary contribution to the commonweal and demonstration that you as a taxpayer were a propertied citizen who both benefited from and contributed to society. Moreover, he thought it was reasonable for the richer to pay proportionately more. He also disapproved of tariffs on imported corn; these raised the price of food for the labouring classes. As Britain embarked on a war to the knife with Napoleon, these were seen as 'political views' that should be separated from the iron laws of political economy. British anti-republicans, conservatives and influential ministers and officials made sure that this dimension of Smith's thinking was suppressed; what they emphasised was his thesis that individualism, free markets and unfettered commerce brought wealth in its train.

In this they were aided by Thomas Malthus, who argued in his 1798 essay 'On the Principle of Population' that Adam Smith's progressive hopes were ill-founded. As soon as living standards rose in the wake of wages rising, courtesy of the division of labour, the birth rate would rise as people sought pleasure and had larger families, but the resulting super-abundance of workers would drive wages down again. Better never to embark on this futile cycle, which also threatened virtuous living as wages rose above subsistence. Don't allow combinations (in today's terms, trade unions) to form and retain the taxes on imported corn that maintain employment in local agriculture – all this in direct contradiction of Smith. Malthus, Burke and the wartime establishment gave Adam Smith a conservative spin, which became entrenched first as classical political economy and, as the nineteenth century progressed, the theory of laissez-faire.

The Rise of Laissez-Faire

Laissez-faire was the ideological backdrop to a string of decisions that gravely weakened British society: the early resistance to trade unionism, the callous response to the Irish Famine and the massive depopulation of the country, replacing the Poor Law with the worse oppression of the workhouse and the reluctance to regulate appalling working conditions. Later in the century, it would justify the refusal to raise taxes to finance a comprehensive national education and training system in the name of the small state. In the case of the free market, it offered primacy to the City of London and its financial priorities. It influenced the early adoption of the gold standard, thus making society dependent on the fluctuation of the quantity of gold. After the First World War, it dictated the readoption of the gold standard in 1925 at the same crucifying exchange rate as before the war. It is a baleful record. In our own times, Mrs Thatcher was able to resurrect it in the form of monetarism, hastening the acceleration of deindustrialisation, financialisation and grave inequality. But, most seriously, it became an unthinking part of British economic officials' culture: the rationale for non-intervention in an ever-more-obviously dysfunctional British economy. It has a lot to answer for.

Yet at first it seemed to work triumphantly as an agent of change and modernity, an essential adjunct to vital political and commercial freedoms and the progress of industrialisation. It was more a liberal than a conservative doctrine. The division of labour is a powerful economic phenomenon, as is a system of decentralised market pricing which fosters it. As first-movers with no competition, the profits were lavish for Britain's pioneer industrialisers – often men from modest backgrounds, like Richard Arkwright or Robert Stephenson, who were able to exploit the comparatively open society of late-eighteenth-century and early-nineteenth-century Britain to make great fortunes. The returns on a spinning jenny, for example, could be nearly 40 per cent a year.[4] A virtuous circle was launched; whole areas like Lancashire, specialising in cotton textiles, captured what twenty-first-century economists would call agglomeration affects. Richard Arkwright would use his profits to go into partnership with Robert Owen's father-in-law David Dale to build a mill – New Lanark – using the fast currents of the Upper Clyde river to turn the mill's wheels. As the steam age succeeded the water mill, Britain would find itself with another advantage to match its fast-flowing rivers: abundant, relatively cheap and accessible coal.

But a lot more lay behind the Industrial Revolution than the division of labour, cheap power and high profits. The fluidity of British society helped. Not only London, but cities like Liverpool and Glasgow, provided well-paid work and the opportunity to service Britain's burgeoning overseas trade, much of it associated with colonisation and slavery. In addition, the wealth created by a dynamic agricultural sector in the earlier decades of the century, through a revolution in agricultural techniques, had created a well-to-do artisan class servicing the prosperous farmers. Robert Owen's father was an ironmonger and the family could afford the investment in young Owen's early ventures; James Watt's father was a shipwright. It was not the scions of the upper classes who drove the revolution in ingenious new machinery, but practical members of the middle class, the 'fabricants'.

Moreover, Britain was a relatively high-wage economy compared to its European peers; there was a ready domestic market for the new cotton, wool and linen clothes and bedwear, and a no-less-vibrant export trade. In the late eighteenth and early nineteenth century, much wool, cotton and linen was exported to the Americas and West Africa. Between 1794 and 1796, 60 per cent of wool textile production, for example, was exported to the Americas and West Africa.[5] In their path-breaking book *Slavery, Capitalism and the Industrial Revolution*, Maxine Berg and Pat Hudson show graphically the degree to which the highly profitable trade with the Atlantic slave and plantation economies helped propel early British industrialisation.

Britain had also been an institutional innovator, in politics, commerce and finance, and developed an early idea of a social contract. The commitment to the rule of law reached back into the seventeenth century; no man is above the law, even the monarch, declared Lord Chief Justice Coke in a famous case in 1610, before being demoted for his pains to become the author of *The Petition of Right*, one of the cornerstones of English and later British justice and liberty. It was a view traceable to the Angevin English monarchs of the twelfth century, inheritors of the Norman conquest, who developed common law as an instrument of decentralised governance, culminating in the settlement of Magna Carta. The practice and understanding of common law had grown deep roots in English civil society. It was matched by parallel developments in the English constitution, brought to a head by the Civil War and the so-called Glorious Revolution of 1689, deposing James II and replacing him with William of Orange. He would govern jointly with the House of Lords and Commons, thus establishing a constitutional monarchy ruling in partnership with a two-chamber Parliament, one chamber of which had representatives who were elected, however primitively. By the end of the eighteenth century, the freedom of the press, freedom of worship and the division of powers into the legislature, executive and judiciary were firmly entrenched. Furthermore, the

Poor Law, which was established by Elizabeth I in 1597, created a nation-wide system of relief for the very poor, in which the better-off in any parish were obliged to offer minimum subsistence to the worse-off. It might incorporate a noxious division between the 'impotent', if deserving, and the undeserving 'idle' poor, but an embryonic social contract embodying the legal responsibility of the better-off to the worse-off had been established. Britain was a European pioneer in this area too.

If this was the legal and constitutional background to the Industrial Revolution, it was not the only innovative institutional development. England (and the Netherlands) had pioneered the idea of the company at the beginning of the seventeenth century, along with early forms of commercial banking. Groups of merchant investors clubbed together to create the capital for an enterprise that could apply for a licence to trade or produce goods and services. The East India Company, founded in 1599, was the first joint-stock company, but by the end of the seventeenth century there were 140 such companies, whose shares were traded in the fast-growing network of City of London coffee houses.

Crucially, incorporation required the company to declare the purpose for which it was incorporating. It was understood that while profit was indispensable, it must flow from the delivery of a purpose – a vital proposition ensuring that capitalism's private values align, to some extent, with social values that has progressively been eroded with the enthronement of profit as the be-all and end-all. (The complexity of how a capitalist enterprise should be conceived has been weakened, and needs to be rethought.) A regulated stock market opened in 1801, creating a single market in shares, boosting their liquidity. Companies could reach beyond their founders and raise money from investors who knew that they could sell shares in the companies in which they had capital, so making it more likely that they would invest, because they could quickly recover their cash. It was a key source of finance, adding financial fuel to the industrial fire – but it accelerated the move away from the pursuit of purpose as the rationale for business; the goal was increasingly short-term profit.

This world of contractual economic relationships, coordinated by freely buying and selling in a way that set market prices (whether in a stock market, in the expanding numbers of shops or workers selling their labour), required unprecedented volumes of money. Yet paper money and coins had to be more than units of account, facilitating ever more exchange; to work, they had to hold their value over time. And, for that, they had to be anchored in the precious metals – gold and silver – that held their value over time.

The creation of the Bank of England in 1694, following the Swedish example in 1668, had been a master stroke. It gave confidence that paper money would hold its value because the Bank of England backed every coin in the realm and overseas colonies with gold and silver. It organised the sale of government bonds to finance what the historian John Brewer calls 'the sinews of war', so creating a new phenomenon: the national debt. Indeed, that was what William III wanted as a quid pro quo for bringing it into existence. The debt would finance Marlborough's armies in their triumphant campaigns during the War of the Spanish Succession against Louis XIV. Later, it would fund the world's most powerful navy. The bank also acted as a backstop to the debt market to ensure that it had liquidity, which also helped the banking system develop.

These institutional developments – in the political, corporate and financial systems – were 'slow-burn' and were accepted as a natural part of the landscape. But they were key foundations on which the Industrial Revolution was built. Smith knew how important the rule of law and private property were to the market system. He understood the value of banks, even if he was wary of their having too much power to create money, describing the Bank of England as the 'greatest bank of circulation in Europe' and writing that 'it acted not only as an ordinary bank but a great engine of state'.[6] He praised how useful the new joint-stock companies were at raising and deploying capital – even if he cautioned that their managers should not be given too much autonomy to run businesses as they liked, independently of their founding purpose.

As the war with France ended with the anti-Bonaparte victory at Waterloo, Britain's commercial, financial and industrial system emerged as another victor. It was the pre-eminent industrial power in Europe, a position that would not be threatened for another sixty years. But the complex skein of institutions that supported all this were taken as givens, as were its relatively high wages and its links with the Atlantic slave trade and plantation economy; what was believed to propel it forward was the free market and the division of labour. This failure of understanding disabled policy at the time, still disables our understanding of the past now and continues to cast a pall over how we act in the present.

The Ideology Hardens but Industry Grows

The decades that followed were the years of the railway boom and accelerating migration from the field to the towns built around factories, mills and mines. By 1852, England, Scotland and Wales had 7,000 miles of railway connecting every major city and town. Yet although it would later be called a revolution, the annual growth of GDP never scaled the heights of today's Asian Tigers; between 1780 and 1860, overall GDP grew at an estimated 1.9 per cent per year.[7] There were revolutionary new industrial techniques, certainly – the steam engine, the spinning jenny, the locomotive, the factory – but their spread was slow and geographically concentrated, noticeably in the textile industry in Lancashire. Industrial production did outpace GDP growth, growing at 2.6 per cent in that same eighty-year period,[8] although the textile industry grew faster, at some 10 per cent per annum.[9] Nonetheless, by today's Asian standards, this is small beer. But what was new and revolutionary was that this was steady growth, year in and year out. By 1830, the cumulative industrial growth meant that around 40 per cent of the working population was employed in manufacturing, overtaking the numbers working in agriculture as early as 1801.[10]

The crucial point for British intellectual and political history was that Britain launched the first Industrial Revolution with no acknowledged help or support from the state. The institutions that supported it – the Bank of England, the Poor Law, the joint-stock company, the constitutional monarchy, the division of political powers and independence of the judiciary, the rule of law – may have been permitted by government but had evolved over the preceding centuries before industrialisation was even a dream. The culture that fostered invention and the economy and society that provided such ready markets – along with Britain's pivotal and profitable role in the Atlantic economy based on slavery – had not been planned. By 1851, the country could marvel at the cornucopia of industrial machinery on display at the Crystal Palace exhibition as positive proof that laissez-faire worked. Glory be to the invisible hand of the market. Indeed, in a battle royal within his own party, in 1846, the Conservative Prime Minister Robert Peel abolished the protectionist corn laws to lower the price of bread for the working classes – and open up markets for British exporters abroad. Smith's view had finally prevailed.

Britain no longer only had a single internal market – it was now committed to extending free trade abroad. Moreover, by linking sterling to a fixed quantity of gold, as it did in 1817, Britain had achieved price stability at the cost of surrendering control of credit and interest rates to movements in its gold stocks. The depression in the years that followed was a warning about where the gold standard could lead. But overall, the results of laissez-faire, free markets, free trade, the minimal state and the gold standard seemed to speak for themselves. British real GDP per head had increased by half from 1800 to 1850 – more than any other country. Britain really was now the workshop of the world and accounted for 40 per cent of all world manufacturing exports.

Cracks in Laissez-Faire Utopia

As the great Austrian economist Karl Polanyi would describe in his brilliant *The Great Transformation*, published during the Second World War, what had happened was the inversion of the relationship between society and economy. By the second half of the nineteenth century, British society had been made subordinate to the market, which had now entered the marrow of society. Britain had become a market society in the sense that all relationships were mediated by fluctuating prices, notably of wages, rents and food. Humanity and its social institutions had become slaves to forces outside of its control. Polanyi's particular object of ire was the gold standard, which by the 1880s was operated by all the major economic powers – including the USA, France and Germany – who joined Britain in pegging their respective currencies to gold. The theory was that international trading and financial relationships could be left to the movements of gold stocks. An internationally competitive economy would find that it sucked in gold as its trade balance soared, which would increase credit and thus inflation until its workers became uncompetitive again. An uncompetitive country would lose gold, credit would shrink and depression would result until the fall in wages would price its goods back into world markets. Suddenly, uncontrollable forces would create booms and busts, with society forced to roll with the punches.

It was an impossibly utopian view of how society worked, Polanyi declared, and it was unsustainable. He attacked the 1834 "reform" of the Poor Law as undermining the capacity of families hit by unemployment to survive unless they accepted degrading labour in the workhouse. There was a double movement, he suggested. The more the market extended its grip and tried to dissolve social relationships, the more society would find ways of fighting back. The fiasco of international financial policy between World Wars I and II was a case in point – rejoining and then abandoning the gold standard was a classic example of how societal reactions made adhering to the total free-market system impossible. It had been a proximate cause of the rise of fascism and communism.

The whole conception of a global free-market utopia was based on the intolerable theorem that society would bend permanently to the dictates of the market as a system – a long-term dream of classical economists and the advocates of laissez-faire. But the double movement identified by Polanyi was already beginning to happen in Britain in the first half of the nineteenth century, and would intensify as it wore on. Society started to fight back.

Organisations of workers, soon to be known as trade unions, were outlawed and strikes prohibited in the 1800 Combination Acts, in part because of the requirements of laissez-faire but also from an anxiety that such gatherings might promote political radicalism and even revolution. But the Acts could only survive until 1824; it had become impossible to sustain them, first against 'Luddites' smashing job-replacing machinery instead of striking, which was now banned, and then against mass strikes in Scotland. Thousands of striking workers could not simply be shot. The Acts were partly relaxed.

But when Dorset farm workers trying to form a union in 1834 were arrested on the trumped-up charge that they had sworn a collective oath of secrecy, which was illegal, 800,000 people petitioned Parliament to pardon their sentence of deportation to Australia. The petition was granted and they were returned to England. One of what were now dubbed the 'Tolpuddle Martyrs' – George Loveless – caught the mood, chalking a call for liberty (rather than socialism) on his prison wall. 'We will, we will, we will be free.'[11]

But the most important sign of society fighting back was the reaction to the 1834 Poor Law Amendment Act, which sought to reduce the claims of the poor on the well-to-do in every parish. Instead, they should work for their subsistence. Every parish would have to establish a workhouse where the poor would be compelled to break stones, chop wood, scrub floors or launder backbreaking loads of dirty clothes. It was a form of slave labour, established so that local middle classes would now be spared paying for relief of the 'undeserving poor'.

Reaction came quickly and in the streets. The Chartist movement was born, building on the momentum of the protests over the arrest of the Tolpuddle Martyrs. It was obvious that there needed to be more MPs in Parliament representing ordinary people to vote against such measures – and that meant further electoral reform. The Charter had six key demands: universal manhood suffrage; no property qualification to vote or stand as an MP; equal electoral districts; voting by secret ballot; annual parliamentary elections; and, crucially, a demand that MPs had to be paid – otherwise, unlike the moneyed classes in both the Lords and the Commons, working-class MPs would have no means of subsistence. If these demands were implemented, Parliament would be transformed; there would be MPs from working-class backgrounds who would speak against the kind of Malthusian political economy that informed Poor Law reform. The Chartists were not apostles of socialism; they were advocates of proper parliamentary democracy, and of putting the slightly more democratic Parliament created by the 1832 Reform Act to work to improve working conditions and radically reform the Poor Laws. Parliament, with its immense legitimacy built up over centuries, was the effective route to change, a view that would be firmly held by trade unionists and radical MPs throughout the nineteenth century and into the twentieth.

From the mid-1830s and into the 1840s, Chartism grew like wildfire. Demonstrations, public meetings and newsletters led to a petition for Chartist reforms that was signed by more than 3 million people. Parliament summarily and inevitably refused the petition, but Chartism had lit a fuse. Widespread strikes followed, organised by the fast-growing numbers of trade unions, industrial action now trying to make good the failure of political pressure. When the Liberal Party was formed in 1859, part of its constitutional radicalism was inherited from Chartism. Nor was the Chartists' faith in Parliament wholly misplaced; between 1800 and 1850, there were at least ten Acts aimed at addressing the working conditions in factories and mills: limiting child and female labour, fencing off dangerous machinery, ending night work and tightening enforcement mechanisms. They were inadequate, but they represented at least the recognition that something had to be done.

Creative responses to the dire realities of factory life came from surprising places. In 1800, Robert Owen, who had already made a fortune in the textile industry, took over the management of the New Lanark mill in Scotland and set about making it an example of a new economic and social model, in which workers laboured no more than ten hours a day, were properly housed and paid, were given Sunday off and had their dignity respected at work. This, in the context of the time, was enlightened private ownership. Children were educated in his school. There was a sickness fund. Get the physical and social environment right, argued Owen, treat people with decency, distribute the rewards of workers' efforts fairly, and the workplace will be highly productive. 'Exchange their poverty for wealth, their ignorance for knowledge, their anger for kindness, their divisions for union', runs his declaration, still posted on the railings of the entrance as you visit the site. It was a rejection of gradgrind working conditions in dark, satanic mills. New Lanark was a success, the mill doubling in value between 1799 and 1810. Owen attracted a syndicate of investors in 1812, including the utilitarian philosopher Jeremy Bentham, who together agreed to take only 5 per cent returns, ploughing any surplus into education, medical care and other communal benefits. Bentham was said to claim it was the only good investment he ever made.[12]

The success helped generate support for one of the first factory Acts – the Cotton Mills and Factories Act in 1819 – and for the Factory Acts that followed. But Owen, for all the sympathy for socialism that he would express in his support for a grand coalition of trade unions in the 1830s, was no soft touch. When you visit New Lanark today you can buy miniature versions of the disciplinary mechanism he used instead of physical punishment and which he would hang over each operative's work station – black for somebody who needed to work harder, white for an exemplary worker and two colour shades in between. Public reward and public shame were more effective than beatings. Every worker was an individual who should be honoured. Owen and his family lived within the mill complex and worked no less hard than the employees. This was enlightened capitalism in action and the results were testimony to how well it worked. It showed that capitalism could have a capacity for agility, and that it could ameliorate the inevitable clash of worker and capital that Marx wrongly anticipated. Its fame among contemporaries spoke to the seriousness of the ills New Lanark successfully sought to address. Capitalism could be done in other ways that were both necessary and possible.

In the 1840s came another societal response: the serious extension of the cooperative movement. The Rochdale Cooperative was launched in 1844 to provide affordable, reasonably nutritious food for its members. It was well-capitalised enough, as well as owning its own stores, to survive and grow – unlike many other attempts that had preceded it. It became an exemplar for the entire movement.

Surveying the horrors of Manchester's industrialisation – child labour, terrible industrial injuries, deplorable working and living conditions, avoidable early death – was a young German mill owner called Friedrich Engels. His *The Condition of the Working Class in England*, published in German in 1845, called for a political rather than a mere industrial response. Socialism – and Engels's later collaboration with Marx – was being born.

Alleviating the Condition of the People

Engels was not alone. Five years earlier, even Thomas Carlyle, the conservative philosopher famously hostile to democracy and a defender of social and political hierarchy as a guarantor of stability, had argued that given the condition of the people, it had to be asked whether the current order could survive. Industrialisation and the society it generated was making workers greater slaves than their ancient counterparts had been; worse, he warned, the degradation of the living conditions of the labouring classes risked causing a revolution unless they were ameliorated. The promise of the apostles of laissez-faire and its philosophical bedmate, utilitarianism, that the general welfare would inevitably be raised was not being met.

The evidence was before everyone's eyes. So poor was urban sanitation and the disposal of human waste that outbreaks of cholera and typhus were common. The threadbare social contract represented by the Poor Law and the minimal civic infrastructure of the towns were simply incapable of handling the volumes of people and demands made upon them. Leeds, Liverpool and Manchester, for example, more than doubled in size in the first thirty years of the nineteenth century. Sanitation was rudimentary; travellers said Preston could be smelled from forty miles away. Drinking water was fouled with faeces. The authorities began to take notice. It took three years from its commissioning by Parliament in 1839, but Edwin Chadwick's landmark 450-page 'Report on the Sanitary Conditions of the Labouring Population of Great Britain' was irrefutable. Disease was caused by damp, filth and overcrowding, he argued. These physical circumstances had to be removed 'by drainage, proper cleansing, better ventilation and other means of diminishing atmospheric impurity'.[13] The heart of his report was a recommendation for a massive public works programme of supplying clean water and disposing of sewage. He was right, even if he was wrong to think atmospheric impurity was the problem, rather than germs spread by polluted water, but dither – rather than action – followed. It took six more years to establish a single national board of health, as he recommended, and not until 1866 was there a Sanitary Act.

In the meantime, the evidence mounted. In London in 1848, 14,000 people died from drinking dirty water – a statistic that had become routine. Smallpox and tuberculosis were widespread.

Engels gave a graphic account of what life was like in the cities.

> The manner in which the great multitude of the poor is treated by society today is revolting [...] they are obliged to throw all offal and garbage, all dirty water, often all disgusting drainage and excrement into the streets being without any other means of disposing of them: they are thus compelled to infect the region of their own dwelling.[14]

What perplexed Engels was why the English working class so supinely accepted these privations. The majority did not join the trade union movement and even those that did restricted their protests to narrow working and wage conditions; a fair day's pay for a fair day's work was a good rallying cry but, argued Engels, it did not address the fact that the root cause was the very operation of capitalism. It could not be reformed; it would have to be overthrown and replaced by communism. The problem was that the trade union movement was already becoming very stratified, with those representing profitable export trades content to demand even better pay rather than political change. Early British trade unions, often small and local, were in the main not politically radical.

Concern about the condition of the people was growing beyond the embryonic self-help organisations of the working class. It was what led Richard Cobden, the free-trader and founder of the Anti-Corn Law League, to campaign to repeal the Corn Laws – as finally happened in 1846. Free trade was good for manufacturers, but also for the people, he argued. This dimension of laissez-faire – that free trade meant cheap food – would become an enduring and popular principle of liberalism right up to the First World War.

Meanwhile, Charles Dickens's hard-hitting, rambunctious novels of the period – *Oliver Twist*, *Bleak House* and so much of the rest of his work – reinforced the growing sense that for all the riches and abundance of manufacturing invention, the growth of slums, the spread of disease, the lack of basic sanitation and the sheer distress of so much of the working class had to be addressed. It was now recognised that the middle classes would catch the same diseases as the workers and slum dwellers. Offering them sermons on religion while their babies died of typhus from drinking foul water would not help, as Dickens's brickmaker explains to the urban missionary in *Bleak House*. By the 1850s, London's Thames was little more than an open sewer; the summer of 1858 was the time of the 'Great Stink', and the pressure to build a proper sewage and water supply system finally became irresistible. Doctors were carefully proving the link between contaminated drinking water and diseases like cholera, which knew no class boundaries. It was in the middle- and upper-class's self-interest that the condition of the people improved.

Moreover as the 1860s unfolded, there were the first signs that laissez-faire was failing on the front it boasted most about – the economy. A second industrial revolution was emerging, based first on oil and later electricity, that would bring new industries to the fore. Britain, enjoying the privilege of being a first-mover, had only slowly realised the benefits of steam power, but that had not mattered in terms of its international position. Now Germany and more especially the USA were industrialising fast. Voluntarism, the small state and a reluctance to govern the market economy – essential components of Liberal leader Gladstone's worldview – were emerging as fatal weaknesses. The doctrine was that the government budget must balance, and public spending must be minimal because it would otherwise demand taxation. Gladstone's approach to finance not only inhibited the pace of vital reform; it became the foundation of the crabbing 'Treasury view' that has palsied Britain for two centuries.

Education was a case in point. Basic literacy and numeracy would be indispensable in the decades ahead, let alone technical, engineering and even scientific skills. Britain's position was dire. In the late 1860s, around half of children had no access to schooling, around a quarter attended voluntarily run schools (often associated with the church) and only another quarter attended state-aided primary schools. The Education Act of 1870 set up new state-aided schools (which would charge a fee to pay for themselves, with the state coming in as a funder of last resort, in line with Gladstone's aversion to spending and taxing) but, like much Victorian social legislation, it left the decision as to whether attendance should be compulsory up to locally elected politicians. By 1876, parents had a duty to ensure that their children attended school, but there was no real way to enforce this. By 1880, schools were required to ensure attendance from the ages of five to ten and empowered to fine the parents of absent children.

It was only in 1891, though, twenty-one years after the recognition that universal primary school education was a national imperative, that the government broke through Gladstonian prohibitions and agreed to pay primary school fees of up to ten shillings, effectively making universal primary education free. It was a game of catch-up, and the priority was always to keep the state small, rather than investing in human capital. British education spending in the late nineteenth century (expressed as a share of GDP) was regularly about half that of Germany and the USA. If universal primary education did not arrive until the 1890s, secondary education was still well behind – and universities even further, with a tiny university student population compared to the USA.

Laissez-faire and Treasury insistence on the small state and balanced budgets would ensure that Britain entered the twentieth century with the mass of its population not only suffering poor nutrition, but semi-educated compared to their international peers. The limitations of Britain's financial system in mobilising the vast sums of capital needed for the new industries, and for re-equipping the old, was equally striking. Britain's trading performance began to suffer, but once again its empire would come to the rescue. British control of India allowed it to cripple the Indian textile industry to benefit Lancashire textile exports, and to commandeer its gold to sustain sterling's place in the gold standard. The imperial laissez-faire ship would sail on, but the fatal cracks below the waterline were widening and deepening.

The Challenges Grow More Serious

By the 1860s, the battle of ideas over how to understand the economics of capitalism, its social impact and potential remedies grew more intense, foreshadowing the debates in the years before the First World War. In 1862, John Ruskin published *Unto This Last*, a passionate denunciation of classical political economy. The founder of the Arts and Crafts movement and a believer in the objective beauty of nature, Ruskin recoiled from the way industrialisation had developed and the privations it imposed. A country's social health could not be independent of how it organised its economy. Wealth, he declared, had many more moral and aesthetic dimensions beyond material riches. A good society had to be judged unto the welfare of its very last member – hence, *Unto This Last*. In effect, Ruskin advocated a government-backed welfare state. Ruskin was not a leveller – as a conservative in many respects, he believed in hierarchy – but society, and the better-off, had obligations to the poor. It was a statement of the case for a form of social contract, rooted partly in Christianity.

Government should ensure the production of goods and services vital for life at affordable prices, Ruskin argued, and train men and women to work in government factories; private enterprises 'would beat the government if they could', but government enterprise should be in the driving seat. The unemployed should be retrained and looked after at the state's expense. 'For the old and destitute, comfort and home should be provided [...] it ought to be quite as natural and straightforward for a labourer to take his pension from his parish [...] as a man of higher rank from his country.'[15]

It was quite a programme for the 1860s; however, five years later, Karl Marx would reframe the entire argument with the publication of the first volume of *Das Kapital*. It would be translated into English twenty years later, but aspects of its thinking began intruding in British left-wing circles beforehand. Apologias and explanations of capitalism that had prompted Luddites, Chartism, strikes, New Lanark, Ruskin-type programmes of reform, Factory Acts and Royal Commissions and petitions were all giving way to full-frontal, systemic criticism.

Karl Marx deplored the same social conditions as John Ruskin, and was equally unconvinced by the arguments for the self-adjusting, self-regulating market that had been promoted by classical political economy. Marx warmed to Robert Owen's faith in humanity and the belief that the ultimate source of value was created by wage labour. He also concurred with Owen's passionate advocacy of getting the physical and social environment right not only for the sake of productivity, but as a basic human entitlement.

But the gulf between Marx and even the most concerned of the Victorian reformers was that he portrayed the developing social disaster as the unavoidable path to an inevitable proletarian revolution that would overthrow the power of private capital. Marx argued that no Ruskinite social contract, however well-designed or well-meaning, no Owenite model factory or well-intentioned Act by whatever parliament (inevitably all in the hands of the bourgeoisie), could redress the ineluctable dynamic of capitalism. He believed that a class of capitalists who appropriated the surplus value created by their workforces was structurally pitched against the objective interests of the vastly larger proletariat. Capitalism was certainly dynamic, and had created machine-driven modernity that spread around the world, but it could not help itself. The drive for profit compelled it to force down wages – the immiseration of the working class – while the division of labour and the selling of labour time for a wage, echoing Carlyle, commoditised productive work. It transformed work into blind, dehumanised labour (wage slavery), alienating workers from the fruits of their efforts. There had to come a moment when the workers' consciousness of their objective position would allow them to throw off their chains and socialise the means of production. Only then could the situation be remedied. Class warfare would lead to the victory of the working class, whose labour was ultimately the source of all value.

Marxism would prove highly persuasive in the last decades of the nineteenth century. Anybody living in an overcrowded, squalid terraced house with limited sanitation, working in grim factories, mills and mines for barely subsistence wages, could confirm the reality of working-class life. Self-evidently, there was a class of bourgeois capitalists living high on the hog, their wealth inextricably linked to the poverty of a proletariat of disenfranchised, exploited workers. Pressing for more democratic representation in Parliament to get relief could only achieve so much; if you wanted fundamentally to challenge the basic dynamics of capitalism, ran the Marxist argument that was so influential in the late nineteenth and early twentieth centuries, you had to accept the logic of class warfare and fight to bring down capitalism as a system.

It was intellectually, politically and emotionally appealing. Marx used the same analytical tools as the classical economists, accepting that the factors of production were land, labour and capital, and that the division of labour, when enhanced by machines, unleashed powerful new capacities to produce goods in extraordinary volumes. But instead of marvelling at Smith's *Wealth of Nations* and the capacity to increase living standards, Marx identified the trends that were leading to the pauperisation of a new working class who had left agriculture for the factories.

He turned the categories of the classical economists against them. And in promising an inevitable revolutionary moment, he gave political economy a transcendent, millenarian, quasi-religious final act, in which believers could literally have faith. All the issues that bedevil the construction of a socialist society, in theory and in practice, could be wished away. Is total equality literally possible? How much does liberty have to be sacrificed to achieve even dramatically less equality? How much do solidarity and fraternity menace individual freedom? And so many more questions. A socialist utopia would dissolve such concerns. A better world was there for the taking, by a brotherhood and sisterhood of the world's working class.

We now know that Marxism was to prove the left's incubus, despite its compelling critique of capitalism that animated the left's first century. Capitalism has not collapsed from its own contradictions; the working class has not been so pauperised that inevitable class conflict would lead to revolution; and communism in government, where it has been tried, has morphed into autocratic tyranny.

Yes, capitalism has a tendency to monopoly and to rent-seeking, as Marx predicted; yes, some capitalist business models depend on a highly contractualised relationship with disempowered, structurally insecure workforces; yes, too much work is profoundly unsatisfying and alienating; and yes, over-financialised economies do oscillate wildly.

On the other hand, some capitalist business models depend on treating their knowledge workers well – and the system, infinitely adaptable, throws up wave after wave of technological innovation. Markets, allowing the price mechanism to function and encouraging experimentation with multiple new technological runners and riders, operates better than the top-down, central plans and state ownership that communism and socialism evolved in the twentieth century. That is not to say that capitalism has solved the production problem; there are inherent tensions between the interests of finance and of producers, and the speed and costs of economic adjustment need to be managed. But public ownership of the means of production as a catch-all solution doesn't work;

production techniques and working practices tended to ossify under such ownership. Capitalism is still here more than 150 years after *Das Kapital* foretold its death.

This stubborn persistence does not mean that the Marxist critique was wholly off-beam. In their path-breaking book *Power and Progress*, Professors Daron Acemoglu and Simon Johnson disown Marx's class analysis of capitalism but address the same problem that Marx did. Capitalism is dynamic and throws up great wealth, largely through the transformatory technologies that its restless experimentation and embrace of the new creates. The problem is that the wealth so generated gravitates to those who are already wealthy. No less problematic, all technologies are malleable. They can be configured to benefit humanity or arranged to benefit a minority. Looking at history, Acemoglu and Johnson do not trace a history of class conflict in which feudalism gives way to capitalism, in turn giving way to communism. Instead, and more persuasively, they observe an ongoing struggle to shape new technologies so they benefit humanity at large – and in so doing share prosperity beyond the incumbent firms and financial institutions. There is no final goal, to return to Willy Brandt's characterisation of socialism; instead, there is a constant struggle over the character of technology and who gets to benefit. The result will depend on a country's particular institutions, the strength and vitality of its democracy and the capacity to set out compelling visions of how the future could be if a progressive path were taken.

For the liberal left, there is a powerful lesson. Capitalism is going to remain; the task is to assemble a coalition that insists on the mode of production being shaped to generate good and satisfying jobs – and that the wealth is shared to benefit as many people as possible. The aim is mass flourishing. This requires a critique of current capitalism, accompanied by a feasible programme of reform, that gives the left an organising, unifying purpose. To be electorally credible and then effective in government it has to offer a forensic critique of what it accepts, even admires, about capitalism – and what it wants to change. It then has to argue for what the great American political philosopher and theorist of social justice John Rawls called an 'infrastructure of justice', to deliver the possibility of living in a good society in which prosperity is fairly shared. There will always be a hunger for some utopia – but centre-left parties and governments can best keep it at bay by delivering the best that is feasibly possible, grounded in a clear-eyed critique of what works and what does not. The story for the last century and a half is the left's incapacity – which is in some respects understandable – to do just that, for long enough to prove its case.

So the next phase of our story begins in 1859. The reforming 'Peelite' Tories who had backed the repeal of the Corn Laws, reform-minded Whigs, former Chartists and radical free-traders all came together to vote down the then Tory government and form the Liberal Party. The politicians who founded the party were in a sense anticipating the Acemoglu/Johnson argument, although their ambition was stymied from the get-go by Gladstone's passionate commitment to stringency in the public finances. Nonetheless, it was obvious that Britain could not continue to be run on the old precepts. The wealth created by capitalism had to be better deployed and shared – on education, on sanitation, on housing and on living standards – even if the pace of change, dictated by the precepts of Gladstonian parsimony, was agonisingly slow. The constitutional settlement had to be reformed and more democracy promoted, which at least came at little public cost. The newly established Liberal Party would start to implement Chartist constitutional reforms, promote free trade and use government power step by step to improve the condition of the people. Lacking a progressive political philosophy, it still genuflected to laissez-faire. But its destiny, surely, was to be Britain's party of reform. It only partially succeeded. If it had done better, we would not be where we are today.

5

THE LOST PROGRESSIVE DECADES

The foundation of the Liberal Party created the modern political system. Britain now possessed a culturally and socially legitimate party of reform, a vehicle that could respond to the growing pressure for change from civil society and to the diagnoses of progressives thinkers, social activists and a succession of Royal Commissions. Taking the eighty-year period to 1939 as a whole, apart from the great reforming government of 1906–14, liberalism failed itself and the country.

There would be no mobilisation of financial, scientific and technical resources to capitalise on the second Industrial Revolution. Britain's participation in the rising industries was indifferent or downright poor. The dysfunctional gap between finance and industry was not addressed. The mass of people remained far too exposed to the hazards of sickness, unemployment, disability, old age and ill-health. Not until 1948 would the Poor Law finally be repealed. Its principles – notably the means test and the division between the deserving and undeserving poor – were still alive as late as the 1930s. There was no systematic effort to invest in broadly based secondary or university education, university in particular remaining the preserve of a narrow elite. With the exception of Lloyd George's People's Budget, the inhibiting injunctions of Gladstonian finance were scrupulously observed. The House of Lords was still populated by hereditary lords, the vast majority of them Tories, recruited from the country's great estates. General elections continued to be held on a first-past-the-post voting system despite efforts to introduce proportional representation in the first two decades of the century. Class divisions remained intense. No political accommodation was reached with the rising Labour Party to hand on the baton of reform either before or after the First World War. There would be no British New Deal. There would be no great programmes to renew Britain's infrastructure or sweep away its slums. Even today, our housing stock, the oldest in Europe, bears the scars. Britain in 1939 was ossifying, about to suffer at Dunkirk the biggest military reversal in its history. Churchill's defiant rhetoric only partially disguised what everyone knew. The economic and social decay going back decades had led to an existential battle for national survival.

The saving grace was that the resources of empire cushioned the full impact of the failure. Britain's growth might have been lower and less dynamic than Germany and the USA, but its economy grew nonetheless. Britain could still muster sufficient industrial and financial muscle to mobilise the country for war, though it had to repudiate totally the doctrines of laissez-faire and adopt state direction to come out on the winning side in the 1939-45 war, as it had in the First World War – relying even more, this time, on American support to clinch victory. But too few enduring lessons were learned. After both wars, the overriding aim was to roll back a largely successful state and restore an unreformed, largely unsuccessful private sector.

In social terms, it was left to civil society and a burgeoning trade union movement, cooperatives, friendly societies, the actions of individual philanthropists and social activists to mitigate the worst failures of minimalist government. Local government chipped in with initiatives to build sewers, distribute clean water, provide schools and alleviate housing distress. But it was all haphazard and piecemeal.

The problem was threefold: the inability to break free from the suffocating attachment to laissez-faire, which was throttling economic and social policy; Tory determination to protect the privileges of class, land and the structures that protected the 'haves'; and the inability of progressive Britain – the 1906-14 Liberal government excepted – to forge a policy programme with different philosophic and economic roots to laissez-faire. It would take the Second World War and an intellectual accommodation between 'new' Liberalism and Labour thinking to turn the situation around and empower the 1945–51 Labour government. But it would not last.

The tensions between the urge to reform and stay true to the tenets of classical liberalism were symbolised by John Stuart Mill's 'On Liberty', which was published in the same year that the Liberal Party was formed. Here was Britain's most influential liberal political philosopher making an absolutist case for individual liberty as essential not only to laissez-faire economics but also to morality. The collective good could only be arrived at if individuals were allowed to make their own choices freely, wrote Mill, experiencing both the rewards and the penalties for their actions. Public authority should stand aside as much as possible, even to warn over the sale of poisons or a footpath approaching a cliff edge. To make the right choices individuals should of course be informed – the case for education and a free press – but the state should intervene, regulate and legislate as little as possible. The possession of individual liberty was everyone's birth-right and the route to the good society.

Mill insisted that if the state had to act beyond the minimalist position, it should only do so within clear limits. The question then remained; how were the economic, social and political exigencies of the late nineteenth century to be accommodated with liberalism's attachment to individual liberty, voluntarism and the minimal state?

The Rise and Importance of New Liberalism

By the end of the nineteenth century, it was impossible to accept that the current economic and social order was working properly. Sanitation was beginning to improve; however, in the absence of a government-led pan-British programme, it was left to individual local authorities to act – exemplified by Birmingham's mayor, the radical Liberal Joseph Chamberlain, who had galvanised the city's efforts in the mid-1870s. Housing need was acute, with virtually no publicly provided social housing, prompting social activists like Octavia Hill to attempt to fill the gap. There was a rising and increasingly activist trade union movement, with growing numbers of strikes and even street riots. Politically, the Liberals had accepted that the worker interest deserved a parliamentary voice to represent 'labour', standing aside in a succession of general elections from 1874 in a small number of working-class, especially mining, constituencies. The aim was to allow the election of 'LibLab' MPs, who would vote with the Liberals but with a licence to speak on labour issues. It was an unsatisfactory halfway house, but it was a start.

Two meticulous studies – and the Boer War – finally brought matters to a head. Charles Booth's seventeen-volume investigation of London poverty, conducted between 1889 and 1903 in meticulous detail, with his colour-coded maps, had shown that 30 per cent of Londoners lived in profound poverty – a statistic that shocked contemporaries. Recruitment for the Boer War had revealed that the majority of volunteers were simply not physically able to be soldiers due to malnutrition and poverty – they were stunted human beings. For example, 8,000 of 11,000 volunteers in Manchester in July 1900 had been considered 'physically unfit to carry a rifle and stand the fatigues of discipline', while only 1,200 of the 3,000 accepted had the 'muscular power and chest measurement' required for soldiering. It was a disastrous ratio, both socially and militarily.[1] Seebohm Rowntree conducted a parallel study in York, published in 1901, to see if the same percentage lived in as profound poverty as the London poor. They did. Winston Churchill acknowledged the impact made on him by the resulting book, *Poverty: A Study of Town Life*, writing to an official of the Midland Conservative Association in December 1901, 'I see little glory in an Empire which can rule the waves and is unable to flush its sewers.' He would refer to it in subsequent speeches – 'I have been reading a book which has fairly made my hair stand on end' – and it was one of the catalysts for him crossing the floor of the House in 1904 to join the Liberals.

Nor could it be argued that, whatever the 'Manchester School' said, free-market capitalism and free trade constituted a perfectly oiled machine, driving the British economy ever upwards. It was already apparent that the system threw up long recessions, or at least very slow growth, such as the one that lasted from 1873 to 1896. These were not acts of God, but rather evolved from the structure of capitalism itself. And as giant American and German companies emerged in sectors in which Britain had a minimal presence, it could not be claimed that free trade, balanced budgets and the minimal state were the guarantees for ongoing economic success. Other countries were coming up with different (and better) answers.

The New Liberals looked these facts in the eye, and were prepared to take on the prevailing orthodoxy. Even John Stuart Mill had recognised that the distribution of the fruits of capitalism needed to be fairer – the 'economics of distribution'. In this way, in his utilitarian terms, could the happiness of the greatest number be assured. Towards the end of his life, he even saw merit in worker cooperatives, and other ways of organising production than pure capitalism, providing they were the products of voluntary individual decision-making.[2] But he did not live through the two-decade-long depression of the 1870s and 1880s. Today's economic historians are warier about its length and depth, but contemporaries saw it differently; a Royal Commission was established in 1886 to inquire into 'the depression of trade and industry.'[3] What was wrong? In beginning to supply answers, the New Liberals laid the foundation of contemporary liberal social democracy and some of the best thinking about the linkages between the inherent flaws of capitalism and social inequality – and how better to redress them while retaining capitalism's essential dynamism, along with individual freedoms. It was a tradition that not only led to the 1906 Liberal government's creation of the early welfare state, but also produced both John Maynard Keynes and William Beveridge.

The Early New Liberal Thinkers: A Very Short Introduction

The stage was set by Oxford University's Thomas Hill Green, who, from the mid-1860s onwards, dared intellectually to challenge the libertarian liberalism of John Stuart Mill, with its primacy of the individual. Instead, he argued that men and women can only be rounded, moral human beings with the capacity for self-realisation – *the* fundamental object of existence – if together they recognise that they share a common purpose which they each have an obligation to help fulfil. Society is not an aggregation of individuals expressing their liberty, the foundation of Mill's thinking; instead, it is a social organism, an identity which, like a human being, is more than the sum of its parts. Every human being is in a constant interaction with their external environment in the form of society, argued Green, which shapes them, and which they in turn shape; they are not blank slates, but self-conscious living entities whose minds and being are in constant iteration with the social world beyond them. The health of the social body, which so influences them, is thus integral to everyone's own health, so that no human being can reflect their humanity if they only pursue their own selfish interest, which will hurt the social body. Holding society together and not pulling away is a common interest and purpose. The common good, and the ability of individuals to live lives they value and find meaningful, are interdependent.

This was the 'politics of obligation', in which it was not enough to do no harm to others in the exercise of individual freedoms, as the Benthamite utilitarians and the Manchester free-trade liberals had argued; the self-actualising human being had positively to assert the common good, collaborating and cooperating with others. It was an 'idealist' philosophy to which both liberals and socialists could subscribe – liberals because individual self-realisation was the objective of liberty, socialists because it stressed the value of shared purpose in living a common life of mutual respect and minimal unfairness. This needed an active state, at both national and local level – certainly circumspect in how ambitious it was not to crowd out individual agency, but nonetheless acting to shape the environment, so that individuals could best put their shoulder to the wheel of the greater common purpose. In particular, the state had an obligation to ensure good levels of education for all.

Although Green's major work, *Principles of Political*

Obligation, was published after an unhappily early death from blood poisoning in 1882, at the age of just forty-five, he (and it) had huge influence. It was not just that his students, like Herbert Asquith and the reformer Arnold Toynbee, were so impressed that they brought his ideas with them all their lives. It represented a comprehensive ethical challenge to laissez-faire thinking; the social body had to be organised so that everyone had a right to exercise their freedom. Green's 'politics of obligation' anticipated John Rawls's *A Theory of Justice* a century later; Green argued in Rawlsian terms that the good society requires the state to ensure that everyone has a chance to participate on an equal footing, so that there is an equal chance to exercise freedom. He created the ethical and moral space for later thinkers to conceive of what this state action would mean in practice. There is a direct line from Green to Beveridge and Keynes and thus the post-war settlement. He deserves wider recognition.

Enter John Hobson, lecturer and social activist, who was convinced that the only viable political vehicle for change was the Liberal Party, despite the doubts of even Fabians like Sidney and Beatrice Webb (the Fabians had been founded in 1884) that it did not have the spine, nor the intellectual convictions, to deliver the change that was needed. Hobson set out to prove them wrong. He would radicalise and transform John Stuart Mill's position. In *The Labour Movement* (1893), he began to go beyond the case for income redistribution from rich to poor that even the classical liberal Mill had conceded. He argued that social ownership of key industries along with forms of cooperative enterprise could both deliver the common good and make economic sense; it would embed workers getting a fairer share through their ownership. Indeed, capitalism needed to accommodate forms of social action and social ownership for its own health and reputation. It should not be against fairness.

But it was his 1894 classic, *The Evolution of Modern Capitalism*, that made his name, the first comprehensive non-Marxist critique of the way capitalism operated as a system. For Hobson, the explanation for the long depression stared one in the face: gross inequality, and thus the underconsumption and oversaving that flowed from it. Britain had a working class that was paid barely more than starvation wages – the low wages and insecure employment, for example, which provoked the successful 100,000-strong strike of London dockers in 1889. A poverty-stricken working class could not possibly spend sufficiently to drive the economy forwards, while the aristocratic elite and upper-middle class were too small to compensate. Instead, they saved, with the savings' surfeit flowing overseas to empire and the financing of other countries' industries. There was, he hypothesised, an ineluctable tendency to monopoly and development of trusts and cartels, which used their power to bid down wages. The solution was to break them up and develop social ownership and public direction of enterprise while simultaneously strengthening trade unions. High wages had not damaged US industry, which was in a virtuous circle of high wages, greater efficiency and higher consumption. Britain should follow suit.

Hobson would later argue that imperialism had the same roots – as a way for Britain's excess savings to find a profitable imperial home. The whole apparatus could be unravelled if the rich were taxed and the state spent the receipts on helping to meet vital social need. Overall levels of consumption could then be better maintained. After all, following Green, the state would only be acting to shape the social body so that it worked better. It was a compelling argument that influenced some of the most prominent thinkers of the early twentieth century, including Keynes, Richard Tawney and even Lenin, at least in his thinking about imperialism. New Liberalism had teeth.

Hobson was not alone. Leonard Hobhouse was a fellow contributor to *The Guardian* (which, under legendary editor C. P. Scott, played a key role in developing New Liberalism) and was London University's first professor of sociology. In his *Liberalism*, published in 1911, Hobhouse argued that individuals needed strong societal structures, succoured by the state, if they were to enjoy proper liberty. He, like Green, was anticipating the ideas of John Rawls in his *Theory of Justice*. Laissez-faire's enthronement of the individual, to be left to him or herself as the sole author of wealth creation, was just wrong; it was self-evident that wealth was as much a civic and social creation, and that the state could legitimately tax it to improve the working of the social whole – whether by regulating working hours, providing education or ensuring that people were looked after in sickness, old age or unemployment. Because wealth was a social creation, it was perfectly reasonable for society to claim back some of what it had created by progressive taxation of income and wealth. As private fortunes had been (in part) created both socially and publicly, the distinction between private and public money was wrong; taxation on great incomes and wealth was thoroughly legitimate.

Hobhouse was the first authentic self-described social liberal, and the link between his thinking and Chancellor Lloyd George's People's Budget of 1909 is obvious. The state must ensure that capitalism worked for the common good, organise decent living standards for the masses, including pensions, and thus save it from its own proclivities. The revolution in ideas launched by Green forty-five years earlier was at last bearing fruit. New Liberalism had provided the Liberal Party with the intellectual ammunition to do what many on its left doubted it could ever do – and it was 'of Britain', rather than some alien political force acting against it.

The Growing and Urgent Call for Reform

The prelude to that reforming Liberal government was a time of intensifying intellectual and political competition. In the early 1880s, both the Fabians and the Social Democratic Federation were founded, creating two of the most inconsistent, opposing strands in socialist thinking. The Fabians were dedicated to gradual, step-by-step social change that would be driven principally by better education, a capitalism organised around cooperation and collaboration and the spread of exemplary personal living and abstention from drink. (The Temperance movement was still very strong.) The Social Democratic Federation, on the other hand, was comprised of anti-gradualists who wanted to spread the Marxist gospel of inevitable class conflict leading to a revolutionary transformative moment. From the very beginning, there was ideological trouble.

On the other side of the political divide, the Conservatives were far from passive. The Primrose League was founded at the same time to promote 'the maintenance of religion, of the estates of the realm, and of the imperial ascendancy of the British Empire'. By the early 1890s, it would have more than 1 million members – more than the total trade union membership at the time.

Pride in empire was a potent political force, skilfully deployed by the Conservative leader Lord Salisbury. Britain should adopt a policy of splendid isolation, he declared, defended by empire, its navy and its commitment to laissez-faire. It was a combination that torpedoed Gladstone's successive attempts to assuage Irish nationalism by offering Home Rule to Ireland. This would be the thin end of the wedge, argued Conservatives and the 'Liberal Unionists' led by Joseph Chamberlain, who had broken from the Liberal Party in 1886 over the issue. Offering Home Rule to Ireland would open the door to offering autonomy to the rest of the empire. And to sustain the empire was Britain's over-riding purpose, even duty – a matter of national pride. It was a formula that allowed the Tories to lose only one general election, for a brief three-year period, over the twenty years from 1886.

But that 1892 election was notable for the left. One Keir Hardie, a successful veteran of Scottish trade unionism, was elected as independent MP for West Ham South, with the Liberals standing aside. He was not elected as a 'LibLab' MP – and so, unlike them, did not have to take the Liberal whip. In Hardie's view, real progress demanded an autonomous Labour Party with grassroots membership around the country and with a tougher, pro-worker ideology. So it was that the Independent Labour Party (ILP) was founded in 1893, with Hardie as chair – independent of the 'LibLabs', but crucially as a 'big tent' coalition ideologically to the left of them. But it was a big tent without any political or intellectual coherence. Hardie's ILP would contain pure Marxists, Methodists, Fabians, elements of the Social Democrat Federation, Christian socialists, as well as moderate and radical trade unionists. All that united them was the general proposition that more of the means of production should be cooperatively or collectively owned for the common good (exact details varied profoundly between the new members), but beyond that it was light on doctrine in order to attract as many left-leaning adherents as possible. The success of capitalism was accepted as a given; the job was to make sure it better served workers by operating more fairly. It was a view the New Liberals shared.

The open question was which political formation, party or combination of parties was the best means to that end – prompting debate and heart-searching across the country. Thus artist, designer, poet and writer William Morris, already in the 1880s internationally famous for his brilliant designs combining romanticised beauty and practicality, was exploring what philosophy and politics would best transform working-class lives – from a radicalised liberalism to Marxism. Neither worked in his view – what was needed was contemporary versions of Mediaeval guilds which had protected the incomes of artisans. In his popular novel published in 1888, *A Dream of John Ball*, about the radical, rebel priest who inspired the Peasants Revolt of 1381, he set out the core of his credo through the imagined voice of Ball. 'Fellowship is heaven, and lack of fellowship is hell: fellowship is life, and lack of fellowship is death: and the deeds that ye do upon the earth, it is for fellowship's sake that ye do them.'[4] They were lines that made a deep impact on the late Victorian and Edwardian left – Clem Attlee among them – but the issue then, as now, is how best and through what political vehicle can fellowship be made economically and socially real.

In 1894, the Rainbow Circle was established to discuss just that, named after the Rainbow Tavern in Fleet Street where its meetings were held. New Liberal John Hobson was a member, but so were Fabian socialists, Liberal MPs and even the young journalist Ramsay MacDonald, who would become secretary of the yet-to-be-formed Labour Representation Committee, which would take forward the work of the Labour Representation League established in the late 1860s.[5] The Circle's main subject of conversation was whether the emerging New Liberal political philosophy was the basis for a unifying reconciliation between liberals and socialists – rather as Whigs, Peelites and Radicals had all come together to form the original Liberal Party – and whether, with a first-past-the-post voting system, a reconstituted combined Liberal and Labour Party could take on and beat the Tories. Hobson launched the LibLab journal *The Progressive Review* with the radical journalist William Clarke to promote a forum for Liberal and Labour collaboration.[6]

Nor was this just an elite debate in London pubs. In the Rhondda, for example, the former miner William Abraham (known by his bardic name 'Mabon' for short) had been elected in 1885 as a passionate advocate of the labour interest in a Liberal constituency, but he would take the Liberal whip. His loyalties could hardly be clearer. Labour, he declared in his campaign literature, created 'the sinew, the bone, the marrow, the life and the prosperity of the community'. Months after his election, he would create the Rhondda Labour and Liberal Association, and continue to be elected under LibLab colours until his last election in 1910 – speaking always for the labour cause but within the mantle of the Liberal Party.[7] He even survived the 1895 election, when every one of Hardie's twenty-eight ILP candidates lost, validating, he would say, his strategy of working with the Liberals.[8] In Oxford, Gilbert Murray, great-grandfather of journalist Polly Toynbee, attempted the same as Mabon; however, as she recounts in her history of her family, he always lost when he stood for election.[9] His experience, rather than Mabon's, would point to the future, though both men would say that had their strategy been followed, the Tory Party would have had less of a clear run in the century that followed.

For Mabon, as much as for Keir Hardie, the assumption was that the capitalist goose would carry on laying golden economic eggs without needing to worry how and why. Its propensity to innovate, invest, compete and modernise were just assumed. The bigger point was that all value was ultimately created by either labour or its expropriation, as Mabon had declared. For socialist thinkers, all that was required to relieve working-class misery was that capital should be owned by the working class. The fundamental issue was not production, but to ensure fair distribution of those capitalist geese's eggs – hence the ILP's policy programme, adopting trade union demands for better working and social conditions. But after the electoral rout in 1895, taking on laissez-faire capitalism and improving the lot of the working class was obviously going to prove a tough task. Tory appeals to empire, splendid isolation and upholding the current social order against working-class agitation had widespread support. The more promising route seemed less like politics and more like the militant industrial action of the fast-growing trade union movement.

Trade Unions to the Fore

Over the 1890s, new unions formed, especially in the unskilled trades, and membership grew exponentially. The dockers' success in the landmark 1889 strike had shown the way. At last, the working class were emboldened to join unions – often local and linked to their trade, which would prove so problematic in the future, with employers having to negotiate with a multiplicity of unions on any one site. It was beginning to be difficult even in the 1890s. Trade union membership would rise from 750,000 in 1888 to 6.5 million by 1918. By 1900, a series of strikes had been won – but, equally, employers were fighting back, sometimes refusing to recognise the newly formed unions as legitimate pay-bargaining partners, resisting wage claims and locking out strikers. The Conservative mantra that trade unions, their wage claims and their strikes were all impairing British competitiveness would become a familiar refrain over the century ahead.

Trade unions at that time did not see the point of a Labour Party and were sceptical about the jumble of ideas that constituted 'socialism' – better to sponsor individual MPs like Mabon within the Liberal Party who would speak for the labour interest. They resisted Keir Hardie's pleas for money to support the ILP. In the 1900 general election, only two ILP MPs were returned. But the House of Lords 1901 Taff Vale judgement, reversing thirty years of trade union law, transformed the political and industrial landscape. A railway union in South Wales was found to have injured the Taff Vale railway company in a nine-day strike through picketing and other attempts to stop the company importing blackleg labour, and the union was compelled to pay swingeing damages. Suddenly, trade unions across the country realised that their industrial power was under profound threat; picketing to support strikes was rendered de facto illegal. Hardie's argument that there needed to be a 'critical mass' of MPs in the House of Commons dedicated to speak for the labour interest to challenge such judgements seemed more prescient. Trade unions were suddenly ready to provide political funding. The Trades Union Congress (TUC) and Liberal opposition combined; they would reverse the Taff Vale judgement. And Hardie's argument needed to be heeded; Labour needed more men in the House of Commons.

The TUC had formed a Labour Representation Committee (LRC) in 1900, with Ramsay MacDonald as its secretary, to boost the numbers of Labour MPs. Pacts had already operated in isolated seats; in 1902, during a by-election in Clitheroe, the Liberals had stood aside for an LRC candidate. Under the secret 1903 Gladstone–MacDonald Pact (Herbert Gladstone, the great William Ewart's son, was the Liberal chief whip), this would be done at scale. In 1904, the LRC decided it would create a fund to pay election expenses and contribute to MPs' salaries – the foundation of the link between unions and Labour that still exists today. Forty candidates stood in working-class constituencies in the 1906 general election, supported by unions affiliated to the LRC, with the Liberals standing down in their favour as their part of the 'Progressive Alliance'. Of the twenty-nine LRC MPs elected in 1906, twenty-four were in seats the Liberals did not contest, including Mabon's in Rhondda. After the election, the LRC MPs changed their committee's name to the Labour Party – but they owed their strength in the House of Commons to the TUC and the pact with the Liberals. Labour had no systematic membership organisation in the country, nor funding independent of trade unions, but the party was born. It had been a liberal landslide victory – 400 Liberal MPs – and the Tories shrunk to 157. Now, reform could begin in earnest.

New Liberalism and Edwardian Socialism

The newly elected Liberal government was a wide, if disparate, coalition, reflecting the complexity and range of Liberal Britain – the Temperance movement, non-conformists, radical free-traders, professionals, small businessmen, trade unionists, New Liberals and 'LibLabbers'. All recognised that the social need was acute; nobody disputed the searing results of Charles Booth's and Seebohm Rowntree's research. There was also a consensus about the growing need for 'national efficiency' in the face of the challenge from the USA and Germany. The former Tory Winston Churchill, Keir Hardie and Mabon all now sat on the governing benches in the House of Commons, part of the same political project led by the Liberals, transparently 'of Britain', rather than subversively against it. The New Liberal intellectuals had argued for an active state, increased spending and progressive taxation to provide the wherewithal for programmes of economic and social improvement. This was what now happened.

One of the first acts of the incoming government was to pass the Trade Disputes Act, restoring the trade unions' legal immunities. It was a moment whose consequences still reverberate today; the union movement was to be placed above the normal operations of commercial and contract law, and it could declare strikes in the confidence that its funds were safe from being sued. The LRC had done its job to reassert the foundation of trade union power – the trade union veto of Harold Wilson's *In Place of Strife* in 1969 and the successful revolt against the Heath government's Industrial Relations Act decades later were direct consequences of this legislation.

The structures that would shape the twentieth-century Labour Party were now in place, but at the time it was not obvious that its destiny was to be a self-standing party pitching for government. It certainly had no overarching ideology that bound its MPs together. Until 1918, it had no individual members, just affiliated bodies and socialist societies. The clue was in the name. It was not called a 'socialist' party, but a Labour Party. Labour MPs' task was to speak for the labour interests of the working classes and trade unions in particular, and to form whatever alliances were necessary to ensure those aims would be met. It was essentially a defensive protector of the workers' interest.

More than a century later, it requires a leap of the imagination to understand the social soil in which socialism and the Marxism that inspired it grew. Working-class lives were grinding, squalid and short-lived (when the state pension was introduced in 1909, male life expectancy was forty-seven). The operation of the Poor Law, which for the entire nineteenth century was the only form of poverty relief, was pitiless – another galvanising element.

One vivid testimony of its effects can be found in *The Ragged-Trousered Philanthropists*, Britain's most successful socialist novel, written just before the First World War by the Irish painter and decorator Robert Tressell. Set in early-Edwardian England, the story's hero is house painter Frank Owen, questing for work on miserable terms; when he finds it, he tries to convince his workmates in a large house where they are all working that the real cause of their misery is the operation of capitalism, with its low wages and insecurity. They should stop believing that a better life is not for them, available only for their 'betters', and embrace the solution: the socialisation of the means of production, so that everyone works for the common good. They should stop accepting criminally low wages, in effect donating profits to their bosses, as the ragged-trousered philanthropists of the title. Owen is heckled and ridiculed by his fellow workers; however, bit by bit, as he outlines the operation of the 'money machine' and the experience of terrible and avoidable accidents, of low pay and of constant uncertainty as to whether there will be a job the following day, he rouses them to take action. Tressell died of tuberculosis before his book was published, but what he described was commonplace. It would influence generations on the left – Jack Jones, the radical general secretary of the Transport and General Workers' Union and opponent of any state regulation of trade unions, would cite it as a major influence.

At the same time, the young Clement Attlee was working in the slums of East London, having just graduated from Oxford.

He was shocked by what he found – as he described in 1905 in remarkably similar terms to Robert Tressell.

> From this [the experience of managing an East End boys' club] it was only a step to examining the whole basis of our social and economic system. I soon began to realise the curse of casual labour. I got to know what slum landlords, and sweating, meant. I understood why the Poor Law was so hated. I learned also why there were rebels. The slums, the suffering, the poverty were not the necessary consequence of the character of the poor. Given opportunities even remotely comparable to the boys who went to Haileybury [Attlee's private school, and whose offshoot in the East End he was managing] the Limehouse lads responded. Most of the poor were poor because they were exploited by the rich. The message for the well-off should not be just 'help the poor who are always with us' but 'get off the people's backs'.[10]

Given the experience of day-to-day working-class life, the moderation of Labour's leaders was striking. Ramsay MacDonald wrote in 1911, 'The Labour party is not socialist. It is an union of socialist and trade union bodies for immediate political work [...] the only political form which evolutionary Socialism can take with the political traditions and methods of Great Britain.'[11] It was the line he had been preaching since the publication of his *Socialism and Society* in 1905, before the election; evolutionary socialism, based on reform, not revolution, was the way forward, which would require iron discipline and sustained moderation.[12] As communism developed as a force, MacDonald would insist that the party must resist infiltration from communists and 'fellow travellers' – and not be associated with industrial militancy. Yes, there were more self-avowedly socialist MPs, like Keir Hardie, who wanted a self-standing party, but even Hardie shared with MacDonald the view that achieving socialism would be an evolutionary rather than revolutionary process – and it would spring from the mutual institutions of civil society: trade unions, cooperatives, friendly societies and Nonconformist chapels.[13] The end game was social justice, and while the state would be essential in achieving that end, it did not (and could not) represent the acme of a socialist society. Echoing William Morris, many of these politicians and trade unionists believed workers needed to live in institutions which they themselves had created, embodying their values and promoting 'fellowship'. For 'fellowship is life', recall that the romantic artist and radical had written, 'and lack of fellowship is death'.

So while the Labour Party's trade union backers looked to Labour MPs to secure practical improvements to working-class lives – and which the Liberal government was trying to do more determinedly than any of its predecessors – Labour MPs themselves entertained an inchoate jumble of bigger ideas. They were not Marxists; instead, their socialism, as one ILP backer of Keir Hardie wrote, was a form of religion in that it demanded 'the right state of our present lives, the right state of our relation to our fellows, the right moral health of our souls'.[14] Socialism was an ethic and a mission, social justice its end. For the early Labour MPs, and Hardie in particular, this was the shared preoccupation. Capitalism, they believed, had solved the production question. The political fight was for fairer distribution – a view the New Liberals, with their roots in Thomas Green, shared. Both MacDonald and Hardie were stressing that Labour, like the Liberal Party, should be seen as making Britain fairer rather than subversively undermining it. In this sense, there was little ideological obstacle to the two political forces fusing, as the Tories feared, and the twentieth century could have been very different.

To Work: The Liberal Government, 1906–14

After restoring trade union immunities, between 1905 and 1908, Liberal Prime Minister Sir Henry Campbell-Bannerman's government introduced free school meals, increased the entitlements for education between the ages of twelve and eighteen, created a scholarship system for bright working-class kids and empowered local education authorities to acquire land to build schools. His chancellor, Herbert Asquith, introduced a differentiated income tax to help pay for it – with a higher rate on 'unearned' income such as rents, interest and dividends. This was pure New Liberal thinking, reflecting what Green had taught him at Balliol all those years earlier. It was a good start, but when Asquith succeeded as prime minister, and David Lloyd George took over as chancellor, the pace of reform accelerated, and the policies of New Liberalism were properly followed through. Nor was it just the influence of Hobson, Hobhouse and Green; the ideas of Carlyle, Ruskin, Morris and even the late Mill, along with the demands of trade unionists, were at last heeded.

The first big move was on pensions. The Poor Law had been a weak enough safety net, but for the over-sixty-fives it was a disaster; Booth had established that nearly half of working-class people over that age fell into paupery. The answer was the introduction of a non-contributory state pension for the over-seventies – which, given that male life expectancy was forty-seven at the time, it was reckoned would not cost much. In the event, half a million people enrolled in the first year, and raising money to pay for the popular pension became even more urgent.

This was the origin of Lloyd George's famous People's Budget, announced in 1909. On top of the pensions, it introduced a National Insurance scheme, with contributions from employers, employees and the state, to create a fund to pay doctors' and hospital bills, sick pay and unemployment benefit. 'This [...] is a war budget', he declared in a four-and-a-half-hour speech to the House of Commons; 'It is for raising money to wage implacable warfare against poverty and squalidness.' The philosophy behind the budget was undiluted New Liberalism, building on Asquith's taxes on unearned income two years earlier. It introduced a progressive surtax targeted at the wealthy, higher death duties, and it taxed land whose value had risen because of the 'enterprise of the community' – an 'unearned increment' piggy-backing on the prosperity brought by town life, or, in the case of mineral royalties, from the good luck of owning land with coal or iron ore beneath it. These were classic New Liberal targets. Pubs and drink were also singled out for punitive treatment, with a tax on pub licences and higher taxes on tobacco and spirits – but, importantly, not beer; the Temperance movement, Nonconformists, teetotallers, socialists and the trade unions were all appeased in one stroke.[15]

Yet these eye-catching and famous measures were buttressed by a myriad of others, before and afterwards. A system of trade boards would set minimum wages, particularly in low-wage industries, as part of the commitment to enforce minimum standards. The construction of back-to-back houses was outlawed. Attempts were made to limit pub opening hours and reduce the number of public houses. The Children's Charter created a duty to protect children's welfare, together with a tax allowance for parents on low incomes. A national system of labour exchanges was established, an idea of the young William Beveridge, to help workers find work.[16] Few areas of social life were left untouched.

The 1909 budget provoked fierce Conservative resistance. The Lords, overwhelmingly dominated by landed Tory hereditary peers, broke reactionary cover. All this, they felt emboldened to argue, was such a radical departure it should be put to the people in an election rather than being tamely passed by the Lords. Ever since the seventeenth century, the constitutional protocol had been that money bills were the sole preserve of the Commons. In the course of 1910, there was a general election in January, a failed Constitutional Conference to sort out the Lords/Commons relationship and then a second general election in December, in which the Liberals and Tories were neck-and-neck for the second election running; however, on both occasions, the Liberals were kept in power by Irish Nationalists and Labour.

In 1911, cowed by the real threat that the Liberals would create hundreds of new peers to pass their Commons legislation, the Lords caved in, and agreed to pass the Parliament Act. The Lords could now only delay a bill for two years. They had been faced down, and in the process the Liberals had conceded to the Labour demand that MPs should be paid, and to the Irish Nationalists that Ireland should finally be granted Home Rule. The People's Budget crisis of 1909–11 had triggered the beginning of the end of aristocratic parliamentary dominance – and raised the funds to finance the precursor of what would grow into the welfare state. It was a moment for which working-class Britain had waited nearly a century.

The Liberals, with Labour's support, now represented the progressive majority in Britain, but with a notable geographical split; there was, as Hobson argued, a 'Producer's England' in the North that voted for the progressive parties and a 'Consumer's England' in the South that voted Tory. Lloyd George, typically, was more graphic: 'the forces of production marshalled against the semi-feudal south'. There were potent challenges ahead – the growth of a more intransigent Irish nationalism, the Suffragette movement and, in industrial Britain, an increasing assertiveness of workers' interests. Trade unionism was becoming more industrially militant – but with more than 1,000 individual trade unions it would be hard to coordinate them into agents for political change. The Liberals, with the philosophy of New Liberalism, had shown they had the muscle, guile and intellectual agility to manage such challenges, recasting if necessary their relationship with a Labour Party that was still far from a national force. In 1914, there was good reason to suppose that Britain had laid the basis of a new potent progressive force that could rival the Tories as a natural party of government. In the USA, the Democratic Party was emerging as a coherent progressive political force. Could the same happen in Britain? Then came war.

The First World War and Its Aftermath

The war upended British politics. Prime Minister Asquith might have been a disciple of Thomas Green, but there was enough John Stuart Mill in him to recoil from the state conscripting men for war – a fundamental offence against the precepts of individual liberty. Men should volunteer from choice. Nor should the state interfere with private business and the operation of the market, even in wartime. And so, Britain began the war with a volunteer army and reliance on the market to provide ordnance, armaments and supplies. It was a stance that could not survive military failures and the carnage of the stalemated trenches. By December 1916, Lloyd George, whose energy had created what was in effect a 'war socialist' economy, manoeuvred to take over as prime minister, backed by Tory leaders, the Tory Party and his loyalists in the Liberal Party. He believed that only he had the proven determination, energy and willingness to mobilise ruthlessly the state to win the war. Asquith, thoroughly outwitted, became leader of the opposition, confronting his former chancellor across the despatch box as prime minister supported by a Liberal rump and the Tories. The Liberal Party, which had split back in 1886 over Irish Home Rule, now split again as the war was reaching its end. The rupture between its two foremost leaders was too much for any party. It was existential; attempted recovery would prove impossible.

When, in April 1917, the USA declared war on Germany, an Allied victory seemed inevitable and discussion began about the post-war political settlement. There would be a new Representation of the People Act – who should vote and how? All men over twenty-one who had risked everything obviously must vote, as should women, acknowledging their fundamental contribution to the war effort. But what should the voting system be? An earlier Royal Commission on Electoral Reform in 1908, commissioned by the Liberals amid the increasing interest in fair voting provoked by the Suffragette movement, had opted for proportional representation (PR) based on the single transferable vote (STV), but its recommendation in 1910 was never acted on. Asquith was not convinced, even if a large element in his party was. Now the Liberals in the House of Commons were split; Tories in the Commons and Lords would determine the outcome. There were voices for the alternative vote (AV), first-past-the-post (FPTP) and STV systems, with the Tories in the Commons attached to no change or to AV. MacDonald calculated that Labour, with the vast extension of the franchise now promised, would be the beneficiary of the existing first-past-the-post system – the miscalculation of the century. It was deadlock; a decision would be deferred. The Victorian electoral system remained in place by default.

At the snap December 1918 'coupon' general election after the war, the coalition led by Lloyd George won a landslide, with Tories making up the lion's share of the MPs. It was a Tory government in all but name, even if Lloyd George remained prime minister. The detailed voting figures reveal the importance of FPTP. Asquith's Liberals and Lloyd George's Coalition Liberal faction both received just under 1.4 million votes, but the former won only 36 seats, while the latter took 127 seats, courtesy of the Tories agreeing not to contest seats held by Liberal MPs who supported the wartime coalition, who were given 'coupons' to show their loyalty. The political reality was that those winning Coalition Liberals were wholly dependent on Conservative indulgence, which, when it was withdrawn, meant they would follow the other Liberal wing into political oblivion – as they eventually did.

The Tory Party had had the guile and self-confidence to mastermind the conditions for its post-war dominance. Other protagonists at the end of the First World War lost empires, went into decline or experienced hyperinflation. Britain's loss was its emergent progressive coalition – and decades of Tory hegemony. The Conservatives had earned legitimacy by supporting the successful wartime leader and then getting behind a post-war national government, had broken the Liberal Party irretrievably and had made first-past-the-post the anchor of the electoral system while dividing the progressive vote. To such victors would fall the coming century's spoils.

The Revolution That Did Not Take Place

Lloyd George had won the war, and he now promised to win the peace – to build 'a fit country for heroes to live in'. If his personal standing was sky-high, his rump Coalition Liberals lacked any national party organisation or political base; the first-past-the-post voting system had made his political position entirely dependent on the Tories. To win the peace he would require a much more progressive coalition to support a big state capable of spending and taxing to deliver on his promise, along with an intellectual consensus to take on the laissez-faire orthodoxy. If the economy was insufficiently dynamic, there needed to be practical radical ideas about how to drive it forwards. None of that existed, beyond left-wing calls for socialist revolution to ape the Bolshevik seizure of power in Russia. The only sure compasses to hand seemed to be laissez-faire, free trade, balanced budgets and the gold standard – all wrong, especially for this moment. If Britain was to live within its means, as the orthodoxy insisted, winning the peace would have to be postponed while public spending was cut. So, between 1921 and 1922, Lloyd George implemented the recommendations of one Sir Eric Geddes, slashing not only defence but all forms of social spending. The unnecessary savagery of the 'Geddes axe' (supported inevitably by the Treasury) passed into legend. The promise of building a country fit for heroes was abandoned.

In October 2022, his government collapsed, and in the ensuing election his now National Liberals only won fifty-three seats, compared to sixty-two for Asquith's branch of the party. Liberalism as a political force was being annihilated. The Labour Party won 142 seats, now the senior progressive party. Together, the three parties had won 8 million votes, compared to the Tories' 5.3 million – the basis for a progressive landslide. First-past-the-post had killed that prospect stone-dead. It was a pattern that would repeated over and again in the coming century. It was not only the voting system and splits within the Liberal leadership that had done for Liberalism. Class had played its fatal part too. New Liberal ideas had led it to becoming the standard-bearer of progressive politics, but the bulk of its leadership was unmistakeably drawn from the upper echelons of British land, business and finance. There could be profound political disagreements, but Liberals alongside Tories were essential buttresses of Britishness. They were legitimate reformers – 'of Britain'. 'How Nature always does contrive – Fal, lal, la!', wrote Gilbert and Sullivan in 1882 in their operetta *Iolanthe*, 'that every boy and every gal that's born into the world alive / Is either a little Liberal. Or else a little Conservative!' Their audience laughed even as it nodded in agreement; Liberal and Conservative were the ying and yang of British politics – part of the whole. Churchill could cross the floor of the House as a scion of the upper class and easily fit in with the great reforming Liberal government.

But class would also prove the Liberal Party's undoing. In industrial Britain, as trade union membership grew alongside belief in socialism, Liberals were seen as members of a class interest that in the end would always uphold an oppressive capitalism. The Liberal government might have passed the Trade Disputes Act but it had not backed Labour's Right to Work bill back in 1906, and unions, recognising Liberal hesitancies, began to affiliate with the Labour Party instead. Industrial action was escalating, after being largely frozen during the war. Between 1919 and 1921, an average 40 million days a year were lost to strikes – with the red flag making more than the occasional appearance, fluttering over Glasgow town hall during its general strike and on the masthead of HMS *Kilbride* when its sailors struck, warning that the rest of the navy would soon follow. In March 1919, Lenin founded the Communist International, inviting all national working-class movements around the world to sign up in order to internationalise the revolution in Russia. In December 1919, the Scottish Divisional Council of the Independent Labour Party voted to join. Where it led, others could follow.[17] Fears of socialism leading to a British-style Bolshevik coup seemed very real; it was to stop the march of Socialism, declared Churchill, that he had returned to the Conservative Party in 1924. In this fight, there was only one side for an aristocrat, an imperialist and a member of the House of Marlborough like him.

Class had deep roots in Britain; the entire House of Lords was still made up of hereditary and mainly Tory peers. Aristocrats, with their grand houses and estates, dominated London 'society'. They were the social and cultural pinnacle of Britain, the automatic first choices to chair banks and prestigious companies and to populate the upper echelons of the military and Indian Civil Service. They were the governing class, overwhelmingly educated in the great public schools and the 'staff college of the old universities' Oxford and Cambridge, as Lloyd George had scornfully called them.

Respectability was powerfully associated with earning the blessing of this aristocratic-cum-upper-class, recognisable then as now by the signifiers of accent and 'gentlemanly' behaviour. In the nineteenth century, Conservative leaders had not trusted the working-class masses to understand how aristocratic stewardship of land and great estates was essential to British institutional resilience and stability as they saw it. This had been at the heart of Tory leader Lord Salisbury's resistance to extending the franchise; demagogy, misrule and assertion of working-class interests, he declaimed, would result if the suffrage was extended.[18] After all, the defence of Britain's great estates was an avowed aim of the Primrose League. While Liberalism could be wrongheaded in Tory eyes, its leaders and party were not social aliens. Labour and the working class were a different kettle of fish.

Labour, as it succeeded the Liberals as the senior progressive party, knew this and yearned to be a respected part of the whole. It was the best platform to advance the workers' demand for a fairer share, equality of treatment and decent living conditions. But the party also talked socialism – making the need to be 'of Britain' rather than subvert it an even harder proposition. Its 1918 constitution called for the labour movement 'to secure for the workers by hand or by brain the full fruits of their industry and the most equitable distribution thereof that may be possible upon the basis of the common ownership of the means of production, distribution and exchange'. How that was to be achieved was less clear; the best guess was that a 'corporate socialism' would unite with 'guild socialism' gradually to take over capitalist firms, who would ensure wage labour received its proper due – but the mechanism was vague. Nonetheless, a Labour Party that was at last rapidly building working-class support saw no reason for more compromises and pacts; it would aim to stand in every constituency. It was a radicalism that in practical political terms was accompanied by an immediate and accompanying desire to reassure; Labour was about no more than gradually achieving its aims within the British parliamentary democratic system and wider British empire. It would proceed by evolution rather than revolution, as both Keir Hardie and Ramsay MacDonald had declared before the First World War.

Thus Labour's first colonial secretary in the short-lived 1924

Labour government, morning-suit-clad James Henry Thomas, made Labour's commitment to empire very clear from his first day in office – but still, like almost every Labour MP, he remained closely engaged in trade unionism. Labour wanted to position itself as bargainer for a better, fairer national deal, rather than as agent of socialist transformation whatever the rhetoric – a tension embedded in its formation in 1900. It wanted to be a legitimate constituent part of the British political and economic order. Nor could a party largely made up of non-university-educated trade union men be very intellectually self-confident. It had neither the zeal to back Marx nor the willingness to dare of John Maynard Keynes.

So, the story is of the revolution that did not take place. The 1920s were a decade of political, ideological and intellectual confusion. Labour, in office and in opposition, was the essence of defensive moderation. It had ideas about how to fund a better social settlement by levying taxes on the rich and the landed gentry, but beyond that it did not dare fundamentally to disagree with the old laissez-faire orthodoxies. It lacked the self-confidence and will to make a dysfunctional capitalism work better. How to put British capitalism back on its feet? How to create jobs? Its answers were paltry. The Tories were equally bankrupt despite their election victories; their only idea was to try to recreate the pre-war world without acknowledging that it had already ceased to work forty or fifty years earlier.

The October 1924 general election, following Labour's first unsatisfactory ten months in government, saw the Conservatives win a 200-seat majority, even though they polled 1 million votes fewer than Labour and Liberals combined – FPTP working its false magic, offering an apparent overwhelming validation of profoundly backward-looking policies. Thus Winston Churchill, by April 1925 chancellor in the new Tory government, took the fateful decision to peg sterling to gold at the same rate as in August 1914, when convertibility to gold had been suspended. This had been the alleged linchpin of British nineteenth-century prosperity – surely it would work again, along with free trade and laissez-faire. It was the chosen path of the Treasury and Bank of

England, not resisted by the Labour Party or by the electorally humiliated Liberals. The result was continued economic stagnation, uncompetitive exports and depressed real wages. But one economist had powerfully and eloquently dissented, and was attracting increasing attention: John Maynard Keynes. At just the moment New Liberalism would throw up some potential answers to the post-war economic crisis, first-past-the-post would deny his party any real political influence.

Keynes: The New Liberal, But With Too Little Purchase on Power

Keynes, a lifelong Liberal and direct heir to the New Liberal tradition, developed that tradition's arguments to define a new intellectual paradigm of economic thought. He had already written one of the best-selling economics books of the twentieth century, *The Economic Consequences of the Peace*, from his position as Treasury insider and Cambridge academic observing the post-war peace conference, warning that the savage peace settlement the Allies had imposed upon Germany contained the germs of a second major war. It would be impossible for Germany to repay the onerous war reparations. No good could come of it. Rather than crush Germany, the sane policy was to put the country back on its feet so that it could stimulate recovery abroad and assuage the rise of political extremism at home.

He made equally prescient arguments about the return to the gold standard in 1925. It was putting the foreign-currency cart before the economic horse. The goal of economic policy should not be maintaining the value of the pound against some arbitrary historic relationship to quantities of gold; it should be to promote employment, investment and growth. In his view British exports could not be competitive given that British wage levels were now being pitched at such high levels in dollar terms; there would inevitably be demands for wage cuts that would rightly be resisted by the trade unions.

Again, his predictions were amply validated. A year later, the mining unions representing over 1 million men came out on strike over proposed wage cuts. Trying to achieve a compromise against intransigent pit owners, the TUC said it would call a general strike in solidarity with the miners. Its bluff was called, so the triple alliance (of miners, iron and steel workers and railway unions) was mobilised along with workers in the energy, building and print industries. Britain found itself in a nationwide general strike – neither to achieve constitutional reform, like the Chartist strikes in the 1830s and 1840s, nor to advance the socialisation of the means of production. Rather, it was a strike in defence of jobs and wages – neither Chartist nor Bolshevik. It went nowhere and, true to its general lack of militancy, after ten days the TUC withdrew its support. The miners would continue their strike, but finally they accepted reduced wages and went back to work. The British Labour movement abjured revolution. Keynes wanted it to stay that way.

That meant there was a moral and self-interested obligation on economic policy-makers to ensure that capitalism worked better – and that did not mean accepting the precepts of laissez-faire. In the wake of the failed general strike, he published his brilliant essay 'The End of Laissez-Faire'. Economists over the previous hundred years, he wrote, had developed the extraordinary doctrine that acts of individual self-interest in free markets will always produce the social interest – thus uniting social reformers, the Church of England, Hume, Locke, followers of Rousseau and the high priests of the City of London around the happy doctrine that the state should do nothing to manage the economy, despite the evidence of the First World War that the state had been supremely successful in doing just that.[19]

The time had come, given the evident malfunctioning of contemporary capitalism, to learn to think differently to promote vital employment and growth. Instead of leaving levels of investment and saving to the choices made by the markets, or the availability of credit, on the grounds that private decisions could reliably deliver the public interest, the state simply had to step in and organise the saving, investment and credit flows that would create employment. Capitalism, properly managed, was the system most likely to deliver prosperity – especially if autonomous institutions could be developed between the state and the individual that incorporated conceptions of the 'We' – the public and social interest. But they should also have the freedom to act autonomously in response to circumstances as they saw them. Such a system had to be organised because it was never going to happen spontaneously. In this way, Keynes argued, capitalism would deliver its promise, provide work and stave off the threat of revolutionary socialisation. Laissez-faire had to end.

He married his public interventions with intense academic work to offer a theoretical basis for better public policy. As the storm clouds grew over the British economy, he worked on his *Treatise on Money* (published in 1930), the foundation of his later *General Theory*. Essentially, the Bank of England, instead of setting the interest rate and the supply of credit to support the value of the pound, should instead turn policy inside-out and use monetary policy to stimulate investment. At the limit, it should even print money and flood the banking system with credit – what he called monetary policy *à outrance*. The pound must simply adjust to what the economy was doing, and not the other way round.

His radical intellectual programme reached its culmination with the publication of the *General Theory of Employment, Interest and Money* in 1936 – in a sense the pure economic distillation of New Liberalism. Capitalism faced an existential dilemma. Economic actors – banks, trade unions and workers, companies, investors – could not know an unknowable future. All they could do was to make the best bet, reflecting their hopes and fears. But the markets in which they operated had different capacities quickly to respond to their actions. Financial markets could react instantaneously, but the markets for workers, products and services responded more slowly. And some markets – principally for big investment goods like machines – were just lumpier in scale than others; they had bigger 'multiplier' effects, driving the economy upwards faster when investment rose, and doing the same thing in reverse when it fell. The proposition of the classical, laissez-faire economists that free markets – rather like the spheres – naturally gravitated to a point of balance that would be the best for all concerned was just baloney. Instead, a capitalist economy was in a permanent state of disequilibrium, with mismatched market reactions and differential cascade effects creating booms and busts, especially the cataclysmic bust of the Great Depression.

The state had to act. It had actively to adjust monetary policy and interest rates, and if that failed it had to raise or lower public spending and borrowing, compensating for what capitalism was not doing. Importantly, this was not a doctrine for always and everywhere increasing public spending, as he would be interpreted after the Second World War. Rather, it was to use public spending to lean against the ups and downs of the business cycle alongside changes in interest rates. It was the state acting to promote prosperity and thus individual liberty, and so legitimising capitalism – turbocharged Green and Hobhouse given economic teeth. But the Liberal schism during the First World War, later sealed by the first-past-the-post electoral system, had marginalised the political vehicle through which Keynes might put his ideas into action.

The effect was dramatised in the 1929 general election. Lloyd George, leader again of the now reunited Liberals, made the aggressively ambitious Keynesian move of a massive public works programme the centrepiece of his manifesto. Unemployment was to be cut by 1 million within a year; public borrowing would climb to whatever necessary level to achieve that target. Labour's manifesto, by contrast, was a timorous affair. Yes, there would be a programme of public works, but on a tiny scale compared with the commitment that Lloyd George had co-created with Keynes. Labour was constrained by its anxiety to balance the government budget and to show its soundness, its respectability and its commitment to the existing order – deeply felt by both MacDonald and his would-be chancellor Philip Snowden. There was a promise to raise unemployment benefit and pensions to encourage older workers to leave the labour market (both aims were abandoned when the party was in government) and to nationalise the coal industry just to show that socialism had not been completely ditched. It was all part of a programme of uncontroversial 'national development', and the party's manifesto sought to reassure voters by insisting that Labour was 'neither

Bolshevik nor Communist. It is opposed to force, revolution and confiscation as means of establishing the New Social Order. It believes in ordered progress and in democratic methods.'

It won 8 million votes and the Liberals 5 million – there was at last the chance of a progressive government with the 59 Liberal MPs giving Labour's 287 MPs a working majority. First-past-the-post was now working in reverse to give Labour an advantage, wildly overrepresented in the House of Commons compared to the Liberals given their respective votes. MacDonald and Snowden, able to govern without inviting Liberals into government, rebutted any embrace of the Keynesian maxims of Lloyd George; their anxiety was to reassure, to play down socialism, to stress their belief in 'ordered progress'. There would be no massive public works programme. The pound must remain convertible to gold at its pre-war rate. If wages had to fall as a result until the economy turned, then so be it. The government would tinker at the margins, but more than a century of laissez-faire orthodoxy could not be wrong. What Labour had to do was to sit tight, trust the process – however painful – stay moderate, win legitimacy from its social betters and redistribute benefits to the working class when the economy finally improved. It could not have been more wrong.

6

DISASTER AND BREAKTHROUGH

If the Wall Street Crash of October 1929 transformed American politics and economics, it caused no profound change in 1930s Britain, despite the impact being similarly traumatic. The purely defensive reaction would instead entrench British economic weaknesses.

The country reeled. Unemployment climbed to nearly 3 million by 1931, a stunning 22 per cent of the workforce, as the economy fell into a deep recession, most acutely felt in areas dominated by traditional industries – coal, steel, rail and textiles. Unemployment in some areas reached 70 per cent. British exports literally halved between 1929 and 1931 as world trade imploded. Real wages, adjusted for inflation, had been under pressure during the 1920s and now they fell still further. Hunger and social distress were ubiquitous.

The newly elected Prime Minister Ramsay MacDonald, his chancellor Philip Snowden and their party were bewildered by events, but palsied into following the orthodoxies. Even in the months before the crisis broke there was little interest in reshaping British capitalism or constructively responding to some of the more progressive overtures of British business. In the wake of the general strike the founder and chair of Imperial Chemical Industries (ICI), Sir Alfred Mond, had initiated talks with the TUC, including the powerful Transport and General Workers' Union, headed by Ernest Bevin, to explore mechanisms through which business and unions could exchange ideas about how to partner rather than confront each other. Bevin, who after the war would design Germany's codetermination structures, was an advocate of such partnership, despite left-wing criticisms that the talks were turncoat compromises with capital. They agreed to create an umbrella body that could bring individual unions and employer organisations together to negotiate. In 1929, a National Industrial Council was established to do just that, but MacDonald was not interested; later as leader of the national government he would let it drop. New Deal-style thinking had no momentum.

But the government did set up the Macmillan Committee, including Bevin and Keynes as members, to assess the causes of the emerging depression and whether the financial system was sufficiently supportive of British business. In the end it did the government's bidding, backing Treasury orthodoxy – despite Keynes and Bevin eloquently arguing for public works programmes and insisting that monetary policy should be designed to boost the domestic economy, rather than supporting sterling. But it did identify the famous 'Macmillan gap' – the lack of close support that British banks and finance offered British industry compared to their American and German rivals. 'Such support', declared the Committee, 'can only be the result of intimate co-operation over years during which the financial interests get an insight into the problems and the requirements of the industry in question.'[1] It was a disengagement that required radically remedying – but again, there was no drive from the top to address the problem. So while American New Dealers would create a wave of new public agencies and regulation to generate a mobilisation of committed, supportive finance for business investment, Britain had to wait until 1945 and the creation of the much more limited Industrial and Commercial Finance Corporation.

Such were MacDonald's attitudes and limitations. The evolutionary socialists did not have the self-confidence or their own worked-out ideas about how better to shape Britain's economic institutions or stimulate its stricken economy. To heed and listen to Keynes and Bevin – or even to Oswald Mosley's plea, while he was still a Labour front-bencher in the months after the Crash, to put the economy on a war footing to tackle unemployment – seemed just too economically and politically dangerous. There seemed to be no alternative to sticking with the orthodoxies. As the crisis deepened in 1930, Snowden – advised by the Treasury and Bank of England, the high priests arguing for balanced budgets, laissez-faire and the necessity of staying on the gold standard to ward off the threat of German-style hyperinflation – stuck doggedly to the conventional line. Anticipating Chancellor George Osborne in eighty years' time, Snowden argued that public austerity was the only route to prosperity. For his part Keynes publicly insisted the policy was unhinged. The correct policy was the opposite: to leave the gold standard and borrow to spend on public works. Continuing attempts to bring down incomes to the level of prices, he wrote privately to MacDonald in early August 1931, would be 'a gross perversion of social justice'. The Independent Labour Party, for its part, countered that socialism and public ownership were the answer. Tory leader Stanley Baldwin and his shadow chancellor Neville Chamberlain had another option – free trade should be abandoned and import tariffs levied to protect British industry.[2]

But Britain's gold reserves kept falling, unemployment kept rising and interest rates kept increasing. On 19 August 1931, MacDonald and Snowden called the cabinet and trade union leaders together for a series of last-ditch crisis meetings to save the pound. Respected City grandee Sir George May had been asked to report, and had recommended another savage retrenchment to correct the expected budget deficit: tax increases on the wealthy, certainly, but the bulk of the pain to be borne by a 20 per cent cut in unemployment benefit and similar cuts in public-sector wages.[3] Only then might American banks provide a loan to support sterling on the gold standard. Would – could – the cabinet and the Labour movement agree to the full extent of the measures? They could not; Snowden was convinced that being forced off the gold standard would precipitate a dangerous inflation, much more menacing to working-class interests and the economy alike. The half-measures the cabinet were prepared to sanction would not relieve the threat. Unable to get agreement on the public austerity deemed necessary to save the pound in the gold standard, on 24 August, MacDonald offered his resignation to the king.

Far from accepting it, the king persuaded MacDonald that the severity of the crisis required him to stay as prime minister, but as head of a 'National Government'. The evolutionary socialist, who believed his party had to be of and for Britain, and accepting of British orthodoxies, could see the king's point. There had to be cuts and the pound had to remain tied to gold. He hoped a good number of colleagues would join him and the rift would be healed after the crisis. He was quickly disabused. A traumatised Labour Party expelled him. Only twelve MPs joined him as 'National Labour', the same 'National' title Lloyd George had used as 'National Liberal'. He was a hostage to the Conservative Party, which could foresee a rerun of what it had done to Lloyd George. Co-opting the Labour leader to the national cause of preserving capitalism would reduce the risk of 'Bolshevism', while the resulting fight between him and his party could only redound to Conservative advantage. The progressives had been suborned for the second time in less than fifteen years. Small wonder, as Ramsay MacDonald allegedly remarked to Snowden, after the National Government's formation was announced, 'tomorrow every Duchess in London will be wanting to kiss me'.

But the National Government had not solved the crisis. As it tried to implement the full range of draconian cuts, a thousand sailors in the British Atlantic fleet mutinied at Invergordon in September 1931 over wage cuts of 25 per cent, with the crew of the flagship singing 'The Red Flag'. The Admiralty backed down, agreeing to 10 per cent cuts for all, and the men went back – but it was too late. The mutiny had prompted an unstoppable run on the pound. No more loans would be forthcoming. Three days later, Britain left the gold standard. The pound did fall 20 per cent, but quickly steadied. Armageddon did not happen. In fact, as Keynes had predicted, it would be the precursor to lower interest rates and economic recovery. 'No one ever told us we could do that', said Sidney Webb (husband of Beatrice), who as Lord Passfield had been MacDonald's secretary of state for the colonies. Being wedded to an orthodoxy that would please every duchess in London was all for nothing. MacDonald and Snowden had split their party, betrayed the progressive cause and imposed unnecessary suffering on the country. Labour and the economy would have been better off if it had had the self-confidence to heed Keynes and pursue different ways of managing capitalism.

There was another lesson. The mutineers at Invergordon may have sung 'The Red Flag', but they went back. There was no revolution, not even the serious threat of one. The Communist Party remained extremely weak. Yet the immiseration of the working class predicted by Marx was unfolding apparently as he predicted. Capitalism's contradictions were now in full view. Wages were being bid down. Class consciousness was rising. There was an example in Russia of how economy and society could allegedly be better organised. This was surely a moment for the working class in their powerful trade unions to storm the citadels of power. It did not happen.

Nor did Britain elect a great reforming government like Sweden's Social Democrats in September 1932 or Franklin Delano Roosevelt's New Dealers in the USA six weeks later. Indeed, the economic programme the Swedes launched, massive public works funded by government borrowing, was textbook Keynesianism (J. K. Galbraith wrote that Swedish Social Democrats should be seen as the real authors of the Keynesian revolution) and would seal Swedish Social Democrat rule for the next forty-four years – rather as the New Deal would for US Democrats. In the UK, such a possibility had already been passed up. In the general election of October 1931, 'National Labour' Prime Minister Ramsay MacDonald found himself campaigning against his former colleague Arthur Henderson as Labour opposition leader, just as 'National Liberal' Lloyd George had against Herbert Asquith nine years earlier. The result could only be a disaster for progressive Britain. The national government was returned by a landslide with MacDonald as its titular head, the Conservative Party winning 55 per cent of the vote and 470 MPs. Labour and Liberals, in refusing to find a way of developing a common programme for the previous thirty years, had handed the government not to a great reformist party, as in the USA and Sweden, but to an administration whose instincts were to be economically minimalist, defensive and conservative.

So Britain had no New Deal. No massive public works

programmes or Swedish-style deficit spending. No root-and-branch reform of the financial system, or even further investigation of the problems identified by the Macmillan Committee. No building on the initiative of Sir Alfred Mond to create institutions to encourage union and business dialogue. Not even baby steps towards planning.

Instead, the government muddled through, doing as little that was actively interventionist as it could – instead looking to empire to save it. In the summer of 1932, the British Empire Economic Conference in Ottawa established the system of 'Imperial Preference' – tariff protection for British producers and the dominions, long mooted by some leading Conservatives. That and the lower pound gave British industry some succour. The Bank of England swung in behind the initiative, keeping interest rates pegged at 2 per cent throughout the 1930s and 1940s – a prolonged period of cheap money – which helped stimulate a house-building boom from 1933 onwards, focused in London and the South-East. The Bank prompted the clearing banks to be more activist in financing the rationalisation and recapitalisation of hard-hit sectors, extending from Lancashire's textiles to the iron and steel industry. What was being created was an essentially defensive economic structure propped up by empire: tariffs behind which monopolies and cartels grew, little stimulus to drive innovation, high profit margins that allowed the financial system to remain disengaged from business except under duress but which also allowed restrictive labour practices to be accommodated. It was a system that by deferring solutions only stored up problems for the future.

But in the meantime the combination of cheap money, lowered competition, tariff walls and more industrial concentration put a temporary floor under the decline of British industry. The same framework helped the formation of new industries – automobiles, aerospace, chemicals, electronics – which all exploited the captive imperial markets. A slow recovery began, marred by the ongoing obsession with fiscal frugality. The government attempted to keep the lid on social spending by means-testing pensions and unemployment benefit – an intrusion into personal lives that working-class communities detested. The cooperative, friendly and provident societies could take some of the strain, but not enough. The means test and the hunger marches would become part of Britain's folk memory.

But if it was not a great reforming government, the National Government and its Conservative successor after 1935 did just enough to give the British economy space to begin a significant transformation, one that it had not enjoyed since international competition intensified in the 1870s. If properly led and managed, and had some Swedish-style Keynesian or American New Deal vigour and experimentation been deployed, there could have been remarkable change. As it was, the gathering economic recovery did enough to ward off any threat from the revolutionary left, but also from Oswald Mosley's fascist blackshirts. It was a very British kind of muddling-through.

Yet the British left did not draw the right lessons. Labour's electorate, drawn from the slums and grim back-to-backs across Britain's industrialised urban areas, were keenly aware that the unions and their Labour Party were the only institutions on which they could rely. But while strikers and mutineers might sing 'The Red Flag', they were not about to man the barricades, nor were even hunger marchers ready to launch a revolution. There was great loyalty to king and country at the same time as wanting a fairer deal, better lives and a job. Nor were the emerging middle class natural supporters of radical socialism, derided by George Orwell in *The Road to Wigan Pier* for the gulf they imposed between themselves and grinding lives of so much of the working class. On the other hand, it was not hard for anyone to see that the capitalist system was dysfunctional and that old orthodoxies did not work – the debate was how practically to do better.

The 1930s: A Second Wave of Progressive Thinking

If there was one common agreement in the Labour Party, it was that there must never be another episode like August 1931. MacDonald had been expelled from the party. A Labour government had to do better. But how and what? For some, notably the Socialist League and passionate critics like the young MP Stafford Cripps, there must be no compromise with capitalism; the task was to promulgate the necessity for taking over the commanding heights of the economy. For them MacDonald – and his colleague in arms Philip Snowden – had colluded in a suicidal betrayal of what Labour should stand for.

If large sections of the party were unconvinced by the Socialist League's remedy, they nonetheless shared the view there had been a betrayal. They were right about that, but it was not a betrayal of socialism. In 1931, there had been no viable socialist programme with widespread political support to betray. What had been betrayed was the forging of a progressive political coalition that could have married the ethic of socialism that had inspired the Labour Party's founders and the New Liberalism that manifested itself in Keynes's thinking – and which could have used Keynesian economics to get out of the crisis.

Over the 1930s, intellectual and political battle was joined, with the Socialist League and radical ILP on the one side and a range of thinkers and politicians quarrying in more reformist terrain. Keynes himself was to publish his landmark *General Theory* in 1936, and some of the more thoughtful in the Labour ranks began not only to accept that he was right, but that this New Liberal's ideas could be successfully married to the Labour Party's ethic of socialism. Political and Economic Planning (PEP) was founded at the height of the 1931 crisis to argue for – and practically demonstrate – that one component of the fusion would be a more carefully planned economy. The Fabians joined in, establishing the New Fabian Research Group with the support of the leading historian of the working class G. D. H. Cole and Richard Tawney to think through what form 'democratic socialism' might take.

Developing an Ethic of Socialism

Tawney, married to William Beveridge's sister and a talented economic historian, had now emerged as one of the left's intellectual stars. In two brilliant books, divided by a decade, Tawney tore into the ethical and moral character of contemporary laissez-faire capitalism. He appealed to first principles of ethics and morality, cast in the progressive new liberal tradition (although he called himself an ethical socialist) to show how unbridled inequalities in private property and the pursuit of profit, justified by the doctrine that individual interests are paramount, wrenched society apart. The books remain masterworks. In the first, *The Acquisitive Society*, published in 1921, Tawney reaches into English social, constitutional and political history. He distinguishes between private 'functional' property used for the purpose of delivering fundamental social functions, which is morally justifiable and economically vital, and 'acquisitive' property used for self-enrichment, creating a worthless class of rentiers who parasitically distort the whole pattern of an economy's consumption and production. Acquisitive societies revere the possession of wealth, and allow the formation of a leisure class and its consumption of indulgent, often futile luxuries. Functional societies honour the act and art of creation that satisfies core human needs.

'What gives meaning to economic activity', he writes, 'is the purpose to which it is directed. All economic activity is not equally estimable.' What counts is the 'functional purpose it discharges'. Too many luxuries get produced to satisfy the demands of the wealthy, displacing necessary production that could meet vital ends.

> It is the social purpose of industry which gives it meaning and makes it worthwhile to carry it on at all. If society is to be healthy, men must regard themselves not as the owners of rights, but as trustees for the discharge of functions and the instruments of a social purpose.[4]

In these terms, he added, citing the New Liberal economist John Hobson, 'It is questionable [...] whether economists shall call it "Property" at all, and not rather, as Mr Hobson has suggested, "Improperty".' He quotes Francis Bacon's great dictum that 'Wealth is like muck. It is not good but if it be spread.'[5]

Tawney was one of the first to see how joint-stock companies were changing the operation of capitalism, separating the owners of capital from the management of the enterprise – and raising fundamental questions about the purpose of business. Was the overriding obligation to maximise profits in order to provide income for shareholders? Or was it to pursue a social purpose, benefiting wider society, positioning any surplus as crucial to the sustainability of the company and thus to the delivery of its purpose? Tawney was uncompromising; 'if the private owner has ceased to perform any positive function', the state had to remove the dead hand and nationalise the company. But 'nationalisation is a means to an end, not an end in itself. Properly conceived its object is [...] to remove the dead hand of private ownership' if it has become functionless.[6] It was a vital distinction between Tawney and the socialist left; capitalism could work for the common good, and only if it did not was there a case to socialise a company or an industry.

In *Equality*, written a decade later, he developed the argument further. Capitalism tried to justify itself by saying that the free market offered equality of opportunity so that those who gained fortune and power deserved their position. But for Tawney equality of opportunity was simply ideological 'decorous drapery'. The truth about capitalism was that it gave more to those who already had. Educational and social privilege begat more privilege, begat access to the top jobs and incomes. Equality of opportunity was nothing more than a cruel joke, the 'impertinent courtesy of an invitation offered to unwelcome guests, in the certainty that circumstances will prevent them from accepting it'. What was required was not merely 'an open road, but [...] an equal start'. The elite would object that efforts to establish an equal start would compromise liberty – but the retort was clear. Real freedom required social justice. Constitutional rights to vote and participate in civic life are meaningless unless people have the means to exercise them.

As matters stood in inter-war Britain, the working classes, trapped in slums and terrible education, had no such means. Equality of opportunity was a mockery when possession of property, wealth and income conferred so much advantage throughout people's lives. These were parallel lives lived in ghettoised silos. Tawney identified public schools as the places where the process began – privileged, expensive, exclusive education as a gateway to the top. 'A public school, in short, is not a school that is easily accessible to the public but a school that the great majority of the public are precluded from entering.'[7] Their widespread existence was an offence against any conception of fairness and equality of opportunity. It meant that those at the top had little or no idea of what life was like for those at the bottom, diminishing both.

The solution? Tawney wanted to tackle the problem at its source: inequality of income and wealth. There had to be progressive taxation on income, taxes on capital and inheritance and the spending of the proceeds on massive social provision. The classes had to be brought together, to share life chances and opportunity. Such was the good society. The muck had to be spread.

Tawney's passion would influence the thinking of the young and increasingly influential Labour intellectual Evan Durbin – a self-styled 'militant moderate' – who was already a member of the XYZ Club (including Dalton, Gaitskell and economic academic Nicholas Kaldor), brainstorming about how to make British capitalism work better and reduce the noxious inequalities of British society that Tawney railed against. Durbin, who became a Labour MP in 1945 and was a lifelong friend of Gaitskell, would write a sentence whose sentiment I have repeated many times: 'Expansion is the great virtue of capitalism; inequality and insecurity are its great vices.'[8]

In his great book *The Politics of Democratic Socialism*, published in 1940, Durbin would argue that Labour should champion a mixture of Keynesian economics, PEP-style planning, a Tawney-like approach to taxation and the fostering of firms with a social purpose, while organising the management of any nationalised companies on decentralised lines. Taught by Hayek, he was careful to insist that planning had to be democratic, experimental and iterative to allow companies and individuals the chance to try out the new and the untested; he recoiled from the kind of directive, centralised Soviet planning which suppressed such vitality.

Echoing Tawney, he observed the rise of joint-stock companies with their multiplicity of shareholders and a new management class – the separation of ownership and control – that gave capitalism a new dynamic. He distinguished between companies that delivered socially useful results and those that were managed to deliver pure self-enrichment for passive, dividend-hungry shareholders – functional property and acquisitive property. The latter, he argued, should be progressively 'superseded' and taken into forms of social control, especially urgent if they had become monopolies. Above all, Durbin believed in the morality and necessity of democracy as it faced the twin challenge of fascism and communism. It was democracy, empowering the majority, that would make a capitalism throwing up intense inequalities politically impossible to sustain. The electorate would demand change. The only way to preserve the best of capitalism was for it to coexist with the institutions of democratic socialism that would create sectors of the economy driven by social priorities. He was under no doubt – democracy would continue to force public spending ever higher. The state's share of the economy could only continue to grow as public spending was ratcheted up by democratic demands.

Durbin himself was drowned in 1948 while rescuing children who got into trouble swimming in Cornwall – a tragic loss, posing one of the great might-have-beens of post-war Labour politics. His book helped underwrite the 1945 Labour government, and meant that the feuds of the 1930s would be resolved in a way that was electorally appealing. But not without wearying struggles. 'After the collapse of 1931', Richard Tawney would write, 'an epidemic of the "infantile disease of Left-wingism" was obviously overdue. It raged for some years like measles in Polynesia, and set thousands gibbering.'[9] Durbin, the militant moderate, had helped lance the infantile disease. But he was not around to do the same in the 1950s.

A Liberal Tory Weighs In

The left's increasingly persuasive thinking was having an impact on the right. An Etonian, five-times-wounded war veteran and Grenadier Guards officer, the Conservative MP for Stockton Harold Macmillan had become an outspoken critic of how British society had developed. 'Housing', he had declared in 1925, echoing Tawney, 'is not a question of Conservatism or Socialism. It is a question of humanity.' Although a Tory, he could see that the economic orthodoxies of free trade, balanced budgets and sound money had led directly to the disastrous economic policies that had accentuated the slump. He also believed that there was a meeting of minds rooted in New Liberal and Keynesian thinking that offered a solution, but which was unlikely to be supported by any political party that was then likely to win power. He had flirted with joining Oswald Mosley's New Party in 1931 because of its commitment to planning, industrial reorganisation and public works but rightly held back, worried about its ultimate direction. Later in the decade, he wondered if a centre party could not be formed out of Lloyd George's Liberals, the reformist wing of the Labour Party represented by moderates like Herbert Morrison and New Liberal-leaning Tories like himself. It was clear that capitalism needed to be reformed and a progressive majority existed for such a programme in the country; there needed to be a party to implement it. As Hitler's menace intensified, he wanted to supplant the National Government with a progressive national government that would square up to the fascist threat. Nothing came of his overtures.

In 1938, he brought together his ideas in *The Middle Way*, arguing that British capitalism and society needed to be reshaped rather than socialised – and attacking the way the current defensive economic system was working. The old orthodoxies were useless, he explained. They had led to the slump and offered no good compass for sustained recovery. He repeated Tawney's argument without needing to cite him, because the truth was obvious; there was no freedom in a democratic society that tolerated mass poverty. The state had to engage with economy and society in a sustained way to ensure growth, prosperity and the elimination of poverty so that some measure of freedom could be exercised. Informed by Keynes's thinking, and quoting extensively from *The General Theory*, Macmillan argued that the state should seek not only to stabilise the economy with an active fiscal and monetary policy; it should act to promote investment and growth. Tackling the Keynesian conundrum that a free-market financial system allowed too much speculation and too much hoarding of idle cash, he proposed a public investment board to ensure that all cash was directed to profitable investment and to take over the task of market-making for all traded shares in order to eliminate speculation.

While the capitalist system could be relied upon to generate a steady flow of new companies, the problem was that as companies matured and grew old they became dysfunctional. There had to be extensive state intervention to deal with the issue. He advocated the creation of a National Economic Council to coordinate and better plan production and investment for maturing companies, working with the Investment Board, and dismissed criticism that such an institution would make mistakes by arguing it could hardly do worse than the 'haphazard' results of the private sector. Where it was obvious that key industries involved in sectors like energy and transport were so intent on pursuing private profits that they neglected their crucial social functions, then they needed to be managed by public boards. He included in this the railways, coal, gas and electricity. Nationalisation would stop there, but he recommended a skein of custom-made institutions beyond nationalisation that would offer a spectrum of public–private collaboration – public utility trusts, water boards, commissions, marketing boards for everything from milk to eggs. He liked the model of the BBC as an autonomous public corporation delivering public-interest outcomes.

There should be a minimum wage and a children's allowance. Unemployment benefit should be comprehensive and err on the side of generosity. Nutritional standards should be established and policed by a Nutrition Board, with a guaranteed supply of essential foodstuffs to every household. The state had an obligation to ensure modernised industry, full employment and reasonable minimum living standards; only thus could democracy flourish and the temptations of totalitarianism of either left or right be kept at bay. This was the Middle Way – a more detailed and practical to-do list than either Tawney or Durbin had produced.

That this ambitious programme for reform was written by a Conservative, albeit a very liberal one, shows the gulf between today's Tory Party and what it once was. It is not just that no Tory MP would currently contemplate such extensive state action and management of the private sector; few would even accept that there is a societal obligation to ensure the wellbeing of those at the bottom of the social scale. Henry Dimbleby's 2021 National Food Strategy, with fourteen recommendations, including proposed taxes on sugar and salt content in food and making the lowering of obesity a national priority, drew from the same ethical foundations as Harold Macmillan's proposals, but it was viciously attacked by MPs and the right-wing press as nannying, intrusive and anti-business. Dimbleby resigned from his post and, as he says in his scathing follow-up book *Ravenous*, little or no progress has been made in implementing any of his proposals. Today's Tory Party may recognise that the issues Macmillan raised still need addressing – collective obesity, ill-health and falling life expectancy – but, unlike him, it is unprepared to act much beyond invocations to individuals to do better by pulling themselves up by their own bootstraps. Macmillan occupied a different moral universe. He was prepared when he became prime minister to live with Labour's post-war settlement because he shared its moral foundations. To anyone who had lived through the 1920s and 1930s, today's right-wing invocations to self-help, dividing the disadvantaged into the deserving and undeserving, would be obviously immoral and nonsensical. Those years were raw and nearer the bone; poverty, hunger and real social need forced politicians, business and intellectuals to challenge the paradigm. It is also proof that when the left begins to acquire real intellectual energy, it has an impact across party boundaries.

Macmillan's fears were borne out. A year later, war broke out and found Britain scarcely better prepared than in 1914. But there was one important difference. There was a growing and shared determination that never again should a decade be so wasted – and so many million lives compromised.

War and Aftermath

War saved the Labour Party. It made national figures of Clem Attlee and Ernest Bevin, who, after Churchill, were rightly seen as co-architects of victory – reliable anchors of the British war effort. Indeed, in late May and June 1940, the unstinting support of Attlee and Arthur Greenwood (deputy Labour Party leader and fifth member of the inner war cabinet) to continue the war was vital in bolstering Churchill's refusal to sue for an armistice, as Lord Halifax and Chamberlain urged him to do. Nor could other senior Labour figures who had been in the war cabinet – Ernest Bevin, Hugh Dalton, Herbert Morrison and Stafford Cripps – be dismissed as unpatriotic, un-British, alien socialists. Churchill's efforts to portray Labour in the July 1945 general election as having to resort to 'some form of gestapo to impose socialism on Britain', echoing Hayek's concerns that a Labour government prefigured individual serfdom, was absurd hyperbole that convinced very few people. The overriding sentiment in the country and the armed services was that, this time, promises to build a land fit for heroes should be honoured, unlike after 1918. No return to the 1930s would have been acceptable. Britain had stood together in war; it would now stand together in peace – Britain's classes thrown together by war, with even Tory households in the shires aghast at what they learned from the millions of evacuees. They were forced to confront what Orwell had condemned them for ignoring. It was obvious who was equipped to lead that process. It should fall to the successful Labour ministers who during the war had argued for state-led reconstruction and a new social settlement.

For the economy had responded well to government intervention and direction. As in the First World War, there could be no success on the battlefield without guns, tanks, ships and aircraft. Their production in quantity could not be left to the vagaries of the private sector. There was a vast scaling-up of the Royal Ordnance factories and a massive state-led expansion of fighter and bomber aircraft-making. British production of military aircraft in the Second World War was astounding, more than trebling between 1939 and 1942, while Germany's only doubled.[10] Britain built an outstanding military–industrial complex during the war, outproducing Germany from a virtual standing start. Rationing and price controls were essential to ensuring food supply at affordable prices. The whole apparatus of price controls, state direction and government manufacture had worked supremely well – and Attlee made no effort to conceal his view from Churchill and the wider public that it would be no less essential to post-war reconstruction.

The differences between the wartime allies were exposed in the reaction to William Beveridge's report on 'Social Insurance and Allied Services' – a flat title for a report that would have far-reaching ramifications. Beveridge was a lifelong New Liberal. His proposals were built on the reforms of Lloyd George's People's Budget, the philosophy of Green, the ideas of Hobhouse and the economic theories of the New Liberal economist John Maynard Keynes. A new Britain, he famously wrote, would conquer 'five giant evils on the road to reconstruction': squalor, ignorance, want, idleness and disease. His proposed comprehensive social insurance system, creating a gigantic national insurance fund to pay for pensions and unemployment benefit, would stand alongside a 'comprehensive health and rehabilitation service for prevention and cure of disease' and a commitment to avoid mass unemployment as part of an interlocking approach to make economy and society work for the common good. The state would act as guarantor of everyone's wellbeing from cradle to grave, but it would do as much as it could to ensure that people did not need the safety net so provided – hence, the commitment to avoiding mass unemployment. The system would be designed to provide national minimum living standards, but 'the State in organising security should not stifle incentive, opportunity, responsibility', wrote the liberal Beveridge; 'in establishing a national minimum it should leave room for voluntary action by each individual to provide more than that minimum'.[11]

It was a captivating vision for a people at war, and the Beveridge Report became an overnight bestseller – sales of the full and abridged versions eventually totalled 600,000. But here is the rub. The proposed social insurance fund was emphatically not socialist; it was based on the contribution principle to ensure that unemployment benefit, pensions and other benefits were never characterised as undeserved handouts but rather as proper insurance payments for people at the receiving end of life's risks – and which society had an obligation to provide, just as Hobhouse and Green had argued. It would obviate any need for the detested means test; benefits were a citizen's right resulting from paying into an insurance fund. Equally, the aim to avoid mass unemployment rested on Keynesian economics, although at this stage Beveridge did not spell out the mechanisms. In *Full Employment in a Free Society*, published two years later, Beveridge would follow through with a fuller account borrowed wholesale from Keynes. The state would use an active fiscal and monetary policy to ensure that aggregate demand was always high enough to ensure full employment, so as to save capitalism from itself – but in a way that protected individual freedoms. The New Liberal conception of the state was not as an agent of control, which its detractors could depict as coercive – Hayek had just published *The Road to Serfdom* and Beveridge wanted to head off any argument that his conception opened the way to totalitarianism. Rather, the state was a referee, a public mechanism to establish collective social insurance and a guarantor of economic and social health and thus fairness, freedom and prosperity.

Attlee was quick to interpret the first Beveridge Report in very different terms – claiming it for socialism. 'Socialism does not admit an alternative. Social security to us can only mean socialism', he told a newspaper interviewer in the wake of the report's publication. Beveridge's report was only part of the socialist ambition to 'create a better and brighter Britain [...] a spring-cleaning to sweep away not only drab industrial areas and deceptive rural slums but scour the very air itself'.[12] He laid out the suite of aims that would later define his government: security against ill-health, unemployment and old age, an adequate and steadily rising standard of living, a decent and well-equipped house in healthy surroundings for every family, full and equal education and complete medical care throughout life. This was socialism, according to Attlee.

These were great and widely shared aims, but Attlee was shoehorning the nation's ache for a better way of life into a socialist category when in truth the people's hopes transcended classes, generations and ideologies. These were equally the aims of New Liberalism, although it did not suit Attlee to say so. Even Churchill was compelled, after initial reluctance, to promise that the Tories would implement Beveridge's reforms in the 1945 election campaign, reminding the country of his earlier New Liberal sympathies. The tragedy for the liberal left was that there was no political incentive or reward for saying in public what Labour knew in private. There was no Labour intellectual to hand who could have done what Beveridge did – having the command of detail, aims and overarching philosophy. It was why Bevin, the new minister of labour, enticed him back to London in June 1940 as a key ally; it was why the following year deputy Labour leader Arthur Greenwood asked him to lead a committee to 'survey the existing schemes of social insurance and allied services' and make recommendations in his own name, exploiting his national prestige.[13] He decided to stand as a Liberal MP in 1944 but the Liberal Party's eclipse was by now nearly complete; he did not win his seat.

There was neither the parliamentary nor electoral heft to claim the Beveridge Report as a product of new liberalism; the only way it would become reality was via a Labour government misnaming it as socialist. Beveridge went along with the deceit. But allowing social insurance to be cast as socialist would later open the way to a Thatcherite Tory Party attacking it for being part of a nannying state. That was never its inspiration. The idea of social insurance has been allowed to wither; National Insurance payments are seen as only marginally more legitimate 'stoppages' than tax deductions. Benefits have been allowed to regress to below-subsistence levels and extensive means-testing has been reintroduced, which Beveridge went to such lengths to avoid. Calling it socialist denied social insurance the broad-based support to sustain it. Words matter.

Labour in Power: the Ethic of Socialism and New Liberalism

But in July 1945, such concerns were far away. Attlee reaped the reward, winning nearly 50 per cent of the popular vote and 393 seats in the general election. The total Liberal vote was 12 per cent of the total but yielded only twenty-three seats (including the rump National Liberals). The greatest reforming Labour government of the twentieth century was launched – one of the most resourceful, determined and innovative in our history, despite the economic constraints and menacing international environment. It established social insurance and the National Health Service (NHS), the backbone of the welfare state. It began a huge housing programme, established the planning system and built new towns. It rolled out the 1944 Education Act, creating a national education system. It nationalised the Bank of England, the utilities and the rail, coal and iron and steel industries. It presided over a massive surge in British exports and the emergence of new industries ranging from computing to jet engines. Internationally, it was an architect of NATO and the United Nations, driving forward the Bretton Woods monetary system and the free-trade order that accompanied it. It gave India independence and organised German reconstruction. And it managed all this within the severest of budgetary constraints. Time and again there were pressures to defer or halt the reforms. But Attlee was indefatigable, as were his senior ministers. There could be no return to the 1930s. They held firm.

And yet. Although the government has passed into socialist legend, this was more a government delivering a coalescence of progressive ideas than the pure milk of socialism. It was responding to a country-wide insistence that there must be no repeat of the mistakes after 1918; there was a near-perfect alignment with its objectives and the popular mood. Moreover, it was building on the structures created during the war and the way the intellectual centre of gravity had evolved during the 1920s and 1930s – the increasing acceptance of Keynesianism, the advance of New Liberal ideas on social insurance and even the concept of the mixed economy. There was now a cross-party consensus that a comprehensive system of social insurance should be established. Planning had worked during the war. It would work now. Macmillan's *The Middle Way* had recommended nationalisation of the utilities and the rail and coal industries because social urgency trumped any case for private ownership and the pursuit of private profit – a variant of the argument for nationalisation that Tawney and Durbin had developed. When, in 1949, the government accepted that a massive sterling devaluation was a necessity given the scale of the trade deficit with the USA, Chancellor Stafford Cripps built on union agreements during the war to hold back a surge of wage demands. Although the Conservatives would vote against the NHS, they too accepted the case for improved health provision. It was the Conservative Rab Butler's Education Act that the Labour government implemented in full and the contribution principle for pensions had been established by Baldwin and Chamberlain. As the leading contemporary sociologist Thomas Marshall conceded at the time, although the arrival of the welfare state was revolutionary, it had 'mixed parentage'. Welfare historian Chris Renwick argues in *Bread for All* that this mixed parentage was the key to the Attlee settlement bedding down and being accepted by the Tory governments that followed. Neither former New Liberal Winston Churchill nor mixed-economy champion Harold Macmillan were minded to unpick the fabric of its achievement.

But if the socialism was not doctrinal, belief in it certainly gave Attlee and his cabinet a steeliness in its implementation. When the Beveridge Report was debated in cabinet during the war, the Tories objected to its expense, a concern that would have been even more acute in 1947 and 1948 as the 'appointed day' approached. Attlee was not prepared to defer or compromise; the social security system would be launched on 5 July 1948 as a comprehensive, universal system on the same day as the NHS was inaugurated. It was a British miracle – at a stroke the whole panoply of Poor Law commissioners, means-testing, ad hoc mean benefits and the patchwork quilt of health provision was abolished and replaced by a comprehensive, universal system. It was and still should be a cause of national celebration, a moment when – a generation before the publication of John Rawls's *Theory of Justice* – a British government brought his ideas to life. Certainly, Aneurin Bevan had made compromises with the British Medical Association to get its assent for the National Health Service – consultants could still continue with private practice and use beds in NHS hospitals ('stuffing their mouths with gold', as he would say) – but they were well-judged compromises to keep intact the vision of a comprehensive health service free at the point of use. It was the muscularity and belief in the values and mission of socialism, combined with the cleverness, grasp of practicalities and ethics of new liberalism, that together achieved what no Conservative administration could or would have done.

Steel nationalisation in 1947 was the next proposed nationalisation, and to avoid this more controversial measure being blocked by the Tory hereditary majority in the House of Lords Attlee navigated the Parliament bill through the Commons, reducing the Lords' blocking powers to just a year. Attacked by Churchill for 'socialist aggression', Attlee retorted that it was only a prudent extension of what Churchill himself had advocated when he 'had stood at this box in 1911'.[14] Curtailing the powers of the hereditary peers in the House of Lords rather than abolishing hereditary peers completely was not socialism and barely New Liberal. Constitutional issues were seen as bourgeois preoccupations, secondary to the real business of economic and social change – the Achilles' heel of left-wing thinking.

It would be a wrangle over what socialism meant that would finally kill off a tiring government whose leading members were visibly ageing – and, like Ernest Bevin and Stafford Cripps, were demonstrably ill or dying in office. Even Attlee was suffering from a duodenal ulcer. The new chancellor, Hugh Gaitskell, wanted to introduce prescription charges on teeth and spectacles in his April 1951 budget, partly to raise funds for what promised to be an expensive war in Korea. Nye Bevan, now minister of labour, was ferociously opposed to this compromise. It was an attack on a free NHS, a cardinal socialist principle, and for which he and the Labour movement had fought so hard. In any case, war in Korea should be avoided if possible, and, if it was to be fought at all, done more cheaply. He resigned and a few months later the government, desperate for a larger majority so as not to be at the mercy of continual internal wrangling, called a snap election. To its surprise, it lost – an undeserving end, given all that it had achieved. Sheer exhaustion was part of the explanation. But renewal in office had required more honesty about the blend of ethical socialism and New Liberalism that had succoured it. Without that, it was wide open to the rancour that ultimately killed it.

7

THE ELUSIVE FORMULA OF
AND FOR SUCCESS

On the left, the 1930s had seen some serious internecine bloodletting over what socialism meant. Now, after Churchill's return to power in 1951, the decade would be consumed by bitter arguments over whether and what kind of socialism could win a general election in an increasingly affluent Britain. After losing his seat in the 1955 general election and in despair of the infighting, Anthony Crosland wrote *The Future of Socialism*. It was published the following year. The aim was to find a shared way forward. He identified no less than twelve different strands in socialist thought, including Owenism, planning, Marxism, Fabianism, William Morris's guild socialism and so on. 'The trouble is', he continued, 'that some of the divergences are not a matter simply of emphasis or the right priorities. They are fundamental and the doctrines mutually inconsistent.'[1] Matters are made worse, he wrote, by the founders of the Labour Party, who, recognising these differences, decided not to spell out what its doctrines were. Quoting G. D. H. Cole, Crosland wrote that this was a socialism 'almost without doctrines [...] so undefined in its doctrinal base as to make recruitment readily among persons of quite different types'.[2] Thus the scope for the wars that had brought the 1945–51 government down and would continue over the decade.

Looking for common ground, he thought that all the varying strands of socialist thought could be boiled down to five elements: the case for workers' control, promoting social welfare, securing full employment, the enmity to economic rent (in particular income from property) and making the case for cooperation. It is in developing those aims, he argued, that the future of socialism lay – and in particular by promoting equality, which underwrote them all – which could be achieved by using Keynesian economics to deliver full employment, higher social spending and welfare, all aided and abetted by good planning.

All of this took wealth creation and economic dynamism as givens – and did not touch on the deep structural weaknesses from which the economy was suffering. Crosland devoted little time to examining how to make British capitalism work better; that could be left to the magic of Keynesianism, which was understood as an endless licence to grow public spending rather than a tool for managing the economic cycle. The real challenge that was becoming apparent over the 1950s was that in order to reshape its economy, Britain needed to dismantle the imperial defensive economic system and become a developmental state. It would take thirteen years in opposition to get even near that understanding. In the meantime, the tumbrils sounded and battle was joined.

The paradox was that the Tory governments after 1951 not only accepted the essence of the Labour settlement, a top rate of tax of 85 per cent to fund the NHS and social security system while denationalising only the steel industry; they went further, launching a major housebuilding programme. Former New Liberal Winston Churchill and New Liberal fellow traveller Harold Macmillan could see – like Eisenhower in the USA – which way the wind was blowing. Over the 1950s, unemployment averaged 2 per cent, while living standards steadily increased; GDP on average grew by 3.2 per cent a year. Keynesian economics worked. Car ownership doubled to reach 10 million by 1960; in the same year, four out of five homes had a black-and-white television.[3] Prime Minister Harold Macmillan could convincingly claim that the British had never had it so good. Prosperity encouraged the Tory hierarchy to accept the Labour settlement, even as its authors locked horns over whither socialism.

These years could have been Labour's achievement had it remained in office. After all, it was Labour's framework and ideas that the Tories were imitating. Over the 1950s and into the 1960s,

Labour could have built on the success of its policies and its electoral dominance, and Britain could have become as enduring a social democracy as the Nordic countries, with a vibrant society and economy. There was popular support. In the October 1951 snap general election, the Labour Party outpolled the Conservative Party with a record 14 million votes. Yet again, given the vagaries of first-post-the-past, a collapsing Liberal vote bequeathed more than twenty seats to the Tories, despite their losing the popular vote. In the earlier 1950 general election, 319 out of 478 Liberal Party candidates had lost their deposits. In 1951, they could only field 109 candidates, decimating their vote share while Labour's votes piled up in its heartlands to no useful electoral effect. Tory candidates were the winners. Labour needed a strategy for a stronger Liberal vote to better manage first-past-the-post, but it could not see past its internal preoccupations to help secure it.

To do that would have demanded a clarity of purpose and vision that was singularly lacking for reasons Crosland described – and even more importantly to have a clear analysis of what reforms British capitalism now needed. The Labour Party, having achieved the welfare state, widespread public ownership, acceptance of planning and the tools of Keynesian demand management, had no shared idea about where to go next. It had no agenda to promote industrial democracy or employee engagement. It had no conception of borrowing from the New Dealers and reshaping British finance to support innovation, investment and growth. It did not concern itself with reforming British capitalism to help create a new cadre of innovative companies and associated industries, even though it was increasingly obvious Britain was being outcompeted.

The Economic Problem

Britain's share of global manufacturing fell from a fifth to a tenth in the first three decades after 1945.[4] It was true that between 1950 and 1973, Britain's labour productivity grew at 3.7 per cent a year – faster than at any period in our history. But other countries – for example, France and Germany – were doing even better. Professor Nick Crafts estimates that even allowing for differing industrial structures and the costs of post-war reconstruction, Britain had a 'growth failure' over those years. By 1973, its GDP was cumulatively 20 per cent smaller than it should have been.[5]

Four interrelated weaknesses stand out, in Craft's view. First, a multiplicity of trade unions operating with legal immunity made linking wage deals to productivity growth particularly difficult. Second, Britain had turned a blind eye to the emergence and dangers of cartels; collusive activity was widespread – after the 1956 Restrictive Practices Act, only 27 per cent of manufacturing was declared free of price-fixing, while 35.7 per cent was cartelised. Third, imperial preference lived on; the average tariff on manufactured imports stood at 14.5 per cent in 1960, compared to 14.7 per cent in 1935, reducing the intensity of competition and supporting super-high profits. Crafts calculates that the price-cost margin in UK manufacturing during 1954–73 averaged over 2, compared with around 1.1 in West Germany (whose tariffs were less than half of Britain's); in other words, profits, secured by cartels, monopoly and tariffs, amazingly, were nearly twice as high for any unit of production compared to Germany. Lower productivity growth in such an environment carried little penalty, and there was too little incentive to invest and innovate.

Finally, company managements had to deal with many uncoordinated, uncommitted shareholders and responded by paying out dividends and supporting the short-term share price, again rather than investing and innovating. It was the defensive system created in 1932 coming home to roost – cosseted, dividend-hungry, rentier shareholders, aggressive shop stewards, disengaged finance and unenterprising managements looking for safety behind tariffs and cartels, rather than putting money into research and new products. To complete the increasingly dismal picture, the performance of the nationalised industries, which accounted for some 10 per cent of GDP, was increasingly disappointing. Labour could see the consequences but could not diagnose the causes.

To develop a convincing story it would have had to break out of

the tortuous conflict that had consumed it from the beginning –
was it a reformist party, guided by an ethic of socialism, trying to
build a broad progressive coalition to reform capitalism, or was it a
vanguardist socialist party? And what exactly should be reformed?
From today's vantage point, after the limitations of planning and
public ownership have been widely accepted, it is obvious what
course should have been taken – but that was not so clear at the
time. Hugh Gaitskell, the social democrat who succeeded Attlee
as leader in 1955, was right to be sceptical that public ownership
and the view that the primacy of the collective should be at the
heart of Labour's policies. Nationalisation, he argued – and in
this he was echoing Richard Tawney and Evan Durbin – was a
means, not an end. Clem Attlee in retirement would have agreed.
His wife Vi knew her husband well when she told his biographer
Kenneth Harris, while on a visit to their home, that Clem was
'never really a socialist, were you darling', and when Attlee looked
up from his paper, making 'a mild dissenting noise', she qualified
her statement: 'Well, not a rabid one.'[6] And that, she obviously
thought, writes Harris, was that. But Nye Bevan and the Bevanite
faction that supported him did deserve the sobriquet. The years
after the election loss in 1951 and again after 1959 were to witness
some of the bitterest clashes in Labour's history as Gaitskell and
Bevan fought for Labour's soul.

The Futile Sectarian Wrangles of the 1950s

Bevan had begun working in the local pit in his home town in
South Wales at the age of fourteen. He was the genuine article: a
self-made, passionate man converted to the socialist cause by his
life experiences and whose oratorical skills matched Churchill's.
When he wrote about the merciless exploitation of workers by
capital in what is still one of the most widely read socialist books
of all time, *In Place of Fear* (published a year after the 1951 election
defeat), his language was a marriage of semi-Marxism and
personal experience.

  In Place of Fear is a flow of socialist consciousness that offers an insight into why he felt compelled to resign over prescription charges, which triggered the end of the Labour government, thus ruining Labour's chances of dominating the post-war period. It also shows how hard it was for the Labour Party to agree on how to build on what it had achieved. Bevan goes for the high ground right from the beginning, asking fundamental questions about what it means to be human in a capitalist society in which the vast majority are poor and powerless. 'What is most essential and who is to decide it?', he asks; 'What are the most worthy objects on which to spend surplus productive capacity?'[7] He does not believe that the answer can come from individual decisions in the market place. It was wrong that society had handed over 'the accumulation of its social furniture to individuals' and not made the decisions for itself – 'a method which produced universal enslavement'.[8]

Instead, there should be collective public spending and public ownership reaching far into the economy to ensure that the social furniture conforms to real wants, especially those of the poor. He dismisses those who want to restrict the public domain and high levels of public spending because they are 'extravagant', while private spending is 'an economy' – a proposition which can only be justified because private ambitions are seen as the 'main purpose of human endeavour'.[9] To accept this proposition is to endorse the continuance of senseless, capricious inequality. This is the basis of his advocacy of the NHS, a universal service free at the point of use. 'No society can legitimately call itself civilized if a sick person is denied medical aid because of lack of means.'

It was a powerful credo with roots, as Bevan acknowledged, in the experience of the working class since the Industrial Revolution. Writing about the iron and steel industry, he argues that if private ownership cannot deliver the necessary investment to sustain its strength, which was so vital to the British economy at the time, then the only option is to nationalise it. Bevan was not interested in the details of governance, the decision-making process or the effectiveness of nationalisation. What mattered was to make sure that strategically important industries were under public ownership. After all, the Bank of England had been nationalised and its court left intact. The same could be done with the nationalised industries.

The book offers a window into Bevan's complex character. Loved and lionised as the great socialist, he thought in great sweeps rather than close analysis – although in office he cut canny deals and compromised to achieve his ends. Richard Tawney, Evan Durbin, the Gaitskellites, every New Liberal thinker and even Harold Macmillan had shared the view that addressing poverty was the precondition for allowing the poor to exercise their rights as citizens. It was a conceit that only he, Nye Bevan, thought in these terms. Nor had he thought as deeply about the joint-stock company or acquisitive and functional property as had Tawney or Durbin – who was now not alive to return fire. He simply deplored all forms of private capital as necessarily exploitative. You can sympathise with him because of what he lived through in South Wales and what he achieved – but Ernest Bevin, who deplored the almost religious sectarianism that Bevan brought to the Labour Party, had had a no-less-tough early life. Had Bevan been as farsighted as Bevin, looking forwards rather than backwards, and had Labour not only held together but broadened its appeal and agenda, the last seventy years could have been very different. Instead, he became a left-wing talisman whose attitudes others were to rehearse no less destructively in the decades ahead.

Gaitskell was compelled to respond. He refused to give *carte blanche* to more nationalisation; each case had to be justified in the terms Tawney had set out. The two rowed bitterly until after the 1955 election had been lost, when a compromise was reached; Bevan accepted that Britain should retain an independent nuclear deterrent – important to Gaitskell and the Labour mainstream – while Gaitskell accepted a modicum of additional nationalisation, especially of road haulage and steel. Social democrats and democratic socialists had arrived at a pact, but a more affluent Britain could see the spatchcock nature of the compromise and wanted none of it. After losing for a third time in 1959, the knives came out. The Bevanites insisted that only full-blooded democratic socialism could win a general election. Gaitskell for his part wanted to rewrite the party's constitution and ditch its commitment to

1918's Clause 4 common ownership. Nationalisation, he argued, was not an end in itself, but a means to express socialist values which had to respect the mixed economy and personal liberty.

It was an argument about ideology even as British capitalism's underperformance was becoming the real issue – but neither Bevan nor Gaitskell grasped that nettle. In the event, both men died, and Harold Wilson was elected as the healing candidate – mainstream Labour but with enough of a Bevanite past (he had resigned with Bevan back in 1951) to satisfy the left. 'Thirteen wasted years' was the jibe Wilson threw at the Tories to win the 1964 election by a hair's breadth. He might as well have said the same of Labour.

From Building Socialism to Managing Capitalism

The reality of Britain's lacklustre performance compared to the rest of Europe was becoming obvious. Britain had become the economic sick man of Europe. It had too few successful companies in most business sectors, especially those that were growing strongly, ranging from cars and aircraft to the whole array of manufactures that were revolutionising the home, from refrigerators to televisions. It had legacy companies in abundance. Trade unions were accused of being overmighty, defending restrictive practices, going on wildcat strikes and bargaining for too much pay in relation to underlying productivity growth. But management was poor. There was little take-up of new science and technologies. The City and the financial system were as disengaged as ever. But the solutions were not seen as reform and repurposing. Instead, there was a growing consensus, captured by Andrew Shonfield's *Modern Capitalism*, published in 1965, that other countries, especially in Europe, were doing better because they were better at planning capitalism. Britain needed to follow suit.

By now, Western capitalism's vastly improved performance compared with the disasters of the inter-war years was bewildering observers and needed some explanation. For Shonfield, economics editor of *The Observer*, the answer was not only Keynesian economics; it was the growing effectiveness of Western governments in supplanting the price mechanism with forms of planned direction of investment and coordination of activity. Dense concentrations of private economic power needed to be counterbalanced and directed by the state into worthwhile investment – given indicative plans of what the state wanted and cajoled and incentivised into doing better, backed up with subsidies and directed credit. This would deliver higher growth rates than Britain was achieving.

An incoming Labour government, declared Harold Wilson, would reproduce this success in Britain. The feeble efforts of the Conservative government – it had established a National Economic Development Council in 1962 – needed to be turbocharged. This would be a perfect marriage of the scientific spirit of socialism – Wilson's solution around which he hoped the left would cohere – and the need for capitalism to be scientifically planned. A Labour government would be midwife to the 'white heat of the technological revolution'. It would create a Ministry of Technology. It would establish a new Department for Economic Affairs to take away economic policy-making from the dead hand of the Treasury, and establish a national plan as France had done so successfully. It would reorganise and consolidate companies to create 'national champions' and intensify tripartite collaboration between government, business and unions. It would manage inflation with a newly established prices and incomes board.

Labour's ambitions were right, even if it underestimated the need to reform finance, tariffs, the unions and too much monopoly, but it failed. Wilson took an early, mistaken decision to maintain the value of the pound. But inflation resisted both deflationary economic policies and attempts to manage the growth of prices and wages by administrative fiat, government direction or union agreement. Import growth outstripped export growth; the balance-of-payments deficit continued to climb to record levels, peaking at 2.5 per cent of GDP in 1967 (though this was low by today's standards). Ultimately, the pound had to be devalued – and in the process the ambitious national plan was discarded. The

National Economic Development Council (NEDC) was already floundering; companies and unions alike were too jealous of the autonomy that more than a century of laissez-faire and free collective bargaining had conferred to want to swap information and plans. The very lack of coordination the NEDC was set up to remedy was a cause of its failure.[10]

The Treasury reclaimed its dominance in Whitehall and the Department of Economic Affairs was wound up in 1969, formally bringing down the curtain on national planning. The Industrial Reorganisation Corporation (IRC) created three national champions – British Leyland, General Electric Company (GEC) and the computer group ICL – whose scale suggested they could be successful. But none of the issues identified earlier were addressed – weak corporate governance, disengaged shareholders and bankers, too many hard-to-coordinate trade unions and a sluggish managerial culture bred by operating for so long behind tariff walls. The companies' fate was sealed. The massive automotive conglomerate British Leyland would collapse, taken into public ownership and dismembered; ICL was a casualty of the 1981 recession; and GEC would disintegrate in the early 2000s. The same cocktail would also finish off other great industrial companies not brought together by the state; by the early 2000s, ICI, Courtaulds, Blue Circle and many others were no more. An active industrial policy was not to blame; the problems were much more deep-rooted.

Britain was trying to be a developmental state without the sophisticated state and financial structures that could make it happen – with no deep shared purpose between government, business and workforce over what the economic mission was – let alone execute it, nor any understanding of how to mobilise private capital for enterprise on the necessary scale. Indeed, far from channelling savings and credit into British business, the City of London was quietly re-establishing itself as the international financial centre it had been in the gold standard era – the hub of the new offshore Eurodollar market, which was cocking a snook at American tax and regulation rules. Backing British national champions or mobilising UK investment was not on its agenda.

Above all, inflation remained stubbornly higher than in comparable countries. Forty per cent of the workforce were members of trade unions, and nearly all Britain's then record 9-million-strong manufacturing workforce was unionised.[11] Both the inflation problem and the problem of weak productivity growth in manufacturing seemed to have their roots in the character of British trade unions, who had been above the law since the 1906 Trade Disputes Act and now had a membership and clout never anticipated sixty years earlier. Something had to be done.

The Trade Union Question

British industrial relations could not continue as they were, even though a commission to inquire into potential reform – the Donavan Commission – had placidly proposed just that. The Tories were proposing to remove trade union legal immunities both because this might prove popular and because the labour market plainly was a problem. Wilson and his secretary of state for employment Barbara Castle decided that Labour should propose a foundational new compact of its own. Castle's *In Place of Strife* self-consciously echoed Bevan's *In Place of Fear* to give the proposals a patina of leftism. Trade unions, above the law since the 1906 Trade Disputes Act, would now be brought within it and a new deal would be struck setting out a framework of rights and responsibilities. Every worker would have the right to join a trade union, which every company would have to recognise. Collective bargaining agreements would not be voluntary but have contractual force, and measures would be taken to strengthen protection against unfair dismissal. There would have to be ballots though before any proposed strike action, a thirty-day cooling-off period and mandatory conciliation if negotiations became deadlocked. If there was an inter-union wrangle, a minister could impose a settlement. It was less an attempt to reduce trade union power than to find a way for it to be used in an orderly fashion – and to open the way to a more constructive workforce–employer dialogue.

The unions were having none of it. The two most powerful

union leaders were Jack Jones, general secretary of the Transport and General Workers' Union, who had been converted to socialism by *The Ragged-Trousered Philanthropists* and had fought in the International Brigade in the Spanish Civil War, and Hugh Scanlon, an ex-communist who was president of the Amalgamated Engineering Union. Both were steeped in Labourism, class warfare, union solidarity and opposition to private capital as a natural enemy. Every weakness in Labour's doctrines and structures over the decades – from union sponsorship of MPs to unresolved arguments over what constituted socialism – was now exposed, and there were ancestral echoes of struggles ranging from Taff Vale to the betrayals of Ramsay MacDonald. The two union leaders' unambiguous position was that the Labour Party should not lift a finger to diminish the power of those who founded it, still financed it and sponsored many of its MPs.

When Scanlon and Jones joined Wilson and Castle at Chequers on 1 June 1969, together with TUC leader Vic Feather, to try and find a way to make a deal, they told Wilson that they were so implacably opposed to the plan because they did not want him 'to become another Ramsay MacDonald'[12] – a betrayer of the Labour movement as a stooge of the right. 'Take your tanks off my lawn, Hughie', Wilson replied, saying that Britain could not continue with a state (the unions and TUC) operating within the state, representing a profound challenge to British democracy. The meeting was a calamity. But the Labour cabinet, in particular the duplicitous Home Secretary Jim Callaghan, was not solidly behind Wilson and Castle – and with 120 union-sponsored Labour MPs, they did not have a majority in the House of Commons.[13] The TUC could not be persuaded either. The argument that the Tories would do worse to the unions did not impress union leaders, who considered themselves powerful enough as the law stood to see off any Tory government. Wilson had to make do with the TUC giving a 'solemn and binding undertaking' it would intervene to stop illegal strikes. It was a valueless commitment. He had been humiliated.

In fact, Feather, Jones and Scanlon, congratulating themselves on being true defenders of the Labour movement, had driven a stake through its heart, leading directly to where we are in 2024 – a government in effect banning strikes in key essential services, and in the private sector a humbled and diminished union movement. They had vastly overreached to protect a nineteenth-century semi-Marxist conception of employee relationships with business. The ragged-trousered philanthropist, no more than cemeteries in Highgate (where Marx is buried), as Wilson himself put it, offered a compass for the last third of the twentieth century.

Certainly, poor industrial relations and strong, decentralised multi-trade unions outside the law were one part of Britain's economic problems that needed to be addressed. In fact, the later Thatcherite assault on trade unions which was meant to unleash suppressed productivity only worked temporarily. It turns out that worker representation and voice is crucial to ensuring workforce engagement. But employers in the 1960s, 1970s and 1980s would not voice such sentiments – and neither would unions who shared the instinctive, reflex opposition to business characterised by Jones and Scanlon. Wilson and Castle had offered a way to modernise and legitimise trade unions which would have opened up a different industrial relations landscape – even one that might have involved industrial democracy, codetermination and workers on boards. It was the road not taken. Instead, as events inexorably played themselves out, the trade union and parliamentary left became accomplices in the unions' progressive demonisation and economic marginalisation.

For the reform of industrial relations would now dominate the next fifteen years of British politics – and in the process fracture the Labour Party. Tory PM Ted Heath, elected in 1970, was quick to pass an Industrial Relations Act in 1971 that went well beyond *In Place of Strife*. The Act took the law into industrial relations with a vengeance and triggered nation-wide 'Kill the Bill' demonstrations, with unions and individual unionists refusing to comply with the legislation. The Tory government, as described in Chapter 3, soon abandoned its free-market Selsdon Man rhetoric and, like Wilson, tried to contain inflation with prices and wages policies, culminating in the debacle of the three-day week and an energy shortage caused by striking coalminers. Labour, holding power narrowly after the 'who governs Britain election' that Heath called in February 1974, repealed the Industrial Relations Act as part of 'a social contract' in which, in return for food subsidies and frozen rents, unions would moderate their pay claims. An attempt to strike out in the direction of industrial democracy, implementing the Bullock Committee's recommendations to put workers on boards, was again resisted by the trade unions as collaboration with capital.

The social contract collapsed in the 'Winter of Discontent'. It was one more failure after *In Place of Strife*, the Industrial Relations Act and the appeal for industrial democracy. Labour, now in opposition as in the 1930s and 1950s, would relapse into internecine political warfare. Tony Benn adopted the same mantle as Nye Bevan thirty years earlier and Stafford Cripps and the Socialist League before him. The lack of an intellectual and political reconciliation between new liberalism and an ethic of socialism to create a workable, successful form of social democracy had weakened policy in government. This would have been hard enough anyway, given the intractable problems of coordinating capital and labour and given the vested interests of the financial sector and the unions. The failure of such an alliance meant that once again the left utopians could take the field claiming that a socialist Jerusalem could be built with just one more determined heave. Let battle begin!

Enter the SDP – and Wilson Reassessed

This time round, there was a difference. In March 1981, four leading Labour ex-ministers decided the moment had come to break with the Labour Party and its endemic capacity to regress to 'absurd exhibitions of self-righteous sectarianism' – as Tawney had stingingly written. Roy Jenkins, David Owen, Bill Rodgers and Shirley Williams launched the Social Democratic Party, or SDP. It would navigate between the extremes of free-market Toryism in the person of Mrs Thatcher and the socialism of Michael Foot, then leader of the Labour Party, with its now powerful Bennite left-wing. The SDP would blend left and right – it would be 'tough and tender'. It accepted the price mechanism and the market, but also crucial social solidarities so aping the German social market economy. It would be pro-European and for constitutional change. Reasonability would be its motto.

If Mrs Thatcher had not so successfully won the Falklands War, it might have broken through electorally in 1983. As it was, it secured 26.4 per cent of the vote, in third place but a mere 0.4 per cent behind Labour. Under the grotesque electoral system, Labour won 148 seats and the SDP won 13. It had succeeded only in dividing the opposition vote and gifting the next fourteen years to the Tory Party. Four years later, having partially merged with the Liberal Democrats to form the Alliance, it would do no better. The party finally wound itself up in 1990. Political scientists Ivor Crewe and Anthony King, in their exhaustive, magisterial book *SDP*, ascribe the failure to two main causes – the first-past-the-post voting system and the failure of the Labour Party to break up, as the Liberals did between 1916 and 1922, which would have opened the way for a third party to exploit first-past-the-post for its own benefit.

Crewe and King are at one level right, but their analysis begs a key question. Why were the Gang of Four not more successful in breaking up the Labour Party, which quivered but ultimately held together? After all, this was the kind of mainstream progressive party trying to combine an ethic of socialism and New Liberalism that Liberals, Fabians and Labour people had discussed in the Rainbow Circle in the 1890s and which had been a recurring theme in the inter-war years. The refugees from Labour even established a Tawney Society as a pivotal SDP think tank. The problem was that it hesitated to identify itself so openly, preferring to define its purpose as not being extreme. What would have pushed the SDP's share of the vote past 30 per cent would have been a harder edge – a genuine fusing of New Liberalism and ethical socialism into a new progressive doctrine that had a bigger project in mind than merely being nicely moderate. Only thus could more of the membership of the Labour Party have been detached from its left. The SDP might even have attracted some unions with such a pitch

– and also found some business backers. It also had a strong appeal to liberal Conservatives – the same terrain that Harold Macmillan had occupied. A broad coalition was there to be built, aiming to do the things that had eluded Wilson and Heath.

For Harold Wilson, to give him his due, had tried – and from the vantage point of the 2020s, when market fundamentalism looks ever more clearly a dead end, was on the right track. *In Place of Strife* and the Bullock Commission could have revolutionised British industrial relations. The attempts by the IRC to create British business champions with stronger City support and better leadership might have succeeded, especially had the union reforms gone through. As noted above, it was not industrial policy that sank the mooted champions, but the wider weaknesses in British capitalism that killed off other great companies. He was right that the Treasury is an over-powerful finance ministry; it perennially ranks short-term budgetary and financial considerations ahead of long-term strategic interests – witness all the stymied recent attempts at levelling up, the lack of a science strategy and the indifferent levels of British training. A Ministry of Technology to champion the diffusion of new technologies is an obvious institutional gap. The notion of a national plan to set expectations and around which investment decisions can cohere is not so stupid: it needed to be more iterative and agile, but the conceptual reasoning is sound.

What defeated Wilson was the profound stubbornness of key vested interests. Bank of England Governor Lord Cromer, Etonian scion of the Baring banking family who chaired the bank during Wilson's first premiership, wrote to him soon after his election suggesting swingeing cuts in public spending. Wilson refused and also refused to devalue sterling – a mistake, but nonetheless his prerogative. Who governs this country, he challenged Cromer; is this a democracy? And he then threatened to call a second general election. Cromer was an unabashed champion of orthodox laissez-faire and the interests of his class. The point of the state was not to advance a conception of the people's interest, but rather to protect the financial interest – better still, put it first.

Five years later, Wilson would adopt the same line in his famous challenge to Cromer's mirror image in the union movement – Hugh Scanlon – to take his tanks off Wilson's lawn. In his view parliamentary democracy was again at stake. Unions no more than the City were prepared to make common cause around shared national objectives. The system worked well enough from their point of view. One of Edward Heath's ambitions was to promote more competition in a highly cartelised British economy, which would be accelerated by joining the then European Common Market. This would jolt a British economy too cosseted from international competition. He, too, was right about that.

The SDP could have spelled out home truths along these lines, along with the fundamental intellectual weaknesses of the twin Thatcherite and Bennite positions, and advocated a compelling new economic and social programme. Constitutional reform could then have been positioned as crucial to the renewal of Britain's ageing state. It did too little of this; maybe it could not, given the character of its leadership. Perhaps it was impossible in the early 1980s for his former colleagues to see any merit in what Wilson had attempted; he was derided more than admired. It was an opportunity lost. But the SDP did leave one legacy: New Labour.

New Labour Finds its Way to the Alchemical Formula – Only to Botch It

The fourth general election loss in a row in 1992 and the prospect of eighteen years of unbroken Conservative rule traumatised the Labour Party. Neil Kinnock as leader had spent nine hard years weaning his party off the 'socialist' policy positions that had split the party and lost the 1983 general election – withdrawal from the EEC, commitment to nationalisation, unilateral disarmament, national planning and massive state-led investment and advocacy of whatever taxation levels were necessary for a big expansion of welfare. In the aftermath of the third loss in 1987, Kinnock would quote Ron Todd, then general secretary of the Transport and General Workers' Union: 'what do you say to a docker who earns £400 a week, owns his house, a new car, a microwave and a video as well as a small place near Marbella. You do not say, "Let me take you out of your misery brother".[14] Kinnock understood that the social ground on which unthinking loyalty to the Labour Party and early-twentieth-century socialism had been built was changing. He very nearly succeeded, but for all his resolve he could not drag Labour over the line.

After his successor John Smith unexpectedly and tragically died in 1994, Tony Blair took over the leadership, determined to carry Kinnock's programme even further. Looking to Bill Clinton's 'New Democrats' and their success in the USA, he would repeat the strategy in the UK – but also learn from the SDP. Labour must lean unambiguously into the political centre to win votes from the newly prosperous and aspirational, but, unlike the SDP, would retain firm anchorage in the left. So Labour would become New Labour, which would have an ideology cast within the socialist tradition while decisively breaking with elements of it. He would distinguish between an 'ethic of socialism' still applicable in an affluent post-industrial society and a class-based socialism rooted in the industrial Britain of the 1890s to the 1970s, although it was clearly weakening even then. An 'ethical basis of socialism', he would declare, is 'the only one that has stood the test of time'.[15] His ethical socialism was a belief in the power of government to do good in areas like health and education, of standing by strong societal and communal institutions that fostered togetherness and belonging, of mutuality and fellowship. It was a 'We' that transcended class; New Labour would not be a party for the working class but a party for the British people. As his chancellor Gordon Brown would put it, 'For the many, not the few'. In that sense Labour would retain its left pedigree.

This 'We', though, was to accommodate a simultaneous and complementary commitment to the 'I'. Labour accepted that with the new prosperity individuals had agency and wanted to better themselves; indeed, a dynamic capitalism, which Labour accepted the country needed, would require a crucial measure of individualism. But it would not be neoliberal individualism. Blair stressed the importance of accompanying obligations. 'We accept our duty as a society to give each person a stake in its future', declared Blair, but in return 'each person accepts a responsibility to respond' and 'to work to improve themselves'. Thus, 'the right to housing carries an obligation to abstain from anti-social behaviour, and the right to education for one's children entails an obligation to ensure they attend school'. For New Labour, 'personal and social responsibility are not optional extras but core principles of a thriving society'.[16] The rewriting of Clause 4 in 1995 to signal that the party no longer wanted to control the commanding economic heights was a powerful symbolic moment. Labour would use 'our common endeavours' – not government or labour movement solidarities – to create a 'community in which power, wealth and opportunity are in the hands of the many, not the few, where the rights we enjoy reflect the duties we owe, and where we live together, freely, in a spirit of solidarity, tolerance and respect'.

It was a formula – a 'third way' – that appealed to a majority of the electorate, from liberal conservatism to the soft left. To recognise the equal importance of both the 'We' and the 'I' is the value system of the British majority. Peter Mandelson and his colleague Roger Liddle would confirm in their book *The Blair Revolution* that Blairism was committed to 'an ethical socialism' which they said, imagining it would confirm its moderation, 'draws on the ideas of Tawney and Ruskin'.[17] It is certainly true that Ruskin was no socialist, but rather a social reformer, and Tawney did not advocate the socialisation of the means of production – nationalisation was a last resort means rather than an end in itself. But Ruskin wanted to better everybody's circumstance, and Tawney, as we have seen, warmly repeated Francis Bacon's dictum, 'wealth is like muck. It is not good but if it be spread', and thought a nakedly acquisitive capitalism (rather than a functional capitalism) so morally repugnant and socially useless that it deserved to have no future. Little of such thinking would surface in the New Labour years.

The incoming government, sorely lacking in self-confidence after eighteen years out of office, seriously misread the runes. Its landslide victory was an endorsement of its new philosophy and voters' enthusiasm to make good the deficiencies of the Tory years, notably on badly neglected public services, the growth of unacceptable inequality and the knowledge that too little had been done to deal with deindustrialisation. But it failed to grasp the nettle. For example, deindustrialisation had torn the heart out of Labour-voting working-class communities, which were still scarred by the Thatcher years; they wanted at the very least the process stopped, if not reversed, and a determined effort made to revitalise them. It was a call for levelling up a generation before Johnson capitalised on the disaffection of those areas. It would be too little heeded.

New Labour offered no signature policies in its first term to demonstrate what it stood for, as all great reforming governments must do – as Asquith, Attlee, even Thatcher and to a degree Wilson had all delivered, or Roosevelt and Johnson had done in the USA. There was no building of new institutions to reshape the British economy, re-engineer work and workplace representation, promote investment and innovation or redesign a new social contract. There were no coherent attempts to reform the constitution, and Blair showed himself quite content to govern with the commanding majority he had received under the first-past-the-post system.

It was a duck-and-weave administration, looking for points of least resistance and choosing not to boast about achievements for fear of upsetting the centre-right ideological consensus, which in fact was in disarray. In practice, its political philosophy offered a highly minimal ethic of socialism, and maximal commitment to individualism, which hardly connected to any form of progressive Liberalism. Blair wanted to be all things to all men, and have the political space to retain the Thatcherite economic model – no rewriting the rules of the 'flexible' labour market, no challenge to financial deregulation, the introduction of private finance into the public sector, not increasing the progressivity of the tax system and not addressing the long-standing weaknesses in British corporate governance. The vested interests he was happiest confronting were not the great investment institutions, banks or companies, but trade unions and the public sector.

For ten years, the implications of the omissions were disguised, although they would leave Blair's heirs with a headache: what was Blairism, really? There was an exceptionally benign international environment, helped by China's accession to the World Trade Organization in 2001, which created the mix of reasonable growth and low inflation – the 'Nice' decade (non-inflationary, consistently expansionary). EU membership was working its balm, promoting competition and inward investment so that between 1997 and 2007 productivity growth matched or exceeded our principal competitors, with wider economic growth averaging 3 per cent a year. A minimum wage was implemented, which did not destroy jobs, as the right had warned.

But the approach had the same Achilles' heel as Thatcherism – a fatal over-reliance on the growth of private credit to drive the economy forwards and a parallel reluctance, shared by previous Labour governments and their leading thinkers, seriously to consider what reforms the basic structures of British capitalism needed, let alone to implement them. Either nationalise private capital or leave it to its own devices is the Labour approach since Keir Hardie; don't reform it. Some of the factors that had inhibited the British economy over the twentieth century had been confronted by Thatcher, notably the labour market; the rest were not addressed. They also remained largely unaddressed by New Labour. Mortgage debt between 1997 and 2007 nearly doubled from 58 per cent to 94 per cent of GDP, while corporate debt jumped from 55 per cent to 82 per cent of GDP. This was the fastest growth of private indebtedness ever incurred in British economic history.[18]

Bad as this was, British banks entered the exploding markets in allegedly risk-free financial derivatives, so that their balance sheets further mushroomed in size. In 2000, every pound of lending by the British financial system was supported by ten pence of shareholders' capital – a ratio of twenty to one, in line with the forty-year average.[19] By 2007, lending had grown to such an extent that the capital underwriting a pound of lending had shrunk to two pence – a leverage ratio of fifty to one. With no separation between commercial and investment banking, it was grotesquely risky, but indulged by a government committed to 'light-touch' regulation and exaggeratedly respectful of the City – witness the quote from Ed Balls cited in Chapter 3. The Great Financial Crisis might have had its origins in stupidly unwise lending in the American mortgage market, but British fragilities magnified the shocks. New Labour cannot shrug off the blame.

The crisis unmasked the failures and omissions of what had gone before. Because it did no more than pay lip service to stakeholder capitalism by introducing a delayed, softened Companies Act in 2006 (with only an invitation for companies to take into account the interests of stakeholders [Section 172], rather than any obligation), New Labour could not begin to reframe the relationship between finance, business and employees – indeed, the party shrank from it. There were no new banking or investment institutions with a mission to promote patient, clever finance, nor institutions dedicated to the creation and dissemination of new technologies. Although productivity did rise steadily up to the financial crisis, too little was sufficiently embedded by investment, innovation, enlightened working relationships and great management; although financial crises tend to cause long-term economic scarring, the degree to which such productivity growth was built on sand and would evaporate after the crisis was striking. It was only then that an industrial strategy was launched.

The reforms to the social contract, although individually good, were piecemeal and did not stack up as a new social settlement. For example, active labour market policies were not put on even a semi-permanent footing until after the financial crisis, and no attempt was made to combine labour market flexibilities with measures to support incomes of the transitionally unemployed and help them to find work through focused training, job guarantees and work programmes. Instead, there were a series of ad hoc New Deals encouraging particular groups to engage in job search, alongside tax credits and tweaks to the welfare system.

The bagginess of the New Labour philosophy had other malevolent by-products – it poisoned the relationship between Blair and Brown over his last years as prime minister. Brown was much more the ethical socialist keen to tackle inequalities, even if he tried to do so under the radar, and Blair was more anxious to keep the coalition together by emphasising the centre-right, union-sceptic, pro-market dimensions of New Labour. An increasingly embittered Brown believed Blair should stand aside; the two could not work together any longer. Blair's focus became reform of public services and foreign policy.

Public service reform combined a welcome increase in resources (public-sector investment trebled over the New Labour years from 1 to 3 per cent of GDP) with the introduction of top-down targets and new frameworks of inspection, enforcement and regulation. It was a mixed bag. By 2007, £68 billion of Private Finance Initiative (PFI) contracts had been signed, mainly to build hospitals and schools, committing future governments to £215 billion of spending to service the contracts – an incredibly costly betrayal of future taxpayers.[20] Borrowing had certainly been kept off the government's balance sheet, but at huge future expense, with inflexible contractual terms and few identifiable efficiencies to compensate for the higher financing costs. The unloved PFI was abolished by the Tory government in 2018. The top-down targets from the centre exposed all the flaws of centralised planning, which felt like bullying, and for all the huffing and puffing productivity growth in the public sector flat-lined over the decade.[21] Offering more autonomy to academy schools to develop their own educational culture was one reform that seemed to work, especially in London. But in the end what made a difference was money. Hospital waiting lists were down to 2.5 million in 2010 following the build-up of health spending, a low from which they have subsequently more than trebled.

Although the disaster of the financial crisis casts a long and deep shadow over any assessment of those years, the cumulative social improvements should be recognised. Living standards rose, as did educational standards and the performance of the NHS. Innovative improvements were made to the treatment of children – the creation of 3,500 SureStart centres and asset-based welfare with the establishment of the Child Trust Fund. Brown's New Deals and tax credits did lift employment levels and incomes of many disadvantaged groups. The newly created Regional

Development Agencies did reduce some regional disparities with London, although they were in need of more accountability and focus.[22] After the financial crisis, an industrial strategy was at last formulated. Britain was a committed member of the European Union, although too little effort was made to sell the advantages of membership. The 2008 Climate Change Act committing the UK to a 100 per cent reduction in carbon emissions by 2050 was passed. Devolution was offered to Scotland and Wales, a London mayor was created, which would become the template for more city mayoralties, the Supreme Court was established and the influence of the hereditary Lords in the House of Lords was curtailed. All worthwhile, but that was as far as constitutional reform went.

Yet ambiguity generated strategic mistakes. Brown was applauded for dodging the bullet of joining the euro – but fatal economic and political consequences followed. The pound remained overvalued throughout the New Labour years, accelerating deindustrialisation, while without the need to sustain euro membership a blind eye could be turned to the Triffid-like growth of the City up until 2007. Worse, it undermined New Labour's support for the EU, muzzling enthusiasm for Europe, and left Britain in a dangerous half-in, half-out position. When euroscepticism took off in the 2010s, euro membership was not there to protect the most important thing: membership of the EU. Non-alignment with Europe would make it easier to side with the USA, rather than sceptical France and Germany, and so take part in the disastrous invasion of Iraq in 2003.

The financial crisis, the lack of structural economic reform, the inadequacies of the social contract and the ambiguities of New Labour's position on Europe damaged New Labour's reputation less than Blair's foreign adventures. Joining George W. Bush with no proper UN mandate to invade Iraq, because of a non-existent terrorist threat and no plan for reconstruction, was close to insanity. The invasion and what was an even worse occupation of Afghanistan had been equally deluded. The only real reasons were to cement the US alliance and consolidate New Labour's reputation on the political right – but at terrible cost and as an abandonment of real British interests. The wars were not just expensive in terms of lost lives and money; they destabilised the Middle East, strengthened Russia's hand and prompted an exodus of refugees which is a proximate cause of the rise of the hard right across Europe. They have made it even harder in the wake of Russia's invasion of Ukraine to rally global opinion to the West's cause. It was obvious double standards. As New Labour former Foreign Secretary David Miliband now acknowledges, Iraq was a first-order mistake.[23]

Blairism was, in sum, an opportunity that was half-embraced only to self-destruct. The boundaries between an ethic of socialism and progressive liberalism were left unclear, leaving too much scope for compromises with the right. It had not been a Rooseveltian New Deal; business and finance had received too little challenge, too little regulation and no new institution-building. Too much had been done to advance consumers' interests, too little to advance those of workers. Yet there were gains. By the end, both Ruskin and Tawney would have found something to cheer. But the ambiguities would allow little to stand the test of time – and the left is still grappling with the aftermath.

Wilderness Years

The two Miliband brothers, both ex-cabinet ministers, fought for the Labour leadership in the wake of the 2010 electoral defeat – Ed narrowly beating David by 50.7 per cent to 49.3 per cent in an electoral college where MPs, unions and members each had a third of the vote. MPs and party members voted for David, who, while accepting the need to address New Labour's weaknesses, wanted to preserve the core political stance and build on its foundations. But enough of the union vote, loyal to the good-old-time religion embodied by union opposition to Wilson's *In Place of Strife*, plumped for Ed. New Labour, he said, was 'dead', indicating he would move in a more pro-worker direction and focus on lowering inequality.[24] Under him the party would more warmly embrace an ethic of socialism, a position he thought was distinct from that of his brother. It was a difference of degrees; but nonetheless they were important, boundary-defining differences.

Yet it was hard to chart a new direction; what did 'socialism' mean in the 2010s? Was there any variant that his shadow cabinet could convincingly unite around, let alone have broad electoral appeal? It was difficult to be sure-footed, especially with an ever-more-confident right-wing media deriding the whole concept. Five years of misconceived, savage austerity should have denied the Conservative Party re-election in 2015, but Labour did not have enough momentum to compensate in England and Wales for the haemorrhage of their seats in Scotland to the Scottish National Party, as Scots rallied to the party after losing the independence referendum.

The Tories profited from the collapse of their former coalition partner's vote, aided and abetted by an aggressive and cynical Tory campaign. The LibDems had little defence; they had betrayed progressive liberalism in joining the Conservatives in coalition with very little to show for it. They were no longer a plausible home even for tactical, progressive voters. The Tories – as they had done so often since 1918 – won a majority of House of Commons seats on a minority of the vote.

In fact, the seeds of disaster had been laid with all the unresolved ambiguities of New Labour more than a decade earlier; indeed, arguably since 1997. To have succeeded against Brown and win the 2010 general election, David Miliband needed to raise his standard in 2007 to contest the succession when Blair resigned, or in 2009 after the financial crisis had stabilised. But what was New Labour? Although tempted, David Miliband could not act, because the very lack of clarity meant it would be seen as a challenge to Gordon Brown as a politician and person – opening a dangerous party split in the run-up to the next election. In this respect, Blair had imperilled his own project by not better defining it, and not preparing the way for his succession. Gordon Brown did not have Tony Blair's electoral charisma, but he undoubtedly stood for a strand of New Labour which he would pugnaciously defend. David Miliband drew back, and events unfolded as they did.

The successor to Ed Miliband was Jeremy Corbyn, now the

beneficiary of the same strand of idealistic socialist thinking that had driven the Socialist League and Stafford Cripps in the 1930s, the Bevan faction in the 1950s and Tony Benn after 1979. The solution to electoral setbacks, he believed, was not to develop New Labour's position, given the new configurations of class and affluence and the incoherencies in the progressive position exposed over the previous sixty years. Rather, Labour would embrace a socialism that the party had never properly tried. Corbyn aimed to fight austerity around a ten-point plan for socialist transformation, democratise the party and build a mass movement for change. Momentum, the campaigning vehicle that grew out of the grassroots enthusiasm for his leadership, would grow still more and combine with a more vocal and convinced trade union movement to make the case for socialism – bypassing a sceptical parliamentary Labour Party and establishment. An enthused membership believed they were voting for a new kind of politics.

But there had been no popular demands for socialism in the 1920s and 1930s when the Royal Navy mutineers at Invergordon had sung 'The Red Flag'. The 1945–51 government, now romanticised as the acme of socialism, was in reality a blend of ethical socialism and progressive New Liberalism whose legitimacy was born of war. But that did not trouble the eurosceptic Corbyn and his allies. They drew their support less from the affluent working class that Ron Todd had described so tellingly back in 1987, but from the highly educated, idealistic young socialist intellectuals and the diehards who dominated the executive committees of some of the big unions, notably Unite. As the Corbyn bandwagon grew, the other candidates for the leadership had no energetic riposte, offering either variants of Ed Miliband's programme in almost managerial terms or trying to rebrand the now-derided New Labour. The die was cast.

Corbyn would have one success – denying Theresa May a renewed majority in the snap election of 2017 that she called in order to have a mandate to negotiate a Brexit that while hard enough to please her right would not be disastrously destructive. He would interpret this as an endorsement of his philosophy and policy; in his world it had not fully succeeded only because it had been undermined by disaffected party insiders and New Labour refuseniks. In fact, it was more May's reverse than Corbyn's gain. The resulting hung Parliament, despite a rise in the Tory vote, reflected tactical voting on a huge scale by the educated better-off to deny May any brand of hard Brexit, confident that the Labour vote would not be strong enough to put Corbyn into Downing Street. There was little popular demand for him or his brand of socialism. In fact, for those daring to look, the slide in the Labour vote in its industrial heartlands that had been evident since the 1960s was continuing. Labour's majority over the Conservatives in the Don Valley and Stoke North, for example, weakening since 1966, fell even further.[25]

In 2019, the party would pay a bitter price. Corbyn's election manifesto, the most centralising socialist programme since 1983, aimed to establish no less than eight national public bodies – a National Education Service, a National Energy Agency, a National Care Agency, a National Food Commission, a National Youth Service, a National Investment Bank, a National Women's Commission and a National Refuge Fund. For every ill, there should be a national response directed from the centre. A Corbyn government would renationalise the big energy firms, rail, water, the National Grid and the broadband arm of BT. It would abolish university tuition fees, lift the minimum wage and pension and freeze the pension age, create a £250-billion green transformation fund and bring forward the net-zero target. It would offer another referendum on Brexit – not a re-run of the in-out referendum but a referendum democratically to validate whatever Brexit deal was finally negotiated.

It was the culmination of decades of 'left' thinking developed in its own echo chamber with too little willingness to look beyond its own categories and slogans. All the policies spoke to real and pressing issues – indeed, it was because Corbyn was so effective at making compelling speeches on them that he won the leadership of the party – but cumulatively the whole was disastrously less than the sum of its parts. In his vision, the state would dominate economy and society, but was it equipped to do what would be asked of it, and do it well? Had the designers of the programme learned anything from the mistakes of the past, or even recognised that there were mistakes? They showed no awareness that they had. How were individuals to express agency, ambition and take responsibility for their lives in this brave new world? Individuals were cast as ciphers with new entitlements from a newly dominant state rather than enfranchised citizens; none of the insights of progressive new liberalism that had animated Attlee's government were acknowledged. Keynesianism, for example, is not about creating a big state; it is about managing capitalism better.

That segued into the big question of the character of British capitalism in a Corbynite world; public and private would become two hostile economic camps, with the public sector the senior empowered partner. Would that be conducive to private innovation and investment, or any kind of capitalist dynamism? Trade unions would be empowered, but as opponents of business, rather than partners. Then there was the question of how to finance such an audaciously expensive programme: not impossible, but requiring a credible fiscal, tax and monetary framework. Little was offered to explain how that might be achieved. Above all, the romantic vision of a nation-wide social movement as the political base for all of this was just that: a romantic fantasy. It ignored the political truth that no such movement existed or was likely to emerge given that it had not done so in the much more propitious circumstances of the inter-war years.

This was a view of British society that had not engaged with the lived experience of tens of millions with their common desire to own a house, build a career and live well. There is certainly acute economic and social need in contemporary Britain; but there are also the apolitical instincts of a majority who take scant notice of politics, let alone want to sign up to a left-wing mass social movement. They recognise the need for change but need to be won over – almost seduced. In any case, neither Corbyn, who was bored with detail, nor his chaotic inner team were capable of organising such a movement even if it were remotely feasible. The campaign, up against someone as slyly effective as Boris Johnson, wholly focused on 'getting Brexit done', was disorganised, collapsing into a blizzard of ever-more-extravagant and incredible announcements.

The right-wing media was mercilessly hostile, reaching new heights of hyperbole. Corbyn during his leadership had given them too much to shoot at, from his decades-long refusal to condemn IRA atrocities, dragging his feet over identifying Russia as responsible for the attempted poisoning of the former Russian spy Sergei Skripal and his daughter in Salisbury, to the painfully slow condemnation of anti-semitism as a problem within the Labour Party – honestly described by Owen Jones, a Corbyn supporter, in his candid assessment of the Corbyn years in *This Land*.

Above all, the compromise on Brexit was too weak to appeal to Remainers, while undermining support in Labour's old industrial heartlands which had voted for Brexit in good faith as a protest against the dysfunctional status quo. Labour was not prepared to respect their vote, but too cautious openly to offer another referendum. The crumbling of the Labour vote in so-called Red Wall seats that had been apparent for decades dissolved into an avalanche. Both Don Valley and Stoke North finally went Conservative. Defeat was inevitable, Labour's electoral performance the worst since 1935.

Blairism and Corbynism were very different, but their twin fates have common roots. There needs to be a feasible progressivism that effectively combines an ethic of socialism with progressive new liberalism – building on the thinkers discussed in the previous chapters – and is unapologetically optimistic about the possibility of universal progress and justice in the best traditions of the European enlightenment. On those terms, both Blairism, for all its electoral success, and Corbynism failed. The task is successfully to combine the 'We' and 'I', and on this progressive ground create a sequence of great reforming governments that will, step by step, turn Britain round.

8

THE 'WE SOCIETY'

Ideas matter; they are the indispensable precondition for action. The challenge, as we have seen, is to create a dynamic capitalism that delivers great companies, jobs and prosperity animated by social purpose and the common good. This needs to be married to a belief in social cohesion, a sense of fairness and personal freedom, and structures that compensate for the sheer bad luck of life's vicissitudes. The two propositions can't stand alone – they are interdependent. A strong economy delivers the possibility of a society to which everyone belongs and in which they have opportunity; a society to which everyone belongs underpins both a strong economy and the democracy which fosters both.[1]

There has to be public agency to bring about these outcomes, and the best agency is democratic government. Apart from the legitimacy and accountability conferred by government of, by and for the people, it is democracies that recognise the pluralism of individual firms and organisations that succour a great capitalism, and it is only democracies that have the feedback mechanisms quickly to change course and respond to the unexpected and unanticipated. But achieving that requires an agile state, and robust institutions through which democracy can work.

By those criteria, Britain falls far short. The long grip of laissez-faire – interrupted only by the thirty-year period after the Second World War – has left a culture of reluctant public engagement based on two palpably false propositions: that economies and societies can be relied upon to self-organise to the best outcomes and that any public initiative should be as minimal as possible so as not to get in the way of those processes. Our progressive tradition, trying to assert fellowship and mutuality, has yet to develop a strong counter-philosophy that allows it convincingly to supplant laissez-faire with something better (as we have seen in the last four chapters). As damaging, Britain is left with an ossifying democracy whose institutions, handed down over the centuries, are largely dysfunctional.

The economic starting point is that the rate of growth of British productivity over the last fifteen years has been 0.4 per cent. In parallel the rate of growth of the capital stock has been 0.2 per cent. Britain is suffering from a crisis of underinvestment, and an inability to keep companies at the forefront of technology domiciled here. Hence our close-to-zero productivity growth and stagnating real wages. Without a serious growth of productivity, which will drive forward more prosperity, every hope turns to dust. Everything that has contributed to these baleful trends has to be reformed.

From this weak platform Britain has to react to the opportunities of the twenty-first-century economy, notably artificial intelligence (AI), which will gradually displace all routine forms of work, causing another surge of inequality and new concentrations of private power. It has always been necessary to act collectively to share prosperity and shape new technologies so that they serve society – not only because it's morally right to do so, but because it sustains the legitimacy of capitalism. Technological progress should not disempower humanity; it must empower us.

Add to this the massive challenge of decarbonising the economy and refashioning how we live so we pass on a liveable planet to the coming generations. Developing a richer progressive public philosophy from which ideas and policies can emerge to confront these challenges, along with a vibrant democracy to deliver them, was always important. Now it is a precondition for turning round what threatens to be unstoppable decline.

British democracy as an instrument for renewal is self-evidently ailing. The House of Commons may have the trappings of a democratic deliberative legislative assembly, but it too rarely functions as such. Rather it is a vehicle for the governing party, elected on a fraction of the popular vote in a first-past-the-post voting system, to whip through ill-thought-out legislation, often after only minutes of scrutiny. The scandalous waste of billions of public money on private contractors peddling often useless equipment during the Covid epidemic, often channelled to Tory donors or insiders, bears witness to a structural lack of accountability. The state has been infantilised by the reflex impulse to contract out both policy analysis and delivery of public service to an array of consultants. Our public apparatus is too weak to deliver consistent good government. Common-sense recommendations to uphold standards in public life have been ignored.[2]

The list of what must be addressed is long. There is too much unaccountable private power. The still-too dominant financial system is biased to wealth extraction and incentivised to make its playmakers exceptionally rich. Private investment in AI dwarfs government investment or regulation. Social housing and public spaces in our cities and towns cannot meet the scale of need. Privatised utilities are too weakly regulated. Disgraceful employment practices are winked at, with minimal risk of any comeback or penalty. The public square is degraded as the mighty right-wing media owners indulge the corruption of basic journalistic standards to serve their political interests. The physical and mental health of too many of us falls far too short of what should be acceptable in a civilised society. And so much more.

To manage problems on this scale has never been easy, yet even more complexity and a need for agile public governance will be the defining characteristic of the twenty-first century. For example a new product today – an iPhone, say, or an electric car – now requires tens of thousands of components, all of which have to be brought together and must conform to rigorous common standards. A new service in the digital age presumes the existence of an interconnected fabric of broadband cable, laptops, software and a host of ancillary services for it to be viable. Companies, exploiting a new digital or proprietary technology, can grow explosively and become monopolies. Social and business risk are ever-present – that the business model can fail or that a rival technology will appear. Ongoing success requires that all these problems and hazards are well-managed.

One of new liberalism's basic tenets, shared with an ethic of socialism, was that business and the better-off were part of a social whole and that the state had an obligation to make society more cohesive by pulling together. If that was true at the beginning of the twentieth century, it is even truer today. The risks are more uncertain and larger. Neither state nor business can know with any certainty what will unfold in the future or the complexities it will throw up. Of necessity, what they do together must be experimental – again recognising a New Liberal argument that private and public power is about constant negotiation. The authority of public power has to be earned by the quality of what it does. Planning may be vital, but planning in this new world will inevitably be by trial and error, iterative, agile and ready quickly to abandon one course of failing action and adopt another more promising avenue.

One analogy is with the way the US Defense Department's Defense Advanced Research Projects Agency (DARPA) identifies projects worth supporting, through constant experimentation and backing the apparently impossible while quickly abandoning those that prove unworkable. Its approach contrasts with the top-down planning of France and Britain in the 1960s. The precondition for success is responsive, open companies and responsive states in a constant dialogue. Britain now has neither.

The Quest for the Holy Grail

Pulling this off will be difficult. Britain is hardly alone in facing a step change in insecurity and inequality as technological change displaces jobs and creates new pools of private wealth and power. The symbiotic interdependence between capitalist dynamism and societal strength is vital in order to deliver wellbeing for the mass of the population. A strong social contract, in which people can trust, is an essential adjunct to the acceptance of the social upheaval that follows in the wake of restless capitalism, destroying even as it creates. Recall the Daron Acemoglu and Simon Johnson argument in *Power and Progress*. They survey the last thousand years, observing that it is successive waves of transformative technologies that not only create dramatic changes in their own sphere, but cause cascading increases in productivity in many other spheres as, say, the railway or the computer both have done. These changes spark the transformations that create great wealth. But the perennial problem is that too much of that resulting wealth is captured by the incumbent elite, who have little interest in sharing it, or shaping what are always malleable technologies into tools that serve the common rather their own individual interest.

That struggle (and the intellectual response to it) has been the subject of the preceding chapters. For the *FT*'s chief economic commentator Martin Wolf, in *The Crisis of Democratic Capitalism*, the issue has become the most profound of our times; the task of liberal democracy has always been to contain capitalism's worst excesses, and to keep the common interest alive, but such is the extraordinary wealth now being generated that democracy itself is in danger of being so captured by the rich (often using populism to serve their ends) that this crucial function is being menaced. This is especially true of the USA, but there are shadows in Britain – think of the influence of donors on the Conservative Party and its unwillingness to propose even modest improvements, say, to food standards or regulate the gambling industry. It becomes increasingly hard to uphold the common interest, to share prosperity, to shape technology – and with those cumulative failings daily life becomes insupportable, making the temptations of political populism irresistible. Democracy itself, Wolf warns, may be at risk.

Public authority must shed the conservative assumption that business and markets will always and everywhere do better than the state. Take the challenge of AI. Either AI can be deployed usefully to be at humankind's service, or become a blind eliminator of work and, as it already is in China, a super-Orwellian Big Brother and author of a stream of fake but nonetheless convincing news. AI now is being allowed to develop unchecked and uncontrolled. Leaving aside the question of whether machines will ever develop consciousness, there is sufficient danger already. There are six key areas where AI is already transforming social and human interaction: image recognition; the analysis of our sentiments and feelings revealed by what we say and how we look; the modelling of language to reproduce texts; the classification of meanings; detecting and recognising objects; and making machines interoperable. These are extraordinary powers, but in 2020 industry, alone or in collaboration with universities, had developed 91 per cent of the leading AI models. In 2021, industry models were twenty-nine times bigger on average than academic models, highlighting the vast difference in computing power available to the two groups – let alone government. Industry's share of the biggest AI models has gone from 11 per cent in 2010 to 96 per cent in 2021.[3] What this means is that one of the great transformatory technologies of the twenty-first century is being captured by business and rich elite universities. For Professors Daron Acemoglu and Simon Johnson, it was ever thus. The perennial struggle is the same: to share the wealth and design the technology so that it benefits humanity as a whole.

Too much AI, they argue – reflecting the statistics above – is being used to deliver unnecessary 'so-so automation' to save unskilled labour. Companies want to engineer quick labour savings into their business models using AI – and the tech corporations supplying the AI respond. Both are following short-term profit signals. The deleterious impact on the labour market is already being felt; blue-collar and white-collar jobs are disappearing and rates of pay are being bid down. There needs to be a redirection of priorities. AI, for example, could have revolutionary beneficial effects in teaching, medicine and the problems of day-to-day life.

The same statistical techniques used to automate tasks can also be used in education for identifying groups of students who have difficulties with similar problems, as well as advanced students who can be exposed to more complex material. The relevant content can then be adjusted for the pedagogic needs of small groups of students; personalisation allows effort to be focused where it is most needed – improving the cognitive and social skills of students from low socioeconomic backgrounds. And AI should not be allowed to displace human agency. The evidence from medical diagnostics is that designing humans out of the loop is a disaster; you need the rapid intelligence of AI, but for the results to be interpreted by doctors and nurses.

Society has risen to these challenges before; it can do so again. Manufacturing techniques in both the USA and Japan were adapted over the last century to allow unskilled and semi-skilled workers to contribute to the production process. In the USA the production line was organised around the creation of interchangeable parts and standardised production to allow unskilled workers more easily to contribute; flexible production in Japan using 'quality circles' allowed any mistakes by less-skilled workers quickly to be spotted and corrected. Machines don't need to impoverish and dehumanise us; they can be made to serve, rather than rule.

But the precondition for any successful remodelling of AI will be a vision of how technology can be used for human betterment, and for the state to get behind such a vision. Given that on some estimates more than 80 per cent of new wealth will have its origins in tech-driven innovation, the need goes beyond AI.[4] It seemed impossible a generation ago that renewable technologies like wind and solar power could end up being cheaper than fossil fuels, but social pressure and the spread of environmental awareness forced governments to offer incentives and make the research and development investments that have delivered the transformation. The same must be done again and again in other spheres.

There will be successor and greater general-purpose technologies, in fields ranging from medicine to nuclear fusion. The pace of capitalism is dazzling in its speed; witness the pace with which vaccines were developed in less than eighteen months – unthinkably fast just a decade ago – as Covid broke over the world, or how the now-failed US Silicon Valley Bank lost a quarter of its deposits in just one day in March 2023. The pace of change is set further to accelerate. Twenty-first-century economies and societies will have to concentrate on generating the knowledge to create firms operating at the ever-receding technological frontier, on financing structures that organise the right mix of equity and debt, on developing educational and training institutions that produce the human beings capable of working in this fast-moving, knowledge-driven environment. We will need smart, agile public and private institutions – and social support structures that underwrite the increasingly risky lives that people will have to lead.

For one of the threatened characteristics of this near-future world is massive inequality; not only will fortunes be made as firms grow explosively, but there will also be more tendency to monopoly, as firms win dominant positions exploiting their very specific knowledge – think of Google or Apple. Moreover, because agglomeration brings great economic rewards, there will be ever-greater differences between fast- and slow-growing cities, towns and regions. These profound economic forces will compel governments to be active in ensuring as much sharing of prosperity as possible. The state will be compelled to get bigger – for all of our sakes.

This was the far-seeing prognostication of British Nobel Prize-winning economist James Meade, writing in the early 1960s. Automation and robotisation, he anticipated, was accelerating and would inevitably put downward pressure on labour's share of national income – and increase the share going to capital. In *Liberty, Equality and Efficiency* he outlined four possible solutions: the trade union state, the welfare state, the socialist state and the property owning state. All are potential mechanisms for sharing prosperity. He rejected both the trade union state which would pitch wages high for privileged trade union insiders while neglecting outsiders and the welfare state because the scale of income transfers would diminish incentives; rather, he opted for an amalgam of a property owning democracy and socialist state. Essentially the state should act in two purposeful ways. Firstly, it should seek to boost the sharing of wealth by encouraging employee share ownership and taxing inheritance, especially of very rich estates, very aggressively. Secondly, it should build up a citizens' wealth fund which, by taking stakes in productive assets or taxing economic rent, would pay out income to compenseate for falling wages. Nor is the idea of a citizens' wealth fund paying out a dividend to citizens so far-fetched: Alaska has its Alaska Permanent Fund, built up from taxing the proceeds of oil drilling licences, that pays out some $1000 a year to every citizen. Norway also has its sovereign wealth fund. Meade's conception was more radical: the state taking equity stakes – topsy turvy nationalisation, he called it – in enterprise across the board to give itself the capacity to compensate for falling real wages by paying a citizens' dividend.[5] Two generations before Acemoglu and Johnson, Meade was thinking in the same terms. Prosperity must be shared.

All this is alien to the ideologically dominant strain in contemporary British Conservatism. It purports to champion free-market capitalism, but its proponents can't engage with capitalist realities. Sharing prosperity, accentuating the common interest, developing social structures to manage risk and actively using the state to drive a high-tech economy forwards rather than offering ad hoc bungs – none of this falls within their blinkered field of view. Yet reality does occasionally crowd in. Boris Johnson as prime minister wanted to use an increase in public investment to level up Britain's left-behind regions and even sanctioned an increase in National Insurance contributions to pay for a national system of social care – but his party balked at both. The National Insurance increase was rescinded, and the new funds for levelling up were trivial. In his tirade when resigning as a MP over the indictment for lying to the House of Commons, Johnson, knowing his party's touch points, reverted to Tory type and called for the restoration of a low-tax regime. Equally, Prime Minister Rishi Sunak, while he celebrates the role of technology in driving growth, is no champion of significant public investment: revealingly, tax cuts were preferred to sustaining already squeezed public capital investment, allowed to fall as a projected share of GDP, in the November 2023 Autumn statement.[6] Anything statist, whatever its merit, is a matter for dread. As for managing the social consequences – dealing with technological unemployment of the type that has already happened in agriculture and manufacturing but is now spreading across the entire economy – no dice.[7]

Meanwhile there is the libertarian, anarcho-capitalist right represented by Liz Truss, who during her forty-nine-day premiership wanted to carpet-bomb an already moderately taxed Britain with a network of even-lower-tax and lower-regulation investment zones. Incredibly, blithely ignoring the disaster over which she presided – Argentina-on-the-Channel, as a former governor of the Bank of England Mark Carney has dubbed it – she is trying to mount a political comeback. The stream of thought she champions, stubbornly resistant to reality, believes that capitalism must be given as much licence as possible, unconstrained by measures to promote the common interest. Contemporary conservatism is a cacophony of competing visions, but the strains and the incapacity to sustain ideological coherence are part of what happens when one order is dying and another is emerging to take its place.

Certainly the electorate is more heterogeneous than the prevailing Conservative ideology presumes. Political scientists Pat Dade and Les Higgins, in their path-breaking categorisation 'Values Modes'[8] developed the notion that populations hold values that can be grouped into three great and broadly equal categories – those who are socially conservative 'settlers', a second category who are achievement- and status-oriented 'prospectors' and, finally, 'pioneers', who quest for change and self-realisation. Conservative majorities since 1979 have been broadly built on socially conservative 'settlers' and status-oriented 'prospectors', but both are under siege from a growing sense of insecurity and so look to government to help pilot society through turbulent times. This trend is also echoed by Electoral Calculus, which divides the electorate into seven clusters. Whether 'strong right', 'young kind capitalists', 'strong left' or 'traditionalists', the polling company discerns a movement to the centre on economic issues – wanting the best of both conventionally right- and left-wing worlds.[9] Certainly, the electoral base for neoliberal market fundamentalism is evaporating.

Instead, there is a willingness to hear new tunes that chime with lived reality, driven home by the cost-of-living crisis. A weakened economy unable to offer decent wages weakens our society, which in turn becomes less capable of creating stronger growth. It does not produce sustained and sophisticated demand for ground-breaking goods and services, nor does it produce skilled and rounded people for the workforces of innovative companies. Over the nineteenth century and into the first decades of the twentieth century, the abject condition of the people worried the best in British society and politics. It should do so again. We need to start looking after our own again, rather than blaming foreigners for all our ills – but to do that, we need to resurrect our economic dynamism.

A New Progressive Philosophy and Its Coalition

The neoliberal era is plainly over, and a newly forged social democratic order needs to solve these challenges. Britain must get beyond the conservative idea of the 'We' defined by a very ancient nation-state, saturated in a complacent sense of its own greatness, seeing public activism as second best to a preferred world in which human endeavour and ambition are private with economy and society, as far as possible, left to their own devices. Instead, the 'We' must be re-surfaced as one that can pursue and deliver more because we work together to achieve shared goals, and which has our back whenever things go wrong in our individual lives. Public and private in this conception are part of an interdependent whole, with the nation-state as the indispensable guarantor of the common good and all our flourishing – whether securing minimum living standards, for example, or acting to contain global warming.

The reset to come must reincorporate the 'We', a shared sense of belonging and collective purpose, back into the DNA of our society; there must be a web of institutions that represent our collective need and common good, while proper space is offered to individual responsibility and agency – but not to libertarian narcissism. Its success might also allow the right, hopefully, to recast conservatism in less destructive terms, and rediscover a conservative philosophy that is less of a menace to our democracy.

For humanity is united in a quest for meaning. Until the very recent past, religious faith offered most people meaning and purpose. In an increasingly secular society, in which the majority no longer truly believes in a life beyond death conferred by a god, purpose has to be found in the here-and-now – our quotidian lives. It was Aristotle who declared that human happiness came less from material goods or being nested in family and friends, and more from being able purposefully to act on the world to make it better, however incrementally.

The populist Brexit right has found its purpose as a surrogate for religion – leaving the European Union, keeping foreigners out, controlling our borders, punishing more offenders more harshly, limiting social obligations only to family and oneself, pushing unregulated free markets, lowering taxes (but still, as if by magic, having great public services). But it is a despairing philosophy of closure and meanness.

The left for its part has not yet offered an aggressive, moral counter-punch. It is consumed either by a defensiveness – we will manage the complexities of the status quo better and more decently than the Tories, without challenging their basic structures. Or it offers a vicarious politics of identity, which so dominated former Labour leader Jeremy Corbyn's political worldview; he was uncritical of the IRA, Palestinian violence, the Iranian regime or Putin's Russia because they were against Western imperialism (as defined by him), and his stance therefore reaffirmed his identity as an anti-imperialist by identifying with them. *Mine enemy's enemy is my friend.* Identity politics may confer meaning for some on the left, but only for the chosen insiders – it is by definition a minority faith, which is the mirror to the minority right's faith in low-tax, deregulatory libertarian capitalism and Brexit. It does not produce a philosophy of public purpose, or a renewal of the 'We'. Parts of the liberal and extreme left seem to feel that the stances taken on identity – race, gender, the legacy of empire – are more secure signifiers of radicalism than challenging capitalism and social injustice.

But Britain does have a great progressive tradition, intertwined with ethical socialism, even if distinct from it, largely rooted in the best of the new liberalism, common law and our early embrace of democracy. Our core values – fairness, tolerance, kindness, openness, admiration for those who dare, championing the underdog – are also fundamentally progressive. The political problem for the liberal left is that it has never marshalled these forces successfully over time into a sustained political project or a single party. British progressivism has been fatally divided.

At the level of political theory, a unifying progressive philosophy will seek once again to integrate new liberalism and an ethic of socialism – which should not be difficult, for the ideas of William Beveridge and Nye Bevan are first cousins to one another, as was obvious at the time; while today, the essentially New Liberal views of, say, Andy Haldane, former chief economist of the Bank of England (now CEO of the Royal Society of Arts), are plainly close to those of the ethical socialist shadow chancellor Rachel Reeves. He might stress the uncapping of individual agency and ambition more than her, and she the need for the We to have our backs by offering security – but the overlap of their views is more extensive than their differences. At a bare minimum and as a small beginning, thought leaders on the liberal left need to own the inter-related pedigree of their ideas and their closeness, rather than accentuating what are in the main second-order differences. Together, the two and two of ethical socialism and progressive liberalism can make a progressive five.

In the day-to-day political vernacular, the conversation needs to stress the building of a 'We' society that has our backs, allows us to live purposeful lives that make the world better and that promotes fairness, security and opportunity. The whole point of the 'We' is to help the 'I'. The inspiration has Aristotelian roots. 'Man is by nature a social animal', he wrote; 'Society is something that precedes the individual. Anyone who either cannot lead the common life or is so self-sufficient not to need to, and therefore does not partake of society, is either a beast or a god.' It is that sociability, the urge to live the common life, that makes us want to have a purpose that makes sense to us and those around us.[10]

Hannah Arendt's conception of the interaction between the public and the private to provide a necessary whole is also an useful insight – she stresses the interdependence of the two domains. I and we need the commonality of public space that is publicly owned; it is where citizens interact, and hold each other to account. I need to participate in the civic life of the public square or enjoy a public park. Equally, I cherish privacy, and the possibility it offers for intimacy, which allows me to do what needs to be out of sight – to be unguarded in what I say or do.[11] To stretch Arendt's analogy with the public garden, I may need the intimate privacy of my private garden to express my gardening preferences and solitude, but its pleasures have limits; the scale of the public park allows for the expression of public virtues, and a larger tapestry on which nature can express its beauty. The park helps me value the privacy of my garden, and the constraints of my garden make me value the necessary attributes of the public space. We need both the public and the private.

Or take the passions aroused by football. Loyalty to a football club offers the fan the chance to share the pleasure of watching the game and the club's ups and downs with others in a diverse collective united by the same passion. It a value system created by 'we-the-fans'. It is in tension with the way some owners regard the club as their personal property, from which they seek to maximise profits by, say, relegating or abandoning the demands of the domestic league and joining an enlarged international league – a permanent temptation. The fan is only necessary to the extent that he or she makes the club more valuable. By contrast, in a completely different sphere, the success of the universities of Oxford and Cambridge is built upon the fellowships of their constituent colleges, academics as college trustees working together solidaristically (if not always in harmony) to uphold academic excellence both within their colleges and with the wider university, while permitting maximum scope and support for individual academics to pursue their research interests. It is the alchemy of the 'We' and 'I' again.*

Importantly, this conception of the 'We' society does not

---

* I experienced academic fellowship in action first hand during my wife's long illness and eventual death when I was Principal of Hertford College, Oxford. The fellowship's solidaristic support was a constant source of succour. They had my back.

seek to write individualism out of the script of what constitutes a good, fair society. Human beings, we now know from multiple controlled tests, have an innate sense of proportionality of deserved reward and punishment for whatever good or bad act they perform. Everyone alive has individual agency and can use it for better or worse – the harder I work, the more I deserve to earn; equally, if I do something profoundly culpable, say, stealing from my trusting clients or being violent in private to my close family, the more I deserve greater punishment.[12] This is a common human understanding written into our DNA – to deny agency is to deny humanity. But individual agency is different from building an entire philosophy of individualism in which only the individual pursuing her or his preferences and interests is deemed necessary for the system to work. This curious mammal, write economists Paul Collier and John Kay in *Greed Is Dead*, who is both endlessly greedy and all-knowing, populates the works of mainstream economic theory – when in fact we know that human beings need to cooperate as much as individually and selfishly compete.

A public philosophy based on the notion of a more generously conceived society tries to capture the necessary fusion of individual agency and the need to collaborate and cooperate. It has the potential to exploit the new electoral geography, creating a political coalition between the increasing readiness of the educated to vote progressively and a recaptured mass of voters who are attracted to social cohesion but whose class affiliation has been weakening. These are the people who have been susceptible across the industrialised West to the lure of the populist, anti-immigration right. The French economist Thomas Piketty in *Capital and Ideology* argues that the 'Brahmin' class of educated voters are newly important, because the sectors of today's knowledge economy in which they work are expanding. They tend to be more tolerant, open-minded and readier to accept policies that promote the common interest, whether on environmental or social issues. They are also readier to have sympathy with 'woke' issues – from Black Lives Matter to respecting trans rights. The political problem is that there is a 'Merchant Right' based in the commercial and financial elite who have successfully persuaded a good part of the traditional working class, whose living standards are under pressure, that the Brahmin class is more preoccupied with 'wokery' and tolerance of immigration than it is with working-class values and interests. Hence the appeal of Brexit in many disadvantaged parts of Britain. Remain was a Brahmin cause; if you were working class, you voted Leave to show them your dissatisfaction.

But eight years on from Brexit and two years on from Russia's invasion of Ukraine, sparking a cost-of-living crisis, that alliance of the working class with the most ruthless section of the financial elite is vulnerable. As many as 85 per cent now believe current levels of inequality are a problem.[13] Under the rubric of the 'We Society' it is possible to imagine a different common programme – measures to make capitalism work for the common good, embed more social fairness and start to lift real wages, which are after all at the heart of working-class discontent. A working class that is more atomised, vulnerable and at risk may now be readier to accept it should look left rather than right.

How to Set About Reform

We should be stressing one overarching principle and two sets of reforms. The overarching framing must be an acceptance of public activism; public investment levels must be dramatically increased in both economic and social capital. Innovative new public institutions in the economic and social realms need to be created and existing ones rejuvenated, and there should be tireless persuasion and debate over how to get the balance between the 'We' and the 'I' right. The quest for the correct mix is ceaseless and the answer will vary from sector to sector. Two focal points for reform should then follow: the refashioning of how our capitalism is conceived and practised; and the building of basic precepts of fairness back into our society.

Capitalism must be repurposed around more rounded moral propositions than individualistic acquisitiveness and networks of contract relationships. The existing approach has failed us. Private property, as Tawney, Hobson, Hobhouse, Keynes, Durbin, Bevan and Macmillan all argued in their different ways, must demonstrate that it delivers a social function. If company directors' sole responsibility is understood to be the maximisation of shareholder value, incentivised by extraordinary personal reward, then companies are trapped into decision-making that biases them towards extracting rather than creating value. Capitalist companies must make profit, certainly – but as a consequence of delivering a social purpose or function. Firms driven by a social purpose have a 'north star' that frames their strategy, informs their values and gives a moral underpinning to the way they engage with all their stakeholders – employees, consumers, suppliers and investors alike.[14] This could be the TV and electronics retailer Richer Sounds looking out to treat its customers, employees and suppliers fairly, the energy company Octopus wanting to re-engineer the entire energy sector to lower prices for consumers, private TV companies and contractors committed to public-service broadcasting or giant insurance company Legal and General's commitment to be economically and socially useful. For a future world in which the intangibles of know-how and problem-solving will have ever-higher importance, such commitments are vital. Nor are the gains just instrumental in terms of improved performance, important though those are; if capitalism is to win legitimacy, it must implant a moral gene currently in eclipse.

The obligation to create a framework in which such moral genes can be generally expressed falls necessarily on the state. It will need to create the legal and institutional framework that supports a purposeful capitalism. The state is all we have to act for the 'We'; it cannot excuse itself from its role as the architect of the capitalist regeneration which will put investment and stakeholder dialogue at its heart. It cannot wash its hands of its responsibilities by saying that markets know best, and that the limit of its ambition is merely to set frameworks. Achieving the aim of net-zero carbon emissions – a hugely challenging task – as well as managing the fourth industrial revolution and addressing chronic inequalities between our regions will require massive responses.

Over the next decade, cumulatively an additional £1 trillion has to be found for investment in infrastructure, in skills, in scientific research and development, for levelling up, for working towards net zero, in corner-stoning the public element of the investment system so it supplies risk capital at the scale required. The right targets have to be established, and action coordinated and integrated, so that every key economic actor is facing in the same direction. This is not centralised planning; this is the continual to-and-fro between every stakeholder in a company and government beyond to achieve desired, shared outcomes – 'experimental governance', as it is described by Charles Sabel and David Victor in their study of how successful strategies have emerged to counter climate change.[15]

New sources of taxation will have to be added to those we have. There are six crucial capitals – financial, intangible, human, physical-cum-natural, together with societal and institutional capital – that have to be deepened, aligned and organised so that they intersect with the particularities of cities, regions and business sectors. Purposeful companies reanimating our capitalism have to know that the wider economy is itself purposed and driving towards common goals. The New Liberals and ethical socialists who called for planning in the middle of the last century to coordinate public and private plans were not wrong. It just has to be done smarter, acknowledging decentralised decision-makers, and more effectively.

This necessarily segues into a second enormous reform agenda. It may be that the depths of human suffering experienced during the nineteenth century have receded – slum housing, endemic disease, hunger and ignorance are in retreat. But the market system and excessive individualism of the last forty years have introduced new forms of suffering – mental illness, obesity, opioid abuse, loneliness on an unprecedented scale – while the old sources of suffering are returning in new guises – reliance on food banks, increased homelessness and vulnerability to the risk of new and more violent pandemics after Covid. As in the nineteenth and early twentieth centuries, and reflecting the powerful arguments of Karl Polanyi, human beings will not long tolerate living under a truly free-market system producing such deformities; society strikes back at rank unfairness. The backlash can come from right or left but it will come. The vote for Brexit, with the Leave vote so concentrated in distressed declining former industrial towns and coastal communities, was a vivid wake-up call.

For society cannot be conceived solely as a competitive arena in which individuals and their families struggle, where losers are neglected and forgotten. Yes, there must necessarily be competition. But, equally, there must be recognition that we cannot flourish solely as winners of a succession of individual battles. Aristotle was right. Human beings are social animals; they crave esteem, respect, reciprocity, affection, love and fairness in their treatment from others. Nor can all risks be borne individually; there must be collective social insurance, and public provision of high-quality key services. There cannot be indifference to how we start in life – to be born into wealth and privilege should not mean a free pass without obligations.

The Fairness Foundation, a think tank, suggests that there are five pillars of a just society (full declaration: I chair its editorial advisory board). Every member should fairly enjoy the essentials of life – food, shelter, warmth. Second, everyone should have a fair and equal chance to succeed, regardless of their class, race or gender (as opposed to having a theoretical chance to do so by virtue of not being discriminated against). Third, financial rewards should be proportional to effort and contribution. Fourth, everyone should pay their dues in terms of taxes and respect the law – and if they need support, it should be there for them. And last, everyone should expect equal treatment, equally influencing decisions made in their name.[16] The sharp-eyed will recognise the influence of the political philosopher John Rawls in this list, who codified the prerequisites of a just society to the extent that it followed three principles.[17] It should offer basic civil liberties and genuine equality of opportunity, and any inequality is only justified if everyone can be shown to benefit. Famously, argued Rawls, society can only be deemed just if, not knowing before you were born into what station you would land, you still would not mind – the 'original position' – from behind a veil of ignorance.

Rawls did not object to inequality per se; he accepted that society recognises that hard work from a fair and equal starting position may result in proportionally more wealth accruing to the harder worker than someone less hard-working. What counts is proportionality, so that income and wealth accrue most to those who have obviously earned their rewards and that it all takes place in a social order which conforms as far as possible to his three principles. That cannot be said of Britain today. It must be said of Britain in future.

The Economics and Politics of Hope: The Moment Is Now

So there is a progressive philosophy and programme to hand, based on two great founding ideas: purposeful capitalism and a just society. This can give us the tools to start digging ourselves out of the pit we are in. Britain's glaring inequalities can be turned around. Our capitalism can be made to work for the common good, and to exploit the opportunities of the fourth industrial revolution. Concerted and coordinated efforts must be made to secure plentiful, good and meaningful jobs. Successive policy mistakes and failure heaped on failure have magnified a pervasive sense of hopelessness. But unless there is hope and optimism that tomorrow can be better than today, we will remain mired in aimlessness and a sense of quiet despair. For what future does a business invest or an individual train for? We need a credible vision for the future, which cannot be more of the same.

That vital credibility about a better tomorrow can be earned if expressed as a credible plan, with credible milestones and credible institutions and policies to achieve it. The rise of market fundamentalism has discredited the very notion of a national plan – an attempt to imagine how we make our shared purpose come to life. But it is ever more obvious that, far from intruding into the freedom of personal decision-making, a good plan helps make sense of personal and corporate decisions; it de-risks them, and shows the paybacks and the dangers.

Britain legislated to make the sale of petrol- and diesel-driven cars illegal by 2035 – a deadline that has been deferred for five years. But there is still no credibility to the aspiration if there is no plan to manufacture enough electric cars and build a national network of electrical charging points. Targets for net zero make no sense if there is no plan to insulate our housing stock. What are our manpower needs over the decades ahead – for doctors, carers, teachers? Are they likely to be met, given current pay scales and training numbers? The Infrastructure Commission identifies pinch-points and deficiencies in our national infrastructure, but independently of a shared national goal of what and who we want to be. Stock market leaders are worried that there are too few new companies coming forward to be listed, especially at the technological cutting-edge, and want to organise a revived flow of new enterprises to sustain its international role as a financial centre. But how? Of necessity there are some plans, but they are hotch-potch and scattered. They need to be brought together into a single plan, regularly revisited and upgraded, so that the claims on resources can be identified and budgeted for – with all interested parties making submissions, and mistakes corrected as evidence emerges of what works and what does not.

The right will attack these notions as a return to failed, centralised corporatism. They are wrong. The response should be that there are many existing plans – but that collectively they make no sense, do not add up and make too little difference. Success will need a state that is both more responsive to its citizens' needs and more proactive in delivering them.

There have been calls for constitutional change for more than a century – we know we have too much centralised executive power, along with a crude and unjust first-past-the-post voting system. But now the need to empower cities and towns outside London is an obvious pre-requisite for levelling up, fairness and growth, as is organising a voting system that places less power in the hands of the over-fifty-fives in a fraction of the country's parliamentary constituencies. The institutions and processes of our democracy need curating, too.

Britain cannot afford to waste any more time. Our backs are against the wall. We must lift investment. We must restock and rejuvenate our bank of companies. We cannot allow the inequities between our towns and cities to continue. Too many lives are being wasted. Too much time is invested in the cul-de-sacs of identity politics, stirring up hate for the 'other', and futile culture wars in the absence of a determined national effort to break out of the trap we are in. We must animate and reshape our democracy so that it expresses the common interest. We cannot afford the status quo. In trade unions, trade associations, companies large and small, the professions, finance and the City of London itself, and so many who work in our public services – not to mention tens of million ordinary people – there is a readiness to come together. The time is now.

9

CHANGING GEAR

Britain has been led into a deep economic and social pit. The baleful truth is that the productivity of the vast bulk of the workforce falls short of our principal competitors and is not growing. The pay and living standards of an average worker do not equal those in even the poorest countries of Europe; for example, the disposable income of the median British household fell below Slovenia's in the early 2020s, with the gap set to widen still further.[1]

Productivity is the heart of the matter. Pay and living standards may have jumped fifteen times since the Industrial Revolution only because of productivity growth – but the story ever since 2008, and accentuated by Brexit, is of productivity growth tailing away to virtually nothing. British labour productivity over the twelve years since the financial crisis has grown at half the rate of the twenty-five richest countries.[2] There is no need to look further for the explanation of zero growth in real wages over the 2010s, according to 'Stagnation Nation: The Economy 2030 Inquiry' (compared to average growth of 33 per cent in each of the preceding decades). Parts of the public sector have even witnessed incredible real wage declines since 2010.

Productivity not only triggers higher living standards; it also opens opportunity, frees up a society and generates optimism. People are more tolerant of diversity and immigration as they grow more confident about becoming richer. As the economy grows there are the resources for improved public services; altruism and generosity expand as horizons broaden. When living standards stagnate or decline, most societies regress – the impulse becomes to hold on to what you have. The mood darkens; it is a world of closure and retreat.

Yet there is no productivity growth without investment – and here Britain's record is consistently dreadful. In the forty years to 2019, total fixed investment in the UK averaged 19 per cent of GDP, the lowest in the G7 group of leading economies, reports Stagnation Nation. Over the last twenty years, the proportion has fallen further to 17.1 per cent. During those two decades, total public investment, so vital to catalyse private investment and thus growth more generally, has on average run at two-thirds the rate of our peer nations. Averaging under 2 per cent of GDP since 1979, the rate has more than halved compared to the thirty years after the Second World War.[3]

The cumulative impact shows up in everything from the second lowest number of hospital beds per million in the industrialised world to low levels of public research and development.[4] Business investment also trails behind superficially similar countries. In 2019, it stood at 10 per cent of GDP – well below the average of 13 per cent in France, Germany and the USA. Even in better times business investment grew only at a bleak 2.6 per cent a year in the decade up to the financial crisis. True, within that total there had been growth in investment in 'intangibles', the term to describe everything to do with intellectual 'knowledge work' ranging from IT and R&D to FinTech. Unlike tangible machines and factories, it constitutes intangible ideas and concepts. This has helped produce so many unicorns. The UK boasts the fourth-largest number of $1-billion start-ups – so-called 'unicorns' – in the world.[5] But since Brexit, growth in all forms of business investment – tangibles and intangibles alike – has tailed off, with a halved growth rate of 1.15 per cent. The Institute of Public Policy Research calculates that had Britain maintained its 2005 position as an average G7 investor, cumulatively business investment would have been £354 billion higher by 2021 – and public-sector investment an additional £208 billion. The country, it says, is trapped in an economic 'doom loop'.[6] The recoveries in business investment hoped for by the Office for Budget Responsibility – first after the Brexit referendum vote and later when the shape of hard Brexit emerged – have not appeared.[7] There is, for all practical purposes, an investment strike. As a result, the growth in the capital stock per hour (adjusting for the rising workforce) – a measure of how much kit in the form of machines, computers or whatever a worker has at her or his hand – has slowed dramatically, from around 2.2 per cent per year to 0.2 per cent. This is not the prelude to a jump in productivity.

The incomes of the poorest households are 22 per cent lower than the poorest in France, and 21 per cent lower than in Germany. The figures are even more threatening looked at through a regional lens. The disparities in British productivity and income per head between different regions are among the largest across advanced economies, and widening. Thus London's productivity was 40 per cent above the national average in 2002, but had grown to 50 per cent above it in 2019 (even while growth in financial services slowed following the financial crash), while Powys in Wales and Torbay in Devon were 20 per cent less productive than the average in 2002, but 30 per cent less productive in 2019.[8] According to the National Institute of Economic and Social Research, the disparities in productivity per hour worked have continued to widen between 2019 and 2024.[9]

Where you are born matters hugely to your life chances. Londoners, London hospitals and London schools outperform the rest of the country in terms of incomes, health and educational attainment. The British government's own *Levelling Up* white paper, published in 2022, sets out the devastating differences in incomes, productivity, health and educational attainment across Britain – as devastating in its way as the work done by Charles Booth and Seebohm Rowntree over a hundred years ago.

The inescapable seriousness of the economic position was driven home in 2023 when, in the wake of the Ukrainian war, British inflation stayed higher for longer than in the EU and the USA. The lack of capital stock per worker meant that there was little scope for firms even partially to absorb price increases, which had to be fully passed on to consumers – a weakness that was intensified by Britain having a proportionally larger, inflation-sensitive, service sector and a proportionally smaller manufacturing sector.

It is also more cartelised, in an economic structure that stretches back to the 1930s and was encouraged by prolonged high tariffs for the forty years that followed, and consistently weak competition policy. Even a more competent Bank of England would have been forced into raising interest rates and holding them high for longer than our peers – with calamitous consequences for mortgage costs in an unreformed mortgage market. To reduce inflation to the international average over the next two or three years will require, if not a recession, then depressed growth at or below 1 per cent per year. Productivity, as the Nobel Prize-winning economist Professor Paul Krugman once famously said, 'isn't everything, but in the long run it's almost everything'. It's time for the British to get real about productivity.

Why?

It can and should be so much better. Britain is a broad-based services economy, built on successful musicians and architects as much as bankers and insurers. We are the second-largest exporter of services in the world, in ICT, culture and marketing as well as finance (whose fraction of total exports fell from 12 per cent to 9 per cent in the pre-pandemic decade). To be a service-based economy is not necessarily to be condemned to low growth and low-value-added activities. Brand, trust and interpersonal relations count for more in many service industries and better protect against low-cost competition than in manufacturing, and global demand for services is high and increasing. In manufacturing, the UK's strong sectors tend to be knowledge-intensive, like pharmaceuticals or aerospace. British economic structures do not condemn us to low productivity, low wages and low investment.

And yet the evidence is that low investment is a problem in all these industries. Services may be less capital-intensive than manufacturing, but even so Britain's service-sector companies invest less than their international peers. French workers in manufacturing and services have over 40 per cent more capital than UK workers, enough to account for the whole productivity gap with the UK. The record on some UK intangible investment is better, but even there the UK is not the best in class, and investment growth has fallen away since Brexit. The overall picture remains the same. We don't invest enough.

Nor can refuge be taken in the argument that Britain has an especially long tail of underperforming companies. The gap between the most and least productive firms is certainly huge; a worker in the top 10 per cent of the firm productivity league table is around sixteen times more productive than one in the bottom 10 per cent. But here is the rub. Recent research suggests the gap is just as bad in other countries, nor is it getting significantly worse overall in Britain.[10]

So what is the explanation for our low productivity and its poor growth? The Institute for Government, in the magisterial overview 'Business Investment, Not Just One Big Problem', written by former Number 10 adviser Giles Wilkes, analyses the array of consensus explanations and finds them all wanting. One favourite argument is that investment depends on macroeconomic stability – and Britain cannot be said to have enjoyed much of that. Certainly, the financial crisis and the war in Ukraine have not helped – but other countries' investment rates have experienced the same crises and proved more resilient than Britain's. Over forty years, even in periods of great stability, the Institute finds that UK investment has been mediocre. Nor does it have much truck with the linkage of higher investment with lower business taxes, a Tory obsession; there is little domestic or international evidence that they make a difference. Both Chancellor George Osborne's lowering of UK corporation tax in the 2010s and then his successor Chancellor Rishi Sunak offering a time-limited 'super-deduction', costing £21–£23 billion, failed to move the dial. The Institute dismisses what little research there is that shows an association between business tax cuts and higher investment as 'publication bias' – right-wing researchers and institutes pouncing on such work but disregarding a canon of other research that proves the opposite. Observing that roughly 70 per cent of UK business investment is financed internally, with the rest funded 50/50 from bank finance and sales of shares, cutting interest rates has little effect; in any case, as companies seek real returns on investment of up to 15 per cent per year, changes in interest rates hardly make an impact. Investment peaked in 1988, when interest rates were high, argues the Institute, and hardly budged in the fourteen years when rates were rock-bottom.[11]

Nor does it believe that British business suffers from an inability to access finance – although the report caveats the judgement. As I argue later, the survey evidence used to justify this assessment cannot reveal what the demand for finance might be in a wholly reshaped, rebalanced financial landscape where British finance actively sought to support British business. Business cannot express a demand for what is not there. UK firms, as demonstrated in Chapter 7, have historically relied on internally generated funds – and not external finance – derived for decades from lush profit margins secured by tariffs and cartelisation. Those target rates of real return of 15 per cent remain high by international comparison. Indeed the aggregate returns on British investment are significantly higher than those in France, Germany and the US; but our companies choose to invest less.[12] The shadows of early industrialisation and empire are long.

But a high level of public investment – if it were forthcoming – would be good news both in itself and as a catalyst for private investment, and this is where Britain's record is also poor. The Institute notes that the returns on public infrastructure spending are significant – a 10 per cent increase in the infrastructure stock, for example, raises GDP by 1 to 2 per cent on the government's own estimates. Raising government R&D spending by 1 per cent raises private business R&D by up to 0.7 per cent. Britain needs to get better at public investment, raising its ambitions and sticking to them over time. Even better results could be expected if Britain were able to combine varying public initiatives and interventions into a coherent industrial strategy and benefit from the self-reinforcing nature of investment. The more private investment is crowded in on top of public investment, the less the risk and the higher the pay-off.

Investment is costly and lumpy, and is thus very influenced by long-term expectations of sales and profits – importantly policy-makers need to be trusted as having the institutional and financial capacity to run the economy well, with a permanent eye on reassuring business that demand will be sustainably as high as possible. That trust does not exist. Moreover, investment decision-making is too segmented into silos in Britain, so that too much risk is borne by individual businesses, banks and financiers. Too little effort is made to identify the spill-overs from investing alongside others. Investment is additive; the more businesses that join an investment, the greater the overall demand, the less risk and the higher the returns from the next investment. In the intangible economy, this is especially true. The evidence, for example, is unambiguous that as more firms adopt digital technologies, the greater the critical mass of adopters and users, the greater the speed of take-up and the greater the returns.[13] Investment works best in a systemic relationship between business, finance and government. Britain has no such system.

Attempts to create coordination of investment decision-making that might create such a system are conspicuous by their absence. The Institute for Government report points to one initiative, the Catapult Network launched by Business Secretary Vince Cable in 2011, which in varying sectors successfully continues to convene business, finance and universities to push forward innovations, as almost the only example of an institutional innovation that has been sustained amid a carnage of failure. The general rule is for public-sector investment projects to be uncoordinated, sporadic (for example, the inability to commit to nuclear power generation), scaled back or even abandoned (the zero-carbon homes policy, Tidal Lagoon Swansea Bay project) and scattered. A classic example of the inability to see public investment projects through is the cancellation of both the Leeds and Manchester extensions of HS2, leaving the project as a high-speed shuttle between London and Birmingham. It is only by building the whole network that the great economic and social returns from linking Britain's major conurbations would have been achieved – not by shrinking from the ambition. HS2 could have been in itself a major spur to lifting British economic growth and productivity, and narrowing spatial inequality. There is a consistent failure to follow through with major projects or allow them to gather momentum. If that is true of public investment, be sure private investment will be very likely to follow suit.

Confronting The Past to Embrace The Future

The prerequisite for growth is investment that drives productivity. This is a truism. Britain does not invest sufficiently. But no business invests in a wider economic, social and political vacuum. Nor, indeed, does government. The heart of the right's failure is that it has no plausible story to fill this gaping vacuum – indeed, it has created this entropic space. What does Britain want to become? What purpose is public and private investment serving? The right's vision of Britain's exceptionalism, rooted in lost nineteenth-century glories of free trade, empire and victory in two world wars, is grotesquely out of kilter with what Britain now is, how contemporary capitalism works and what vision might inspire the bulk of our entrepreneurs and people. Yet for the last fourteen years they have defined the national debate, vainly trying to ape the market-fundamentalist revolution Mrs Thatcher began, and in the process trashing one obvious partial solution to the question. Britain should be part of Europe and its economic and political structures. Instead, Conservatism gave us Brexit, the chimera of 'Global Britain' and an attempt to transmute a very European country with social democratic values into a Hayekian utopia. It convinces no one but a shrinking echo chamber of ideological obsessives and cranks.

By contrast, post-war Conservative politicians had lived through the shock of the 1929 financial crash and being forced off the gold standard. They knew how laissez-faire economics, in undermining our productive capacity in the 1930s, had led to the debacle of Dunkirk – an epic defeat, not a victory – as Britain conserved its then inadequate airpower for the desperate Battle of Britain that was to come. They had had to accept decolonisation and the end of empire as inevitable. The majority of the party, its members, its donors and its media would have then known that pretensions to strut the world stage as 'Global Britain' would have been ludicrous. It was Prime Minister Harold Macmillan, who had served in the First World War and was author of *The Middle Way*, clear-eyed about British realities (and backed by his party), who made Britain's first – if unsuccessful – application to join the Common Market. There would be little or no criticism of Harold Wilson for standing aside from the Vietnam War. They knew the future lay in making common cause with Europe – joining the Common Market (as it then was) was more of a Conservative than Labour cause.

In fact, the Common Market, morphing into the EU, did answer the question of national direction, even if at the time the case was made more in terms of economic benefits than addressing the existential question of Britain's national purpose. That was implied rather than openly argued. The beast of looking backward to past glories remained un-slayed, with consequences with which we live today. Yet the economic benefits were real enough. The launch of the single market on 1 January 1993 had a particularly stimulating impact on the UK, which became an increasingly attractive destination for multinational investors – full access to a European market of 450 million but from a comparatively low-cost base and 'flexible' labour market, with the least demanding contractual requirements of any workforces in the EU. The UK car industry was reinvented, for example, around European and Japanese car manufacturers investing in order to export to the EU, with car production peaking at 1.75 million in 2016. Financial services also boomed, with the City of London becoming Europe's financial centre. By the eve of the financial crisis, British investment levels equalled the G7 average; the productivity gap between the UK and France and Germany had narrowed to 6 per cent. British household incomes were actually higher than in both of those countries.

Britain was becoming a fully fledged European economy, increasingly integrated into EU supply chains, and benefiting from its role as the service-sector champion of Europe. London in particular was becoming the New York of Europe – not only its de facto financial but also its services capital. Professor Nick Crafts, it is worth recalling, estimated that membership lifted British GDP between 8 and 10 per cent higher than it would otherwise have been. Not enough had been done to ensure that the prosperity was shared around the country, although the European Investment Bank was lending aggressively in Britain's poorer regions. The UK's deep problems – the corporate governance regime, the structure of the financial system, the propensity to create monopoly, the poor quality of so much training – were masked. But no leading politician, few commentators and only a handful of businesses spoke up for the EU as a driver of the new prosperity – let alone how central it was to Britain's destiny.

Then the financial crisis, most acute in the UK, with its overlarge and overleveraged financial sector, rocked the economy with a shock that was then multiplied by Brexit. The UK's productivity deficit with France and Germany has almost tripled since 2008, from 6 per cent to 16 per cent – equivalent to £3,700 in lost output per person. Typical household incomes are now 16 per cent lower in the UK than in Germany, and 9 per cent lower than in France. Brexit has lowered investment by between 11 and 13 per cent, according to the Institute for Government. Automobile production fell by 1 million to 775,000 in 2022, of which 57 per cent is exported to the EU, recovering a little in 2023 but still far short of the 2016 production peak. The LSE/Resolution Foundation show that the collapse of trade openness following Brexit will mean a 24 per cent fall in UK exports by 2030 compared to what they would have been had we remained an EU member.[14] The City of London is suffering accelerating decline. Had Britain remained in the EU, by 2030 we would have been an economy co-equal, if very different, to Germany's. As it stands, the post-Brexit decade will be a lost decade. It is a tragedy.

To turn the economy around demands above all an intellectual and cultural readjustment – an honest recognition of what Britain can reasonably be, and agreeing to claim exceptionalism only when it is earned. Vainglorious boasting about being 'world-beating' or 'world-class' in almost every sphere, however extravagantly at variance with the truth, imagining that past imperial glories can be reinvented, posturing as buccaneering 'Global Britain', invoking special and largely fantastical notions of our indigenous entrepreneurial prowess, dismissing the European Union as an economic corpse – all this has to be derided and buried. Britain has to be more knowing and honest about its past, then reckon with its present before it can build a renewed future.

Take the empire. Maritime Western European powers – Portugal, Spain, France and the Netherlands all built great overseas empires. Britain's was the biggest, certainly, but it was part of a larger European story of overseas expansion. European explorers and seamen opened up the world of which the British were part, helped by our geographical standing as an enormous offshore European island. Magellan circumnavigated the globe fifty years before Drake. Amerigo Vespucci discovered the New World. Abel Tasman discovered Tasmania and New Zealand a century before James Cook. Jacques Cartier and Samuel de Champlain opened up Canada.

Nor was the British empire genial, liberal and generous, as some wild-eyed conservative historians have claimed. We may have left India a national railway system; little is said about the crucial role that monumental British trade surpluses with India for the fifty years up to the First World War, throttling its textile industry in order to control its gold, had in sustaining sterling on the gold standard. Nor, to take one example from everyday life, that on long-distance journeys travelling conditions in third class for native Indians were so overcrowded that passenger deaths were not unusual. Like other European powers, Britain's overseas expansion was exploitative, extractive and racist. If Portugal pioneered the transatlantic slave trade from Africa to Brazil, after the middle of the seventeenth century the British overtook it to became Europe's leading slave trader. Bristol and Liverpool rose to prosperity on the proceeds of slavery. Nantes, Europe's third great slave port, memorialised its apology for the victims of slavery in 2012. Gradually, and too often against right-wing resistance, Britain is making similar, if belated, steps. Liverpool now has a slavery museum. In June 2020, the statue of Bristol slave trader Edward Colston was toppled into the harbour in a public protest; it now is no longer on public display but part of Bristol Museum, at the express wish of the majority of Bristolians. Tate Britain has recently rehung its paintings, carefully describing their associations with empire and slavery. The National Trust in 2020 set out its approach to colonialism and slavery, identifying some ninety properties in its charge that had such links. Typically, the Common Sense Group of twenty-six Tory MPs and two peers attacked it for cultural Marxism, wokery and for even daring to drag Chartwell – Winston Churchill's home – into its denigration of our past.

This is no denigration. It is an essential part of the necessary acknowledgement of the realities of empire, and its deep and continuing impact on our culture and institutions. The Lancashire cotton industry was built on cheap imported cotton from the slave plantations of the American South, and re-exports of textiles were part of the Atlantic slave economy. Our financial system, only today beginning to engage with its domestic hinterland, owes its internationalism and, until recently, essentially extractive approach to finance to the experience of empire. If Britain is to become what it can be – a progressive, front-rank European power with a vigorous economy and fair society, committed to European peace and the achievement of net zero – it can no longer be trapped by its past. It must strike out anew – and every museum, art gallery, public protest, public commemoration, history course or book that pushes back against the deadweight legacy of a jingoist interpretation of our history is helping to embrace the future.

This is not 'unpicking our history', as Prime Minister Rishi Sunak told the House of Commons in April 2023, when pressed to apologise over slavery; it is looking at it in the eye to keep our feet squarely on the ground. It means looking at the worst, but also honouring the best, in our past – whether being the first European country to abolish the slave trade within its empire in 1807, or the extraordinary worldwide impact our great poets, writers and dramatists have had through their mastery of the written word. We build a future not by inventing a fantasy la-la land of yesteryear, but by rooting ourselves in shared truths.

The Mission

The aim must be to create an environmentally sustainable, high-productivity Britain that is less unequal, fairer and economically dynamic, and which, while global in its reach, is firmly anchored in its own continent. That is what Britain must invest for – a 'We Society' around which the private and public sectors can coalesce.

But the price tag is big. The Climate Change Committee calculates that achieving net zero by 2050 will require spending £50 billion a year from the late 2020s onwards largely on transport, housing and renewables – cumulatively, a cost of over £1 trillion. The *Levelling Up* white paper for its part says that its twelve aims (including raising productivity, spreading increased R&D spending around Britain more fairly, making sure that public transport and digital connectivity is as good in our regional cities as in London and radically improving health, housing and education) will cost another £50 billion a year. At the end of twenty years each British region would then have a globally competitive city as a magnet for growth. But that means £1 trillion will have to be found to meet such ambitious targets. The current £2.5 trillion of national debt already equals British GDP, which as the Office for Budget Responsibility warns has risen threefold since 2000.[15] The bill for these two mammoth national investment projects – a cool £2 trillion – will nearly double it again over twenty years, although national output will rise too. The National Infrastructure Commission, set up in 2017 to attempt to build a national consensus about our infrastructure needs, endorses the needs in its detailed 2023 National Infrastructure Assessment. Britain, it says, could afford and had the will to build a strategic electric 'supergrid' in the 1950s and a strategic road network in the 1960s and 1970s. Now it must have the bravery and gumption to do the same to meet today's strategic challenges.[16] It is essential for economic growth.

For can Britain afford not to drive to net zero and to continue to tolerate growing regional inequality? The Climate Change Committee argues that the cumulative savings will exceed the costs around the middle of the 2040s. The *Levelling Up* white paper argues that if worker productivity in the bottom quarter of every part of the UK could be lifted to the median, the boost to productivity would be £2,300 per worker – worth £50 billion a year. If Britain could pull off these twin feats, the ratio of national debt to output might rise, but containably – because GDP would be very much higher and the net-zero commitment would have paid for itself.

And there would be a crowding-in effect. Former MP Chris Skidmore, once a co-author of the free-market libertarian tract *Britannia Unchained*, was commissioned by his fellow author Liz Truss – when she was briefly prime minister – to assess how to achieve net zero. His 2023 independent review – 'Mission Zero' – is a wholesale repudiation of the neoliberal worldview in which public investment 'crowded out' private investment. He was reflecting the views of the many businesses to which he spoke. Echoing the Climate Change Committee, he calls for a massive twenty-year programme of public infrastructure investment – in solar, the grid, onshore wind, nuclear, industrial decarbonisation, raising recycling capacity and recasting of the housing stock's energy efficiency. But, crucially, he argues that public investment will crowd in opportunity for British business; achieving net zero will be the 'business growth opportunity of the twenty-first century' – a potential £1-trillion global market up to 2030 alone.

To delay is to damage the planet, incur further climate change costs and forego potential growth and tax revenues; the report estimates that a decade-long deferral of action will lift the national debt by 27 per cent of GDP. The faster we move, the quicker we drive costs down – and compete with the EU, the USA and China. But it is crucial, he argues, that the effort is credible, sustained and that it commands cross-party support; the private sector, if it is to invest at scale, will want to see a clear road map, a believable funding plan and a coherent strategy. To achieve that, he proposed that an Office for Net Zero Delivery should be established. All this was to be in place by the end of 2023, Skidmore recommended.

Fat chance. Skidmore's sense of urgency and his proposed mechanisms are correct – and proof of a remarkable personal conversion. But today's Conservative Party is too divided to heed the message. Reflecting right-wing US Republican views that coordinated collective action to combat climate change is backdoor 'socialism', a powerful strand on the Tory right and in the media echoes their views. Prime Minister Sunak, anxious to keep the temperature down in a brutally divided party, kept the government's responses to Skidmore's more-than-a-hundred recommendations as low-key, inexpensive and minimalist as possible. In September 2023, Sunak went further, directly contradicting any urgency by diluting and deferring the government's existing commitments, notably deferring the ban on the sale of diesel and petrol cars to 2035 and delaying the ban on gas boiler sales. What triggered Skidmore's resignation as a Tory MP in January 2024 was a further retreat by Sunak: a bill to mandate regular annual auctions of oil and gas licences – going against the recommendation of the Intergovernmental Panel of Climate Change. Skidmore explained he could no longer condone or support an action he knew to be wrong.

These were especially important because together these are significant retrograde steps. Transport and housing emissions are two areas where the UK most needs action if it is to have any hope of meeting net zero by 2050. The Climate Change Committee had warned in its 2023 Progress Report that its confidence in the carbon targets being met had declined 'markedly';[17] now, there is little or no chance of meeting them. The 2037 interim target was already virtually impossible to meet, and too much of the rest depends on hoped-for technological breakthroughs. Sunak had never made achieving net zero one of his five pledges, even though he pays lip service to it being a growth opportunity. Given that so much investment, especially in the car industry and its supply chain, had been predicated on cross-party commitment to net zero, his protestations that the decision was driven by pragmatism and not politics were wholly spurious. After the Uxbridge by-election in July 2023, narrowly won by the Conservatives partly because of a reaction to the constituency becoming part of London's Low Emission Zone, there might even be votes in being climate-change-sceptic, dressed up as 'pragmatism'. It dramatises the short-termism and expediency that governs British public investment decisions. There will be no change in environmental infrastructure spending on the scale necessary under Sunak's government – it would offend the Tory right's sensibilities. Better, literally, to risk keeping the economy fossilised.

It echoes the approach to levelling up. The fact that Boris Johnson set so much store by this policy is another sign of the waning of the neoliberal order. Decades of low public investment have left the stock of British physical infrastructure at the low end of the international league table, with Britain's regions particularly neglected. In 2019, the Office of National Statistics estimated that the UK's infrastructure stock stood at 47 per cent of GDP, compared to France's 54 per cent and Italy's 52 per cent.[18] Spending on roads between 1995 and 2020 was among the lowest of any industrialised economy, annually running at a mere 0.3 per cent of GDP.[19] The British motorway network is underdeveloped, causing more hours of delay than any other country except Germany.[20]

Investment in rail has been higher, but heavily biased towards London, where over the last twenty years it has run at twice the level of regions outside the South-East.[21] International comparisons show just how dismal public transport is for much of the country; the number of people in British cities that can reach their city centre within thirty minutes is 23 per cent lower than the average in Western Europe. Whether by car or by rail, a research paper by the Kennedy School at Harvard notes that compared to the USA or Western Europe, British commuting is more time-consuming – which limits the 'effective size' of cities and weakens their capacity to come together dynamically.

There is little embedded resilience in British infrastructure, and it has too many pinch-points. The dreadful punctuality of our railways is legendary. The problems extend to energy. The lack of investment in gas storage capacity was cruelly revealed as gas prices soared in the wake of Russia's invasion of Ukraine – Britain had the lowest reserves in relation to consumption in Europe.[22] The approach to infrastructure has been one of penny-pinching, of underestimating demand, of undervaluing resilience. We are generally behind the curve. At a minimum, says the National Infrastructure Commission, the run rate of public infrastructure investment needs to rise from some £20 billion to £30 billion a year until 2040. And private-sector investment needs to rise in tandem by the same proportion to £40–£50 billion a year over the same period. The necessity cannot be denied.[23]

The *Levelling Up* white paper endorsed all this – along with addressing lower life expectancy, poor training and lack of social mobility. But again the Conservative government could not rise to the challenge – even though the then Prime Minister Boris Johnson recognised the need, and indeed had won over forty 'Red Wall' seats in the December 2019 general election, partly on the promise that along with getting Brexit done he would act on levelling up. Those who worked on the white paper told me off the record and privately that Rishi Sunak, then the chancellor, simply blocked any new spending commitments, however important – and, although the paper called for an end to the system in which local governments are forced competitively to bid against each other for limited funds in varying funding pots, to be replaced by a fair and comprehensive system, Sunak stuck to the existing processes. They allow the party in government to divert funds for what it imagines is maximum political impact – to Tory marginal seats – even if in economic development terms such spending works against creating multiplier effects, let alone targeting need.

The New Towns Fund, established in 2019 to help left-behind towns address structural disadvantages, is an egregious example. Professor Chris Hanretty of Royal Holloway University, surveying 101 towns selected for New Towns funds from a long list of 541 since 2019, found an enormous bias in favour of Tory-held constituencies, with the chance of a Tory-held marginal being allocated funds a full forty-five points higher. The rules used by civil servants were not based on objective levelling-up criteria, but were palpably 'adventitious' so as to retain the discretion for funds to be allocated on political grounds. It was pure pork-barrel politics. Hanretty called for a prime ministerial formal investigation, in particular into two 'levelling-up' ministers, Robert Jenrick and Jake Berry.[24] It was later learned that both ministers had directed Towns Fund monies to their own constituencies, with Jenrick's Newark only the 270th most deprived in the country.[25] Needless to say, no investigation has been undertaken. But the scandal dramatises the need for profound constitutional and institutional change.

Pulling Off Big Ambitions

Sustained public investment on the scale required over twenty years is something the UK has never done. It was complacently assumed that the country's great power status and ongoing economic strength guaranteed there was little need. Markets would provide. Now, after Brexit has accentuated every adverse trend, the UK has its back against the wall; the need has become pressing and urgent. The prize would be huge and would transform the country. Success would boost productivity and raise living standards, creating a tax base for otherwise unaffordable public services, increase resilience in the face of shocks and make every part of our island a more congenial, sustainable place to live and work. The political philosophy I've outlined in this book is a crucial enabler – feeding the will to act and encouraging both the intellectual case and finding the means.

First, it is clear that, however it is framed, this strategy requires an acceptance of a vastly scaled-up role for fiscal policy – and in particular a rejection of the deep Conservative conviction that public spending and borrowing are a priori bad and that tax cuts are a priori good. There is a role for tax incentives in driving forward business investment in R&D, innovation and sustainable business models – but clean public transport, expanded electricity grids, networks of electricity charging points, refitted housing, digital connectivity and all the rest are infrastructure projects that need subsidies, grants, guarantees and public spending. Although that is incontrovertible, Britain can be much smarter with how it uses its public balance sheet to promote investment. For example, the recently created UK Infrastructure Bank (UKIB), wholly owned by the state, has £22 billion of notional financial capacity to lend; but crucially, only a risk capital buffer of a mere £4.5 billion needs be 'scored' as public spending. Much of the balance of that financial capacity comes in the form of a 'Sovereign Infrastructure Guarantee' to the loans of private sector banks to fund infrastructure projects. Every one pound of 'scored' risk capital thus buys more than four times the amount of 'guaranteed' private sector lending.

Boosting UKIB's risk capital would thus vastly scale up its guaranteeing capacity to achieve the levels of infrastructure spending needed to drive levelling up and the path to net zero – and must all be part of a reframing of fiscal policy. Plainly, there should be fiscal rules, but the current rules which set artificial limits for national debt in relation to national income are intellectually absurd. They take no account of the growing need for what economists call 'public goods' as economies grow richer and more sophisticated and which underwrite our economy and society; citizens expect that hospitals, schools, policing, universities, cyber and pandemic defences should be state-of-the-art – not trapped in decades-old technology because of artificial prohibitions on debt-to-income ratios.

Spending on public goods will thus tend to rise over time, and so will national debt. This is natural and should be permitted. As Andy Haldane, former chief economist of the Bank of England, has argued, liabilities on the national balance sheet should be assessed alongside the creation of these public-good assets. At the moment non-financial assets, whether tangible (roads, schools, ports, hospitals) or intangible (data, intellectual property, code), are not included. The focus is wholly on debt and liabilities with no counterbalancing assessment of assets. But national accounting must be able to record the wealth and resilience of the nation.[26] Alarm bells should already be ringing: Britain's public net worth has been declining for more than forty years, went negative around the financial crisis in 2007/8 and is now – including liabilities for unfunded public sector pension funds – seriously negative at some 100 per cent of GDP. Only Portugal scores worse. This is unsustainable and needs to be reversed.[27] What really matters to sustain financial market confidence is knowledge that the country to whom the markets are lending has public assets growing faster than its liabilities, coupled with a level of public debt that can be reliably serviced from a secure and growing tax base. The greater the growth rate, the more buoyant potential tax revenues – a reality that financial markets recognise. The fiscal rules on which to focus are thus the public balance sheet's overall net worth, the affordability of debt service in relation to tax revenues and current public spending, and credible forecasts that reasonable growth will be sustained.

Second, it must be accepted honestly that in today's circumstances, the only prospect of achieving tax cuts is by stifling public investment and degrading public services, which will more than offset any small economic stimulus tax cuts might provide. Public investment, finds the IMF, is significantly more stimulatory than tax cuts.[28] Strategically the necessity is thus the opposite to tax cuts. Taxes, given the condition of Britain's public finances in 2024 and our dependence on the kindness of strangers to hold sterling and buy our debt, will first have to rise to play their part in financing much-needed public investment and avoid more damaging austerity hitting public services already in crisis. This does not mean tax increases must shoulder the entire burden of financing the investment stimulus; public borrowing can rise, but only to the extent it adds to public sector net worth and is supported by projected tax revenue growth to service it. To ensure that public investment will leverage more private investment and so lift economic growth as much as possible, careful attention has to be given to both our institutional 'plumbing' and where the public investment is directed. The less indebted companies are and the more they have access to plentiful loans and equity, the more they will invest – thus the importance of the reshaping of the financial system proposed in the next chapter. Macro-economic policy also has to be got right – but it needs to be reinforced with smart micro-economic policy.

The more public investment is directed to areas like health-care, transport and housing (both with strong environmental impact), the greater the multiplier, or in plainer English, ricochet effects. Only once growth has been firmly lifted from today's abysmal levels is there any hope of reducing the tax take. Put bluntly tax receipts may have to rise by between one to two per cent of GDP above current levels to achieve growth, and may have to stay there for a prolonged period before there is any prospect of their proportional reduction. The brutal truth is that unless there is a sharp acceleration of growth, given the intense demand for public goods – health, education, transport, care, justice – which all require more public investment, tax receipts will have to stay at current levels or higher. Nearly a hundred years ago, US Supreme Court judge Oliver Wendell Holmes, Jnr famously declared that taxes are the price paid for a civilised society; that is even more true today. Taxes buy vital public goods that richer societies prize even more, are capable of affording and underpin vital public investment. Taxation should be not be demonised as a coercive burden; it pays for what we hold in common, so enlarges the scope of our lives and our capacity to exercise our freedoms.

The proposition that the tax take is already excessively high and that if it was lower it would stimulate growth is demonstrably false. According to IMF figures, Britain's tax revenues as a proportion of GDP were lower than most other EU countries and Canada in 2006, and remained lower in 2022 – yet the growth rate of almost all of these comparable countries has been higher.[29] Part of the reason is that taxes are not very influential in business investment decisions, as we have seen; the other reason is that the UK tax system is exceptionally poorly designed, full of loopholes and perverse incentives, and politicians shy away from rationality, so that economically efficient tax-raising often does not happen. Because, for example, the residential values for council tax have not been raised since 1991, stamp duty has increased to punitive levels to compensate for the shortfall – deterring people from moving house and downsizing. Fuel duty has not been increased for fifteen years. Corporation tax, still not high by international standards, has little or no impact on business investment – except if business can completely and clearly offset investment spending against corporation tax. This, now government policy, is likely to have some impact on investment, but it is small.

There are plenty of rich pickings to be had. The proportion of revenue raised from wealth, now more than seven times national income compared to three times forty years ago, is unchanged.[30]

Council tax must be reformed and replaced (as I'll discuss in Chapter 12); gift and inheritance tax reshaped and raised, and pension fund tax breaks for higher earners (worth annually some £21 billion) must be removed. There is more beyond that – substituting fuel duties with a mileage tax so that electrically powered cars pay tax along with petrol and diesel cars; reducing the scope for tax avoidance; lifting some VAT exemptions; scaling back relief on corporate debt interest payments; and raising environmental taxes. With more resources, the think-tank Tax Watch argue that HMRC could go significantly further in closing the estimated £35.8 billion annual 'tax gap' – the gap between what should and what is being collected.[31] Altogether estimates of the potential increased tax revenue range up to £50 billion, or 2 per cent of GDP.[32] Britain is more than rich enough to finance its economic and social rejuvenation. It just has to want it enough.

There is also a case for creating a sovereign wealth fund from earmarking a proportion of oil revenues from any new oil and gas field production (as in Norway and Alaska), so that over time the returns from the investments it makes can be used to support key public spending priorities – or even pay out a citizens' dividend as James Meade proposed (see Chapter 8). It would be some compensation for continuing oil and gas exploration and production – forty years late, but better late than never. The public fund would work closely with the proposed private wealth fund, backstopping risk and stepping in to provide liquidity – all part of organising Britain's financial plumbing to stimulate growth. The Bank of England, custodian of the monetary and financial system, should adopt a twin responsibility: not only for hitting a pre-agreed inflation target but also supporting growth and employment. With this twin mandate and targeting inflation in a range of 1 to 3 per cent (rather than the current rigid 2 per cent), monetary policy would be better adapted to support economic growth.

Finally, the machinery of government needs a root-and-branch overhaul. Coordination and integration of decision-making are imperatives when public spending is on this scale, as is the capacity to change course and adjust as circumstances change and new information comes to light. Above all, there cannot be continual stopping and starting; these are plans for a span of twenty years. Treasury concerns to secure value for money will certainly be important, but its culture is endemically hostile to sustained long-term public investment. It is a powerful finance ministry suspicious of capital investment – not an investment and growth ministry. I suggest in Chapter 13 that it should be divided into an Office of the Budget and Economic Strategy Ministry; it has been palsying Britain for too long. There needs to be a new institutional mechanism – for example, a Growth Council – with powers established by statute that brings together the Treasury in its new guise, the Bank of England, the Climate Change Committee and the Departments of Communities and Levelling Up, Business and Education on equal terms. It will be particularly important to identify projects that advance both the net-zero and levelling-up agendas – for example, in public transport, energy, housing and R&D. The Treasury should not be able to exercise an automatic veto; hence the case for its division. The government should be obliged at the beginning of every parliament to publish an Investment Act (as suggested by the Resolution Foundation's *Ending Stagnation Report*) setting out framework targets and milestones for public investment, and should be regularly held to account for meeting them by a joint committee of both the Commons and Lords. If Britain is to succeed in delivering big ambitions, every institution and mechanism will have to be enlisted in the task. The alternative is too dire to allow for failure. The next step is to enlist – and transform – the private sector.

10

THE BREAK OUT

An audacious public investment programme is vital in its own right, but to work fully, by leveraging more private investment, the opportunity must be taken to reshape British business and finance for the better, which is today a mix of the good, the monopolised bad and the over-financialised ugly. The government will want trusted contractors and partners to deliver its goals, and new business models will inevitably be invented as these new projects come into being. A financial system that has never put its muscle behind the British economy must be induced to do so.

British capitalism certainly needs to change. The laissez-faire tradition in Britain runs very deep; recall its grip on nineteenth-century politics and business, and how even Ramsay MacDonald's Labour Party wanted to hang on to the gold standard, free trade and balanced budgets in that desperate summer of 1931. It then prevented Britain from adopting New Deal-type interventions in the 1930s, and although submerged by the post-war settlement, laissez-faire was disastrously revived by Mrs Thatcher. As Britain changes gear to become a developmental state – more like an emergent than a developed economy – what is obvious is that the legacy of laissez-faire leaves it very few public agencies to do the job. The British Business Bank has little power to lend independently on the scale necessary; the UK Infrastructure Bank is small and undercapitalised. Apart from the Pension Protection Fund and NEST (the National Employment Savings Trust) there are no public agencies in the savings and investment sector. All have to be scaled up and new institutions invented to join their ranks.

It's also clear that British business needs a makeover in its culture, corporate governance and ownership. Ownership is typically highly dispersed; very few companies can point to four or five shareholders who together account for between a quarter and a third of the equity – and this kind of committed shareholding is crucial as a platform for investment and innovation. Company law is still built around a primitive view of property; shareholder property rights reign supreme. This is wrong. Great companies have to bind together all their stakeholders in a common enterprise. And the job of a company cannot be simple profit maximisation; complex trade-offs have to be acknowledged and delivered.

One of the great myths of the market-fundamentalist era was the axiom that risk-taking private business must not be interfered with by government; business, it was alleged, is crowded out and constrained by too much public activity. It was a complete inversion of reality. Business carefully assesses risk, and is willing to assume it if the likely payback is high, but its central preference is for managing risks and trading them off with lower but more certain returns. In this sense business is less a profit-maximiser than a profit-'satisficer' ('finding satisfactory solutions for a more realistic world', in the words of the term's inventor[1]) – it needs enough profit given the risk rather than a maximum profit which might put the organisation in peril. Partnering with the state or accepting the myriad means by which the state can mitigate risk – from tax breaks to grants and subsidies and including the creation of market franchises – are crucial to private-sector business models. Almost every leading company has had its business model supported one way or another by public agency. And every firm knows that recurrent orders for whatever good or service depend on delivering a useful social purpose. These are truths that the best in business and finance know, but they have to genuflect to a right-wing culture that tries to deny them.

All of these deformations have been made worse by the extraordinary financialisaton of the non-financial economy in the years before 2008 – the hangover remains with us still. The mantra was that the purpose of all business was the maximisation of shareholder value, so prioritising financial metrics: artificial financial engineering schemes involving extraordinary levels of debt or trying to build monopoly market positions through takeover, were the order of the day. In the financial sector, financialisaton took the form of making money from money rather than engaging with the real economy, of which the global financial derivatives market was one astonishing manifestation – now worth notionally over $600 trillion on some estimates.[2] The purpose of derivatives is to lay off risk and boost returns, but, as we learned in 2007/8, the system cannot insure against systemic risk. Leverage ratios of 50:1 have consequences. There is an extensive economic literature that acknowledges the crucial role a good financial system can play in driving growth, but warns that if it grows too large it can suck talent and resources from the rest of the economy without adding much social value in return. Lord Adair Turner, ex-chair of the Financial Conduct Authority, famously described much of this activity as socially useless, while the president of the American Finance Association, Luigi Zingales, said in his 2015 presidential address: 'there is no theoretical reason or empirical evidence to support the notion that all the growth of the financial sector in the last forty years has been beneficial to society'.[3] Today, US National Security Adviser Jake Sullivan admits that allowing the financial sector to grow so large, so weakly regulated and so globalised was a mistake.

What financialisaton in general and the derivatives markets in particular have undoubtedly done is enormously boost the profitability of the financial sector, inflating bankers' bonuses which have then become the pace-setting benchmarks for all directors' pay. Since 2008, there has been closer scrutiny of chief executive pay, both because of its dismaying size – often 100 times more than the salary of a median worker – and its imperviousness to poor performance. As a result, ratios have stabilised, but still at a very high level.

The moment has come for a reset. Financialisaton to achieve profit must become secondary to genuine value creation. The entire structure must be organised to ensure that flows of credit and equity go where they will support the national necessity of boosting growth. Smarter regulation, new public investment agencies, the repurposing of existing ones along with the reorganisation of our insurance and pension system will all be part of the story.

British banks hold some £3 trillion of financial derivatives, £2 trillion of loans to households (the vast bulk of that in mortgages) and around £500 billion of loans to business, of which around a third is to small and medium-sized business.[4] This does not suggest that supporting British business is high on the banks' list of priorities – but in fairness, the ranking is better than it was ten years ago. Then, the banking system held an amazing £5 trillion of derivatives. In terms of savings and investment, British pension funds and insurance companies again show less-than-overwhelming interest in supporting British business. In 2000, over 50 per cent of pension fund assets were held in British shares; now, it is a meagre 4 per cent.[5] Meanwhile, 60 per cent of their assets are held in fixed-income securities, up from 15 per cent in 2000 – again, the highest and most risk-averse in the world. Their returns to savers are indifferent – but then only 7 per cent of their investments are in high-return assets (property, infrastructure, start-ups, venture capital and private equity), compared to an international average of 19 per cent.

This risk aversion is embedded in the structure of our pension funds in particular: 5,800 so-called defined-benefit (DB) pension funds, worth £1.5 trillion in aggregate, which guarantee that the ultimate pension is keyed into people's final salaries, and over 27,000 tiny defined-contribution (DC) pension funds, worth in aggregate £650 billion, which will pay out a pension from the pension pot the individual has saved for over their life. These provide no guarantees on the size of the final pension. In addition, savers have accumulated £850 billion in Self-Invested Pension Plans (SIPPs), and there is the rapidly growing but still small £20-billon National Employment Savings Trust. All contributions to pensions attract tax relief up to certain limits, and Britain is fortunate that 57 per cent of adults below retirement age save for retirement even if their contribution rates need to be higher – an imperative, given that the state pension is so inadequate. Such is a snapshot of the British banking, saving and investment system in the middle of the third decade of the twenty-first century – hardly capable of supporting existing economic structures, let alone an ambitious programme of national economic development.

Reinventing British Banking

Let us start with banking. Lending is a power relationship. Any individual borrower must accept the terms – the rate of interest, the collateral required, the length of loan term and how onerous the terms will be if for any reason the borrower is struggling to repay. When times are good, the lender loses power and relaxes those terms to win business; when times are fearful, the opposite is the case. In both cases the upswing and downswing are hugely amplified. Here the state cannot stand idly by. Roosevelt recast the US banking system in the 1930s to protect against the risk of a similar devastating credit crunch in the future. After the most recent financial crisis the UK, which was disproportionately badly hit by its banking system's excesses, some of the toughest rules in Western banking were correctly established.

Three reforms are essential, building on a necessary partnership between government and finance better to manage risk. First, the Prudential Regulatory Authority should be much more proactive about the risk weightings it requires banks to attach to categories of lending, and thus the amount of their own equity capital they are required to set aside in their balance sheet. As matters stand, there is too much emphasis on the risk to the individual bank of any particular loan, and too little emphasis on societal risk and potential societal advantage. Mortgage lending attracts too low a risk weighting because property is deemed 'good' collateral; the costs to society of excess mortgage credit bidding up house prices is not factored into the weighting.

Lending to small and medium-sized enterprises (SMEs) requires proportionally more capital, with regulators (overseen by negligent government) making little judgement about the societal rewards from stimulating lending to create a vibrant British *Mittelstand* – the SMEs that form the backbone of the

German economy. To support this flexibility and give regulators confidence in encouraging vital but allegedly risky lending for any one bank, we should borrow from the model of Roosevelt's New Deal, which set up specialist and refinancing banks to backstop mortgage and commercial lenders, providing liquidity if needed.

'Fannie Mae' and 'Freddie Mac' protect the US mortgage market, standing behind lenders, ready to buy packages of mortgages as need be. The USA today enjoys a mortgage market where twenty-five-year fixed-rate mortgages are widely available as a result – very different to Britain's Wild West, where the rule is generally two-year fixed-rate mortgages, exposing buyers to the vagaries of violent short-term interest rate changes. The Reconstruction Finance Corporation (which was discontinued in 1957, under Eisenhower), rather like the German Kreditanstalt für Wiederaufbau, had successfully backstopped American industrial lending for a generation. The UK had a smaller version of a similar scheme, the Industrial and Commercial Finance Corporation, created after the Second World War, but it was allowed to morph into 3i and ultimately (and inevitably) was privatised. The directors got a great windfall; Britain lost a key public financial agency. We now need to build an institutional framework of this type but also to make it highly decentralised to support house-buyers, SMEs and start-ups, and bringing decision-making as close as possible to the borrower. Banks are being permitted far too much latitude in closing down their branch networks and stripping out the middle-management layer who held relationships with borrowers, replacing that with arbitrary, automated AI-driven processes whose decisions cannot be appealed. To speak to a human being about your financial needs is becoming close to impossible, involving time-consuming waits and navigating automated AI telephone answering systems. This does not need to be how banking is done – but customers' complaints are insufficient. Equally, business surveys that show little dissatisfaction with the availability of finance merely capture the existing power relationship and terms of business; a world in which banks build strong relationships with customers along with plentiful long-term loans is unimaginable in the present scheme of things.

Second, both the assets and liabilities of banks are too inflexible, particularly if things go wrong – borrowers threatening to default on their debts (their liability but the banks' asset) or a bank being unable to honour borrowing it has undertaken on its own behalf (liabilities in the form of deposits and loans it has incurred to lend on to others). The bank's capacity to continue as a going concern is then threatened – bank runs are more instantaneous and terrifying today than ever before – so governments and taxpayers are forced into guarantees and bailouts, triggering intense public resentment, especially if bankers have been pocketing vast bonuses before the crisis. Instead, building on the arguments of Nobel Prize-winner Professor Robert Shiller, there needs to be much more flexibility in both the banks' assets and liabilities so that they can respond to varying contingencies. A proportion of bonds any bank issues on its behalf should be hybrid, so they can be turned into equity if the bank gets into trading difficulties; it would then be bondholders who face losses as their bonds are automatically turned into shares, rather than taxpayers'.[6]

Reciprocally long-term bank lending should also be hybrid, so that if borrowers are unable to repay on the existing terms they have the legal right to renegotiate the terms of the loan. Indeed, loan repayments could be formally linked to the borrowers' capacity to pay as income-contingent loans – repaying more when flush with cash but having the capacity to defer payment when hard-pressed. Finance would cease to be society's master; instead, debt write-downs and reorganisations would be built into the warp and woof of banking – giving more parity of power between banker and client. Bankers will thus have an incentive to look after and curate their clients, rather than offer credit recklessly; existing shareholders and bondholders will have an incentive to ensure that banks are soundly run, delivering their social purpose, rather than 'chasing the alpha' of extreme profitability.

And last, Britain needs to equip itself with a network of publicly created specialist banking institutions, expanding on the suggestions above. Incredibly, a Conservative government created the Green Investment Bank in 2012, then privatised it 2017, only to create the UK Infrastructure Bank in 2021 to fill the gap it itself had created. This is a fundamentally frivolous attitude towards financing environmental infrastructure – a flip-flopping that springs from the free-market faith that the market will and should provide when the evidence is overwhelming that it won't.

Infrastructure financing, combining government grants and matching long-term funds with long-term needs is sophisticated and specialist – and beyond the competence of the typical UK commercial bank. The UK Infrastructure Bank has made a creditable beginning, and the model of offering sovereign guarantees to commercial banks' lending has rich possibilities, as argued earlier. Britain's mainstream banks are keen to play ball. But if it is to plug the gap left by the European Investment Bank, its risk capital must be at least doubled. It is the same story with the British Business Bank, which with sufficient capital could play a vital role in building up business lending in Britain's regions. Both institutions represent the 'We' in banking; both are only backed half-heartedly by the Conservative government – here repeating its pantomime-horse contortions of conceding the case for public intervention but doing it half-heartedly because it does not want to admit the failure of laissez-faire. The result is a halfway-house stasis. It needs to be swept away.

Organising Ourselves to Take Risks

Capitalism needs risk capital, investors who come forward to invest in a company's equity, accepting risk for higher rewards. Owners shape the character of a country's capitalism. Here, the UK has a related equity and ownership crisis. British investors, notably institutional investors, are in wholesale retreat from investing in the public markets. Not only are there a diminishing number of British owners with skin in the game who want properly to steward and engage with the companies in which they invest; the mechanisms by which they can exercise a collective and constructive voice are weak and by default shareholder value maximisation is still the dominant credo. Companies in the so-called intangible economy are also suffering from the equity strike.

They take greater risks and lack much tangible collateral, but they may yield potentially high returns, which should make them better candidates for equity investment than bank loans – but equity is not forthcoming on any scale. Venture capital and some parts of private equity are still relatively strong – Britain leads the EU in the strength of its venture capital flows – but investment tends to be highly geographically concentrated in the South-East and in a few fashionable sectors (FinTech, the computer programmes used in banking and financial services, and consumer goods). The overall picture is dire.

The value of shares quoted on the London Stock Exchange is still below the levels of 2007 – the only major European country to be in that position. The UK stock market has sunk from third-biggest in the world in 2000 to tenth today. British company valuations have collapsed compared to peer companies quoted on the European, Asian or North American stock markets. The valuation gap for like-for-like companies has been as high as 40 per cent, according to the *Financial Times*.[7] Michael Tory, former Morgan Stanley banker and Co-founder of the investor advisory consultancy Ondra, calculates in 'Britain plc in Liquidation' that in 1990, British pension funds owned more than a trillion pounds worth of British companies; now they hold less than £100 billion. It is a wrong-headed attempt to make pension funds so safe they are killing our economy, and paradoxically themselves. Since 2006 Tory finds that the valuation of a like-for-like company quoted on the London stock market compared with any other stock market in the US or Europe has fallen on average by a third. British companies are under-invested-in, undervalued and thus fatally wounded lame ducks.[8] The retreat extends to start-up investment: 63 per cent of investment into UK tech in 2020 came from overseas, up from 50 per cent in 2016.

The public markets play a very limited role in raising capital. The Tony Blair Institute report 'Investing in the Future' writes that the

> last material (ie greater than $1 billion) primary equity issue by a widely held UK company was in 2019 by AstraZeneca.

Even though the funds were to fund expansion in its heartland oncology business [...] it prompted widespread suspicion. The general reaction was that UK companies should not attempt to raise equity any more [...] AstraZeneca's share price has almost doubled due to the success of the issue, in which there was almost zero participation by domestic UK Investors.[9]

Corporate strategies, expansive in the 1980s and 1990s, have become largely defensive. New capital is not raised, investment is curtailed and to try to stop the rot British companies become very short term. They surrender markets to hoard their profits, don't develop new products and try to assuage their rag-bag of remaining shareholders with big dividends and buying back shares at or above the prevailing share price. Publicly quoted companies are exposed to takeover by foreign companies or private equity on a scale unequalled anywhere else in the world. With under 3 per cent of global GDP, Britain accounted for a quarter of all cross-border takeover activity between 1997 and 2017; fifty companies that would have been in the FTSE 100 are now foreign-owned.[10] Since Brexit, the pace has accelerated; foreign takeovers have increased by 400 per cent. Some foreign takeovers can boost investment, but the overall evidence for their beneficial impact is scant.

The Tony Blair Institute, in a second impressive paper, 'Transparency, Accountability, Predictability: Protecting National Security through the Foreign-Takeover Regime', argues that many high-tech companies, valuable directly or indirectly for national security, are taken into foreign ownership only to be dismembered and the valuable parts sold off or repatriated to the host country; this has happened in varying degrees to the defence companies Cobham, Ultra and Meggit and the IT company Arm, all of which have recently been taken over. Britain has the third-highest stock of inward investment in the world – but that has not been reflected in markedly better productivity or improvement in economic performance.

Around half of Britain's £3-trillion pension fund assets are held by DB schemes, all but 450 of them closed to new entrants.

A combination of regulatory, tax and accounting 'reforms' over the last twenty-five years, along with very low interest rates, drove them into huge deficits – their liabilities to pay guaranteed pensions (hence the name 'defined benefit') far outstripping the pension funds' projected assets. The sponsoring companies could not accept the growing burden of topping them up, so they closed them down. Advised to crystallise their assets compared to their liabilities during what is sometimes a forty-year run-off period, they have sold off equities and invested largely in government bonds, along with a smattering of corporate bonds which have predictable values. The portfolio may be safe, but the returns are indifferent. The sum of £1.5 trillion has in effect been placed in investment cold storage. Over 1,000 DB schemes have been taken over by the Pension Protection Fund (PPF) when companies have gone to the wall. Interestingly, the PPF as a superfund has not taken the same hyper-risk-averse view; as a large fund, and destined to grow larger, it could spread risk, and so it continued to invest in a balanced equity portfolio – producing annualised returns half as high again, at 9 per cent, compared to the 6 per cent returns earned by the fossilised, refrigerated DB pension schemes still at large. In 2023, it had an investment surplus of £12 billion.

The current structure is madness, and has begun to attract the attention of both Chancellor Jeremy Hunt and the shadow chancellor Rachel Reeves. There needs to be a shake-up – valuations of British shares need to be lifted to those of peer countries and in the process UK companies given the opportunity to recruit more anchor shareholders to support their purpose through dialogue with superfunds with the resources and incentive to assume that role. If domestic investors will not invest in you, it is a poor platform from which to gain international support.

Two proposals are on the table as I write. The first (proposed by the Tony Blair Institute) is to help the myriad of schemes struggling to meet their liabilities by investing in bonds. Britain does not need over 5,000 of such tiny fossilised DB pension funds; they should be consolidated into four or five superfunds, capable of investing in a spread of British and overseas shares, as the PPF does. Companies should be allowed to transfer their pension funds initially to the PPF – and other new superfunds when it has grown sufficiently large – without first going bust. In the 2023 Autumn Statement it was announced that going-concern companies would be able to transfer smaller DB schemes to the PPF; a long overdue cross-party consensus is emerging that Britain must move in this direction. The objection to this is that it may risk lowering small DB schemes' already-low returns – a partly self-serving concern from the insurance industry, which manages many of the small funds and wants to retain the management fees. But there are long-standing, proven investment virtues in pooling risks, and this is easier the larger the fund; superfunds can have a spread of risk and thereby raise their returns. And the evidence is before us. The PPF's returns are 50 per cent higher than the DB average. A PPF superfund will also have the scale, resources and incentive to invest in UK equity. It could be biased towards investing in companies which take their declared social purpose seriously, commit to achieving net zero by 2050 and to float and issue share capital in London. Everyone would win – future pensioners, purposeful companies, the standing of the City, the economy at large and the environment. The only potential loser would be some insurance companies, trying to cling on to their fees as they pursue sub-optimal but allegedly less-risky investment strategies which deliver poor returns.

The crucial issue is that more UK companies need engaged owners who buy into and support their purposes, and who have the voting power to turn that support into reality by engaging with the company over the longer term. A company thus needs a small number of such 'blockholders', in the jargon of the market, to whom it can explain its business model along with the material risks and opportunities, and upon whom it can rely for at least 25 per cent and up to 50 per cent of the votes.[11] In this important area, Britain is at the low end of the international scale, even if many British companies do have a couple of blockholders. Indeed on one assessment of thirty-two leading countries, Britain is the worst ranked.[12] There is no escaping the reality that British shareholder structures are dysfunctional and must be remedied. For the evidence is that blockholders, as long as they have the resources to reciprocate the company's willingness to open up and engage in an ongoing dialogue, improve corporate performance significantly. Because they are a large shareholder they have skin in the game – they can advise, scrutinise, provide a reality-check and share information about best practice from other companies in which they invest. As London Business School professor Alex Edmans has explained, fragmented shareholders have too little at stake, for example, to analyse a company's intangible assets, such as culture. They thus focus on freely available, published short-term earnings – 'the market sells first and asks questions later'.[13] The presence of engaged blockholders, whether someone like Warren Buffett or a large insurance company like Legal and General, with the resources to manage the relationship, imparts a long-term bias to company strategy that would not otherwise be there.

Britain needs to organise its pension funds to perform this role. The majority of the equity in our companies is owned by overseas investors, often in low-cost and poorly resourced tracker or index funds. They simply cannot afford the teams of specialists to engage with companies.[14] Britain desperately needs more engaged shareholders and the creation of a network of British superfunds would be a great step towards that goal. This should be aided and abetted by offering tax credits for British domiciled investors investing in British listed companies as the Australians and Canadians do; Britain should follow suit. Investment Savings Accounts (ISAs) should only be tax exempt if investment is made in UK shares. The whole approach needs to be turbo-charged.

We also need funds prepared to take stakes in illiquid but potentially high-growth entities and assets – especially start-ups, scale-ups and infrastructure companies. Here, a second proposal is highly relevant. If 5 per cent of current DC and SIPP funds were allocated to a UK Sovereign Wealth Fund, it would quickly grow to over £50 billion. Forty years after Mrs Thatcher failed to create a wealth fund as the Norwegians did, this would be a belated catching-up, albeit on a smaller scale, and not from oil revenues – a massive opportunity foregone. The fund would have a different mandate from the superfunds; it would be to plug the start-up funding gap, and more readily invest in long-term assets on the basis that the economy needs this. And if it's done right, such companies produce higher-than-average returns to investors. The additional risk makes it a more suitable investment vehicle for open-ended DC funds which can take a long-term view, but which do not have to guarantee a minimum pension pot on retirement (the payment or contribution to the fund is defined, but not the future pension or benefit) – so they can take risks in return for really high performance.

The wealth fund would be managed independently of government, identifying opportunities among the intangibles, green technologies and other enterprises. Already in July 2023, Chancellor Jeremy Hunt leant into this agenda, announcing that nine DC pension funds were voluntarily and independently allocating 5 per cent of their funds in this category of investments in the so-called Mansion House declaration. They were baby steps in the right direction. We need both a wealth fund and a cluster of new superfunds. Critics object that any government attempts to make investment in the wealth fund compulsory would be tantamount to confiscating private assets and deploying them wastefully – first cousin to the objections over creating superfunds. One obvious retort is that the opt-in principle should be adopted; 5 per cent of DC and SIPP funds would be presumed to be opted in with an option for individuals to opt out – the approach taken to building up NEST, which has worked so well. The model would work better, as advocated by Nick Lyons, chair of Phoenix Insurance, if a public-sector wealth fund, funded by tax revenues (say partly from newly licensed oil and gas fields) and bonds, could be established alongside it to co-invest and potentially backstop the liquidity of the main private fund. One such fund has been suggested by the Labour Party, along with a promise that every £1 it invests should be matched by £3 from the private sector. This would be a great deal easier to achieve if the public and private funds were comanaged symbiotically. It is crucial that the funds are invested purely on long-term commercial and business grounds – investment decisions should not be driven by political interventions. One such governance structure respecting this principle has been developed by the Canadian Pension Plan, now worth over $500 billion. As for being wasteful, the current low rates of returns on these funds are a disgrace.[15] It is long overdue that more 'We' is inserted into the structures of British savings, investment and finance. Britain can and must do better.

Advancing the Intangible Economy

Such equity investment is especially important to business models that rely on intellectual property, increasingly the most important and dynamic in the brave new world of intangibles. Investment in everything from information technology (IT) and AI to architectural designs and brands has been higher than investment in so-called tangibles (machines, bricks and mortar) since the turn of the century. With intellectual property underpinning most intangible business models, they are always vulnerable to the next wave of new ideas, and the firms may not last long unless they prove exceptionally agile. Nor do they offer bankable collateral in the same way as tangible assets; the intellectual property (IP) on which they depend has no ready market as matters stand. Banks, who have hardly distinguished themselves lending in the world of conventional, tangible manufacturing, are even more risk-averse with intangibles. In any case, given the risks, overloading intangible companies' balance sheets with too much debt is wrong in principle.

Again, public action in the name of the 'We' to protect and free up the investment process is an imperative. Public markets in intellectual property rights (IPR) to establish IPR market values need to be developed at government instigation, and then the state should develop a system of insurance guarantees – analogous to those proposed earlier for the mortgage and business loan markets and already developed in export finance – based on the now-identified market value of the intellectual property. Britain's R&D spend needs to double, but there needs to be a quid pro quo for all this investment. Intellectual property that the state has helped to develop or agreed to patent must be used commercially, rather than hoarded or left idle. One promising solution is to develop public IP markets so that intellectual property such as patents and copyrights can be traded, rather as shares and bonds are traded. This will give a value to IP that can be used as bankable and investable collateral, and which the wealth funds in particular can deploy to open up finance and financing channels for domestic and foreign equity investors alike. Britain could become a world leader in IP trading, stimulating a new generation of unicorns.

But the starting point is weak. Economists Jonathan Haskel and Stian Westlake argue in their latest book, *Restarting the Future*, that the dearth of equity, accelerating since Brexit, has created a crisis in the intangible economy. There were already specific difficulties in this area – Britain hugely underspends on R&D, polices competition weakly, especially of the type thrown up by the intangible economy, where monopolies quickly get established, and has saddled itself with an antediluvian approach to intellectual property that stresses ownership rather than openness. But the drying up of equity investment has proved a tipping point. The current economic crisis, they argue, is de facto a crisis of the intangible economy.[16]

One key issue is the tax privileging of debt over equity. There needs to be a rebalancing – withdrawing the tax advantages of debt and directing the savings so created to give tax credits on dividends, thus making equity investment equally attractive in tax terms. Here, the UK is not alone. Three main options have been implemented or are under discussion across the industrialised world. The most aggressive is the complete removal of interest payment deductibility by developing a comprehensive business income tax. Another is to set a limit on the amount of debt eligible for tax deductions, as Germany and Italy now do – or alternatively to allow a deduction on returns on equity, as Belgium, Italy, Latvia and Portugal propose. Italy is pioneering both approaches, which is the direction the UK should take. Given that multinationals will route their profits to the kindest tax jurisdiction, these types of tax reforms require strong international coordination – another reason Britain should never have left the EU!

Purposeful Business and Twenty-First-Century Capitalism

The evidence borders on unambiguous. Companies driven by a 'north star' of purpose – that is to say, delivering on an ambition to improve the world in some way – perform better than their less-principled peers. They organise their strategy, values, operating model and approach to their customers and workforces around their purpose. Leaders of purpose-driven companies attest to greater employee engagement, customer loyalty and organisational resilience by being purposeful – as two reports for the business think tank The Purposeful Company ('The Purpose Tapes' and 'Advancing Purpose') vividly display through the personal testimony of a variety of CEOs.[17] (Full disclosure: I am co-chair of this body.) Purposeful companies tend to invest and innovate more – and certainly better manage the difficult trade-offs in day-to-day business life. Purpose-driven companies were especially attentive to the needs of their employees during Covid.

Legal and General declares that its purpose is to be 'economically and socially useful', which, says former CEO Sir Nigel Wilson, is one of the reasons behind its growth to be Britain's leading and most profitable insurance company. Unilever's purpose is 'to make sustainable living commonplace'; the National Grid's is 'to bring energy to life'. ITV, Aviva, Pets at Home, the NHS, Lloyds Bank, Phoenix Insurance, Anglia and Severn Water all agree that the primacy of purpose in their affairs has helped them perform better. In the much-criticised water industry it is socially purposed Anglia and especially Severn which consistently come out best in environmental, reliability and consumer satisfaction ratings. Niklas Zennstrom, the founder of Skype, now runs a $5-billion venture capital fund, Atomico, dedicated to finding young tech companies like Skype which are animated by trying to disrupt and do something new to make the world better.

No social purpose can be delivered without the engagement of employees, the support of shareholders, the supply chain and the approval of customers; success requires the company actively to engage all its stakeholders in a continuing dialogue. Some companies establish consumer challenge groups; all recognise trade unions; all report systematically on their purpose and the material obstacles ahead; some go out of their way to recruit shareholders who buy into their purpose. All work hard at promoting investor–company understanding.

Certain asset owners and managers, notably Legal and General, Fidelity International, Phoenix, Aviva, Generation Investment Management and Federated Hermes, responsible for more than £3.5 trillion of funds under management, all concur in these values. They choose to invest in purposeful companies because that leads to above-average investment performance. But purposeful capitalism also addresses the riddle posed by Richard Tawney a hundred years ago; society, he argued, must distinguish between legitimate property rights, based on useful social function, and the amassing of property as a route to simple acquisitive wealth. All associated with the ownership and management of purposeful companies are deploying privately owned assets and wealth not to become materially rich as their primary motivation, but to deliver a socially useful and justifiable function from which they seek to earn good and sustainable returns. Interestingly, since the establishment in 2016 of the seventeen UN Sustainable Development Goals, there has been an explosion in so-called environmental, societal and governance (ESG) investing, with £3 trillion of funds under management in London earmarked for such investment. It speaks to a new concern among savers to see that their savings support objectives other than pure profit-maximisation. Purpose and ESG are of course not the same – purpose answers the 'why' of a company, while ESG addresses the 'how' – but they are closely related. The aim is to achieve a triple whammy of improving performance, legitimising capitalism and answering the question haunting every individual alive: what is the purpose of my life?

In this sense, purpose is the most important 'intangible' of all – a prerequisite for success in the knowledge-driven, data-rich twenty-first-century capitalism where agility and the ability to enlist the hearts and minds of all employees are key reasons for success. The necessary but insufficient condition for any successful economic strategy that aims to 'go big' is to ensure as far as possible that the private sector's companies are purpose-driven; here are the roots of innovation, adaptability and organisational energy.

Already Section 172 of the 2006 Companies Act rather tamely invites directors to consider that their responsibility is to all the members or stakeholders of a company, rather than just shareholders (the timid concession to stakeholding made by the Blair government), but in difficult cases the courts still view the first obligation as being to shareholders. The Corporate Governance Code, as another step, now requires its volunteer signatories to declare their purpose and report on it, but the Financial Reporting Council has noted that only 21 per cent of the FTSE 350 companies which declared their purpose did so in any way that was useful. It is time to go beyond polite invitations.[18] All companies should be legally required to declare their purpose as part of their articles of association, and to report on it systematically in their annual audited report, accounts and strategic report. Shareholders should hold them properly to account. Sir Nigel Wilson believes there is a strong case for the creation of an investable asset class of purposeful companies. This would be an avenue to that goal.

One very important sector to deploy purpose should be the regulated utilities. In each particular industry there are examples of the best, but too many privatised companies have not accepted that as monopolistic utilities they have obligations to citizens that have not been reduced because they now have private rather than public shareholders. Asset-stripping, tax avoidance, underinvestment and sheer neglect have been scandalously prevalent – witness Thames Water's underinvestment, loaded with £14 billion of historic debt largely to pay dividends through tax havens to shareholders and now lurching towards crisis, or the wider disgrace of polluted beaches and rivers. One solution, if expensive renationalisation is ruled out (which, at best, has a mixed track record, as Gaitskell recognised seventy years ago), is for every utility to incorporate as a company consecrated to delivering social purpose or public benefit – reliability, affordability, resilience, commitment to net zero, respect for biodiversity, delivery of social tariffs and payment of taxes, employee and customer engagement with the purpose flexed for each utility's particular circumstances. This should be accompanied by credible regulation, with regulators insisting that a commitment to social purpose is the foundation for receiving a licence to operate, and that it will be toughly implemented, with a well-understood pyramid of interventions, from fines to the withdrawal of licences for persistent offenders. This would include a much more activist approach to locking up companies' cash to prevent dividend distributions if rigorous financial and social-purpose performance criteria have not been met. At the limit, companies may need to be taken into temporary public ownership on penal terms if they fail to meet their social purpose. Never again a Thames Water.

All companies should be required to list a quarter of their shares on public markets so that the same standards of transparency and accountability required of public companies apply to all utilities. To be owned by private equity or a private consortium should not allow any utility to escape high standards of scrutiny. In this new universe utilities and regulators would have a common purpose, citizens could trust that key services were being provided with their benefit first and foremost in mind, and shareholders would buy shares knowing that their price performance would unlikely be more than modest, but very reliable. The same principle could be extended to other areas deemed critically important – for example, social media and digital platform companies. It is long overdue that society cared about how companies are governed.

There is pushback. In the USA, the political right, already sceptical of climate change, have ESG investing in their crosshairs. It is socialism by the back door, they argue. Investors have only one fiduciary duty: to maximise the value of their investments. Companies have only one fiduciary duty too: to maximise their profits. Muddy the waters with commitments to the environment, society or good governance and it becomes an excuse for disguising poor performance for what in effect are 'socialist' goals. Attorneys from twenty-one Republican-controlled states have written to over fifty leading US investment managers challenging whether they are right to vote at annual general meetings in favour of ESG policies. President Biden has had to veto Congressional moves to follow up with legal prohibitions.

The best defence is that the alleged conflict is non-existent, and ESG investing makes long-term excellent commercial sense. Electrical vehicles are the future. Fossil fuel companies risk sitting on unburnable oil and gas reserves and need to change their business model. Companies that play fast and loose with employee safety or products that are unsafe, like drugs or chemicals, expose themselves to enormous fines, regulatory risk and reputational damage. Consumers and employees alike care about the integrity of from whom they buy and for whom they work. Moreover, as governments gear up their infrastructure spending to respond to climate challenges, there are straightforward profitable opportunities by being a business partner committed to the same goals. ESG investors that promote such attitudes and behaviour are enormously valuable, promoting the companies which take the agenda seriously. In the UK and Europe, ESG investing continues to grow for just these reasons.

Purpose has been largely insulated from these attacks, but the changing American environment does create a scepticism that requires robust answers. For example, the 2023 resignation of Alison Rose, CEO of NatWest, over the 'unbanking' of former UKIP leader Nigel Farage has raised doubts in some quarters. A few critics allege that NatWest's commitment to purpose – 'to champion potential, helping people, families and businesses to thrive' – which had underpinned the extraordinary commercial transformation of the bank, had on occasion become close to echoing wokery. That was the real reason Farage lost his account at Coutts, as he had self-interestedly argued – not good commercial criteria. The case certainly exposed a risk; the point of purpose is to offer a compass for business strategy, embedded in the business model, that mobilises and animates a business – exactly the role it had played in transforming NatWest. Purposeful companies have to be alert to their critics and the danger of how they can be perceived, but must stick to their principles. The best way to achieve genuine value that underpins sustainable profitability is to make it part of a greater purpose. It works.

Holding monopolies or near monopolies to account for delivering their purpose is only a start. The yeast driving the rapid growth of the West Coast tech giants is because what they offer – digital platforms to search information, deepen personal connections and buy almost anything instantaneously, mobile phones, apps – can reach extraordinary economic scale very quickly, and once they achieve that scale they become virtually impregnable to potential competitors. An extraordinary one-fifth of the value of the US stock market is represented by the big five (Amazon, Meta, Alphabet [Google as was], Apple and Microsoft). They can reinforce their position by protecting their services with restrictive long-term patents, along with protective patents in adjacent technologies, so that the holder can sit on an innovation or invention – or roll it out very slowly – because there is no competition or competition authority that forces it to do otherwise. Beyond that, there is growing fear of how unconstrained AI could be deployed destructively, with misinformation and fakery becoming routine. But society, as I argued in Chapter 8, has a choice; technology is malleable and can – must – be shaped to serve rather than dominate humanity. Here, again, there is a necessity to assert the 'We'.

Here, I suggest a five-pronged approach based on the policies I've suggested on companies' purpose and on the utilities. All companies using AI must be required to incorporate as public benefit companies, stating that their purpose is to use AI for societal benefit. A new regulator – a machine intelligence commission – must be established with powers to hold them to account for their use of AI. Data unions should be created in which individual members can collectively hold data only to be used as they choose and by companies of whom they approve. The Competition and Markets Authority must act not only to break up existing monopolies (requiring close collaboration with the EU and USA) by separating out digital platforms from the capacity to provide key services, notably messaging and imaging; it must also pre-empt the growth of monopoly by ruling out big incumbents taking over rapidly growing innovative small companies who have the potential to become super-competitors in future. That is what we want – even if the incumbents do not. And last, just as the BBC was created a hundred years ago to ensure probity in the infancy of broadcasting, so today (as proposed by Professor Diane Coyle) we should build a public service social media platform, openly transparent, to compete with private social media platforms and keep them honest.[19] All this, note, would be more effective if it was done internationally. One of the great benefits of the EU single market is that the mutual recognition of each Member State's non-tariff rules, especially in the intangible economy, allows proper scope for the surveillance and regulation of AI. Whether or not Britain likes it, we are condemned to work with and follow the EU lead – or none of our intangible, AI and data-driven companies will be able to trade in Europe.

We also need to be eagle-eyed on competition in the analogue economy, where over the last forty years too many companies have been able to make profits above the average rate because they can charge prices higher than would be the case if competition existed. This is known as 'economic rent', and Britain suffers severely from it. As Brett Christophers explores in *Rentier Capitalism: Who Owns the Economy, and Who Pays for It?*, Britain has market structures that are dominated by one or two companies whose power is such that they can set monopolistic prices – from food retailing to banking, from digital platforms to the utilities. One of the problems, identified by David Halpern and his colleagues in the Behavioural Insights Team, the ex-No. 10 'Nudge Unit', is that consumers simply stay far too loyal for too long to indifferent goods and services offered by such rentier companies, and out of ignorance do not switch to the better products offered by others. Good companies' potential growth thus gets choked off, while the rentiers hold their position. What is needed is a massive public and private investment in third parties who rate goods and services independently to give consumers a better steer: this alone could double productivity growth they claim.* Rentier capitalism goes hand-in-hand with ossifying capital markets in which it is

---

* The argument will be set out more fully in 'The shrouded economy: A think-piece for boosting the UK's productivity and growth', to be published by the Behavioural Insights Team in March 2024, but after this book went to press.

hard to secure external finance – so firms price for high margins to generate cash flow themselves. To reduce – even eliminate – rentier capitalism requires movement across all these fronts: the governance and financing of companies, how they interface with regulators, how they exploit data, the encouragement given to challengers and how big they are allowed to grow. One of the many sad consequences of leaving the EU is that it has reduced trade flows and thus the intensity of competition – one of the notable benefits of membership of the single market.

Richard Tawney's distinction between socially functional and purely acquisitive capitalism is even more relevant today, but it is still widely ignored. Today, the danger of IP being used to construct monopoly concentrations of political and economic power, and abuse society, is intense. We need openness, open access, open innovation and multiple sites of power – not closure and monopoly. The answer to today's challenges cannot be the assertion of the 'I' via private property rights, strengthening them in IP law, and ceding the social to the rule of the market. The 'We Society' demands differently.

Openness – so crucial not just to innovation, but to the good society – cannot be allowed to take its chance in a brutish world of increasingly giant companies uncommitted to social purpose. That in turn means maintaining a society which can produce such values, can live a common life, address chronic unfairness and educate the men and women who have the skills to navigate today's multiple threats and turn them into opportunities. It is to that we now turn.

11

IT'S SOCIETY, STUPID

'No man is an island entire of itself,' wrote the great seventeenth-century poet John Donne; 'any man's death diminishes me, because I am involved in mankind. And therefore never send to know for whom the bell tolls; it tolls for thee.' Aristotle had the same message over 2,000 years earlier; recall his injunction that anyone who declared independence from society was either a god or a beast.

The architects of the post-war settlement understood this, and wanted to equip Britain with social institutions and processes that would better bind British society together. For the 1945 Labour government, no man or woman was an island, a god or a beast. The state would provide social insurance, a National Health Service, housing and education. It was a decisive break from the pre-war world, a self-conscious effort to create a social contract and a stronger social fabric. British citizens would pay tax and National Insurance as their obligation; reciprocally, they would all become entitled to the crucial props to their lives as and when they were needed.

The understanding was that a strong society and a strong economy go hand-in-hand, born of the bitter experience of the 1930s and needless economic and social waste. It's not only an ethical imperative that men, women and their families should know there is a floor underneath their lives beneath which they can't sink. It's also an economic question. The more people turn up to work fit and well, the greater the level of production in a society. Today, a weakened NHS means that 2.6 million people are taken out of the UK workforce because of long-term sickness. Academic performance in schools is weakened; hungry kids from distressed homes are less able to concentrate.[1] At the extreme, as demonstrated during the Covid pandemic, pockets of disadvantage incubate a virus that can infect and even kill the better-off; a virus knows no boundaries. Rates of mortality from Covid-19 in England between March and July 2020, reports the Office of National Statistics (ONS), were twice as bad in the most deprived areas, with mortality rates rising as deprivation rose and living conditions worsened.[2] This had knock-on consequences for the better-off; the risks from infection grew and lockdown lasted longer.

Just as importantly, ambition, innovation, enterprise and aspiration are empty words for those who have to fight a day at a time for survival. One American study finds that children born into the richest 1 per cent of society are ten times more likely to be inventors than those born into the bottom 50 per cent, with a dramatic effect on aggregate levels of innovation. Level up, and there would have been four times as many inventors – millions of 'lost Einsteins', as the study characterised them.[3] We all have an interest in a strong society.

The social contract is a foundation for social and economic strength, and creates more of what social scientists describe as social capital – a collective belief that we have a joint interest in each other's fate. Obligations and responsibilities to the other are accepted, with the others expected to reciprocate. One good turn deserves another. Once again, this is not only an ethical and social benefit, but an economic one. Social capital helps rally employees behind a common business purpose; it is social capital that allows business and workplace agreements to be secured on a handshake, which is more effective and cheaper than expensive legal contracts. It is easier to raise capital because investors take company promises of their intent at face value; it is social capital that makes people readier to pay taxes if they know others are doing the same – they are shamed into doing the right thing. Where there is social capital, there is trust, and to the extent that makes regulation, law and enforcement less necessary, so the efficient allocation of resources is promoted more cheaply. High-trust economies fare better over time than low-trust economies.

More broadly, the more social capital, the more the police and judiciary will function effectively, the more political stability there will be, and the more democratic legitimacy. Governments can better raise tax revenues and provide more public goods. In society at large, social capital is what enables communities of individuals to make common cause to achieve mutually beneficial outcomes in which they all believe. It is, after all, whole societies which encourage the culture of innovation – accepting both the risks and rewards – from which productivity and wealth originate. If we want a strong mutually supportive society and all that flows from it, we need strong social capital as the necessary if insufficient condition to underpin it.

It is a virtuous circle. It falls to government to create the social contract that nurtures the structures that underwrite our lives, which in turn create more social capital that drives the economy forward. Up to the election of Mrs Thatcher, Britain had governments that more or less understood this relationship, but from then onwards British Conservatism has taken a different course. Thatcher herself wrestled with how her commitment to individualism could be reconciled with an idea of society and the creation of vital social capital. In Chapter 3, I cited her famous remark in an 1987 interview with *Woman's Own*: 'Who is society? There is no such thing! There are individual men and women, and there are families and no government can do anything except through people and people look to themselves first' is certainly a paean to individualism and the uselessness of government action. But it was immediately followed by an acknowledgement of necessary reciprocity.

> It is our duty to look after ourselves and then also to help look after our neighbour and life is a reciprocal business and people have got the entitlements too much in mind without the obligations, because there is no such thing as an entitlement unless someone has first met an obligation.[4]

But there was to be no role for government in this framework; it was not to operate as the upholder of a social contract and of reciprocity. Thatcher did understand the importance of social capital to a market economy. Her ideological blind spot, shared by all her Conservative successors, is the belief that social capital should just grow spontaneously out of the sinews and processes of society itself. The good society would be propelled forward by the 'I' of individual action – with government as the 'We' cast to the sidelines rather than attempting to create the common good.

What that failure of understanding has ushered in is a toxic antipathy to society and the very idea of social capital. Sky-rocketing inequalities interact with an increasingly tattered, neglected social contract – from workplace insecurity through underprovided healthcare to lack of affordable housing. There was a pause to these malign trends in the New Labour years, with at least some repair to the social contract – although too many remained ill-equipped to manage the headwinds of globalisation and deindustrialisation – but since 2010 the decline has accelerated. Britain's unchecked income inequality is the highest of all the large European countries and is superimposed on an absolute growth in the wealth gap; an adult in the richest 10 per cent of the population now owns £1.4 million more than the average (compared to £960,000 in 2006–8).[5] In 2021, for example, the richest 1 per cent of Britons owned 70 per cent of all wealth.[6] Only 10 per cent of our wealth is now in public hands, down from 30 per cent in 1970.[7] And recall, overall wealth has more than doubled in relation to national income over the last forty years.

Part of the story is the boom in executive pay, which is linked to bonuses keyed into undemanding performance criteria; another element is the asset price inflation of the last fifty years, with low levels of property, capital gains and inheritance tax – to those that are given, still more is given. Winner-take-all effects abound in a globalised economy – from Premier League footballers to dealers in contemporary art. The British economy is more cartelised than most in the EU, as we have seen, which is reflected in wretched productivity and lower pay. The growth in income inequality may have recently levelled off, as has wealth inequality, but both remain stubbornly high. At the same time poverty for those in or out of work has climbed as the social contract has degenerated.

Moreover, these severe economic and social inequalities are overlaid with inequality of access to the digital world, information, health, education and housing, which eat into the very marrow of our beings – the disadvantaged start to believe they are not worthy of esteem, the advantaged that the high esteem in which they hold themselves and others hold them could not be more deserved. We live in tiered, stratified, siloed networks defined by entry barriers impossible to overcome without the necessary precondition of sufficient income, wealth and educational or digital wherewithal.

At the end of the USA's gilded age in 1899, Thorsten Veblen published *The Theory of the Leisure Class*, in which he argued that the wealthy were in a race to show ever greater conspicuous opulence which had no other purpose than to demonstrate wealth and status. At the top of today's wealth pyramid we have returned to a world Veblen would recognise. The sealed world of private wealth, for no other purpose than showing off wealth, is breathtakingly opulent – paintings, décor, furniture, fittings, yachts, live-in servants, coiffured animals, private cinemas. Some of the assumptions of that world are on weekly display in the *Financial Times*' 'How To Spend It' supplement, which entices the very rich with staggeringly expensive gadgets, clothing and accessories. But you cannot build relationships of reciprocity on which trust depends with folk with whom you never interact. All this has an impact on economic growth, as the IMF argues in an important paper on the links between inequality, poverty and growth.

> The evidence is that the more social inclusion (the IMF's proxy for social capital and an effective social contract) – on education, on healthcare, on justice, on access to finance, on physical safety – the more the entire population is enlisted to produce growth as educated, healthy workers, consumers and innovators. The danger of social unrest and political instability is reduced.[8]

For over two decades, Britain's apparently strong economic performance, largely attributable to EU membership attracting inward investment, combined with a reckless credit-cum-asset price boom, staved off serious objections to this growth of inequality. The academic evidence is that people generally accept the proposition that the more you contribute, the more you deserve to get back; it is your just desert and reflects a deep human instinct in favour of proportionality.[9] It is not an urge to equality that fires people up, but rather fairness, and although there was growing inequality before the financial crisis, the apparent robust vitality of the financial services industry and its tax revenues earned less criticism. It is not inequality per se to which people object, if it is felt to be earned fairly, in the sense of winners receiving their due, especially if there is a social contract and a sense that the upward tide is floating most boats, however imperfectly, as it was in the run-up to the financial crisis. It was an imperfect economic and social bargain, but at the time it fell within the rubric of being 'fair' inequality. For a period, neoliberalism could just about get away with it.[10]

The Great Financial Crisis and the £1-trillion bailout of banks, with extravagantly paid bankers suffering no penalty for their profligacy and incompetence, moved the dial decisively. The scale of bankers' remuneration was palpably, unfairly disproportionate and hugely undeserved, given the disaster the banks had imposed on the wider economy and society. As provocative was their culture of entitlement. There was little collective bankers' remorse at the reality that there was no alternative to bailing them out; the deal they struck was a one-way street – profits were private, losses were nationalised and risks were socialised. Leading psychological researcher Dacher Keltner, director of the University of Berkeley's Social Interaction Lab, has mounted experiments showing that the richer people become, the less they are willing to behave reciprocally and observe common codes of behaviour; they come to believe they have earned the right to behave solely in their own interest. The more powerful and rich, the more likely they are to act selfishly and ignore the consequences of their actions on others.[11] Drivers of more expensive cars, for example, cut off pedestrians 45 per cent of the time, compared to almost never by drivers of the least expensive cars; it is the rich who tend to cheat, not believing that tax evasion is wrong or just being unabashedly greedier. They consider it their just desert. Very rich bankers had come to believe they lived by a different code, endorsed by the lack of penalty for their obvious vices.

George Osborne's ruthless attacks on the social contract when the coalition government took office in 2010 then savaged the sense of a societal compact and exacerbated the disaffection. By 2015, social contract disbursements had reduced by £18.9 billion compared to 2010 – freezing child benefit, reducing the earned tax credit, stopping eligibility for aid with council tax, the infamous bedroom tax and the capping of benefit increases to 1 per cent a year. These cuts made life worse for as many as 7 million households. This came on top of the withdrawal of substantial funding for local authority services. The University of Warwick's Thiemo Fetzer, in a devastating paper, 'Did Austerity Cause Brexit?', to which I alluded in Chapter 3, shows that by 2016 the financial loss for a working adult in an economically and socially deprived local authority like Blackpool was £914 a year; in the City of London it was just £177. Moreover, the more hard-hit local authorities tended to be – those with relatively large private-sector manufacturing operations badly impacted by globalisation – the more the hurt was then compounded by the rollback of benefit payments. Risk was being displaced from the public realm to the shoulders of individuals least able to bear it. Fetzer carefully shows that the larger the social contract financial loss, the larger the Brexit vote, so that inevitably Blackpool voted for Brexit by one of the largest majorities in the country. He concludes:

> Austerity policies from late 2010 onward are key to understanding 'Brexit.' The welfare reforms are a strong driving factor behind the growing support for the populist UKIP party, contributed to the development of broader anti-establishment preferences and are strongly associated with higher levels of support for Leave.
>
> The results suggest that the EU referendum either may not have taken place, or, as back-of-the-envelope calculations

suggest, could have resulted in a victory for Remain, had it not been for austerity.[12]

Voters in Leave areas felt that cruel financial losses were imposed on them, along with additional risk. A force from without had stripped them of vital financial support. Of course they responded to appeals to 'take back control' by voting to leave the EU. Britain is now experiencing lost output of some £100 billion a year as a result of Brexit, along with up to £40 billion of lost taxes annually, set to rise in the decade ahead[13] and, as the IMF warned, has suffered chronic political instability. Britain is less investable, not only because of our lack of access to the EU single market, but because both UK and overseas investors are wary of the political stasis that has resulted. A strong social contract matters; weakening it has consequences that affect us all. It will matter even more in the decades ahead as our economy and society contends with technologically driven transformations, climate change, raw material shortages and pandemic shocks. We can't risk more Brexits.

What should a social contract do? It must attend to education, to health, to housing, to justice, and to making good shortfalls of income from unemployment or disability, and provide pensions and care in old age. It must reduce exposure to life's risks and vicissitudes, and offer a platform to take opportunities as they arise, to participate in civic, social and work life, and in the process empower – an empowerment that can and should be expressed in neighbourhoods and communities. Strong local government can allow this empowerment to make itself felt.

But the cornerstone of economic and social wellbeing is the ability to work, not only for the income it brings, but for the psychological and social wellbeing that accompanies work. Human beings want and need to act on the world – this is a universal impulse. To work is to be valued, to contribute and to have purpose. It is the entry ticket to society, available to everyone regardless of race, creed, gender or disability. It was Harry Hopkins – one of the principal architects of the New Deal and in particular its work programmes – who famously said, 'Give a man a dole and you save his body and destroy his spirit. Give him a job and pay him an assured wage, and you save both the body and the spirit.'

When William Beveridge, similarly scarred by the 1930s, designed his social security system, he shared the same view that work certainly provided the financial wherewithal to live, but to contribute was a psychological imperative. It was rarely, if ever, the fault of the unemployed in the 1930s that they were unemployed, but they internalised the derisive accusation that they were in some way scroungers, skivers, moochers. That unfair sense of guilt should be avoided at all costs. His proposed social security system would be designed so that benefits were felt to be a matter of right in return for insurance premiums paid. And it would not get in the way of working, which he regarded as central to human existence, and as described in Chapter 6 he looked to Keynesian economics to ensure that as far as possible the economy delivered full employment.

The social contract for the 2020s and the decades beyond will be built on the same foundation of a healthy employment market created by managing the economy so that demand is pressing the boundaries of production as much as possible. Men and women should have the capacity to acquire the qualifications and skills to participate in the workforce, and be supported in retraining and finding work – work that is fulfilling, meaningful and respectful of individuals, allowing them to co-create a great workplace. The labour market will not invent these conditions spontaneously. The social contract designers have to step in and start the dialogue that will guide businesses into creating better.

The Troubled Workplace

Britain in the early 2020s has very high levels of employment; at the time of writing, 76 per cent of the adult population are in work and unemployment stands at 4.2 per cent, although the proportion is rising the more the economy stagnates.[14] William Beveridge might have allowed himself a small smile. He would have smiled less at the state of the British workplace. Employees are increasingly likely to be treated poorly – at risk of summarily losing their job, of being intensely and counterproductively micromanaged, of having to accept terms of employment uniquely favourable to the employer, of being fired and rehired on worse conditions, of having no voice in the workplace or of suffering an increasingly insupportable gap between unemployment benefit and their wages. It is a gap worse than it was a generation ago. Moreover, real wages in Britain have not risen since the financial crisis. Had previous growth rates continued over the last fifteen years, the average worker would now be £10,700 a year better off.[15] Workers may be in work, but they are more disempowered, more at risk and less well-off than they could and should be. The lower the income distribution, the more acute the gathering squeeze. The 1.8 million people who are paid at or near the wage floor, for example, receive no pay slips and are six times more likely not to receive paid holidays – even though it is a legal entitlement from day one of employment.[16]

There is a large pool of full-time employees – more than 40 per cent of all in work – who enjoy reasonable salaries, secure work, the opportunity for progression and the full panoply of associated benefits – pensions, good sickness pay, maternity and paternity leave and holiday entitlement. They report good levels of job satisfaction. But a darkening shadow hangs over them. Job insecurity is extending into even what hitherto were considered 'safe' middle-class, professional jobs. For example, 80 per cent of the country's journalists may be graduates, but their average salary in 2022 was £28,000; many were forced to be self-employed, with 36 per cent in 2015 claiming state benefits or tax credits – and the proportion will be greater now.[17] The TUC estimates that over 11 per cent of the adult working population – just under 4 million – are in varying forms of insecure employment, from zero-hours contracts to agency work. Insecurity is certainly biased to 'working-class' jobs, so that a fifth of those working, for example, as process and machine operators are categorised as insecure, but so are a fifth of skilled workers and even 8 per cent of managers, directors and senior officials.[18]

Storm warnings abound; the situation is likely to get much

worse. The UK, after the USA, possesses the least regulated labour market in the advanced world. Enforcement is scant. Proposals to merge the Employment Agency Standards Authority, minimum-wage enforcement and labour-abuse regulators to improve matters have been stalled for four years – but then, there have been four secretaries of state for work and pensions over the same period, and nine since 2010. Successive Conservative governments may pay lip service to ensuring that standards are met, but their actions betray an astounding lack of urgency and an underlying attachment to laissez-faire economics. Interference is a vice. Anything should go. Britain ranks twenty-seventh out of thirty-three OECD countries with only 0.29 workplace standards inspectors per 10,000 employees; between 2017 and 2022, exactly four labour market enforcement orders were issued.[19] Lack of enforcement accentuates not only insecurity, but low pay, driving millions into poverty. Roughly one in five working-age adults – around 8 million people – live in poverty, as defined by the Joseph Rowntree Foundation. But 68 per cent of them work; 5.4 million are working adults, whose financial resources are well below their material needs.[20] One in four children live in poverty-stricken households. During the Covid crisis, these were the homes most affected by the virus. Beveridge's recipe of good work as a foundation, supplemented by National Insurance benefits paid as a matter of right when they are needed, is in tatters – nine out of ten benefits are now means-tested and benefit rates barely offer even subsistence.

The cause of so much misery is a labour market where trade unions have been weakened or banished. Nor are workers offered a capacity to empower themselves and maintain their living standards via the so-called flexi-security model pioneered by Denmark – flexible work contracts but security offered via generous welfare benefits, training and work guarantees. The result is that a fifth of jobs are paid below the national living wage – a stunning indictment of the lack of enforcement and the way the labour market has been allowed to develop. In the EU, nine out of the eleven countries who boast the lowest rates of workers earning low pay are those with industry-wide collective bargaining agreements covering at least 70 per cent of the workforce. Finland, Denmark and Sweden have such collective bargaining agreements but no minimum wage; they enjoy the lowest levels of low pay and in-work poverty.[21] In Britain, just 13 per cent of private-sector workers are covered by collective bargaining agreements; when the public sector is included, the proportion rises to 27 per cent.[22] Thirty years ago, the overall coverage was 36 per cent and the private sector stood at 23 per cent. It's been a story of continual decline and rollback.

Trust levels at work are falling and micromanagement is increasing. Thirty years ago, more than three-fifths of workers reported high levels of task discretion at work; now, it is under two-fifths.[23] The less regulated the labour market, the more the micromanagement increases – although the stagnation of productivity suggests it is not producing much in the way of results. The initial applications of AI have mainly been used to micro-monitor individual workers' attendance, facial attitudes on Zoom calls (which became normal during Covid) and how much productive time is spent on their laptops. Working from home, inaugurated during successive lockdowns, opened up more fault-lines of micromanagement. Most blue-collar, unskilled and even skilled work in the service sector must take place five days a week in the same physical workplace, but white-collar workers tied to a laptop have the option of working from home – increasingly the choice for part of the week. Working flexibly does not necessarily lead to enfranchisement; it can mean poorly designed work stations, loneliness, absence from the collective workplace and at the same time it is an opportunity for firms to reduce the cost of office space and displace it on to their workforces. Much depends on the character of the firm and the work. For many companies, cost minimisation and micro-controlling workers from a distance serves their purpose of maximising shareholder value all too well – but of course it also alienates the workforce.

This has to be turned around. Part of the answer was provided by the last chapter – above all, stimulation of the emergence of purposeful companies who take workforce engagement and participation seriously. They do not want alienated employees.

But more interventions have to be in place – the encouragement of trade unions as a countervailing force in the labour market, the recreation of a genuinely supportive social security system, the eradication of bad workplaces and a drive to create good workplaces, brilliant training and the maximum chance to work.

Solutions: Collective Bargaining

Industry-wide collective bargaining agreements securing good wages and good work, reproducing what has happened in the best of the EU, are one obvious way forward. But such agreements depend on the existence of trade unions to negotiate them. In 2022, only one in eight workers in the private sector were members of trade unions, and one in two in the public sector – where collective bargaining covers more than three-fifths of the workforce. Overall, just 22 per cent of the working population belongs to trade unions, a proportion that has been falling for more than thirty years. It is certainly difficult and expensive to organise trade unions in today's multiplicity of small workplaces, but the very best incentive for workers to do so would be the knowledge that they, via their unions, have representation in negotiating pay agreements. If business was prepared, or compelled, to negotiate collective bargaining agreements by sector, trade unions would gain a major rationale for existing. Collective bargaining deals would become their *raison d'être*.

The failed initiatives of the late 1960s and mid-1970s – *In Place of Strife* and the Bullock Report – need to be revisited; recall that the proposed bargains were that union recognition, legal requirements to have collective bargaining agreements and unions represented in strategic decision-making, were to be the quid pro quo for accepting legally enforceable contractual obligations, and using mediation rather than strikes to settle disputes, which would only be a last resort. Trade union culture at the time was fiercely opposed to such compromises. It implied supping with the capitalist devil and losing the precious freedom to strike at will.

Today, the bulk of the union movement would and should seize the opportunity. The most important building block in addressing in-work poverty and creating good workplaces would be for the government to resurrect the *In Place of Strife*/Bullock framework to ensure that every sector is covered by a collective bargaining agreement and that workers become involved in company decision-making.

Paradoxically, the decline in trade unions has cleared the workplace decks to make such a world easier to construct. In 1945, Britain had 1,000 trade unions, so making free collective bargaining arrangements stick was like herding cats – the system was plagued by free-riding and opportunistic cheating. Today, there are 124 trade unions and only twelve have a membership of more than 50,000.[24] If unions want to rebuild their memberships, this is one certain way. Nor are members so suspicious of capitalism; it has become obvious that the way forward is to work with business, Ernest Bevin-style, rather than try to overthrow it, Hugh Scanlon- or Arthur Scargill-style. From the employers' point of view the evidence is clear; the more workers can be involved in decision-making, the more innovative the company. The twenty-first-century company is more than ever a social organisation aimed at complex problem-solving; enlisting employees to the cause makes perfect sense. And while British business remains suspicious of workers on their boards, it is a great signifier of good intent – and international evidence suggests that it is beneficial for all concerned, with very few downsides.[25] A first step, rather as service delivery company Capita has done, is to invite employees to serve on, say, the audit and remuneration committees. 'Why wouldn't you want an employee on the Audit Committee?', asks outgoing CEO Jon Lewis. 'They have insights about what is going on in the organisation that the chair would not otherwise realise.' As for the remuneration committee, he argues, it is good for workers to see the pros and cons of the considerations driving remuneration.[26] It keeps everyone honest. Capita is a pathfinder. In the decades ahead, twenty-first-century companies will increasingly have employees on their boards.

It is all part of trade unions coming of age, becoming partners and problem-solvers in the workplace, rather than being structurally hostile to business. For its part, business would have to drop its two-century-old suspicion of trade unions as socialist trouble-makers – but as the numbers of purposeful, stakeholder companies reach critical mass, that should be more than possible. The inclination would be reinforced if employee share ownership could be strengthened by developing and extending employee ownership trusts.

Nor need gig workers be left out of the equation. Typically, gig work is distributed through digital social platforms. Any employer hiring a gig worker should be mandated to provide details on the platform about which union they can join to represent them – and unions like the Independent Workers' Union of Great Britain, which specialises in representing gig workers, should be actively encouraged. Any tax credit or benefit for which an employee qualified as a full-time worker should be transportable to part-time, self-employed or gig work. Following Martin Sandbu's suggestions in *The Economy of Belonging*, employees' acquired rights should be portable too. Last, as the University of Bristol's Professor Alan Bogg argues, there should be a Labour Enforcement Act; if employers set aside their legal obligations, for example, firing staff with acquired rights and decent pay to rehire workers on gig terms, not following proper processes, then there should be much more severe consequences than there are now. The P&O case, when, in spring 2022, 786 staff, many of them unionised, were summarily sacked in a few hours with no pre-notification, to be replaced by non-unionised agency workers on much lower pay, shocked the nation. The company should not be allowed to get away with it, said Prime Minister Boris Johnson. But P&O did escape scot-free, recognising the illegality of what it was doing anticipating that the low fines and short-term loss of reputation were no more than an associated low business cost. Instead, firms should be exposed to legal redress, much heavier fines than those provided by current law and trade unions should be freed to take strike action in response, along with secondary picketing, without all the hoops they currently have to go through.[27] Employers and some employees do value the flexibility of gig work, but bad workplaces and bad employment practices have to be confronted. There is no reason for workers on highly flexible contracts to be treated like Wagner's Nibelung dwarves in some hellish underworld. They are human beings, deserving of respect.

Solutions: A Social Security System That Offers Security

Next, the social security system. The designers of the post-war settlement believed no one willingly shirked or would prefer to be on the dole. Unemployment benefit should never be considered as a handout; rather, it should be a right, part of a system of social insurance based on something for something. The benefit should not be so generous as to be a viable alternative to working, but neither so mean that unemployment becomes a form of desperate financial punishment.

The impulse was closer to Elizabeth I's Poor Law and its adaptation in the later Speenhamland system, which took as a starting point that poverty was not a lifestyle choice, as conservative American commentator William Buckley would claim, but brute bad luck which society had to a duty to alleviate (even if with barely subsistence help). It was a direct refutation of the later Victorian workhouse, with its brutal assumption that the poor were morally undeserving and had to be compelled to live and work apart – the spirit that lived on in the 1930s means test. In 1948, when the National Insurance system was launched, the weekly pension and unemployment benefit were fixed at the same rate: £1 3s per week, or around 20 per cent of the then average weekly earnings. Both would be paid as a matter or right – and not means-tested. Today, the weekly pension at £203.85 is 240 per cent higher than the equivalent weekly Universal Credit, as it is now called (in fact, it is paid monthly). Pensions are pitched at 31 per cent of average weekly earnings. Universal Credit (or job seekers' allowance) for a single childless worker has declined to a mere 14 per cent of average weekly earnings – compared to an average in OECD countries of some 55 per cent. We have moved from the culture of Speenhamland back to the culture of the workhouse in two generations.

'Beveridge envisaged a system of non means tested flat rate contributory benefits for those unable to work', writes IFS Director Paul Johnson. 'What we have is a system of means-tested benefits largely paid to those in work.'[28] Universal Credit, which is withdrawn in a taper the more you earn, did prove an effective and fast way of getting financial resources to the poorest during the pandemic – but nobody can argue it is generous. Indeed, not only is it mean, but the rate at which it is withdrawn remains astonishingly penal.

Philip Alston, the then UN commissioner on extreme poverty and human rights, commented after his 2018 UK investigation that the government's intent has been

> to reduce benefits by every means available, including constant reductions in benefit levels, ever-more-demanding conditions, harsher penalties, depersonalization, stigmatization, and virtually eliminating the option of using the legal system to vindicate rights. The basic message, delivered in the language of managerial efficiency and automation, is that almost any alternative will be more tolerable than seeking to obtain government benefits. This is a very far cry from any notion of a social contract, Beveridge model or otherwise, let alone of social human rights.[29]

The Covid pandemic exposed the system's weaknesses and triggered a reappraisal of the role of social security for the wider population. The furlough scheme allowed firms and workers to receive 80 per cent of their former earnings, while Universal Credit was increased by £20 a week. Everyone's health depended on the observation of lockdowns to slow the transmission of the virus, and that in turn meant that there was a collective interest in everyone having the financial capacity to stay isolated. Hotspots of infection were concentrated in poorer districts with a concentration of multi-occupied homes. It was obvious that the furlough scheme and Universal Credit increase were an indispensable part of the fight against the pandemic.

But the generosity was short-lived. The government rescinded both the furlough scheme and Universal Credit uplift as fast as possible. Little or no attempt has been made to capitalise on the experience – or to make the case that those out of work through no fault of their own should not be pushed into desolation row. It may be impossible routinely to compensate for job loss at furlough rates, but surely we can do better than fix relief at levels that impose such incredible privation.

In particular, reports the Joseph Rowntree Foundation, throughout the last twenty-five years, children, sometimes a third of them, have consistently suffered the highest poverty rates. This is now set to rise again, given the two-child limit to child credit introduced in 2017, the operation of the benefit cap and the freezing of Local Housing Allowance (LHA) rates – all of which drag down incomes at the bottom of the distribution. Factor in housing, and the sheer neglect of those at the bottom is shaming, recognised in the 2023 Autumn Statement when the LHA was finally restored to the hardly generous levels of 2016. But even so, the Resolution Foundation forecasts that relative child poverty in 2028–9 will climb to the highest level for thirty years (since 1998–9), with large families especially exposed; poverty for three-child families is set to exceed 40 per cent during this decade.[30] Yet, bar the occasional revelatory film or book, like Tom Clark's *Broke*, which documented the daily struggle to live, and the agonising trade-offs between shelter, clothing and going hungry that are imposed on millions, it has been until recently a secret trauma. The cost-of-living crisis since the Russian invasion of Ukraine has brought the issue more alive for millions. Food insecurity and hunger are spreading their malevolent tentacles.

Britain needs to pitch its benefits rates above today's subsistence levels and repair its social contract. At the very least, Universal Credit rates need to be increased, the system administered more flexibly and the withdrawal from it more generous. Child credit must be extended to larger families. But the issue is how to pay for it. Levels of personal taxation are already deemed to be close to as high as the public will accept, although few politicians and 'thought leaders' dare to try to move the dial on this consensus by explaining the necessity for higher taxes, still modest by European standards. Further tax increases have to be well-designed and well-argued; perhaps the easiest case to make for a tax increase, or foregone tax cut, is if it is earmarked to pay for child credit to be extended to three- and four-child families.

National Insurance contributions are one way forward, still seen as a valid way of contributing towards increased benefits. Boris Johnson's government proposed a health and social care levy to pay for improved social care based on National Insurance contributions (it was subsequently rescinded). In 2002, the Blair government raised National Insurance by 1 per cent to pay for higher NHS spending. Covid will not be the last pandemic of the twenty-first century, and we need to be ready to pay for our response to it.

Social security would have more legitimacy if the government established a new National Insurance Fund specifically to cater for the risk of job loss with the onset of AI and automation – call it the Twenty-First-Century Fund. Everyone will be able to contribute at varying rates to receive varying benefits to supplement payments for unemployment and sickness (where the benefit at the moment is the lowest in the OECD). The fund would be first cousin to the new sovereign wealth fund proposed in the previous chapter. It could even invest in a range of UK and international assets, retaining a conservative risk profile but venturing a little to invest with the same purpose – to achieve great returns for its potential beneficiaries. This would be Beveridge for the twenty-first century – a means to de-risk otherwise increasingly risky working lives while investing in ourselves.

Solutions: The Good Workplace

Julian Richer, founder of Richer Sounds, is one of the most successful entrepreneurs and retailers in Britain. He explains his success at the outset of his career as reading and implementing Tom Peters and Robert H. Waterman's famous 1982 management book *In Search of Excellence*, one of the best-selling business books of all time. Richer's take-away was simple. All great businesses flourish because customers believe that the business provides a great service – but great service is impossible without committed, engaged staff. Richer built his business on always paying above the market rate, always treating his staff respectfully, offering them training and support and the scope to innovate. Richer Sounds' philanthropic donations as a share of profits are the highest in the UK. As he entered his sixties, he gave three-fifths of his shares to an employee ownership trust, along with bonuses to all his staff depending on length of service. The foundation of business success, he insists, is a fair workplace that offers dignity and respect to workers. He is a twenty-first-century example of the principles that inspired Robert Owen in New Lanark, the Cadburys in Bourneville and the Lever Brothers when they created Port Sunlight. Treating workers properly and with respect is not only right – it produces results.

It is a lesson that has had to be repeated over and over. Zeynep Ton made the same point in the best-selling *The Good Jobs Strategy* in 2014, and again in 2023 with *The Case for Good Jobs*. Keep jobs focused and simplified, she argues. Standardise processes as much as possible so the maximum number of people across all ability ranges can do them. Cross-train staff. And 'operate with slack' to allow employees greater autonomy – giving them time to solve problems and create innovations. Customers, she says, rehearsing the same argument as Peters, can best be served by contented, motivated staff. Walmart is a convert, going from a micromanaging low-payer to an advocate of good jobs. Julian Richer would say he was convinced forty years ago.

The evidence is mounting that he is right, and not just from his own experience. There is a causal relationship between employee wellbeing and productivity. In research undertaken with British Telecom, a group of researchers at Oxford University found that feeling better by just one point on a ten-point scale translated into 13 per cent more weekly sales at BT call centres.[31] All this is increasingly recognised by enlightened employers, where the link between engaged, satisfied employees and the satisfaction of customers – indeed, wider organisational performance – is identified, measured and encouraged. In interviews for the

Purposeful Company's 2021 paper 'The Purpose Tapes', the CEOs of NatWest, Unilever, Capita, Severn Trent and the National Grid all highlighted this relationship, as did the senior partners of EY and PwC. The open question is how to achieve more.

The case for good work is so important that Harvard's Dani Rodrik and Columbia's Charles Sabel argue that government should adopt a strategy of 'building a good jobs economy' with three, mutually reinforcing components.

> Increasing the skill level and productivity of existing jobs, and the competitiveness of firms, for example through provision of extension services to improve management or cooperative programs to advance technology; increasing the number of good jobs by supporting start-ups, the expansion of existing, local firms or attracting investment by outsiders—what the many state and local programs (of greatly varying quality) currently directed to this last purpose refer to simply as 'economic development'; and active labor market policies or workforce development programs to help workers, especially from at-risk groups, master the skills required for good jobs.[32]

Readers will recollect the advocacy in this book of a £50-billion fund to support purpose-led start-ups, and in the next chapter I discuss how training could be deployed to support a good jobs economy. There are building blocks available. As for active labour market policies, in Britain they are conspicuous by their lack of consistency, typically rolled out only in an emergency and quickly discarded. Thus the 2009 Future Jobs Fund, which was launched after the financial crisis, disbursed significant grants and more than paid for itself, but it was dropped three years later. Or the 2021 Kick Start programme, in which tax credits were made available to employers taking on unemployed sixteen- to twenty-four-year-olds for six months during the pandemic to provide work experience and training. But the Conservative government was a reluctant promoter of such an active labour market policy, hidebound by its belief that the state should only act *in extremis*. Take-up was poor and the scheme was dropped. Grants and determination will work in this territory; tax credits, the default option for laissez-faire governments, are ineffective, despite their ideological appeal. Britain needs purposeful intervention, with the state itself spending cash in public programmes.

Britain should create a Civilian Conservation Corps modelled on the New Deal example – repeated again by President Joe Biden – which would partner with employers to achieve social goals ranging from conservation to caring. While the state would pay half or more of the wages, employers would both pick up the balance and design the work, together with appropriate training. One important by-product is that, open to all social classes, it would tend to create more social capital by breaking through class divides. It could be part of a wider jobs guarantee for all who are unemployed for longer than, say, twelve months. One such three-year-long job guarantee programme piloted in a local authority in Mariental, southern Austria, produced stunning results; the evaluation found that everybody out of work for more than twelve months (150 people in all) and offered work on the programme found long-term work subsequently, with a remarkable impact on their psychological and mental health. The cost of each job guarantee was lower than paying unemployment benefit, so the scheme paid for itself. Long-term unemployment was eliminated.[33] It is telling that the best example of a purposeful, grant-led programme that gathered job guarantees together was not in the UK.

The spirit of all these proposals is within a social contract framework – something for something to underwrite all the risks and the bad luck life throws at us. A counter-proposal is that because new technologies, notably AI, threaten to create mass unemployment, a better alternative is the establishment of a universal basic income (UBI), payable to every citizen as a universal entitlement. It is certainly true that UBI can produce good localised results for, say, left-behind teenagers; in one pilot in Wales, unemployed teenagers were given £20,000 a year, which the majority used to make themselves employable and find work. The problem with any wider application of UBI is the incredible cost for any worthwhile payment when scaled up to a working population of over 30 million, and that UBI drives a coach and horses through two basic human dispositions: the belief that income should reflect a just reward for effort, and the very basic human need to want to contribute through work. New Dealer Harry Hopkins was right; shred those and we shred a basic conception of what it means to be human – nothing is done for what Hopkins called a man's spirit. UBI will quickly lose legitimacy. Nor can we assume that the future is going to be plagued by unemployment; human wants are infinite, as are potential sources of work. Better to make the labour market work for everyone along social contract lines, but the reforms needed to achieve those goals go much further than putting the 'We' back into the operation of the labour market. Read on.

12

SPREADING MUCK TO
FILL THE CRACKS

It is not for nothing that the ONS defines 'human capital' as 'the stock of knowledge, skills, competences, health and other attributes embodied in people during their life'. People's knowledge-acquiring ability begins the moment they leave the womb, at the same moment they begin to experience what are often crucifying and disabling inequalities.

By the time a middle-class child is three, he or she will have heard millions more words – the so-called 'word gap' – and experienced more verbal explanations and non-verbal cues from parents than a child in a more disadvantaged home. More resources will have been spent on toys, nursery education, books and a variety of food, drink and visual stimuli. The middle-class baby will be equipped with a greater vocabulary and will be on the way to a level of articulacy and a better understanding of the reciprocities that matter in our day-to-day life. Babies nurtured like this are set to learn, to be educated, to acquire professional and skill capabilities that will both enhance their own lives and add to the economy's productive capacity. Society cannot look upon this complacently, but instead must act to remedy the injustice, and not because of a desire to appease the gods of John Rawls. Educational inequality hurts individuals, of course, but us, the 'We' of the wider society, too. The task is to put in place the best education and learning system we can for everyone and limit inequality in our best interests.

It is a demanding task. Had the governments since 2010

built on some of the initiatives taken by the Blair and Brown governments, Britain could now be nearer to achieving that goal. Instead, the opportunity was squandered – partly because of an obsession with shrinking the state, so that education spending over the last fourteen years has fallen markedly in real terms, partly because the contemporary Conservative mind is indifferent to inequality and does not believe in state action to mitigate it, and partly because building a great state education system has not been a priority. The core Tory electoral constituency, after all, is the elderly and the school-fee-paying middle class. Two-fifths of Tory MPs elected in 2019 were educated privately, and two-thirds of both Boris Johnson's and Rishi Sunak's cabinets also attended what are still ironically called 'public' schools. State education is a foreign land to them. They may protest their attachment to state education and training; their actions speak otherwise.

The first act of destruction was the evisceration of the Sure Start programme. Set up in 1999 by the then children's minister Tessa Jowell, it had grown to a network of 3,600 centres around the UK to provide one-stop-shop support for the under-fives, spotting health problems in young children and correcting them, and offering childcare and education. The idea, confirmed by a wealth of evidence, is that early-years development is a fundamental determinant of life chances – everything from future careers to good health.[1] Indeed, researchers at the Institute for Fiscal Studies found, in an evaluation of Sure Start, that it not only improved educational outcomes but also, by increasing hospital treatment for the very young, spotting illness early, reduced hospitalisations by 13,000 a year for eleven- to fifteen-year-olds – this alone offsetting 31 per cent of its cost even before other benefits are factored in.[2]

Sure Start Centres were popular, and also an important means for people from different socioeconomic backgrounds to make friends – parenting young kids can be lonely and very demanding. They were social capital creators, as well as giving all kids a fair start in life. None of that, nor their role in promoting great health and education outcomes, cut any ice with first the Tory-led coalition government and later Tory governments. Funding has been slashed by two-thirds and 2,400 centres have closed. Of the many acts of economic and social vandalism committed by the right since it assumed power in 2010, this comes close to the top.

Time and money spent in the Sure Start Centre, nursery, classroom, lecture theatre or apprentice workshop is not inessential, as in the mindset of Chancellor George Osborne and his successors. Education is an investment in ourselves; it should be seen as utterly indispensable capital spending. Its financial returns are measurable. The greater an economy's stock of human capital, the more it can innovate, adapt, invent and produce. Human capital as a concept may be criticised as instrumentalising our humanity, but it is also a recognition that investment in ourselves is the point of it all.

The UK Office for Science, for example, has tried to identify the financial returns deriving from education. The average return to degree-holders is estimated (varying with the degree) to be 21 per cent for men and 29 per cent for women, while there are positive (if lower) returns for holders of vocational qualifications.[3] For employers, there are also measurable effects; every 1 per cent increase in training raises the value added per worker by 0.6 per cent an hour and wages by 0.3 per cent.[4] For the economy as a whole, each additional year of education is estimated to lift GDP per capita by up to 10 per cent. The evidence is also clear that the more anyone receives formal education and training when young, the more they will benefit as they grow older by updating their knowledge. The better a workforce is educated and trained when young, the more it can adapt and change as it grows older.

The upper-middle class have always known the value of investing early to build their children's human capital, without ever requiring the investment to be justified by formal rates of return. The evidence stares them in the face. The grip of the privately educated on the upper echelons of the British economy and society has been with us for more than a century. Using data from 1926, Richard Tawney noted in his 1931 book *Inequality* that:

71 out of 80 bishops and deans, 139 out of 181 members of the judicial profession, 152 out of 210 highly placed members of public departments, 63 out of 88 members of the Indian Civil Service and Governors of Dominions and 99 out of 132 directors of banks and railways had been educated at public schools.[5]

Nearly a hundred years later, Robert Verkaik lists the comparable figures for today's public school alumni in *Posh Boys*: '74 per cent of senior judges, 71 per cent of high ranking officers in the armed services, 67 per cent of Oscar winners, 55 per cent of permanent secretaries in Whitehall, 50 per cent of cabinet ministers [...] and a third of Russell Group university vice-chancellors'. He adds that 44 per cent of the captains of industry and business listed in the *Sunday Times* 'Rich List' were privately educated.[6] The appeal of private schools to those who can afford the fees is in part the good exam grades achieved by such establishments, in order to meet admissions criteria for the selective universities. Smaller class sizes and high-quality teaching buys results. But just as important is learning the cultural signifiers of class, buying into those networks and embedding the assumption that status and achievement are in your own hands if you want to try for them. You become one of the chosen, to whom still too many British people doff a metaphorical cap. Britain's private schools, educating a mere 7 per cent of the school population, are proportionately the biggest and most influential of any in the advanced world. It is social engineering on such an immense scale that it could be seen, if telescopes could ever reach such sophistication, from outer space.

The private school shadow overhangs the education and training system as a scarcely visible but ever-present shroud; inequality is so entrenched that it seems the natural order of things. GCSEs, and especially A-Levels, are the 'gold standard' of academic excellence, it is claimed, that cannot be challenged; from the private school's point of view, they are the 'objective' measurements that justify their incredible fees, which for boarders can exceed £40,000 a year. For them, it was an investment that paid off handsomely during the pandemic, when teacher-assessed grades replaced examinations; 70 per cent of private school students were deemed to have achieved A or A+ grades, compared to 39 per cent in comprehensives.[7] Teachers reported intense pressure from parents to deliver the desired results.

There is near universal agreement among educationalists and businesses that the curriculum should be broader between ages sixteen and eighteen than the narrow spectrum of A-Levels. The gulf between the academic and vocational needs to be reduced. Better still, vocational training should have parity of esteem with academic education. But all such initiatives have foundered on the same rock of compromising 'excellence', a campaign typically orchestrated by the *Daily Mail* and *The Telegraph* with quiet support from the Headmasters' and Headmistresses' Conference, the private schools trade union.

We excessively privilege the academic, and woefully underinvest in the Cinderella world of apprenticeships, further education and training, in which there is a constant chopping and changing of certificates. The BTech, offering students the capacity to pick and mix with A-Levels, is now out, after twenty years, and the T-Level is in, posing sixteen-year-olds with an even more dramatic choice between the academic and vocational. In October 2023 the Sunak government announced yet another proposed change: T-Levels, hardly established, are to disappear to be subsumed in a proposed 'Advanced British Standard'. This will combine T-Levels and A-Levels, the avowed objective of which is to ensure both English and Mathematics are de facto taught to A-Level. There is still too little recognition of the value of the practical and vocational apprenticeship; once again the academic is over accentuated and privileged. The way in which the vocational is undervalued is bewildering; despite university being wholly inappropriate for many young people, that is where they are destined to go. As Paul Johnson writes in *Follow the Money*, 'Only about 56,000 young people under the age of nineteen started an apprenticeship of any kind between August 2021 and January 2022 (this being the six months during which most apprenticeships begin). Compare that to over a quarter of a million eighteen-year-olds heading off to university.'[8]

The low priority the Tories accord to developing human capital is underlined by the remarkable turnover of ministers. In 2022 alone, for example, there were five education secretaries. Only Michael Gove, successfully completing the roll-out of academies over his four-year tenure, could be described as effective, but even he connived in shocking real spending cuts – not protecting Sure Start, for example, and scrapping the Schools for the Future programme, exposing schools to closure in 2023, notably those built with weak concrete in the decades after the war and whose structural weaknesses thus went unaddressed. The Institute for Fiscal Studies wrote in 2021 that 'the cuts to education spending over the last decade are effectively without precedent in post-war UK history, including a 9% real-terms fall in school spending per pupil and a 14% fall in spending per student in colleges'.[9]

Emblematic of the government's priorities is the poverty of efforts to compensate for lost learning time during the Covid epidemic, which has been feeble by international comparison. In 2021, Sir Kevan Collins, then in charge of the government's attempts to catch up after Covid, proposed 100 extra hours of compensatory teaching for every pupil at an estimated cost of £15 billion. The government responded by offering a paltry £1.4 billion – or £22 per child – after children had missed an estimated 115 days in school. He resigned in protest. The National Institute of Economic and Social Research has shown that 'the total learning losses in education could equate to lifetime earning losses of between £8,000 and £22,000 per pupil'.[10] It was a vivid example of the attainment gap between children from advantaged and disadvantaged homes that persists throughout education.[11]

If schools have been hard-pressed, Further Education, with its bias to vocational learning, has been devastated. The Institute for Fiscal Studies commented as follows a year later, in 2022:

Colleges and sixth forms have seen a long-term decline in spending per student relative to schools. Further education spending per student aged 16–18 in 2022–23 was £6,800, which is lower than spending per pupil in secondary schools and only 11–12% greater than in primary schools, having been more than two times greater in the early 1990s.[12]

The Bad News Continues: Bright Spots Are Rare

The calamitous education investment declines over the 2010s and early 2020s bode ill for the future. But the earlier investments in the 2000s have produced some good results. The opening up of university access via the student loan programme boosted both revenue and student numbers. Britain has proportionally more world-class universities than any other country for its size, with seventeen in the world top hundred, while in England 42 per cent of the workforce now have level-4 skills (equivalent to the first year of university or college). Primary schools remain relatively well funded. England's nine- to ten-year-olds are fourth in international league tables for reading (because primary school education is impacted less by real spending cuts).

The story changes with secondary education. The 32 per cent achieving 'upper-secondary' qualifications as their highest level of attainment is below the OECD average of 42 per cent (France and the USA are also around this level), and far below the share in Germany (55 per cent). Moreover, it has fallen since 2014. Parallel problems show up in those parts of the education system where spending is of even more critical importance – in secondary school for low achievers, or in areas of the country where economic and social disadvantage is concentrated.

Those who do not get to university are bereft; just over a third of the school population (33.59 per cent) achieve only level-2 skills or below.[13] Sixteen- to nineteen-year-olds in England have the lowest levels of literacy inside the OECD, while England is the second-worst for numeracy after the USA.[14] The geographical differences are stark. A child on free school meals in London, where the academy school programme has been successful, has more than twice the chance of going to university at nineteen than a child on free school meals elsewhere in the country.

The obvious concern is that fourteen years of shameful

educational neglect will mean these poor figures worsen, while recently universities have been suffering real resource cuts on the same scale as the rest of the system. The freezing of student fees at £9,250 at a time of double-digit inflation has meant that universities in 2022 on average lost £1,750 for teaching each undergraduate, a loss which is set to rise to £4,000 in 2025, according to the Russell Group of research universities.

With research income squeezed by the three-year delay in rejoining the European Horizon programme of collaborative scientific research, and then only as an associate member, British universities will have to curtail British student numbers in favour of profitable international students who pay bigger fees. They will have to spend less on research. This is already happening; more than a quarter of the places at Russell Group universities went to overseas students in 2022, compared to 16 per cent between 2012 and 2017.[15] Conservative ministers show little urgency or concern about this; doubtless they are aware that university graduates are mostly not Tory voters. Universities are central to places where growth can occur; the costs of neglecting them are vast.

The Skills Gap: Crocodile Tears

British employers consistently report that they cannot find people with the requisite skills – but do precious little to remedy the situation themselves. Thus, the UK's Employer Skills Survey in 2019 reported that the greatest challenges were finding suitably skilled candidates in 'skilled trades' occupations; 84 per cent of those recruiting failures were at least partially caused by a lack of technical or practical skills. Internationally, technical skills shortages have been more prevalent in the UK, while such skills are in surplus in France, Germany and the USA.

But despite all the evidence of its importance, the average number of days an employee spent training in Britain fell by 18 per cent between 2011 and 2017.[16] Since 2022, firms have had to give back £3.3 billion in unspent apprenticeship levy to the Treasury, with no promise that the unspent monies will be earmarked to support other elements of education and training.[17] In particular, training rates have fallen for younger workers and have been persistently low for those with lower skill levels. And while the number of apprenticeships has risen in recent years, the overall quantity is pitifully low, as we've seen – and the quality uncertain. Not only has there been a steady falling away of younger apprenticeships; the time offered on an apprenticeship has shrunk. The government was forced to respond by mandating a minimum apprenticeship length of twelve months from 2017, but the approach remains thin and parsimonious.

The bald fact is that there is an outrageous, discriminatory class bias in the way university and further education are funded. While the so-called Robbins principle applies to university – anybody who applies to university can expect a place so that funding is demand-led – the reverse is true for vocational training. Funding is capped, so places are capped. An important paper from the LSE's Centre for Economic Performance, 'Skills for the "Other 50 Per Cent": Applying the Robbins Principle', is a scholarly *cri de coeur* about the implications. Funding for further education is 50 per cent of what it was in 2010, while the tariff rate per student remains frozen at 2013 levels. Imagine the outcry if students applying to our top schools and universities had been treated the same way. The system is, they conclude, one of the unfairest aspects of our current society – and it is a cause of both inequality and low productivity.

It is a generalised problem. Too many British employers seem indifferent to creating good work or in training their people. There are exceptions, notably those committed to achieving a social purpose, who are leading a more enlightened approach to the value of training. But in general British corporate commitment to training is patchy, with a poverty of ambition and a long tail of underperforming firms.

If firms are not going to initiate training themselves, and the usual laissez-faire proposals incentivising firms to do better by a tax credit do not work, then the state must step in. A proposal by Sheffield University's Professor Michael Jacobs to create a dozen vocational universities based in towns that do not at present have a university – like Penzance in Cornwall or Blackpool in Lancashire – would galvanise training levels.

Human capital is vital in all its dimensions and it is going to become even more vital as the twenty-first century unfolds, but Britain falls short in owning the concept – and is far too reliant on a few centres of excellence to raise its educational and training standing to anything approaching the international average. If some of the gains made before the investment drought of the last fourteen years could be reinstated and accelerated, the country could be challenging the best in Europe, South Korea and Japan as a human capital leader.

Instead, Britain is in an already poor position that could slide into an avalanche of failure and disappointed hopes. There is no escaping the reality: we need to spend more. Sure Start needs be revived. Further education colleges should be cherished and the funding organised so that every student who wants a place can get one. Vocational universities should be founded. Vocational and academic qualifications should have parity of esteem. The charitable status of private schools should be removed. If tuition fees are not to be raised, then additional university funding has to be provided. The structures, public institutions and good intentions are in place. What is lacking is commitment to the cause – and, above all, the resources. Britain is betraying its young, the biggest betrayal any society can make.

Sickness and Health

Health is essential in any assessment of human and social capital. In the wake of the Covid-19 pandemic there has been a startling rise in absenteeism because of long-term sickness. It is worth repeating that 2.6 million people reported long-term sickness in 2022 as the reason for their economic inactivity, up from 2 million in 2019. Obesity, and the risk of diabetes it triggers, is also a major cause of absenteeism, premature death and poor performance at work.[18] Nearly one-third of the UK population is obese, the highest rate in Europe besides Turkey and Malta.

The implications for the workplace are obvious. And health is incredibly unequal geographically; poor health as a reason for not attending work affects just 2 per cent of the workforce in prosperous southern towns like Wokingham, Maidenhead and Windsor, but 9 per cent in towns like Glasgow, Port Talbot and Blackpool.[19]

Grievous health inequality in the UK is nothing new. Our high income inequality means that on an index combining the varying measures of social deprivation – shortened life expectancy, high infant mortality, obesity, teenage births, homicides – Britain scored near to the worst compared to other leading countries. Kate Pickett and Richard Wilkinson's influential book *The Spirit Level* documented the devastating effects on the country. Some of the figures within Britain are even more dramatic. Men in the most disadvantaged communities can now expect to live for 9.5 years less than those in the wealthiest areas, while for women the difference is 7.5 years. People living in the most deprived areas spend nearly a third of their lives in poor health, the King's Fund reports, compared with only about a sixth of those in the least deprived areas. In the pandemic, Black men were 3.3 times more likely to die from Covid than white men. A child in year six in the most deprived part of the country is twice as likely to be obese as their counterparts from the most well-off areas.[20] In 2020, leading public health expert Professor Michael Marmot published a follow-up review to his path-breaking 2010 report 'Fair Society, Healthy Lives'. He found that life expectancy had failed to increase across the country for the first time in more than 100 years; for the poorest 10 per cent of women, it had actually declined.

There should be a multi-pronged response. First, as Michael Marmot, the King's Fund, and Kate Pickett and Richard Wilkinson all agree, Britain has to do better on the metrics discussed in this and the preceding chapters: real wage growth, especially for those in the bottom 20 per cent; better housing; better income support; better attention to nutrition; better education; more good workplaces. Deprivation leading to bad health outcomes has to be attacked at source.

A second prong lies in contesting the hyper-individualism that

has allowed the crankish anti-vaccination movement to grow –
perhaps one of the most dangerous consequences of the Ayn Rand-
inspired conception that selfishness is good and of the insistence
that the collective 'We' has no moral claim upon the individual
'I'. One of the inspiring lessons of the Covid pandemic was the
speed with which scientists were able to develop new vaccines, a
technology that can be used again and again to improve health
outcomes. Professor Sir Andrew Pollard, director of the Oxford
Vaccine Group, believes this breakthrough in vaccine technology,
which allows for speedy and agile responses to transmittable
disease, is a health game-changer. The approach can and must be
applied to a plethora of health conditions. But it is dependent not
only on government commitment and scientific breakthrough,
but also a collective social acceptance of the very principle of
vaccination to unleash the benefits as the greatest endeavour
of our generation – a classic case of the need to recalibrate the
relationship between the 'We' and the 'I'.

The third prong is a step change in the performance of the NHS.
Here, the *Financial Times* data journalist John Burn-Murdoch has
gathered some dismal and telling comparative facts. Since 2010,
he reports, the NHS's capital investment has run at some 0.3 per
cent of GDP – well below the rate of all eleven comparably rich
countries (Germany, France, Finland, Norway, Austria, Denmark,
the Netherlands, Sweden, the USA, Canada and Switzerland).
Britain is bottom of the league table in almost all areas – including
beds or MRI and ICT scanners per million people. Social care
spending was no higher in real terms in 2022 than it was in 2010,
despite the numbers of over-seventies climbing by 30 per cent and
those with multiple health conditions increasing by more than
twice that rate.[21]

The social care system, unable to accept more people, forces the
NHS to keep them in hospitals – one in seven beds is occupied by
people who could be discharged but are bottled up in hospital. The
blockages gum up the entire system, so that new arrivals at A&E
have to be kept waiting for beds. Death rates are unacceptably
above the long-term average. The Royal College of Emergency
Medicine estimated that the excess death rate in the autumn of

2022 was 'roughly' between 300 and 500 a week, as 600,000 people waited more than four hours for treatment in A&E.[22] England is short of 4,200 GPs.[23] Talk of reform and of increasing preventative public health are important but, given the scale of the crisis, are only part of the solution. The NHS has been neglected for too long; it and the care system need to be integrated and properly funded. It took fourteen years to reach this sorry pass. It will take fourteen years to put things right.

Roofs Over Our Heads – At a Price

Britain has organised too much of its capitalism around ever-inflating house prices and home ownership but has not had the bravery to insist that the prime point of a home is just that – to be a home. Nor has it ensured that there are sufficient affordable homes to rent for those unable to buy, who form an increasingly large part of the population. The effects are drastic. At their most acute, homeless, penniless people resort to foodbanks; a third of those referred to foodbanks have been homeless in the last year. To have nowhere to live is to be condemned to live at society's margins; without an address, getting a job, building relationships, even holding a bank account or receiving welfare benefit are impossible. A home is the 'gateway right' to other rights, yet some 271,000 people have no such gateway, including 123,000 children.[24]

The housing market that so cripples both society and the economy has toxic effects right up the income scale. People are unable to find a reasonably priced home to rent or buy. Renters are five times more likely to struggle financially than homeowners.[25] Buying a home is ever more elusive. Forty years ago, it took the average couple three years to save for a deposit to buy a home in the UK. Today, it takes nine, rising to fifteen in London. Young couples especially are so devastated by high rents and mortgages that consume up to two-fifths of their household income that they defer having children. Parents, at least those who have the resources, step in to compensate. Two decades ago, about a quarter of first-time buyers in Britain said their parents had given them a financial leg up with help on a deposit to buy a house, but by 2019 that figure had climbed to 54 per cent. The lottery of birth has become decisive; £11 billion a year is transferred by the over-fifties, who own three-quarters of Britain's housing equity, to help their children get on the housing ladder, part of a wider £100 billion a year passed on in bequests.[26] As a result, by the age of thirty-five, a UCL study finds, homeownership levels are three times higher for those lucky enough to have high-income parents who can help them buy compared to the unlucky remnant whose parents are poorly educated renters. By the age of thirty-five, the lucky group holds approximately ten times the level of housing wealth compared to the less fortunate.[27] The number is set to double again in the decades ahead. Britain is creating a network of mini family dynasties driven entirely by unearned good luck. The unfairness could hardly be more vivid.

Nor is that all. Housing space is used irrationally; older people live in homes too big for them, but with no incentive to downsize. Releasing the land to build homes is difficult for politicians because the new estates may offend incumbent homeowners' sensibilities and threaten their house prices. This is a permanent drag on new building. Because so many can't afford to live there, the migration to high-productivity, fast-growing cities does not happen on the scale necessary to sustain their growth; instead, the migration works in reverse, as people move to stagnating towns where house prices are affordable. In inner London, schools are closing as the exodus mounts. On current trends, tracts of the city may literally become childless as young couples cannot afford to live there.

Housing policy is killing British culture and its social capital. Every deformation in right-wing thinking over the last forty years has come together in the British housing market. It can be seen in the lily-livered, craven refusal to revalue property prices, which are frozen at 1991 levels, so that council tax receipts are pathetically low; in the refusal to accept a duty of care for the less-well-off by building enough social housing; in the hyper-laissez-faire approach to a Wild West mortgage market; in the indulgence of feudal forms of tenure; in the way the future is compromised to reward those alive today through council house sales and not building to replace them; in the vendetta against local government; in the way that planning gives 'not-in-my-back-yard' nimbys a veto over home-building; and in the refusal to redirect the financial system's excessive bias to lending with property assets as collateral. The rule is never to think or act long-term. The Conservative Party fiercely protects its old and late-middle-aged homeowning electoral base and damns everyone else.

As a result, we have a privileged caste of homeowners, typically in their fifties or over, who have paid off their mortgages on their grotesquely overpriced homes as a result of a fifty-year inflation in house prices. Property prices, notwithstanding recent falls, remain the highest they have been as a multiple of average earnings since the late nineteenth century and have more than doubled over the last thirty years. Owner occupation is falling – at 64 per cent today, compared to a peak of over 70 per cent in 2005.[28]

Putting this right requires public engagement everywhere – a willingness to tax, to direct, to build, to plan, to create new public institutions, to provide incomes that allow everyone to have access to a home. It is to assert the 'We' over too much destructive individualism. Start with the least advantaged. Beveridge knew the devil was in 'the problem of the rent', as he put it – how the variation of housing costs from household to household could make even well-designed and apparently generous welfare benefits useless unless there was some flexibility in allowances to help pay housing costs. Today, there is almost no such flexibility; high rents are crushing welfare recipients, while the £58-billion expenditure on supporting low-income renters exceeds the defence budget.

What to do? Enforcing labour market rules and extending collective bargaining agreements would ensure that adults in work at least receive the minimum wage, which over time should be raised to the living wage – a wage that would feed the income earners and their households. Universal Credit should be built around a careful, independent assessment of essential needs, as advocated by the Trussell Trust and Joseph Rowntree Foundation, and the judgement should be guaranteed to be respected by government.[29] It would rise from the current £85 per week to some £120 a week.

The problem is rent, as we have seen. Housing allowances to top up Universal Credit are often not enough to pay for private rental even after the 2023 uplift, which in many parts of the country, given social housing shortages, is all that it is available. The aim should be to lower rents and raise incomes. The rate of withdrawal of credit as wages rise should be much less penal. The right to buy council houses should be suspended until there is a cast-iron guarantee that the stock is replenished with new houses; 4.4 million have been sold and not replaced since the programme was launched by Mrs Thatcher in 1980.

Britain, according to one respected estimate, is 4.3 million homes shorter on all forms of tenure than if it had built homes at the same rate since the war as the European average.[30] We have the oldest housing stock in Europe, as well as the most overpriced.[31] We need to build more social homes, starter homes, homes for key workers, homes for our police and soldiers, homes for people who are downsizing, homes for the elderly. Planning needs to be reformed so that building is allowed within clear rules rather than at the discretion of local authority planners, and so that development gains are shared with local communities. And social housing should be as important as private housebuilding.

Former Deputy Prime Minister Nick Clegg recalls in his memoir *Politics: Between the Extremes* that either George Osborne or David Cameron (he says he can't remember which) – then chancellor and prime minister, respectively, of the 2010–16 coalition government – said that they didn't understand why he pressed for more social housing; it only created more Labour voters. 'They saw housing as a petri dish for voters. Unbelievable', he told the *Daily Mirror* when trailing the book.[32] The building of council housing has virtually ceased, with the provision of social housing falling on the shoulders of housing associations. The problem is that under current rules new social housing has to compete for scarce land with private housebuilders. When local planners give planning permission to landowners or developers, they trigger a ten- or twenty-fold increase in the value of land, but there is no land tax over and above simple capital gains tax – and none directed to the local area. Housing associations find themselves having to charge high rents in order to service the debt they assume to build homes on expensive land. They need to be able to build on cheaper land. Planning and land taxation needs to change. One simple reform would be a 'use it or lose it' approach to land for which planning permission has been granted; if it is not built on, then it should be sold to someone who will use it within two years.

What of those buying homes? Seven and a half million people hold a record £1.7 trillion of mortgage debt and are more exposed to short-term movements in interest rates than in any other advanced country; 95 per cent of British mortgages are either variable, linked to every quirk in interest rates, or on a mere two-year fixed rate. Two years after Russian tanks rolled into Ukraine in February 2022 and interest rates started climbing, 3 million households are coming to the end of their fixed-rate deals. For example, a household borrowing £300,000 on a twenty-five-year mortgage will now face a 50 per cent rise in monthly repayments – from £1,200 to £1,800 – as a consequence of interest rates increasing from 2 per cent to their current average of some 5.25 per cent.[33] The Resolution Foundation think tank estimates that by the end of 2024, over £15 billion extra will be bleeding out of household budgets. Given that so few households have more than £2,000 of savings, the Institute for Fiscal Studies forecasts that 2.9 million mortgage-holders will exhaust their savings completely.

The contrast with the US mortgage market is stark. Over 80 per cent of American mortgages are fixed for between fifteen and thirty years at rates between 2 and 3.5 per cent, insulating the vast majority of borrowers from the impact of rising short-term interest rates. Why? The American mortgage market used to be like Britain's, but the New Deal completely reshaped it. Britain needs to reproduce those Rooseveltian reforms, creating the same risk-sharing through specialist public funding agencies with widely available fixed-rate ten-, twenty- and even thirty-year mortgages. Only complacency, inertia, surrender to mortgage lenders' lobbying, belief that free markets never make mistakes and indifference to the interests of mortgagees have prevented the same happening in Britain.

As if all this was not mad enough, there is tax. Council tax is regressive, out of date and yields far less than it should. Politicians continually shy away from the revaluation of 1991 house prices on which the system is based – the kind of surrender to vested interests that characterised other civilisations in decline, like seventeenth-century Venice or eighteenth-century Spain. If the UK is still basing council tax in 2091 on 1991 residential values, be sure it will be a failed country. The nettle must be grasped. The regressive unfairness alone is breath-taking. The top band H council tax for high-priced property means it only attracts three times as much council tax as the least valuable in band A, despite being worth at least eight times more! The average property in Westminster pays council tax worth 0.06 per cent of its value; the average in Kensington and Chelsea pays 0.1 per cent. These are the richest boroughs in London. At the other end of the country, the average council tax in Hartlepool is levied at 1.3 per cent of the property's value – thirteen times as high as in Central London. At the very least, the arbitrary bands should be done away with as part of a revaluation, even if the aim is just to be revenue-neutral. The impact, calculates the Institute for Fiscal Studies, will be to lower bills for less-valuable property price households in the North and Midlands, including rented accommodation, and above-average property price households in London and the South will pay more.

The system currently yields £31 billion a year – proportionally far short of the revenue raised at the end of the 1980s, before Mrs Thatcher tried to substitute it with a poll tax. Widespread riots put paid to that, and contributed to the sense she was overreaching herself and should go. Council tax was the hastily cobbled-up alternative to the poll tax. Now we must go beyond reshaping it to root-and-branch reform. At the very least, let's review property values. If there had been regular revaluations since 1991, one estimate provided to me by an IFS researcher calculates that council tax receipts would now be a third to a half higher – between £10 billion and £15 billion annually. One feasible approach would simply be to levy a proportional tax on up-to-date property values subject to regular three- or five-year reviews, as proposed by the Mirrlees Review in 2010 – a proposal allowed quietly to rot. More radical still is Oxford University professor John Muellbauer's proposal to launch a split-rate property tax – partly based on the value of the land and partly on the value of the property, but with a discount for energy use. The greener the property, the lower the property tax. Households that are property-rich but cash-poor could defer paying the tax until their home was sold either to move on or on the death of the owner.[34] As he says, evidence marshalled by the OECD shows that economies in which property taxes are levied at current market values tend to have greater macroeconomic stability and higher growth.[35] Such a reform would yield greater local authority tax revenues, impose fairer property taxation, embed incentives to green energy use and achieve higher economic growth.

Above all, we need to regear the financial system so that it does not prioritise property lending so much. Too much of British banking is constructed around lending against residential property collateral – even for small business and start-ups – part of the distorting effect that property now has, not only in our personal lives but more widely. The regulators should give property lending higher risk weightings, and act to damp down lending growth by tightening risk weightings when the market booms – and, conversely, ease them when the market slumps. Britain does not need to live with a ludicrous property market that has become a destructive monster. Its reform is one of the preconditions to creating a saner economy and society.

Justice

It should not need to be said that any good society needs a functioning criminal justice system. In a letter to his eighteen-year-old self, the 'Secret Barrister' writes in *Nothing but the Truth*:

> Criminal justice means more than ever-increasing measures of punishments ... It is pervasive and effervescent and permeates every second of every day of every human life,

whether we are aware of it or not. It is the philosophy of what we do to each other.

The justice system does not exist on a discrete plane, populated by those unlike us and hermetically sealed from Middle England. 'We' are not merely an audience; justice runs through our society, and its quality affects us all.[36]

Everyone needs to know that basic principles of proportional, reciprocal human interaction will be upheld and that the rule of law will prevail; that contracts can be enforced; that obligations will be met; that fraud, theft and violence will be dealt with quickly and fairly; and, above all, that everyone, in whatever station of life, will respect the law and suffer sanctions speedily and fairly if they do not. Everyone should have recourse to legal advice, support and the courts if it is needed – a foundation of citizenship. Social capital will flourish in such a society; it will wilt if such principles are neglected.

The last fourteen years have seen these principles shamefully shredded. At the time of writing, the backlog of outstanding cases in the Crown Courts is 62,511 – with 29 per cent becalmed for more than a year, an all-time peak. The statistics were growing worse before the Covid pandemic; in both the Magistrates' and Crown Courts, the number of cases waiting to be completed after the original offence had climbed to disgraceful numbers. Now it is worse still. In the first quarter of 2023, the median time between offence and resolution in the Magistrates' Courts was 187 days, and in the Crown Courts an astounding 398 days.[37]

Meanwhile, Britain has the highest prison population per head in Western Europe, with more than 81,000 prisoners. Overcrowding and violence are rife; rehabilitation is ever harder. Prison sentencing is a nightmarish cat's cradle of conflicting injunctions, with guidance running to over 1,300 pages. The probation service is still reeling from the attempt to privatise it in 2013, farming out complex and demanding work to contractors who tried to turn probation into a low-cost mass process. It had to be abandoned. Now the supervision of over 100,000 high-risk offenders, reports the HM Probation Inspectorate, is being done inadequately, with six out of ten probation officers seriously overworked; the number of offences committed by those on probation continues to rise. Every dimension of the system is crippled by the swingeing spending cuts imposed by austerity – many courts are physically unusable for safety reasons, and there is a chronic shortage of prison capacity.

Britain has churned through eleven justice secretaries since 2010. The justice and prison system – out of sight for most of the public, with no consistent ministerial advocate and being a cause in which contemporary conservatism does not believe – suffered the biggest real spending cuts of more than a quarter over the 2010s (only social care suffered as much). The most dramatic casualty was legal aid, following the 2012 Legal Aid, Sentencing and Punishment of Offenders Act, which removed support for cases involving housing, welfare, medical negligence, employment, debt and immigration. The numbers receiving legal aid dropped from 1 million in 2009 to 130,000 in 2011/2.[38] The entire ecosystem offering citizens support to secure justice has shrivelled. In Tory circles, these were almost all seen as vexatious cases, succouring the incomes of 'lefty lawyers' who took up cases only because of the availability of legal aid. Doubtless there was some abuse – but surely better to have policed legal aid more effectively than simply to remove some of the most important cases, like welfare, housing and employment, from eligibility altogether. But ambitious Conservative politicians have not advanced their careers through protecting a just society and a functioning criminal justice system. They get on better by attacking human rights, in particular the European Court of Human Rights, assaulting judges as the enemies of the people, devising ever-more-punitive sentences, radically reducing access to the law and allowing the court system to decay. It is performative politics, playing to Britain's immensely powerful right-wing media. Britain is a less just society as a result.

The Good Society?

Growing inequality and a broken social contract would make for a weaker society in any circumstances, but it is their interaction with other pernicious forces that has driven society to the edge. Our cities are increasingly defined by siloed, self-contained houses and blocks of soulless flats, riven with social divides. We have sealed neighbourhoods of either owner-occupied or social housing with too little public space, and diminishing capacity to associate freely with one another. Think of London's South Bank, the concentration of tower blocks in Vauxhall or Manchester's Salford Quays – and there are many more around the country. Over the last forty years, there has been a surge of gated communities and privately owned 'public spaces', and a steady sell-off of public land and property – including school playing fields, publicly owned real estate, accommodation for the police and military near where they work and, of course, those 4-million-plus council house sales since the Right to Buy was introduced in 1980. Social media and the Internet mean people retreat from face-to-face communication; clothes, books, groceries and electronic devices are delivered to our front doors, rather than being bought in-person on the High Street, while we scroll through our social media accounts recording likes and hurling out insults. It has never been easier to be alone, and already in 2016 – four years prior to the pandemic – 9 million Britons reported that they were always or often lonely.[39] All of this reinforces the deep undercurrents that are producing a more gummed-up and stratified society.

Social capital is best created by face-to-face interaction, especially social interaction across class, ethnic, income and educational divides. This is the finding of an extraordinary study – 'Social Capital and Economic Mobility' – into the networks and neighbourhoods of up to 20 million people in the USA by four Harvard researchers.[40] The key determinant of children's social mobility is the degree of cross-class economic connectedness – the extent to which, for whatever reason, from the character of the schools to the quality and quantity of sports clubs and the openness of its bars, coffee shops and restaurants – people from different backgrounds make friendships. The more friends people from lower-income backgrounds can make with those in middle- and upper-income backgrounds, especially when they are young, the greater their social capital and the greater their chance of faring well in life.

That is less likely in contemporary Britain. It is not only the way we organise ourselves physically, but socially. The more common phenomenon is not cross-class connectedness, but 'opportunity hoarding', the way parents in upper-income groups try to maximise their children's advantages through private education, tutoring, membership of exclusive clubs and other social and educational tricks to give their kids that bit extra – as if they need it. Social mobility implies people moving down as well as up, but all the evidence, as the Sutton Trust amply proves, is that those who have intend to use every stratagem to ensure that their children will also have. It takes five generations for people from low-income backgrounds to climb to middle-income jobs in Britain, so tough are the obstacles, compared to one generation in Denmark, says outgoing LSE Director Minouche Safik.[41] It is not good enough.

To do better begins, as argued earlier, with serious investment in education and promoting schools and universities as sites for cross-class interconnectedness. At least a third of the intake of private schools should be made up of kids from middle- and lower-income families on bursaries. Reform of our housing market, complete with better designed taxation of it and the wealthy more generally, must begin to cap inequality. Grants need to be made available to all forms of civic association – tennis clubs, choirs, book clubs, rewilding groups – that might promote social interconnectedness. One advantage of the proposed Civilian Conservation Corps, and its variant, a National Youth Corps focused on work experience and training for sixteen- to twenty-four-year-olds (I led an informal group proposing this in 2021), is that both would recruit members from all classes of society.[42] It was the movement of 4 million evacuees during the Second World War, recall, that gave the better-off in larger houses away from the threat of bombing a better sense of what life was like for the poor in the bombed-out inner cities, and increased solidarity and empathy as scales fell from their eyes. The Corps could do a similar job today.

It is one way, with many more needed, of living what author Jon Yates calls in his book *Fractured* a 'common life', so that we lean against the proclivities that pull us apart. Our cities and towns must reassert public and civic space – libraries, parks, open shopping centres, affordable housing, teenage clubs, sports fields, concert halls and strict limitations of gated communities and private roads. The BBC and other public-service broadcasters represent the 'We'. They need to be supported, not starved of funds. They can become the model for public-interest social media platforms in which data privacy is respected and which can only be shared with individuals' agreement; there would be strong rules of engagement to ensure truthfulness and the policing of online bullying and trolling. Local and city government should be properly empowered and resourced; it should aim to create more physical and social space for social interaction. Flexible hybrid working should be mandatory, to free up time for all workers. Public transport needs to be reinvigorated outside London so that it takes the majority thirty minutes or less to get to the city centre, rather than enduring today's disastrous travel times. A stronger national network of Sure Start Centres and well-respected new vocational universities could promote yet more cross-class connectedness.

There is a lot that can be done, none of which comes easily to the libertarians in thrall to laissez-faire. The 'We' must reassert itself. We must not only reduce inequality and repair our social contract, but unapologetically promote social capital in the broadest sense.

International comparisons confirm the story of Britain's weak performance. A comprehensive world ranking of social capital on fifteen criteria, grouped under equality, health, crime, satisfaction and freedom, places Britain 51st out of 160 countries. Britain as a developed country should be above the global average, but it is still well below the global best. In Europe, only Hungary and Bulgaria scored lower.[43]

But there is a caution. As acknowledged by the leading theorist of social capital, Harvard's Professor Robert Putnam, there is negative social capital as well as positive. Social capital that grows within a framework stressing classic European Enlightenment values of tolerance, freedom, non-violence, celebration of debate and mutual respect is likely to support the other five capitals – physical/natural, financial, innovative, social and institutional. In this case membership is open rather than closed; the aim is to build bonds of openness, bridge divides and to link people.

But there is also a form of social capital constructed by groups using hostility to 'the other' to cement the togetherness of their own closed membership; here, the aim is to oppose, factionalise, differ, exclude and separate, drawing the insiders together. As Kenan Malik argues in his important book *Not So Black and White*, it is an anxiety to 'other' on the basis of skin colour that creates racism; human beings' more generous first instinct is to ignore skin colour and assess people by their qualities and attributes. But the phenomenon of our time has become identity politics, based on stressing the differences between groups, with the political right often stressing ethnically driven difference, with 'whiteness' the most superior. There is the angry obsession with being 'anti-woke', of 'Making America Great Again', and, on the left, the defining of identity through one's stance on the environment, the empire, slavery, Palestine or trans rights. These are groupings that create social capital which pulls society apart, rather than emphasising what we hold in common. Malik argues that the best response is to argue for the universal values of openness, tolerance and inclusion – citing Salman Rushdie's call for 'hybridity, impurity and intermingling'. It is the only response consistent with the 'We' society, with achieving the best that social capital can offer – to stand by the indivisibility of fellowship.

For democratic societies are based on argument, and more argument; progress demands debate. The merchants of identity politics have to be argued out of positions they hold; to coerce or ostracise by no-platforming is to play the game by their rules. As John Locke argued in 1689 in his famous letter 'On Toleration', you cannot coerce people into belief; they have to be tolerated, to be argued with and to find their own way to beliefs they want to stand by and can defend in open argument. 'We-ness' based on exclusion, differentiation and socially created differences is a dead-end and a civilisational threat; it reduces rather than increases social capital. We need connectedness, interaction, argument and a capacity to listen to each other.

But how argument is structured by political institutions and the media is crucial; it cannot be a shouting match from behind siloed stockades, in which deafness is celebrated. Great political debate can create positive social capital, rather than diminish it. The social capital needed to navigate the world we're facing will come from those societies and cultures that one way or another find a route to resolving difference amicably – as crucial as learning to live together well. One precondition is to build a robust society on the principles of fairness that underpin a social contract – all the elements identified in the last two chapters. Another is to build great democratic institutions to frame the public square. How best to do that? This is the question to which we now turn.

13

THE DEGRADED PUBLIC SQUARE

Britain must do democracy, public argument and government better. What follows in the wake of democratic failure is bad governance. If Britain is to launch a New Deal-style partnership between government, finance, business and employees in the decades ahead, it needs an agile and effective democratic state supported actively by citizens whose consent is won and rewon in a vigorous public square. Such dynamic democratic processes do not exist in 2024.

There is already a trust deficit; citizens have heard so many undelivered extravagant promises that they have become suspicious not only of Conservative politicians, but of all politicians. Too much performative politics, playing to the right-wing gallery, has degraded the entire process of political communication. Politicians habitually do not level with a public that they know does not trust them. In this atmosphere it is best to avoid straying into the 'wicked issues' that involve intractable and painful trade-offs and to instead say things that you think people want to hear; there are few dividends in candour. The British, for example, have been allowed to believe that they can enjoy European levels of high-quality public services with American-style low taxation. In reality, this is an impossibility.

Too many discussions follow the same path, and we end up not confronting, say, the financing of social care any more than the costs of the drive to reduce our carbon emissions. It is obvious that capital and wealth need to be taxed more fairly – after all wealth has more than doubled over the last generation in relation to national output but the proportion of tax raised from wealth is the same. Brexit has imposed needless frictions on trade with the EU, which are self-damaging. Again, there is simply silence or aggressive, wearisome point-scoring.

It is a degenerate political culture, made worse by a highly centralised structure of government whose politicians are elected by a first-past-the-post voting system. As a result power is concentrated on a single party with a minority of votes but a majority of MPs. Cynicism about voting is accentuated because in large parts of the country there is no point in voting for a politician who shares your values. First-past-the-post guarantees that they lose, and your vote has served no purpose. To add insult to injury, smaller towns and rural areas with geographically dispersed voters have an advantage over cities. Urban Labour votes are concentrated in fewer constituencies, piling up uselessly large majorities.

For the smaller parties the unfairness is even more gross. In the 2019 general election, it took 336,000 votes to elect a LibDem MP and 866,000 to elect a Green MP, which gives voters a sense of helplessness and unfairness.[1] Because the occasions on which the major parties have to find compromises, make common cause or respect each other are so rare, they are locked in a permanent bitter rivalry in which the quest is to find sharply dividing issues. From this political culture a powerful, partisan and unaccountable media takes its cue, becoming the cheerleader for one side or the other – usually the very right-wing position given the bias in our press – so that the public square is degraded.

For the stakes are high. To become the government of the British state is the most complete prize of any democracy, in a way that is impossible in very few other countries. Control the House of Commons, and an unrivalled degree of patronage and power falls into the governing party's lap. If you are prepared to push it – as Boris Johnson showed so brazenly – there is virtually no limit to the winning party's capacity to shower honours, jobs and money on its friends, to challenge the courts and rule of law, to bend the parliamentary, electoral and constitutional rule book for party advantage and to reward donations with favours. Politics is a rough trade in any democracy, but in Britain it is rough for the most primitive of purposes. In Britain the winner takes all. The Conservative Party has taken this truth to heart more than its rivals, becoming a machine for winning and wielding power to the advantage of its supporters. But the paradox is that so much discretionary executive power leads to consistently bad government, bad policy and bad outcomes. It does not even allow policy experimentation outside central government because local power is so minimal; good ideas do not get a chance to breathe.

Defenders point to the presence of countervailing political power, in Parliament formally the task of the official opposition and the House of Lords. But this is trivial and ineffective against the party holding a Commons majority. It ruthlessly controls Parliament's timetable and business. The party's own MPs will be reliably compliant lobby fodder who, partly out of tribal loyalty and partly from hopes of preferment, will vote for almost any legislation as it is drafted and rarely properly scrutinise, let alone challenge, it. In any case, British MPs are not funded, as they are in most other democracies, to equip themselves with research support for such legislative work. Their role is circumscribed to representing their constituents, evolving into super-ombudsmen and women dealing with constituents' problems with housing, employment, welfare and crime. The assumption is that the devising of policy and drafting of bills will have been done on high by the minister and officials, reducing MPs to ciphers.

'You're humiliated by the whips, who force you to vote on the party line day in, day out', former Tory cabinet minister Rory Stewart says. 'There's barely any point reading legislation. It becomes clear your promotion has nothing to do with expertise. It's about loyalty and defending the indefensible.'[2] The notion that the self-styled mother of parliaments is the envy of the world and leads to well-oiled government has never more obviously been a noxious conceit. In reality, a form of feudal power persists, only today it is exercised by ministers who don't claim the divine right to rule absolutely but rather by virtue of being elected, enabling them to assume a power that is still drenched in monarchical absolutism. Thus the executive is described as having so-called Henry VIII powers – and contemporary governments have been extending the spheres they rule much as Henry VIII might have done.

Law in Britain is lawful once it is passed by Parliament and signed by the monarch – who will unfailingly comply. But the continuing constitutional presence of the Crown means that regal prerogative power is delegated to ministers who then act as surrogate mini-monarchs. Processes theoretically designed to ensure integrity, like the Advisory Committee on Business Appointments or the Committee on Standards in Public Life, are established within this framework of delegated regal authority. They have the capacity only to advise an absolutist prime minister, so that he or she can ignore their recommendations – as Johnson did almost as a matter of routine. Even an institution that is on a statutory footing, like the Electoral Commission, can find the scope of its investigations defined by the prime minister. Equally dispensable is advice on ministerial conflicts of interests or from your own ethics adviser, both of whom Johnson also ignored and treated with contempt, leading to their twin resignations. As a schoolboy at Eton, an incubator of overweening ambition, Boris Johnson said he wanted to be 'World King'. He ended up with a good second option, being de facto king in Britain.

So much in the British constitutional and political system rests on a willingness to abide by conventions and codes of decency – to behave, as Professor Peter Hennessy once dubbed it, as 'good chaps'. These gentlemen's agreements have long since disappeared. The Conservative Party in government has dispelled any last illusions. It uses the system to raise money from whatever dubious source – members of Russian oligarch networks, Middle Eastern kleptocrats of dubious provenance – and rewards donors with peerages and honours, with few questions asked. It has even changed the voting system to favour itself, by requiring the showing of photographic ID in order to vote – allegedly to suppress voter fraud (which is negligible in Britain), but in fact to disenfranchise some of the young, poor and ethnic-minority voters who tend to vote Labour. It worked, up to a point. In the English local elections in May 2023, 14,000 voters were turned away from voting and another 4 per cent of those who did not vote

– estimated to be up to 400,000 – said that they did not bother even to try because of voter ID, in the estimate of the Electoral Commission.[3] All to stop perhaps a dozen fraudulent votes.

True, the courts have a degree of independence, and civil society organisations or businesses may launch a judicial review of government actions, but in the main they can only challenge the process rather than any particular law. It was important that the Supreme Court ruled against Johnson's prorogation of Parliament in the autumn of 2019 in order to reduce time for parliamentary scrutiny of Brexit, but in doing so it also recognised the principle of prerogative powers. It was just that prerogative could not be used overtly to trump the sovereignty of Parliament, ruled the Court. Johnson had been prepared to do just that. Indeed, in the earlier test of prorogation in Scotland's highest court, before the case went to the Supreme Court, it had ruled that Johnson had in effect lied over his true motives – to the Queen, to Parliament and to the electorate.[4] Such legal intervention was portrayed by Tory leaders and the party's megaphone press as an outrageous intrusion by lawyers and judges into 'democracy' – a view expressed with even more passion when the rulings of the European Court of Human Rights intrude into the UK. Set up after the Second World War to be the guarantor of human rights, with energetic support from the British government, there is now a growing element in the Tory Party who would rather that Britain leave the European Convention on Human Rights complete with its court, most recently over its ruling that the government's plan to deport asylum seekers to Rwanda without appeal offended basic human rights. In Britain an elected government should suffer no constraint on its actions by any judge. Parliamentary sovereignty is to be interpreted as the government having the right to be above the law, an argument the right deployed to harden proposed legislation to overcome legal objections to Rwanda deportations in December 2023 into new realms of disregard for law. Over immigration the British government should exercise unrestrained prerogative powers. Even as it was the legislation proposed virtually no opportunity for redress or appeal against its rulings and allowed the government to set aside important legal duties to observe human rights. The right, launching a battle over what constitutes democracy, has exposed the frailty of Britain's constitutional settlement and its capacity to regress to authoritarianism.

The Civil Service is a weak instrument for constraining untrammelled executive power. Historically, it saw its role as turning a governing party's electoral mandate into effective government action, steering ministers away from obvious pitfalls; a permanent secretary would serve their minister well by speaking truth to power. Today, after a succession of firings, notably of the Permanent Secretary to the Treasury Tom Scholar by the short-lived Chancellor Kwasi Kwarteng in September 2022, permanent secretaries are cowed into being super-administrators. Sir Philip Rutnam, permanent secretary at the Home Office, resigned and brought a charge of bullying against the then Home Secretary Priti Patel, which the government expensively settled – and only after the ethics adviser, Alex Allan, had similarly resigned over Johnson's backing for Patel. Young, callow, highly politicised special advisers fill the gap. This is democracy as farce, wide open to manipulation to achieve the kind of executive dominance and discretion which autocrats around the world already possess and of which the ultra-right in the USA and Europe can only dream.

Monarchical centralisation reaches its apogee in the evisceration of local government. In British constitutional terms, sovereignty can only be loaned to local government by a sovereign monarch. Thus the relationship between Westminster and the localities is constitutionally the same as the one devised by William the Conqueror, the warrior monarch who subjugated England. Local government's powers to tax, borrow and spend are minimal. It is reduced to providing refuse collection, care for the elderly, homeless and neglected children, street lighting, libraries and some planning functions. As an agent for local economic regeneration and growth, it is enfeebled. Only 2 per cent of all capital and current spending in the UK on economic development is spent by local government; start-up companies know that the idea of local government acting to compensate for the absence of locally based equity and credit funding is a pipedream – it has neither the capacity nor power to change anything. Britain is thereby economically disabled.

Despite the interest in expanding devolution with the spread of city mayors, spending has become even more centralised in Britain over the last decade – and dramatically cut in real terms. Real core local government spending between 2010/11 and 2022/3 fell by an astounding 27 per cent.[5] Raising taxation locally to compensate? Not a chance. Local government raises around half of what comparable local governments in other countries can raise from tax; taxation on property accounts for 99 per cent of all local government revenue and the rates and valuations are set by central government, and the total they can raise is capped. It is a financial straitjacket. No local taxes on income or spending are allowed. By comparison, reports the Centre for Cities, Paris has nine local taxes, Tokyo has seventeen, Berlin has eighteen and New York City has at least twenty-two.[6] Intense pressure to finance fast-rising adult and child social care costs interacting with the savage real cuts in central government grants and no local revenue raising powers are now provoking an escalating number of local governments to issue Section 114 bankruptcy notices declaring themselves nothing less than bankrupt – Nottingham and Birmingham the largest and most recent in 2023. Local government is entering a full-scale crisis.

Centralisation is further embedded by the system of local government competing with other local governments to bid for funds from central 'pots'. Competitive bidding wastes enormous amounts of local authorities' limited time and resources, often for no reward. Its purpose is to ensure that central government decides what local authorities should be doing in their local areas, rather than trusting local government with the resources required to deliver on local priorities. Combined with the sheer churn in funding pots, with 18 per cent of all revenue grants and 30 per cent of all capital grants for local authorities being wound up every year, responding to economic conditions or planning for long-term priorities is close to impossible.[7]

There are baby steps towards change. Devolution deals for the combined authorities of Greater Manchester and the West

THE DEGRADED PUBLIC SQUARE

Midlands in 2023 are a recognition that centralisation has gone too far. Both areas will establish a joint governance board for technical education, co-design future employment support programmes and take part in the governance of local rail services. But in essentials the regime remains the same; Greater Manchester and the West Midlands have more discretion over how some public money in both areas should be spent, but that's it. In essence local government remains as dependent and subservient to Westminster as their predecessors were to the first Norman kings. As central government appoints commissioners to take over the running of cities and towns bankrupted by the current financial and political order, that is not hyperbole but an all too obvious reality.

Epic Misgovernance

In their path-breaking book *The Blunders of Our Government*, published ten years ago, Professors Ivor Crewe and Anthony King set out the catalogue of disasters that had defined thirty years of British government up to that moment. Some were large-scale – entering the European Exchange Rate Mechanism at too high an exchange rate, the poll tax, the still-bungled attempt to bring IT into the NHS or the fiasco of the now-abandoned public–private partnership for the London Underground. Others were more modest in scale – the abortive attempt to launch grotesque 'super-casinos', the launch and withdrawal of home information packs and individual learning accounts after widespread fraud or the disaster of the Child Support Agency, which proved unable to get maintenance money from unwilling separated fathers.

Since 2013, matters have hardly improved. Crewe's challenge to me when we met was to name one successful policy from the last decade. The large-scale epic failures are obviously Brexit and austerity. Brexit happened partly because an ill-designed referendum did not even require either side formally to set out their case, let alone earn a super-majority for such a seismic constitutional and political rupture. Then Prime Minister May triggered Article 50, setting a two-year deadline to leave the EU but without even a framework for what leaving would actually mean. It has been a disaster, socially divisive and economically destructive. Austerity, a wholesale, unwanted and unnecessary assault on public services and the disadvantaged, was rammed through, again with little deliberation. Since then the talismanic policy of levelling up has shrivelled to virtually nothing. The reduction of the much-vaunted high-speed rail project HS2 to little more than a shuttle between stations outside London and Birmingham was cited in an earlier chapter. Public services languish. The Lansley reforms of the NHS were costly, disruptive and produced no improvement in performance. The probation service was privatised in 2015, only for it to be reversed in 2018 after, as Crewe writes, 'having destroyed the national rehabilitation system, forfeited the confidence of the courts, and bankrupted the private providers'.[8] Successive efforts at limiting immigration have failed.

Nor have British military efforts been notably successful, which is sobering for a country that prides itself on the efficiency of its elite forces. There is embarrassment in the 'shame' of Iraq, as the army privately acknowledges, and expensive ineffectiveness in Afghanistan before a scuttle that left many thousands of Afghanis who had worked for Britain exposed to the tender mercies of the Taliban. Famously, the then Foreign Secretary Dominic Raab only belatedly returned from holiday in the days before the fall of Kabul.

There are a few successes in the long litany of failure. Pensions are one bright spot, with the launch of the Pension Protection Fund successfully saving over 1,000 company defined-benefit pension plans, and then the opt-in to stakeholder pensions, which has grown to give most adults a small top-up to the state pension. When Covid struck, the single-minded focus on vaccine production and its subsequent roll-out, with the NHS providing the vaccine and local government finding both sites and volunteers, worked well – a near miracle, as the King's Fund called it.[9] It was a great example of how local energy and local decision-making can be harnessed with the centre.

Despite flashes of effectiveness, the general story has been one of sustained blunder after blunder. Success in vaccines during the pandemic are offset by great scandals. The discharge of elderly NHS Covid-sufferers into care homes caused thousands of premature deaths, as former health secretary Matt Hancock told the Covid Inquiry. The spending of £3.7 billion on questionable PPE contracts to contractors in the preferred 'VIP lane' (largely the contacts of ministers, Tory MPs and donors), among which Baroness Michelle Mone and her husband making £100-million profit on defective and unusable PPE equipment and surgical gowns was only the most egregious, is but the latest example of the trend. Britain is chronically and systematically badly governed.

The Heart of It

The heart of the problem is our overly majoritarian political system, which places little emphasis on implementation, and makes politics primarily an arena for career advancement and striking ideological attitudes rather than governing effectively. As Ian Dunt writes in his scathing *How Westminster Works... and Why It Doesn't*, first-past-the-post 'fails in two distinct ways. First, it fails on the most basic possible level imaginable by ignoring the majority of votes. Second, it fails by creating a form of government with no need to compromise.'[10]

The 2022 British Social Attitudes Survey, for the first time in its forty-year history, found a 51 per cent majority in favour of electoral reform – witness to the growing recognition that the current system does not fairly represent the diversity of views in the electorate and encourages a politics that doesn't work for the majority.[11] As we saw in earlier chapters, for over a century it has produced governments that do not actually receive the majority of votes, wholly distorting the course of our history. Defenders of the status quo stress the importance of the constituency link in anchoring MPs in neighbourhoods, allowing local electorates to build a relationship with an MP they know and in conferring majorities in the House of Commons on a single party, which avoids the horse-trading and unseemly bargaining associated with more proportional voting systems. Governments, it is argued, can get on and govern. Unfortunately, the most relevant and unanswered criticism is that the governments born this way deliver consistently poor government.

Britain now has over 13 million voters living in Scotland, Wales and London who vote for members of the Scottish Parliament, the Welsh Senedd and the Greater London Assembly, using a blend of constituency voting with numbers in the assemblies topped up in proportion to the overall share of votes cast. The world has not fallen in. Indeed, arguably all are governed better than the system that preceded it, especially in Wales. Citizens seem more politically engaged and readier to turn out more in elections. Certainly, smaller parties, like the Greens, have a better chance of winning representation, which has led to a more pluralistic and inclusive political landscape – and their better exposure to serious scrutiny. The Well-being of Future Generations Act in Wales has come to be seen as something of a landmark internationally, incubated in what in British terms is a very distinct pluralist political climate. Fewer votes are wasted, because even if a party or candidate does not win a majority in a constituency, their votes will contribute to the overall seat allocation, which reinforces engagement and participation. Instead of fair voting leading to political fragmentation and instability, it has forced parties to work together, and increased collaboration, negotiation and compromise. As for the argument that proportional representation empowers fringe and extremist parties, the fate of the Brexit Party in the Welsh Senedd is telling. Faced with the reality of explaining and justifying its position, it has imploded. It would have been much better for democracy if Nigel Farage had been in the House of Commons having to argue his position rather than mounting a destructive populist insurgency from the sidelines. The extremists can be defanged by exposing them to democratic argument and scrutiny in a national parliament.

More representative membership of our Parliament would help create a culture of serious governance, currently conspicuous by its absence. The House of Lords takes scrutiny of bills more seriously than the Commons, where it is not unusual for whole bills to attract just minutes of examination. In the Lords there is no guillotine. But for all that, it is an astonishing anachronism – 'a weeping sore on the face of the British constitution', as described by former Electoral Commissioner David Howarth. Its replacement by an elected chamber was mooted as long ago as the debates leading to the 1911 Parliament Act. More than a century later, we still wait, with apologists insisting that somehow 'it works'. It does not. It is dysfunctional.

It is not endearingly eccentric that in 2023 Britain leaves scrutiny of its legislation to ninety-two hereditary peers and some 700 lifelong appointees, as the parties vie with each other to secure political control. The Lords is the second-biggest legislative assembly in the world after the Chinese National Congress. Only half of its nominal members ever turn up. If Labour win power and wish for parity with the Tories, it will have to appoint another 100 Labour peers; if it wants an overall majority, it will have to appoint another 250 peers, sending total membership spiralling to over 1,000. Scrutiny? Only 10 per cent of cross-bench peers, whose knowledge and wisdom is deemed so precious to the Lords, bother to sign in for their £300 attendance allowance. And when push comes to shove, as with the 2023 Immigration bill, the government will whip its Tory peers to suspend their independent judgement in the same way it does Tory MPs in the Commons.

As for the character of the political appointees to the Lords, here is another example of the way monarchical power suffuses the constitution. The monarch used the power of appointment to sell honours to raise money from the late Middle Ages onwards. Charles II also did it to reward his mistresses. Inveighing against the appointments system because Conservative prime ministers in particular use it to reward donors – the going rate for a peerage under the Tories has been estimated at £3 million[12] – is to miss the point; the system is being used exactly as it was always intended, to raise money and offer patronage to friends and loyalists. Of course, too many appointees are of doubtful worth, enjoying the personal coat of arms, the flim-flam and social status that being a Lord confers, while others take their responsibilities as super-scrutineers seriously. Most peers do their best within the confines of what is possible, and the majority accept the need for reform as a quid pro quo for a more serious constitutional role. The independent House of Lords Appointments Commission may vet the prime minister's nominees to its number, but within the British system it can only advise. 'King' Johnson simply chose to overrule it in the case of his appointment of Lord Cruddas.

The Civil Service does its best, but it has been weakened by continual attacks from influential Tories; for example, Tory Chair Greg Hands in a leaked email claimed that the Civil Service constitutes an obstructive 'blob'. Cabinet Secretary Simon Case observed to the Public Administration and Constitutional Affairs Select Committee that the language was 'dehumanising', undermined Civil Service morale and was 'self-defeating cowardice'. He is right. It is much easier to blame the Civil Service for the unworkability of policy rather than accept that its political authors were wrong.

The most powerful department of all, the Treasury, is endemically penny-wise and pound-foolish, which makes long-term strategic policy all the harder to fashion. Its officials, all too often very young and only a year or two out of university, soon become saturated in a spirit of sceptical disengagement. The Treasury's default position is to play the role of critical, unfriendly banker to spendthrift departments in the name of protecting the taxpayer from any public initiative. Proactive policies are always doomed to be over-budget, and can be expected not to succeed in their avowed aim; this is the habitual Treasury mindset. Its unwillingness ever to throw its weight behind public purpose translates into the department becoming an institutional enabler of blunders. Tax policy is shrouded in such absurd secrecy that the result, in the words of one influential 2016 report, is 'an ever-lengthening tax code, beset by a series of problems, confusion for taxpayers, poor implementation, political reversals and constrained options'.[13]

The culture is a hangover from more than a century and a half of attachment to laissez-faire economics and the Gladstonian small state, which the Treasury has never really shed. 'Free trade and sound money', declared Robert Chalmers, permanent secretary to the Treasury in the early 1900s, 'are really two sides of the same coin',[14] a refrain echoed a generation later by senior Treasury official Sir Otto Niemeyer, adding the need for balancing the budget, as he piloted Britain back onto the gold standard. Senior officials supporting Chancellor George Osborne's austerity drive eighty-five years later were singing from a 150-year-old hymn sheet. Importantly, trust in free trade, sound money and balanced budgets excuses non-specialist officials from having to engage with practical issues of policy implementation, for which, in any case, they lack the appropriate skills. Attempts to remedy the situation, for example, a 2002 recommendation to allow more experts to have Treasury careers, 'died a quiet death', in the words of the report's author, Sir John Kingman.[15] Instead, officials continue just to say 'No', leaving others to worry about the consequences.

Government reacts to crises and issues as they come up, with an ingrained instinct to interfere as little as possible with the private sector, which is assumed to know best. Nye Bevan's complaint, in his book *In Place of Fear*, of the culture where private ambitions are seen as 'the main purpose of human endeavour' rings as true in the 2020s as it did in the 1950s. In this world, public spending is always extravagant and private spending is virtuous and ever-efficient. There is little developed institutional capacity, or parliamentary incentive, to do what all other good organisations do – road-test ideas, assess risk, work across government departments if necessary and then implement policy, adjusting as feedback is gathered. Indeed, pilot schemes have fallen out of use over the Tory years. The Treasury does not invite such an approach, nor is Parliament able to offer scrutiny of real material risk. Instead, the entire emphasis is on retrospective and sporadic questioning and audit, represented in Parliament by the Public Accounts Committee and in the Civil Service by the National Audit Office. In fairness, they both quite effectively do their job of looking in the back mirror and holding departments and officials to account – but in so doing, they further embed risk aversion. Don't act unless you have to; and, if you do act, cover your arse.

For these reasons, contracting out and the use of consultants come easily to the British state. By using one of the big four accountancy partnerships, top management consultancies or leading public-service contractors, an official can say they did their best to deliver high-quality results; they cannot be blamed – they're covered. They took the best advice, at eye-watering cost. Not only is this an expensive surrogate for in-house capacity; what it means in effect, as the former cabinet minister Lord Agnew acknowledged in 2020, is the further infantilisation of the Civil Service.[16] Young, intelligent graduates in the Civil Service contract out work to young, intelligent but better-paid graduates in one of the major consultancies. Neither side is truly experienced or knows much about creative enterprise; they recycle the latest transient business school wisdom or fad from the World Economic Forum. The civil servants are just as able as the consultants, but are not trusted to do the work themselves.

The state robs itself of the capacity to act, as Mariana Mazzucato and Rosie Collington argue in the *The Big Con: How the Consulting Industry Weakens our Businesses, Infantilises Our Governments and Warps Our Economies.*[17] Instead, the state becomes the prisoner of slick PowerPoint presentations and transient consultants peddling quick-fix solutions, which (however well-meaning) are no substitute for deep institutional knowledge, learning by doing and having skin in the game – to avoid paying the price for failure by straining every sinew to make sure that policy works. Nor are consultants indifferent to the sheer profitability of the work. McKinsey charged £563,400 to provide 'vision, purpose and narrative' for the UK's Covid test-and-trace programme, led by Dido Harding (herself a former McKinsey consultant)[18] – an expensive price-tag for framing a programme that would ultimately cost £37 billion and which the House of Commons Public Accounts Committee judged made no difference at all to the management and spread of the epidemic.

Rapid ministerial turnover, always a feature of British politics, has become habitual as the Conservative government enters its protracted death throes, and makes matters worse. The general picture – in fairness, there are some exceptions, like Michael Gove at Communities and Levelling Up, Ben Wallace when at

Defence or Jeremy Hunt at Health – is of ministers lasting little longer than eighteen months or less, in thrall to theatrical right-wing gestures to please party members and the right-wing media, passing through on their way to imagined greater things. The doctrine of ministerial accountability means that civil servants serve their transient minister rather than the government as a whole. The central apparatus around the prime minister and the cabinet office, while strong enough to promote and demote, veto and initiate, is not equipped to ensure delivery of policies, while the permanently sceptical, secretive Treasury holds the purse strings. It is as if British government is set up to fail.

Controlling the Narrative

It is no accident that all autocratic states make sure they control the means of information. There can only be one message – there is no alternative to the supreme leader, and of course no limit to their wisdom. But while democracies may be constructed around the contest for power, democratic leaders throughout history are no strangers to wanting to control the message. Politicians and political parties strain every muscle to ensure that as far as possible it is their words, their message, their spin that frames the public argument – knowing that most citizens don't have the time and energy to mine the truth. Frame the argument and control the narrative, and you are more than half the way to winning elections and afterwards sustaining yourself in office. Half-truths and even lies are all part of the currency. It is up to your opponents to expose you.

It is vital that there are some guarantors of fact in the information ecosystem, that a bias to honesty is maintained in the no-holds-barred fight between the parties. Overstep the mark in telling lies, and the ecosystem should find you out. There should be penalties for mendacity. But that is no longer the rule. For, here, the right has been extremely active and in its way creative (often in the most banal and literal sense), weakening what was once a halfway reasonable system that guaranteed a minimum threshold of media integrity. Instead, it is becoming ever more vulnerable to fake news, manipulation and overt lying in the service of the desired right-wing controlling narrative. British newspapers, serving their right-wing proprietors, were always biased to the Tory cause – recall Northcliffe in the early 1900s or Beaverbrook in the 1940s and 1950s – but strong public-service broadcasting in the form of the BBC and a public-service regulatory requirement on private broadcasters of news and current affairs meant that right-wing papers could not stray too far into total propaganda. The broadcast media kept them semi-honest.

In the 2020s, that constraint has shrunk alarmingly. First of all, the barriers between opinion and news reporting in newspapers have steadily eroded – partly in the search for sales and revenue as print circulation has declined, and revenues from digital online papers are harder to deliver, and partly because of the growing recognition that the prioritisation of some stories over others because of their political value combined with unrestrained inflammatory commentary serves the right-wing cause. In the absence of regulatory constraint, the press has continually pushed the boundaries of what is acceptable. Every new nadir, like the shameless front pages of the *Daily Mail* heightening immigration fears in the weeks before the Brexit referendum, is surpassed by another – the *Mail*'s accusation months later that the Supreme Court's decision that Brexit would first need the approval of Parliament made the court the 'enemies of the people'. The language of Stalinist Russia and Maoist China was blazoned across the front page of a British newspaper.

Next, since at least 2010, the BBC has been consistently weakened. Licence fee revenues have been allowed to fall by 19 per cent in real terms since 2010, and having to fund a free licence for the over-seventy-fives imposed a further penalty. This and the relentless Conservative attacks on the BBC had an additional effect, encouraging evasion of payment of the fee, all grist to the Tory mill.[19] This increase in evasion is conveniently used as an excuse to launch a review of the BBC's funding in order further to disable and shrink it. Yet, although trust in BBC news is falling, it still stands at 55 per cent of its audience in 2020, alongside the same percentage for the public-service ITV news – vastly higher than either *The Sun*, at 12 per cent, or the *Daily Mail*, at 23 per cent, according to the 2022 Reuters Institute Survey of Journalism. Few actually believe what they read in these fulminating tabloids. Small wonder the Tory Party and its outriders seek to undermine the BBC at every turn – not merely its funding, but its integrity. A classic of the genre was the furore in 2023 over *Match of the Day* presenter Gary Lineker tweeting that he considered the policy of summarily deporting asylum seekers to Rwanda to have echoes of 1930s Germany. Had he or had he not infringed impartiality guidelines – and what were those, exactly, for a high-profile presenter of a sports programme? The sheer scale of the coverage, lasting days, was vastly disproportionate. Some months later, the BBC sensibly adjudicated that presenters outside its news and current affairs programmes could express political views – but not campaign on them. But by then the damage had been done. The BBC had suffered another question mark over its integrity.

Last, the emergence of well-funded, loss-making right-wing TV stations has created a new platform for extreme-right-wing views. In fairness, regulator Ofcom tries to ensure that their news coverage is free from bias, which is an almost comical idea. But even its limited interventions are limp-wristed and in any case do not extend to comment and current affairs. Ofcom failed to take persistent offender Russia Today, an actual organ of Russian state propaganda, off the air until the Ukrainian war made its lack of impartiality impossible to tolerate. Potential and actual fines are no deterrent, a trivial business cost as these imitators of Fox News seek to increase their audience. Beyond the not-terribly-well-policed boundary between news and comment, anything goes. At the time of writing, GB News employs five serving Tory MPs, including the hyper-partisan former deputy chair of the Tory Party, Lee Anderson, as presenters; this is a crossing of the line between politics and journalism (laceratingly detailed by LBC presenter James O'Brien in his book *How They Broke Britain*) that neither democratic political parties nor democracy-supporting news organisations – nor regulators for that matter – should entertain. It is the slippery slope to direct political influence over a free media. The funders of these channels hope that as trust in the BBC and its capacity to report news declines and the corporation is shrunk still further on a different funding model, a gap will open that they can occupy. Their capacity to shape the national narrative in the interests of one political party and philosophy will have been enlarged. GB News losses in 2022/3 were £31 million on revenue of £3.6 million. Why else endure such losses?

The Power to Persuade

Human beings are social animals; we learn from others, and the more social standing an individual commands, the more we are likely to accept that what they say makes sense – a reality confirmed by countless controlled social psychological experiments. Economists Daron Acemoglu and Simon Johnson, in their influential *Power and Progress* (I referred to their work in Chapters 1 and 8), use such evidence, along with historical examples, to go even further. They argue that if anyone has won the capacity to shape an agenda through having a prominent voice in the media, then of necessity society will deem their ideas worthy of attention. The fact that a person has a position from which they have the chance to persuade you reinforces the feeling that they have social and political standing. The power to persuade is of course about loquacity, verve, passion and speaking effectively and urgently to issues that concern an audience. But do not neglect the virtuous circle effect. If you are in a position to persuade, that reinforces your social standing and thus the readiness of your interlocutors to hear you. The visions and ideas that animate a society are as much mediated by the standing of those propagating them as their intrinsic merit, Acemoglu and Johnson claim. Social, political and media power go hand-in-hand. The genius of the BBC is that it is an institutional circuit-breaker in this chain of causation; it represents the 'We'. Its commitment to truth, balance and impartiality forces argument to be based more on intrinsic value and potential truth than the social and political standing of the persuader.

The right want to be the most convincing persuaders – and are beginning to succeed. The agenda-setting capacity of the Conservative media was evident for decades before 2016; however, with Brexit, a Rubicon was crossed in terms of ampage, recklessness and sheer scale of partisanship – a willingness to bend facts or ignore them to make a plausible case for Brexit which even at the time was plainly flawed. The right-wing media had become the national persuader, despite the weaknesses of the case.

Eight years on, the flaws are obvious, and Brexit is increasingly recognised to be a self-harming calamity, though that can't be openly admitted by right-wing commentators even as Rishi Sunak attempts to claw something from the wreckage with his Windsor deal on Northern Ireland and his belated re-entry into the Horizon science programme. Yet, at the time of the referendum, a climate was created in which the broadcasters, especially the BBC, trod very carefully. Almost every major factual claim by the Leave campaigns turned out to be at least contestable and more often false. Vote Leave protagonists were not only allowed to broadcast palpable lies, but a cowed BBC retreated from its role as public-interest circuit-breaker. It decided that 'balance' meant giving both sides equivalent air time, however outlandish or false their claims – from the Leave campaign's claims that there would be a post-Brexit boom in trade and investment, to the spurious amounts of cash that would be freed up to spend on the NHS. The entire discourse was pulled to the right.

The rise in social media has aided and abetted this process, devaluing the intrinsic value of accurate information and accentuating what plays instantly to the emotions, however doubtful its provenance – and at lightning speed. False news that surprises us because of its improbability travels much faster and further than the truth; people are more likely to share unlikely, surprising news, however fantastical.[20] Researchers show that false stories are 70 per cent more likely to be retweeted than true ones; true stories take about six times longer to reach 1,500 people than false ones.[21] And all this is amplified by bots retweeting the material at the direction of influencers, some of whom will retweet in turn.[22] It is an ecosystem that amplifies the false and the weird. The companies owning the platforms on which all this happens want to dissociate themselves from the content – an attitude summed up by Nick Clegg, vice-president of global affairs and communications for then Facebook, now Meta (and former British deputy prime minister), who in a major speech compared his giant company with a tennis court: 'Our job is to make sure the court is ready – the surface is flat, the lines painted, the net at the correct height. But we don't pick up a racket and start playing. How the players play the game is up to them, not us.'[23] This is the washing of hands in the digital age.

And it isn't good enough. Hannah Arendt presciently wrote that when people in democratic or non-democratic countries alike get bombarded with falsehoods and propaganda, they stop believing anything. That process is well advanced in the USA, and Britain is catching up. Although the arrival of the Internet and social media were meant to democratise news, they have developed into a means for those who already hold media power to amplify their message, especially if it is lurid enough. The right's dominance of the analogue world has been transferred to the digital realm, where firestorms break every few days; thus, the 2023 Tory retention of the Uxbridge by-election was so magnified in significance by digital social media that it triggered Rishi Sunak's retreat from the cross-party consensus about the measures needed to achieve net zero by 2050. Car owners in an outer-London suburb, irritated by the prospect of having to pay a small charge for ageing, polluting vehicles, which in any case most of them did not own, were allowed to change the climate policy of a major Western country.

The lens through which increasingly every subject is seen – immigration, climate change, tax – has become heavily skewed to the right. Britain is not as far-gone as the USA, where the right-wing TV channels colluded with Donald Trump's lie that the US presidential election had been stolen. Fox News in 2023 had to pay Dominion, the voting machine manufacturer, $787.5 million in settlement for wrongly suggesting that it had rigged its machines to favour the Democrats. But by then the damage was done; a majority of Republicans at the very least had bought into Trump's narrative. TV anchors, after all, have authority and social standing as persuaders; their political status derives from that authority. The aim of the British right is to occupy the same position: to be Britain's persuaders-in-chief.

To expect Athenian democratic debate is to cry for the moon. But there should be some minimal rules of engagement in our democracy. It should be possible for argument to be heard properly, and for claims to have some relationship to the truth. Over and above that, there should be some consensus that the parties are able to spend roughly equivalent amounts on general elections. There should be transparency about the identity of donors, whether money came from abroad, who donors are and what favours they receive for their donations. Constituency boundaries, election rules, voting processes, access to airtime and news coverage should be broadly fair. The electorate deserves that degree of respect. But too much of our media is so keen to be an active participant in the public square that it has no interest in safeguarding the integrity of the institutions that mark off the square. It's as if a wealthy and unruly section of the crowd was constantly invading the tennis court invoked by Nick Clegg, helping one player and intimidating the umpire into silence.

This also suffocates debate about the profundity of the issues facing the country. Becoming an international debtor can't be allowed to continue at such a rapid pace. Our trade relationships with Europe have to be repaired. But an informed discussion, whether on public spending or tax, is close to impossible. It is apparent that the upward pressure on public spending – from social care and education to defence – is not going to lessen. It is equally apparent that household wealth in the UK, around some seven times national income, is very lightly taxed.[24] For example, council tax, as argued in the preceding chapter, is regressive and its yield is running at a fraction of what it should. Capital gains and inheritance tax are also too low. The tax code is full of anomalies. The entire tax system, writes Paul Johnson, director of the Institute for Fiscal Studies, should be reorganised around the recommendations of the Mirrlees Report of 2011, so that it is fairer, more understandable and less riddled with unfairness. It would also yield more.

In particular, we have indulged the anonymous foreign owners of British property assets and London's role as an international centre for money laundering for too long. Too many former British colonies and jurisdictions operate as tax havens – a network mapped out brilliantly by Oliver Bullough in *Butler to the World*. 'Whether the mismatch between gambling taxes in Gibraltar and the UK or the discrepancies between company law in the British Virgin Islands and elsewhere', he writes, they allow assets and even the existence of their owner to be hidden; 'Britain should iron these differences out.' He adds, in a sentence that should ring out for any of our decent politicians: 'Right now Britain's territories opt into the bits of Britishness that are profitable and out of the bits that require sacrifice. That has to stop.'[25]

Johnson and Bullough are right, but even with the access that the respected Johnson gets to TV and radio, he might as well not open his mouth. Change requires a recognition of reality, and that in turn requires the kind of focused, relentless energy the *Daily Mail*, *The Sun*, *The Telegraph* and *Daily Express* deployed in the Brexit referendum campaign and later into defending Boris Johnson's indefensible prime ministership. When they write about tax, it is not to educate their readers about the plain truths spelled out by Paul Johnson; it is to back the Tory right, and to call for tax cuts that simply cannot be afforded if the country is to have quality public services, justice and security. They encourage fantasy.

But this has the virtue, in their eyes, of putting the Labour Party and progressive politics permanently on the defensive. They are a self-appointed firewall around the least competent British government of modern times. The national conversation is not defined by how to improve everyday lives, the performance of our economy and the fairness of our society, but rather by the preoccupations of the current Conservative hegemony, despite its nugatory achievement. Politics is tribal, but this is tribalism taken to destructive excess. So how to turn things round?

How and What to Reform

Britain needs a serious, urgent conversation about how it is governed, and the fairness of the information ecosystem in which governance is framed. Good government is the precondition for any kind of successful state-led economic and social transformation. Democracy, if it is to serve the people, must reflect the will of the majority and governments must be held to account for the success or failure of what they do. The veteran socialist MP Tony Benn used to say that there were five questions to be levelled at anyone in power: what power have you got? Where did you get it from? In whose interests do you use it? To whom are you accountable? And, most importantly of all, how do we get rid of you?

It was the great German sociologist Max Weber who wrote: 'politics is not an ethical business. But there does nevertheless exist a certain minimum of shame and obligation to behave decently which cannot be violated with impunity even in politics.'[26] To ensure decent behaviour, democracy must live in a media ecosystem that gives the public the flow of information they need to make good judgements about how they are governed. How else can we hold our governors to account and decide whether to get rid of them?

We do not possess such an ecosystem, but nor do we possess institutions that offer checks and balances, and ensure an essential minimum of integrity in our media. These weaknesses in British democracy and government have to be addressed. They can no longer be ignored as we muddle through. There may be no likelihood of a revolutionary constitutional moment like those that coincided with the American War of Independence or the deposition of the French Bourbons, but acting is still an urgent necessity. Manifestos matter in British politics, so what a progressive coalition promises to do by way of action in its manifestos is fundamental. They give leaders the political space to act and to insist that their MPs and cabinet colleagues agree with what the manifesto promises. So constitutional reform must follow from enacting commitments made in the winning party's manifesto. Some issues may require the creation of a constitutional convention to search for consensus, but a lead can be given by the elected government enacting its manifesto commitments.

An incoming reforming government may plead that the most urgent task is to fix the economy and not divert itself into controversial, time-consuming constitutional questions. It could not be more wrong. Economic vitality and a social contract, as I've argued throughout this book, depend upon an apparatus of good government and effective democracy. Moreover, a new Labour government, for example, might reflect that the most enduring legacy of its predecessors has indeed been institution-building – whether the NHS, the Open University or, in the case of the Blair government, the creation of the Supreme Court, devolved government, elected mayors and the Freedom of Information and Human Rights Acts. An ancient country like Britain deserves and needs better democratic institutions; the arbitrary proroguing of parliament in 2019 to sterilise debate over Brexit and the wild assertions made by the Tory right over the Rwanda bill in 2023/4 about parliamentary sovereignty being effectively limitless dramatise the dangers and vulnerabilities. The work of constitutional change can take place alongside initiatives on the economy and society – they are not mutually exclusive, and none of them are indulgent sideshows.

Britain does not have a written constitution; it has not had reason to write one. They are composed in other countries after cataclysmic events like revolution, winning national independence or defeat in war. But what it can have (as argued by former prime minister Gordon Brown's Commission on the UK's Future) is a statutory constitutional commitment to certain guiding principles: that the UK is a union of nations; that while power is shared, decision-making should be as close to the people as possible; that the political, administrative and financial autonomy of local government should be respected by central government; and that living standards and social rights should be equalised across the country. Within that statutory constitutional framework there are twelve key areas for action.

1. Enhance the capacity of the executive to make strategy and deliver policy, in particular by turning the cabinet office into a strong Department of the Prime Minister and splitting the Treasury into an Office of the Budget and an Economic Strategy Ministry.

The executive needs formally to be equipped with greater capacity for strategy, policy formulation and implementation. The cabinet office should be transformed into a Department of the Prime Minister, housed in its own building and incorporating strong and intelligent strategy, policy and delivery units.[27]

The Treasury should be broken up into an Office of the Budget, confining its focus to spending, tax and borrowing policy but within a framework in which laissez-faire no longer dominates economic policy-making. One immediate focus should be the simplification of the tax code and the reform of tax policy. It must work with the enlarged Department of the Prime Minister and a newly formed Economic Strategy Ministry to ensure that all economic plans are coordinated and properly integrated.

The Economic Strategy Ministry should work with the Office of the Budget, the Bank of England, the Climate Change Committee and the Departments of Business, Levelling Up and Education to devise an ambitious economic and social programme, and to revise and deliver it in the light of events and the test of reality.

As a rule, the convention should be that the governing party can change its leader, and thus the prime minister, only once in any Parliament. Attempting to install a third prime minister should necessitate a general election.

2. Give Parliament the capacity for forward-looking scrutiny of proposed laws, and establish equal control of the parliamentary timetable and four-year fixed-term elections.

Prime ministers' extensive powers of action and patronage need scrutiny, oversight and checks and balances. Such plenipotentiary executive powers are at the root of bad governance. The House of Commons needs to be empowered to co-organise the procedural timetable with the government in power, so that there is always the opportunity for bills to be properly scrutinised. Arbitrary guillotines cutting off debate are not a feature of the House of Lords, and the Commons should follow suit.

To make scrutiny properly effective, the executive must supply Parliament with a map of expected risks and rewards for each legislative and regulatory proposal along with how it would respond if the risks materialised. MPs must be given the funding to staff their offices with professionals who are able to support them in their scrutiny function. This should be their priority, not having second and third jobs outside Parliament. House of Commons committees should have greater power, with the executive obliged to comply with their recommendations – or explain why they disagree. They should hold ministers to account, following Ian Dunt's suggestion in *How Westminster Works... and Why It Doesn't*, for up to six years after they have left an office of state. Exercising power has long-term consequences. There should be four-year fixed-term Parliaments, removing the discretion of general election timing from the incumbent party.

3. Entrench the powers of local government, cities and regions and underwrite the independence of the Civil Service.

Pushing government as close to the people as possible, local governments should be given greater long-term financial certainty to invest more confidently in their areas' futures, as well as more capacity to generate their own revenues with new fiscal powers, and they should be able to initiate local legislation. The same principles should apply to the combined authorities, so that their mayors become serious local economic and social actors. A Civil Service Act should reaffirm the independence of the Civil Service, set limits to the use of external consultants and special advisers, develop careers for civil servants with specialist knowledge, notably in science, technology and social science, and ensure competitive pay.

4. Replace the House of Lords with an elected Assembly of

Nations, Regions and Cities with four-yearly elections held in between general elections to the House of Commons.

British democracy needs a second chamber to balance and act as a check on the House of Commons as the primary chamber. The majority should be elected and no more than a quarter of its members appointed. Elections would be on a different timetable to those of the House of Commons. Its responsibility should be to revise national legislation, with its power of delay extending to blocking powers only over constitutional and international treaty changes and proposed associated laws, not over policies in the governing party's manifesto. It should have no formal power over money bills. It could, for example, block the exercise of Henry VIII powers, or prevent a referendum which does not require a super-majority for a major constitutional or treaty change. It should also be able to block or delay constitutional changes, say, on voting or qualifications to judicial independence, proposed by the House of Commons.

The elected representatives should mostly come, as the Brown Commission recommended, from Britain's four nations, cities and regions, including the mayors of combined authorities. The existence of cross-bench, independent 'peers', appointed only after agreement by the Assembly's Appointment Committee and the party leaders, would ensure that majorities for most measures would be won through good argument, rather than brutal whipping.

5. Replace the first-past-the-post voting system with a proportional voting system. Parties should receive state funding, with a cap on contributions by donors and an overall cap on party income.

The simple majoritarian, first-past-the-post voting system was already past its sell-by date in 1918, when reform was proposed as part of the Parliament Act. It has made political representation unfair for more than a century, with the baleful results described in earlier chapters. Reform is now an imperative. Every citizen's vote should count, not only those who live in marginal constituencies, as a core democratic principle. The complexion of the House of Commons and the Assembly should reflect opinion in the country.

Constituency elections should be by a single transferable vote, in which MPs are elected when they reach a majority of votes cast through second and third preferences. In addition, a number of seats should be set aside, as in the Scottish, Senedd and London assemblies, to ensure that the final shape of Parliament conforms to people's first preferences. State support for parties should be scaled up and donations from individual donors capped. There should be an overall income cap.

The aim is to encourage political parties that are open, deliberative, serious and accountable between elections, and biased towards governing inclusively for all. Proportional voting would be a giant step away from parties functioning as isolated institutions for political career advancement, in which adherence to ideological purity pushes you up the political career ladder while producing partisan policy and encouraging ministerial 'musical chairs' when in government.

6. Establish ground rules for referenda, with voting thresholds for issues of constitutional importance and clear rules of engagement.

Referenda sit uneasily in a parliamentary democracy – they are incredibly crude instruments for settling often very complex questions. The whole *raison d'être* of a reformed Parliament that would better reflect national opinion is that it would deliberate and scrutinise better and make the right calls on everyone's behalf. Referenda should be a last resort in a well-functioning parliamentary democracy, rather than a get-out-of-jail card for a prime minister under pressure, like Harold Wilson in 1975 or David Cameron in 2016 over entry into and continued membership of the EU, respectively. A referendum should only be binding on the government of the day if there is a super-majority of two-thirds of votes cast and the turnout exceeds 75 per cent – then at least half of the electorate will have voted for the change.

If those criteria are not met, the Assembly of Nations, Regions and Cities will have the constitutional obligation to block the enactment of the referendum result if the House of Commons tries to push it through.

7. Merge committees and commissions overseeing ethics and integrity in government into an independent commission with statutory powers. Guarantee judicial independence.

The Committee on Standards in Public Life, varying appointments commissions and ethics advisers should be merged and given statutory independence. The Electoral Commission's remit as a guarantor of the election process should be independent of the prime minister.

In addition, following John Bowers's recommendations in *Downward Spiral*, the independence of the judiciary, judicial appointments and the right to judicial review should all be statutorily protected. Judicial independence should be ensured by the double lock of protection by statute together with approval by the Assembly of Nations for any proposed change.

8. Entrench independence of the BBC with proper funding and extend Ofcom's powers to guarantee impartial public-service broadcasting of news and current affairs in all broadcast media.

Trusted and well-sourced information is the lifeblood of democracy. The diminution of the BBC must be stopped in its tracks, and the corporation reinvigorated around a system that guarantees its real revenues independent of government interference. Its independence must be entrenched. A chair should be appointed by the governing party, and a deputy chair by the opposition. It is everyone's BBC.

Ofcom should be given the resources to ensure that all broadcasters observe its guidelines on balance and impartiality, with the power to withdraw a licence to operate if rules are systematically transgressed.

9. Implement the Leveson recommendations for independent self-regulation of the press, ensure access to justice for victims of press abuse and provide greater protection for journalists against harassment, intimidation and libel.

Press freedom is indispensable; however, on the one hand, it is menaced by suffocating libel laws and legal instruments to suppress journalistic inquiry, and on the other by the willingness of some newspapers to set aside ethical standards in pursuit of salacious stories, their own political agendas and targeted attacks on selected individuals. In 2013, after a year-long public inquiry chaired by Court of Appeal judge Sir Brian Leveson, Parliament agreed that high ethical standards in the written media should be assured through a self-regulatory framework reinforced by backstop powers. This involved the setting up of a Press Recognition Panel (PRP) through the mechanism of a Royal Charter, charged with assessing whether a press self-regulator met statutory criteria for independence and effectiveness. An essential ingredient of this framework was measures to incentivise publishers to join a recognised self-regulator. Those measures, despite being passed into statute, were never initiated by the Tory government. The Charter framework was effectively neutered.

There has been regulatory stand-off. In order to have some fig leaf of regulation and industry-wide process to handle complaints, a group of mainly right-wing newspapers set up the Independent Press Standards Organisation (IPSO) – in effect an upgraded version of the former Press Complaints Commission – which is widely regarded as no less feeble than its predecessor. After all it was the weaknesses of the Press Complaints Commission which Leveson attempted to remedy. Paid for by the industry, IPSO is not independent, has never carried out any regulatory acts (such as investigations or sanctions) and is answerable to no one but its paymasters. The argument that Leveson's proposed measures would have infringed press freedom is nonsense. What offends the right-wing press barons is not a threat to public-interest press freedom, as they protest, but to their right to slant any story as they see fit, with no effective redress for inaccuracy. A minimum requirement is for press self-regulators to comply with the terms of the revived Royal Charter, so providing an independent standard for how regulation is conducted and a mechanism of accountability.[28] In addition, the majority of votes of proprietors and shareholders in UK media companies should be exercised by individuals or organisations domiciled in the UK.

New measures must be adopted to protect journalists from intimidation, legal threat and harassment. A public-interest defence was introduced in the 2013 Defamation Act, but it needs to be better codified and made much more robust. The courts should be empowered to strike out so-called strategic lawsuits against public participation (SLAPPs), which are designed to impoverish and intimidate any journalist investigating the affairs of rich individuals and corporations to bring whatever questionable conduct into the public domain for public-interest reasons. Legal costs should be capped. Together, these are minimum measures to restore the public square to health.

10. Reform social media and digital platforms

The providers of digital platforms do not see their role as being guardians of responsible content, despite more activist moderation in the last few years; Facebook (now Meta), for example established an oversight board in 2020. But a public-interest circuit-breaker function needs to be triggered when a social media bubble inflates dangerous and false content. A digital regulator (the Office for Digital Content, or OfDC), reproducing Ofcom's functions, should be created. The public should be enlisted in the creation of e-rules and the better enforcement of existing legislation and standards via verification, fact-checking and trust marks.

A public social media corporation should be formed to create a trusted digital platform with an accountable moderation system for preventing online trolling and abusive content. The rules applying to the written and broadcast word should apply to the digital word.

11. Open up and democratise the regulators.

British regulation has not distinguished itself, whether over the utilities or the financial services. There needs to be a drastic change in all regulators' engagement with the public they serve to ensure more responsiveness, and to avoid regulatory capture – the regulator-gamekeeper turning into a submissive creature of the powerful poacher they're meant to be policing. Each regulator should have meaningful and appropriate power, to include the scrutiny and capacity to block 'unfit' owners and ensure that, where directed, voting is exercised by owners domiciled in the UK. Regulators should be obliged to convene 'citizen juries' as a representative group of stakeholders provided with expert information and background on policy issues. They should have enough information to debate, co-deliberate and to help set policy. Citizens can act as diffused networks tracking the degree to which regulatory bodies really implement their policies effectively. They should sit on oversight boards.

12. Establish an Office of EU Relations.

Finally, Britain's relationship with the EU will have to be repaired over time. Economic growth, security and the achievement of climate change goals will all require collaboration – provided for in the existing Trade and Co-operation Agreement, but yet to be acted on. At a minimum Britain will need to align with the vast majority of EU regulation, particularly in the single market, and only disengage from it if there is a clear interest in so doing which has been explained to the EU. This framework is vital if trade with the EU is to resume and grow at the same pace. Already, whether re-joining the EU Horizon programme of collaborative scientific research or lobbying aggressively for a three-year deferral of EU rules of origin requirements on car imports (so that the UK automobile sector is in effect in the single market), the direction of travel to re-association is clear. An Office of EU Relations must be created systematically to coordinate with the European Commission over proposed EU law and regulation, demonstrate that British goods or services regulations conform with EU standards and make representations in the British interest where EU proposals cut across our interests – and explain any UK decisions to diverge. It will hold the ring in the varying consultative bodies to be created under the Trade and Co-operation Agreement, and take the lead in any negotiation about associate membership in a reconfigured EU. Britain cannot stand aside from our continent and hinterland, and the Office will be an expression of British willingness to create good working relations, closer involvement with EU policies, regulations and institutions and – who knows? – eventually even to rejoin the European Union.

The world we live in requires agile, effective government and the self-confidence offered by democratic legitimacy. We need the knowledge freely gathered by democratic engagement to govern experimentally and well. It is how the 'We' is expressed in the way we are governed and how our economy works. Today, it is more obvious than ever that good government requires reliable, honest data which is best garnered in a democratic environment. Democracy, when it works well, is deliberative and lives off feedback loops freely offered because the process serves a 'We' that is open and inclusive. This is in stark contrast to the oppressive top-down 'We', the totalitarian version of the collective that is exemplified by China, where a Maoist party dictatorship has fused to create Leninist capitalism. Our best way forward is not to continue to allow our democracy to degenerate so that the outward form of democracy hides a discretionary, autocratic and too-easily-corruptible heart.

These measures taken together will reinvent our democracy, our government and the vitality of our public square. Something like this reform programme has been in the air for more than a century. Many opportunities to implement it have been lost, and too many dead-ends have been explored. It is now imperative to act.

Conclusion

The Conservative Party is now an association of cults – five right-wing 'families' and a bloc of mainstream 'One Nation' Tories – none of whom command a majority in the party, let alone the country. This presents non-Tory Britain with an all-too-rare opportunity. But Tory disarray may not last. The forces of the rational centre-right may be in headlong retreat, but there is every prospect that this now very-right-wing party will next coalesce around an extreme programme of rabid hostility to immigration and aggressive tax cuts. Tax cuts are still seen as a universal panacea, notwithstanding the fiasco of the Truss government (leader of the 'Conservative Growth Group' the Tory 'family' she inspired, Truss is now portrayed as an influential kingmaker in any future Tory leadership contest and even as a candidate herself). Violent opposition to all things 'woke', with no trace of liberalism or pro-Europeanism, will complete the political stance. Withdrawal from the European Convention on Human Rights is the next anti-European frontier – there is always some sinister European menace on the horizon – to be replaced by a proposed all British Human Rights Act. This will doubtless allow any number of core rights to be overridden at the discretion of a sovereign parliament – confidently expected to be in right-wing Tory hands almost permanently – and removing their independent legal entrenchment by almost abolishing appeal to the courts over immigration and asylum rulings. Even discussion about climate change and the environment, once an area of cross-party consensus, has become toxic, now seen as a dividing line with the opposition parties. More inequality, social division and environmental damage may follow – but no matter. They may pay electoral dividends.

Thatcher and her vastly overegged achievements remain the shibboleth to which any aspirant Conservative politician must genuflect. The playmakers on the right have translated Thatcherism into outright populism and libertarianism, backed by a powerful media that is many times more 'feral' than when Tony Blair dubbed it such on leaving office. The readiness to exaggerate to the point of falsehood, a feature of Brexit, has now become a regular trope of Conservative discourse. Such language, which was once condemned even by Conservatives – as when Enoch Powell spoke of 'rivers of blood' if immigration continued unabated and was dismissed from the shadow cabinet – now routinely crosses poisonous boundaries with no reproach; a 'hurricane' of immigration threatens, a cosseted 'liberal elite' menace 'the people', 'lefty lawyers' traduce the intent of elected lawmakers. This dark dimension to the Conservative hard right translates directly into policy; another term of office will lead to further attacks on civil liberties and the rule of law, the radical undermining of public-service broadcasting and even-more-intense screening of appointments and surveillance of anybody it considers threatening to its project – journalists, academics, publishers, NGOs, lawyers, public-service broadcasters, trade unionists, independent civil servants. Orwell directed much of his concern about the distortion of language to serve authoritarian ends to the left. Today, he would surely be equally concerned about the manipulation of language by the right.

While a progressive opportunity is opening, it will quickly come under assault. Perhaps the only unexpected benefit of Brexit is that it has been such an obvious failure; Tory populists in its wake will struggle to find majority electoral support in rallying to protect it. Thus the temptation to alight on immigration as a surrogate cause. Yet the country has seen where populism leads, and it has little appetite for more, at least so far. A Tory populist revival can be kept at bay until the party is reclaimed by those representing its better angels – as long as a progressive government actually delivers.

The best prophylactic against a right-wing revival is to run the country well, in pursuit of a vision of inclusive prosperity in which the mass of British people flourish, or can see that there is an opportunity to flourish, grounded in values of fellowship, mutuality and an insistence that there is such a thing as society, in which everyone has both a stake and reciprocal obligations. Such is the marriage of the 'We' and the 'I', of collective solidarity and creative individualism, of ethical socialism and progressive liberalism – values to which the majority of the British still adhere. The recurrent argument in this book is that the successful non-Conservative administrations of the last 125 years have managed, rarely acknowledging the philosophic roots of what they were doing, to bring together these twin progressive strands. Whether Herbert Asquith and Lloyd George relying on Labour votes to pass the Parliament Act, the Attlee government commissioning a New Liberal to devise a comprehensive National Insurance system or Tony Blair convening a weekly meeting with the LibDem leader Paddy Ashdown to discuss and monitor constitutional reform, the interdependence of the two philosophies is striking. But the temptation is to deny this truth or the attractiveness of what it offers. When Tony Blair claimed, on the death of Mrs Thatcher in 2013, that he had always seen his mission as in part building on her achievements, it showed how lost he had become, even allowing for the hyperbole of funeral rites. Instead of consolidating a progressive intellectual alliance, he had drifted with the prevailing right-wing tide.

It cannot happen again. Britain is at a decisive moment in its national fortunes. More of the same and we condemn ourselves to drop out of the front rank of nations, in every sense – in terms of personal and social wellbeing, economic performance, social cohesion and international influence. The position is precarious, as described in earlier chapters. There is scarcely a dial on the economic, social and democratic dashboard that is not flashing amber or red. None of these trends can continue for another twenty-five years.

The culprit is not hard to identify. It is a continuing inability to invest in ourselves purposefully – in our businesses, our public services, our infrastructure, research and development, our young, the preservation of nature and everything that makes life worth living. That failing has two key roots. The first is the grip that free-market, laissez-faire, set-the-individual-free economic thinking continues to have on the national discourse and on policy-making, ever since the election of Mrs Thatcher. The people may want collective action and investment in great public services; the Conservative establishment resists because it is unwilling on principle – it does not believe in the 'We' – and because such investment is incompatible with cutting taxes, the automatic preference if there is any fiscal latitude. The situation is made worse by the failings of our state structures as they have built up since the middle of the nineteenth century. Britain does not have the public institutions and official mindset to want to invest in and develop its economy. As observed throughout this book, a belief in laissez-faire and the self-organising market has never really died. Social and economic success in the twenty-first century demands a very different approach.

The necessary direction of travel is clear: towards a stakeholder capitalism serving the common good supported by a step change in public investment triggering more private investment. Such a system would embrace the new, the continual experimentation and the problem-solving vital to the private and public sectors alike. Well-funded research and development would be celebrated, and the companies driven by purpose who commercialise it would be backed by a refashioned financial system capable of mobilising latent multi-billions of pounds of loans and equity investment. Workplaces become more humane, offering workers pride and purpose. People take more responsibility for their lives. As investment and productivity rise, there will be growing confidence that tomorrow will be better than today. The forces promoting closure and hostility to the other – the menacing foreigner, the enemy within – will ebb. Immigration levels must be managed, certainly, but humanely and within the rule of domestic and international law. Britain can become a kinder and more generous society again.

No less essential is to repair our fraying social contract. The new risks and inequalities that every citizen will confront in an ever-faster-moving environment need to be mitigated and managed by a social contract that ensures those good workplaces are underwritten by great education, health and housing and indispensable income support when, for any reason, it becomes impossible to work. There must be a proper system of social care. Societies need to pool risk in the name of the 'We'; in particular, it is a disgrace that people as they reach the end of their lives may or may not have to pay for their care by themselves, depending on the lottery of their health. Nor can we have children going hungry in their millions, with schools, training institutions and further-education colleges allowed to decay. Many of our citizens live in disgraceful conditions. Housing – from owner occupation to social housing – requires a major overhaul.

'The other half' are part of the 'We', of the society of which we are all members, and their wellbeing includes how well they eat, their access to education and training and the circumstances of their lives. These things are of universal concern. It is certain that the country is losing precious potential Einsteins as matters stand; but, worse, too many of our fellow citizens are locked into lives that are far too hard and demanding. The resulting drug abuse, knife crime, domestic violence and unsafe streets blight all of us. The criminal justice system, from overwhelmed courts and prisons to the dramatic curtailing of access to legal aid, is a standing reproach to what claims to be a civilised country. Churchill was right all those years ago when as home secretary in 1910 he said, 'the mood and temper of the public in regard to the treatment of crime and criminals is one of the most unfailing tests of the civilisation of any country'. The repressive policies pioneered by Home Secretary Priti Patel and her short-lived successor Suella Braverman would horrify him.

To remedy all of this cannot be done in one Parliament. It has taken fourteen years to reach this sorry pass, building on foundations laid in the Thatcher years, so turning this around is a generational task – although improvements should be obvious by the end of the first Parliament of a new reforming administration, if it is serious about change. The money can be found. Fiscal policy needs to be remodelled with investment as its centrepiece. The national investment balance sheet needs to be measured and the steady improvement in the net worth of the public sector as investment rises recorded and monitored. Financial markets actually approve of investment and higher growth rates; they will buy British government debt to finance it. New revenue sources, particularly derived from taxing environmental harms and wealth, can be created. The overall tax take will first have to rise to finance vital additional public investment, rescue public services in crisis and so catalyse more growth. But as growth rises, so the country will enter a virtuous circle of growth begetting the tax revenues for another cycle of public improvement and higher private investment. Britain is more than rich enough to fund its own renaissance, and as it draws away from today's abyss there will be scope to organise the tax system more fairly, even to begin to lower the tax take.

All this will need strategic direction, striking the right balance between central and local government, implementing step by step all of the reforms to the constitution, state apparatus, regulation and the media outlined in the previous chapter. The degraded public square can be made saner and more civil; Scotland can be persuaded that with more control over its destiny it should make common cause with England, Wales and Northern Ireland in a rejuvenated and more federal country. Britain used to have a reputation for good government, rather than for presiding over an endless series of blunders and serial incompetence. That reputation can and must be regained.

The UK cannot get this right by itself. We are a European country, and we need to recover the trade and investment flows – along with the commitment to high and common European standards – that accompanied our membership of the EU. And the global environment is very different to 2016, when the country was hoodwinked into leaving. Britain must be part of the emergent European defence and security architecture based on EU collaboration – whether organising aid to Ukraine or the development of European defence, military and weapons industries. Every significant twenty-first-century challenge – artificial intelligence, climate change, international migration, managing pandemics, energy security – requires collaboration across borders. Our best shot at confronting and managing any upsurge in international migration, for example, is to work with other states on our own continent. To have excluded ourselves from the councils in Europe where the responses will be decided was an act of vandalism. We need, as a character in the great musical *Hamilton* sings, to be in 'the room where it happens'. The British were deceived by politicians who appealed to the electorate's demons rather than its better angels. Reassociating ourselves with the EU is vital – it cannot be dodged, like the refusal for thirty years to revalue residential property. The approach may be touching stones to cross the river, as the old Chinese aphorism puts it, but the steps must be touched and the river crossed.

As I write these words I am keenly aware of the objections – that Europe is turning rightwards and inwards and that the pressures encouraging right-wing movements across the West, from immigration to stagnating real wages, are intensifying. Donald Trump may win the Republican nomination for the US presidency and then even win the presidency. To imagine a different order is to live in dreamland, the cynical will say. And yet. To hate, to exclude, to divide, to set men and women against each other on the basis of their colour or ethnicity, to pull up the drawbridge, to endorse closure – none of this leads to the good life. They cannot be purposes that enhance our humanity. I warm to Attlee's answer when asked to describe in his first major television interview in 1954 what he thought the Labour Party had to offer – how his brand of socialism should be understood. 'You know there's nothing better than the motto we have in this Borough, by our greatest citizen, William Morris – Fellowship is Life.' Attlee continued, 'we believe in the kind of society where we've fellowship for all. You can't get that in a totalitarian society, you can't get while there's grave inequalities of wealth. That is the hope of the world'.[1] Today, we are diminished by denying our urge to fellowship – the effort to put ourselves in the skin of our fellow human beings, try to see the world as they see it and stand shoulder to shoulder in redressing injustice and offering opportunity. New Liberal thinker Thomas Green was right. Men and women, he declared, can only be rounded, moral human beings with the capacity for self-realisation – the fundamental object of existence – if they recognise that they share a common purpose of human betterment with every other human being, which each individual has an obligation to help both themselves and others fulfil. Attlee's ethic of socialism grounded in fellowship and Green's new liberalism are not antagonistic visions; they are overlapping and complementary.

The legacy of empire and the Industrial Revolution, creating profound divisions of class and life experience, made it impossible for that complementarity to be realised in a single political formation. British progressivism became divided; too many Labour people saw progressive New Liberals as their class enemy. Liberals returned fire. But in the 2020s it is even less likely that capitalism will collapse under its own contradictions than it was in the 1920s or in 1867 when the first volume of *Das Kapital* was published. Now empire is behind us and the divisions of class less acute and more fluid, the task can be seen not as socialising capitalism but as harnessing and humanising it, so that it serves the common good in a society where everyone can flourish. To achieve this outcome is, or should be, a joint project of ethical socialists and progressive liberals. Get it right and Britain could be the most dynamic economy in Europe, with a multicultural society and a vigorous democracy. Britain could become a model for the rest of Europe to emulate. Internationally, it could justify its membership of the UN Security Council and its privileged position in the IMF and World Bank which, if matters continue to slide, it will be under pressure to surrender. It could become a force for good, living its values, in a world that is more dangerous and menacing than at any time since 1945.

Why not try? Britain retains great assets on which to build, and above all a great tradition of tolerance and fairness – fundamental building blocks of the twenty-first-century order. But first there has to be a progressive government. The first-past-the-post electoral system, for over a hundred years the curse of British democracy, forces the issue – both voters and the opposition parties have to recognise that for this next election and the one that follows the normal rules cannot apply. The stakes are too high. The precondition for change is that voters exercise their right to vote, especially the under 50s whose participation tends to be lower than their elders – but whose lives will be most directly affected by more economic and social failure. Tactical voting has been a feature of general elections and in particular by-elections for decades, but this time every vote must count. Electors must vote tactically for their second-preference progressive candidate if they are the one most likely to win. The political parties cannot pretend that this is not the calculation of most non-Tory voters, and go through the pantomime of competing against each other, dividing the vote. At the very least, there must be an informal understanding not to compete in seats which are obviously winnable by the other party. Then the party manifestos must be drawn up so that there is a huge overlap in priorities, including the emphasis on environmental imperatives, not only because of their intrinsic importance but because many Green voters also need to be persuaded to vote tactically. They, alongside Labour and LibDem voters, need to know that the sacrifice they are making in not voting for their first-choice candidate is not so great – a lot of what they want will be in every opposition party manifesto.

There is a case for going further still. The Liberal Party took the calculated risk in the last decades of the nineteenth century of allowing trade unionists to stand in heavily industrialised Liberal constituencies in order to represent the 'labour' interest, LibLab MPs who would support the Liberals in government. The thinking in 1903 was that the non-Tory vote in a crucial general election that might end two almost-unbroken decades of Conservative rule must not be divided – hence the Gladstone–MacDonald pact. Two dozen Labour MPs were elected as a direct result, and proved an important part of the coalition to achieve badly needed reforms. What was done in 1906 can be done in 2024, and again in subsequent elections. The parties could and should stand aside for each other in a critical mass of seats until the voting system is reformed. Britain cannot afford more of the same any more today than it could 120 years ago.

Such an arrangement would be a bold political statement in its own right. The dominant political narrative should be that the great task of national renewal – our New Deal moment – goes beyond party, that the philosophical differences between the opposition parties are too small to argue about and that there are times in national life when politicians and people must come together for the common good. It is a framework that allows the political debate to go up a gear, opening the space to talk about the seriousness of our situation. It also would give the better Conservatives a chance to make a parallel case in their own party.

What the next government must do is obvious, and it needs to have as big and as wide a mandate as possible – helped by supportive MPs from other sympathetic parties. We can rebuild an attractive country with an uniquely dynamic, purpose-driven capitalism grounded in an economic philosophy that recognises the interdependence of the private and public spheres. We can all lead lives we have reason to value underwritten by a vibrant social contract. We can revive our democracy. We can stand by the values – fellowship, tolerance, fairness, kindness, belonging – we hold dear while at the same time respecting the urge for individual self-betterment, ambition and action. The 'We Society' must offer both a floor and a ladder. We can hold our political union together. We can remake our relationship with the EU. The life of a nation is no more preordained than that of an individual; we have choices and agency. This time, no mistakes.

Acknowledgements

These ideas have been gestating over the whole course of my writing career, so in a way this is a life's work. My intellectual heroes remain John Maynard Keynes, his great interpreters Axel Leijonhufvud and John Kenneth Galbraith, and on the good society John Rawls, Hannah Arendt and William Beveridge. Through writing this book I can add Richard Tawney's name to the roll call. My political heroes are Franklin Roosevelt and Clem Attlee (the ethical socialist and *sotto voce* new liberal combined) – but also Lloyd George and Roy Jenkins (who temporarily helped secure our position in Europe), and even Harold Wilson deserves a place in the pantheon. Another reason writing was solitary rather than lonely was that a number of generous people accepted my request to read sections, chapters and sometimes a sequence of chapters, always offering useful feedback and wise comments. So (in alphabetic order) my thanks are due to Steve Barnett, Sid Blumenthal, Alan Bogg, David Cannadine, Jagjit Chadwa, Ivor Crewe, David Halpern, Evan Harris, Michael Jacobs, Bob Kuttner, Richard Layard, Molly Meacher, Adrian Pabst, Steve Richards, David Riemer, Alan Rusbridger, Emma Smith and Liz Macfarlane (particularly for the New Lanark visit), Will Snell, Andre Stern, Christopher Tyerman and Paul Webster. The encouragement of David Miliband in the early stages and Neil Kinnock's upbeat texts to the evolving ideas were also important, Julian Richer, a latter day Robert Owen, is an inspiration and living exemplar that stakeholder capitalism works. Working as Co-chair of The Purposeful Company, writing and reviewing its reports, debating with steering-group colleagues and, through its network, meeting a range of business leaders committed to delivering great purposes has been richly illuminating. Fellow members of the Progressive Economic Forum were a great source of stimulus, too; we agree on the vital importance of progressive macro-economic policies if not every detail, and I never leave one of our regular online meetings without being stimulated. Thanks also to the fellows of Hertford College Oxford, where I was Principal for nine years, for bringing to life the conception of fellowship that runs through this book: fellowship and individual agency are not incompatible values. It was also fascinating to learn from my fellow grandfather, David Evans, about his family's relationship to the Rhondda Labour and Liberal Association via its LibLab MP William Abraham's agent William Evans. I also acknowledge my debt to social science, a community I am privileged to represent, in the structural and systemic insights it brings to bear on economic, social and political questions and from whom over the decades I have learned so much. Thanks to everyone. Any mistakes are mine and mine alone.

My two researchers deserve special thanks. Seth Alexander Thévoz, who joined me from the beginning in late 2022, for his research and excellent guts of key books and texts; he is a considerable historian in his own right, understanding quickly what I was trying to do and finding ways constructively to criticise drafts without deflating me. Our weekly catch-up meetings in a Crouch End café were a pleasure. Then in April 2023, six months before completion of the first full manuscript, Philippe Schneider stepped forward to join Seth. Incredibly well-read and among the cleverest people I know, he too pointed me to key sections in articles and books he considered important, with no less excellent summaries of key arguments, and offered sometimes uncomfortable but always valuable comments on early chapter drafts. A 'truth-seeker', I value his unflinching intellectual honesty and commitment enormously; over the years we have developed tried and tested ways of working and understanding each other. Importantly, both he and Seth were fully intellectually supportive of what the book aims to do.

I was also lucky that Neil Belton agreed not only to publish the book, but to offer his unmatched skills as an editor, both conceptually and in literary terms, going through the text line by line. He did the same for *The State We're In* and I wanted, like the partnership of one late-middle-aged and one ageing gun-slinger, to repeat the experience nearly thirty years on. He did not fail me, and his last ten days of virtual sleepless editing were incredible. What can I say but 'Thank you!'? Not only to him, but the rest of the Head of Zeus team, including Karina Maduro, Kathryn Colwell and Oliver Grant.

I always hold in mind my love and gratitude to my daughters Sarah and Alice, and my son Andrew. I hope the book may trigger changes that will improve all of your lives, and of those you love. And last but certainly not least, thanks to Helen, whose unstinting support and understanding of my steady retreat into the obsessive cocoon that all books ultimately demand were essential foundations for fifteen months of work. But, better still, she read the whole thing in draft, telling me what worked and what didn't. Above all, she wanted me to remain true to my optimism about a possible progressive and better future. I hope that shines through. It is not only possible – it is a must.

Notes

Chapter 1

1 Figures and statistics in this paragraph supplied to the author by the National Institute of Economic and Social Research.

2 Burn-Murdoch, John, 'Is Britain really as poor as Mississippi?', *Financial Times* (11 Aug. 2023).

3 NIESR, 'Economic Outlook Summer 2023 Series A. No. 11', National Institute, August 2023. See also www.niesr.ac.uk/wp-content/uploads/2023/08/JC737-NIESR-Outlook-Summer-2023-UK-v10-AC.pdf. For among the shortest five year olds in Europe, see *Economist*, 'Are young children getting smaller?' 29 June 2023.

4 Resolution Foundation, Centre for Economic Performance and Nuffield Foundation, 'Ending Stagnation: A New Economic Strategy for Britain', *The Economy 2030 Inquiry: The Final Report* (London, 2023), pp.40–1.

5 Koo, Richard, 'Balance sheet recession is the reason for "secular stagnation"', VoxEU CEPR (11 Aug. 2014). See also www.cepr.org/voxeu/columns/balance-sheet-recession-reason-secular-stagnation

6 Bank for International Settlements, 'Structural changes in banking after the crisis', CGFS Working Paper No.60, January 2018. See also www.bis.org/publ/cgfs60.pdf

7 Crafts, Nicholas, *Forging Ahead, Falling Behind and Fighting Back* (Cambridge University Press, Cambridge, 2018).

8 Atkinson, Andrew, 'Brexit is Costing the UK £100 Billion a Year in Lost Output', *Bloomberg News*, 31 January 2023; Ryan Wain at the Tony Blair Institute's 'Future of Britain' conference 2023.

9 Bieller, Susanne, Bill, Marina, Kraud, Werner and Müller, Christopher, *World Robotics Report* (International Federation of Robotics, Frankfurt, October 2022). See also www.automation.com/en-us/articles/

october-2022/ifr-presents-world-robotics-report-2022

10 Booth, Robert, 'Cost of Grenfell Tower disaster soars to nearly £1.2bn',
    Guardian (30 Jul. 2023).

11 Sturge, Georgina, 'Asylum Statistics', House of Commons Library (Sept.
    2023). See also https://researchbriefings.files.parliament.uk/documents/
    SN01403/SN01403.pdf

12 Calculations for the author by Seth Alexander Thévoz.

13 Sullivan, Jake, 'Remarks by National Security Advisor Jake Sullivan on
    Renewing American Economic Leadership at the Brookings Institution',
    White House website (Apr. 2023). See also https://www.whitehouse.
    gov/briefing-room/speeches-remarks/2023/04/27/remarks-by-national-
    security-advisor-jake-sullivan-on-renewing-american-economic-
    leadership-at-the-brookings-institution/?utm_source=substack&utm_
    medium=email

14 De La Baume, Maia, 'Orbán, Le Pen, Salvini join forces to blast EU
    integration', *Politico* (2 Jul. 2023). See also www.politico.eu/article/viktor-
    orban-marine-le-pen-matteo-salvini-eu-integration-european-superstate-
    radical-forces//

15 Hogarth, Ian, 'We must slow down the race to God-like AI', *Financial
    Times* (13 Apr. 2023). See also www.ft.com/content/03895dc4-a3b7-481e-
    95cc-336a524f2ac2

16 World Economic Forum, 'Nature Risk Rising: Why the Crisis Engulfing
    Nature Matters for Business and the Economy', New Nature Economy
    series, WEF (Jan. 2020). See also https://www3.weforum.org/docs/WEF_
    New_Nature_Economy_Report_2020.pdf

17 The King's Fund Responds to the Latest ONS Mortality Data (London:
    December 2022). Note that even on age-adjusted excess death rates, the
    UK performed worse of comparable Western EU countries (Figure 4,
    ONS Bulletin, December 2022).

Chapter 2

1 Kuttner, Robert, *Going Big: FDR's Legacy, Biden's New Deal, and the
   Struggle to Save Democracy* (New Press, New York/London, 2022), pp.42-
   3.

2 Mont Pelerin Society website. See also www.depts.ttu.edu/
   freemarketinstitute/mps.ph

3   Phillips-Kein, Kim, 'One Notion: Individual Two lives of Ayn Rand', *Harpers* (Dec. 2009).

4   Rand, Ayn, *The Virtue of Selfishness* (Signet, New York, 1964).

5   Boaz, David, *The Libertarian Mind: A Manifesto for Freedom* (Simon & Schuster, New York, 2015).

6   Blumenthal, Sidney, *The Rise of the Counter-Establishment: The Conservative Ascent to Political Power* (Union Square Press, New York, 2008), p.10.

7   Kuhn, David Paul, 'Capitol Mourns Political Icon', *Politico* (27 Feb. 2008), https://www.politico.com/story/2008/02/capital-mourns-conservative-icon-008741

8   Kuttner, op. cit. p.96.

9   Blumenthal, op. cit. p.259.

10 Gingrich, Newt, 'Language: A Key Mechanism of Control' (GOPAC Working Paper, Washington DC, 1990). See also https://uh.edu/~englin/rephandout.html

11 Graffeo, Emily, 'Warren Buffett warned 18 years ago about the financial instruments that triggered the Archegos implosion', *Business Insider* (2 Apr. 2021). See also https://markets.businessinsider.com/news/stocks/warren-buffett-archegos-implosion-warning-derivatives-total-return-swaps-lethal-2021-4-1030272114

12 Sullivan, op. cit.

13 Gerstle, G., *The Rise and Fall of The Neoliberal Order: America and the World in the Free Market Era* (Oxford University Press, Oxford, 2022).

14 Swan, Jonathan, Savage, Charlie and Haberman, Maggie, 'Trump and Allies Forge Plans to Increase Presidential Power in 2025', *New York Times*, 17 July 2023.

Chapter 3

1   Tinline, Phil, *The Death of Consensus: 100 Years of British Political Nightmares* (Hurst & Company, London, 2022), p.229.

2   Thatcher, Margaret, 'Interview for "Woman's Own" ("No Such Thing as Society")' (23 Sept. 1987). See also the Margaret Thatcher Foundation website.

3   R. Jones, op, cit. p.84.

4   Jones, Russell, *The Tyranny of Nostalgia; Half a Century of British*

Economic Decline (London Publishing Partnership, London 2023), p.84.

5   Jones, op. cit. p.64.

6   Jones, op. cit. p.64.

7   Crafts (2018), op. cit., figures from chapters 5 and 6.

8   Rice, Patricia G. and Venables, Anthony J., 'The persistent consequences of adverse shocks: how the 1970s shaped regional inequality', *Oxford Review of Economic Policy*, 37/1 (2021), pp.132-151.

9   Jones, op. cit. p.67.

10   The Equality Trust, 'The Scale of Economic Equality in the UK', Equality Trust website. See also https://equalitytrust.org.uk/scale-economic-inequality-uk

11   Crafts, Nicholas, 'The Growth Effects of EU Membership for the UK: Review of the evidence', SMF-CAGE Global Perspectives Series: Paper 7 (Apr. 2016), University of Warwick, p. 93. See also https://warwick.ac.uk/fac/soc/economics/research/centres/cage/publications/policybriefings/2016/the_growth_effects_of_eu_membership_for_the_uk_review_of_the_evidence/

12   Jones, op. cit. p 85.

13   Shoben, Carl, 'New poll: public strongly backing public ownership of energy and key utilities', *Survation*, 15 August 2022, https://www.survation.com/new-poll-public-strongly-backing-public-ownership-of-energy-and-key-utilities/

14   Elliott, Larry, 'UK "missed chance to build up £450bn sovereign wealth fund"', *Guardian* (27 Feb. 2008).

15   Balls, Ed, City Minister, Bloomberg Speech, 14 June 2006.

16   May, Theresa, 'Full text: Theresa May's conference speech', *Guardian* (7 Oct. 2002).

17   The Conservative Manifesto 2010, 'Invitation to join the Government of Britain' (Conservative Party, London, 2010).

18   Tinline, op. cit. pp.215-18.

19   Fetzer, Thiemo, 'Did Austerity Cause Brexit?', *American Economic Review*, 109:11 (2019), pp. 3849-86.

20   Shoben, op. cit.

21   Partington, Richard, 'Flip-flopping has cost the UK billions', *Guardian* (17 Nov. 2023).

22 The other three 'families' are the Conservative Growth Group, the Common Sense Group and the New Conservatives.

Chapter 4

1 Sassoon, Donald, *One Hundred Years of Socialism: The West European Left in the Twentieth Century* (I. B. Tauris, London, 1996), p.765.
2 Smith, Adam, *An Inquiry into the Nature and Causes of the* Wealth of Nations (Wordsworth, London, 2012 [first pub. 1776]).
3 Rothschild, Emma, *Economic Sentiments: Condorcet, Smith and the Industrial Revolution* (Harvard University Press, Cambridge, MA/London, 2022), p.12.
4 Allen, Robert C., *The British Industrial Revolution in Global Perspective* (Cambridge University Press, Cambridge, 2009).
5 Berg, Maxine and Hudson, Pat, *Slavery, Capitalism and the Industrial Revolution* (John Wiley, Oxford, 2023), p.143.
6 Smith, Adam, op. cit. pp.318-20.
7 Crafts, op. cit. p.13.
8 Crafts, op. cit. p.13.
9 See Allen, op. cit.
10 Crafts, op. cit. p.14.
11 'Tolpuddle Martyrs: The Story'. See also https://www.tolpuddlemartyrs.org.uk/story
12 Trincado, Estrella and Santos-Redondo, Manuel, 'Bentham and Owen on entrepreneurship and social reform', *The European Journal of the History of Economic Thought*, 21:2 (2014), pp.252-77.
13 Renwick, Chris, *Bread for All: The Origins of the Welfare State* (Allen Lane, London, 2017), p.30.
14 Acemoglu, Darren and Johnson, Simon, *Power and Progress: Our Thousand-Year Struggle Over Technology and Prosperity* (Basic Books, London, 2023).
15 Crafts, op. cit. p.13.

Chapter 5

1 Renwick, op. cit. p.96.
2 See Capaldi, op. cit.
3 Weldon, Duncan, *Two Hundred Years of Muddling Through: The*

Surprising Story of Britain's Economy from Boom to Bust and Back Again (Little, Brown, London, 2021), p.90.

4   Morris, William, *A Dream of John Ball* (Reeves & Turner, London, 1888), Chapter 4.

5   Renwick, op. cit p.67.

6   Diamond, Patrick and Radice, Giles, *Labour's Civil War: How Infighting Has Kept the Left from Power (And What Can Be Done About It)* (Haus Publishing, London, 2022), p.30.

7   Williams, Chris, *Democratic Rhonda, Politics and Society 1885-1951* (University of Wales Press, Cardiff, 1996).

8   Bogdanor, Vernon, *The Strange Survival of Liberal Britain* (Biteback Publishing, London, 2022), p. 229.

9   Toynbee, Polly, *An Uneasy Inheritance: My Family and Other Radicals* (Atlantic Books, London, 2023).

10 Crafts, op. cit. p.20.

11 Bogdanor, op. cit. p.247.

12 Diamond and Radice, op. cit. p.31.

13 Bogdanor, op. cit. p.227.

14 Bogdanor, op. cit. p.249.

15 Renwick, op. cit. pp.75-8.

16 Renwick, op. cit. pp.176-80.

17 Marquand, David, *The Progressive Dilemma* (Phoenix, London, 1991), pp.40-1.

18 Pinto-Duschinsky, Michael, 'From Fear of Democracy to Political Expediency: Lord Salisbury and the Second and Third Reform Acts', *Revue Francaise De Civilisation Britannique*, 3:3 (2017), pp.65-75.

19 Keynes, John Maynard, 'The End of *Laissez-faire*', *Collected Writings*, Vol IX, (Hogarth Press, London, 1926), p.4.

Chapter 6

1   Hutton, Will, *The State We're In* (Jonathan Cape, London, 1996), p.127.

2   Tinline, op. cit. pp.20-3.

3   Weldon, op. cit. p.162.

4   Tawney R. H., *The Acquisitive Society* (G. Bell, London, 1920), p.8 and p.51.

5   Tawney R. H., op. cit. p.58.

6   Tawney R. H., op. cit. p.104.

7   Tawney R. H., *Equality* (William Pickering, London, 1931), p.74.

8   Diamond and Radice, op. cit. p.62.

9   Tawney, R.H., *Equality* (William Pickering, London 1931) p.225.

10 Statista Research Department, 'Annual number of combat aircraft produced by the major powers during the Second World War from 1939 to 1945 (in 000s)' (1998), https://www.statista.com/statistics/1336929/wwii-combat-aircraft-production-annual/

11 Beveridge, William, 'Social Insurance and Allied Services Report" (HMSO, London, 1942), p.7.

12 Harris, Kenneth, *Attlee* (Orion, London, 1995), p.220.

13 Renwick, C., op. cit. pp.217–30.

14 Harris, op. cit. p.35.

Chapter 7

1   Crosland, Anthony, *The Future of Socialism* (Jonathan Cape, London, 1956), p.87.

2   Cole, G.D.H., *A Short History of the British Working Class Movement, 1789-1937* (George Allen & Unwin, London, 1937), pp.22-6.

3   See Weldon op. cit.

4   Slobodian, Quin, *Crack-up Capitalism: Market Radicals and the Dream of a World Without Democracy* (Allen Lane, London, 2023), p.42.

5   Crafts (2018), op. cit. p.85.

6   Harris, K., op. cit. p.56.

7   Bevan, Aneurin, *In Place of Fear* (Heinemann, London, 1952), p.59.

8   Bevan, op. cit. p.59.

9   Bevan, op. cit. p.57.

10 Wood, Stewart, 'Why "Indicative Planning" Failed: British Industry and the Formation of the National Economic Development Council', *Twentieth Century British History*, 11/4 (2000), pp.431–59.

11 Weldon, op. cit. pp.225-7.

12 Thomas-Symonds, Nick, *Harold Wilson: The Winner* (Weidenfeld & Nicolson, London, 2022), p.303.

13 Tyler, Richard John, 'Victim of our history', *Contemporary British History*, 20:3 (2006), pp.461-476.

14 Collier, Paul and Kay, John, *Greed Is Dead: Politics After Individualism*

(Penguin, London, 2022), p.67.

15   Blair, Tony, 'Let us Face the Future', Fabian Pamphlet No. 571, 1995.

16   Bevir, Mark, 'New Labour: A Study in Ideology', *British Journal of Politics and International Relations*, 2:3 (2000), pp. 277-301.

17   Mandelson, Peter and Liddle, Rod, *The Blair Revolution* (Faber & Faber, London, 1996).

18   Jones, op. cit. p.134.

19   Jones, op. cit. p.147.

20   Jones, op. cit. p.131.

21   Jones, op. cit. p.145.

22   Larkin, Kieran, 'Regional Development Agencies: the facts', Centre for Cities, (Dec. 2009). See also https://www.centreforcities.org/wp-content/uploads/2014/09/09-12-08-RDAS-The-facts.pdf

23   Miliband, David, speech to the Hay Festival (27 May 2023).

24   Jones, Owen, *This Land: The Struggle for the Left* (Allen Lane, London, 2020), p.40.

25   Collier and Kay, op. cit. p.77.

Chapter 8

1   This argument underpins the book, Sandbu, Martin, *The Economics of Belonging*. Sandbu, M., *The Economics of Belonging: A Radical Plan to Win Back the Left Behind and Achieve Prosperity for All* (Princeton University Press, New Jersey, 2020).

2   Committee on Standards in Public Life, 'Upholding Standards in Public Life: Final Report of the Standards Matters 2', (Sept. 2020). See also https://www.gov.uk/government/collections/standards-matter-2

3   Ahmed, Nur, Wahed, Muntasir, and Thompson, Neil, 'The growing influence of industry in AI research', *Science*, 379:6635 (Mar. 2023), pp.884-6. See also https://www.science.org/doi/10.1126/science.ade2420. See also European Parliament, 'Artificial intelligence: How does it work, why does it matter, and what can we do about it?', Panel for the Future of Science and Technology (Jun. 2020). See also https://www.europarl.europa.eu/RegData/etudes/STUD/2020/641547/EPRS_STU(2020)641547_EN.pdf

4   McKinsey, 'Growth Strategy & Innovation', McKinsey website. See also https://www.mckinsey.com/capabilities/strategy-and-corporate-finance/

how-we-help-clients/growth-strategy-and-innovation

5 White, Stuart and Seth-Smith, Niki, *Democratic Wealth: Building a Citizens' Economy*, openDemocracy (24 Mar 2014).

6 Pope, Thomas, Tetlow, Gemma, Hoddinott, Stuart, Bartrum, Olly and Pattison, Jeremy, 'Six Things We Learned from the Autumn Statement', Institute for Government website (22 Nov. 2023). See also https://www.instituteforgovernment.org.uk/comment/six-things-look-out-2023-autumn-statement

7 Susskind, Daniel, *A World Without Work: Technology, Automation and How We Should Respond* (Allen Lane, London, 2020).

8 The Values Modes' model was first created by Pat Dade and Les Higgins in 1973.

9 Electoral Calculus, 'Three-D Politics 2021' (Mar. 2021). See also https://www.electoralcalculus.co.uk/pol3d_2021.html

10 Collier and Kay, op. cit. p.91. Aristotle sometimes refers to man as a political animal or creature, but in this quote he uses social creature. For him politics was an outgrowth of human belonging to society.

11 Arendt, Hannah, *The Human Condition* (University of Chicago Press, Chicago, IL, 1958.)

12 See the discussion of fairness in Chapters 2 and 3 in *Them and Us* which I wrote published by Abacus in 2010. See Hutton, Will, *Them And Us: Changing Britain - Why We Need a Fair Society* (Abacus, London, 2010).

13 Fairness Foundation, 'Fairly United: What Britons Think about Inequality and Fairness', Fairness Foundation website (3 Jul. 2023). See also https://fairnessfoundation.com/fairly-united

14 See The Purposeful Company, *The Purpose Tapes: purpose driven leaders in their own words*, Purposeful Company website (9 May 2021). See also https://thepurposefulcompany.org/wp-content/uploads/2021/05/TPC_The-Purpose-Tapes_May21.pdf; The Purposeful Company, *Advancing Purpose: How purposeful companies and investors can make better common cause*, Purposeful company website (23 Feb. 2023). See also https://thepurposefulcompany.org/wp-content/uploads/2023/02/TPC_Report-Advancing-Purpose_23FEB2023.pdf

15 Victor, David. and Sabel, Charles, 'How to Fix the Climate', *Boston Review* (Dec. 2020). See also https://www.bostonreview.net/forum/charles-sabel-david-g-victor-how-fix-climate/

16 These are the five fair necessities established by the Fairness Foundation. See also 'The Fair Necessities', https://fairnessfoundation.com/fairnecessities

17 See Rawls, John, *A Theory of Justice* (Harvard University Press, Cambridge, MA, 1971); but also Chandler, Daniel, *Free and Equal: What Would a Fair Society Look Like?* (Penguin, London, 2023).

Chapter 9

1 Burn-Murdoch, John, 'Britain and the US are poor societies with some very rich people', *Financial Times* (16 Sept. 2022). See also https://www.ft.com/content/ef265420-45e8-497b-b308-c951baa68945

2 Thwaites, Greg and Tomlinson, Daniel, *Stagnation Nation: Navigating a Route to a Fairer and More Prosperous Britain – Interim Report of the Economy 2030 Enquiry* (Resolution Foundation, London, 2022).

3 Chadha, Jagit S. and Samiri, Issam, 'Macroeconomic Perspectives on Productivity', The Productivity institute working paper no. 030 (2022). See also https://www.productivity.ac.uk/wp- content/uploads/2022/12/WP030-Macroeconomic-Perspectives-FINAL-131222.pdf

4 *Ending Stagnation*, op, cit. p.13.

5 Beauhurst, 'UK Unicorn Companies' (Sep. 2022). See also https://www.beauhurst.com/research/unicorn-companies/

6 Partington, Richard, 'UK economy in growth "doom loop" after decades of underinvestment', *Guardian* (20 Jun. 2023).

7 Wilkes, Giles, *Business Investment: Not Just One Big Problem* (Institute for Government, London, 2022), p.10.

8 *Bridging the Gap, The Economy 2030 Inquiry* (Resolution Foundation, London, 2023), p.5.

9 National Institute of Economic and Social Research, 'UK Heading Towards Five Years of Lost Economic Growth', NIESR website, August 2023. See also https://www.niesr.ac.uk/publications/uk-heading-towards-five-years-lost-economic-growth?type=uk-economic-outlook

10 Oliveira-Cunha, Julianna, Kozler, Jesse, Shah, Pablo, Thwaites, Gregory, and Valero, Anna, *Business time: How ready are UK firms for the decisive decade?*, The Economy 2030 Inquiry (Resolution Foundation/Centre for Economic Performance, London, November 2021).

11 Wilkes, op. cit.

12   Bell, Torsten, Clark, Tom, Fry, Emily, Kelly, Gavin, and Thwaites, Greg,
      Ending Stagnation – A New Economic Strategy for Britain, The Economy
      2030 Inquiry (Resolution Foundation/Centre for Economic Performance,
      London, 2023). See fig. 36, p.153.

13   Sorbe, Stéphane, Gal, Peter, Nicoletti, Giuseppe, and Timiliotis, Christina
      'Digital Dividend: Policies to Harness the Productivity Potential of Digital
      Technologies', no. 26 (OECD Publishing, Paris, Feb. 2019).

14   Bell et al., op. cit. p.74.

15   Hughes, Richard, Miles, David, and King, Andy, *Fiscal Risks and
      Sustainability Report 2023* (Office for Budget Responsibility, London,
      Jul. 2023). See also https://obr.uk/docs/dlm_uploads/Fiscal_risks_and_
      sustainability_report_July_2023.pdf

16   Armit, John, Prescot, Julia, Besley, Tim, Coleman, Neale, Green, Andy,
      Hall, Jim, Morgan, Sadie, Willard, Kate, and Winser, Nick, *The Second
      National Infrastructure Assessment* (National Infrastructure Commission,
      London, Oct. 2023). See also https://nic.org.uk/app/uploads/Final-NIA-2-
      Full-Document.pdf

17   Climate Change Committee, *Progress in Reducing Emissions: 2023 Progress
      Report to Parliament* (28 Jun. 2023). See also https://www.theccc.org.uk/
      publication/2023-progress-report-to-parliament/

18   Martin, Josh, 'Experimental comparisons of infrastructure
      across Europe: May 2019', Office for National Statistics
      (May 2019). See also https://www.ons.gov.uk/economy/
      economicoutputandproductivity/productivitymeasures/articles/
      experimentalcomparisonsofinfrastructureacrosseurope/may2019

19   Stansbury, Anna, Turner, Dan and Balls, Ed, 'Tackling the UK's regional
      inequality: binding constraints and areas for policy intervention',
      Contemporary Social Science (Aug. 2023), p.29.

20   'International Journey Time Benchmarking: Strategic Road Networks',
      Office of Rail and Road (23 Nov. 2017). See also https://www.orr.gov.
      uk/sites/default/files/om/international-journey-time-benchmarking-
      analysis-report-2017-11-23.pdf

21   Stansbury et al., op. cit. p.29.

22   Millard, Rachel and Oliver, Matt, 'Inside the "crazy" decisions that left
      Britain with no gas storage and vulnerable to Putin', *Daily Telegraph* (14
      Aug. 2022). See also https://www.telegraph.co.uk/business/2022/08/14/

inside-crazy-decisions-left-britain-no-gas-storage-vulnerable/

23   See Amrit et al., op. cit.

24   Hanretty, Chris, 'The Pork Barrel Politics of the Towns Fund', Political
     Quarterly blog (6 May 2021). See also https://politicalquarterly.org.uk/
     blog/the-pork-barrel-politics-of-the-towns-fund

25   Busby, Mattha, 'Labour calls for investigation over funding for Robert
     Jenrick's constituency', *Guardian* (10 Oct. 2020).

26   Haldane, Andy, 'The case for rethinking fiscal rules is overwhelming',
     Financial Times (16 May 2023). See also https://www.ft.com/content/
     d57567c3-cd97-4cbe-be00-6cf50886b308

27   *Cutting the Cuts, The Economy 2023 inquiry* (CEP and Resolution
     Foundation, 2023), figures 6 and 7, p.17.

28   Espinoza, Raphael, Gambola-Arbelaez, Juliana, and Syl, Mouhamamadou,
     'The Fiscal Multiplier of Public Investment: The Role of Corporate
     Balance Sheet', IMF Working Paper: Fiscal Affairs Department (Sep.
     2020).

29   IMF figures cited in Wolf, Martin, 'British politicians owe voters some
     candour on tax', *Financial Times* (17 Sept. 2023).

30   'Ending Stagnation', op. cit. p.218.

31   TaxWatch, *HMRC 2023 Tax Gap Report*, June 2023.

32   Tax Research have some interesting ideas, some of which I have used.
     See Murphy, Richard, 'The Taxing Wealth Report 2024', Tax Research (6
     Sep. 2023). See also https://www.taxresearch.org.uk/Blog/2023/09/06/
     launching-the-taxing-wealth-report-2024/

Chapter 10

1   Simon, H.A., 'Rational choice and the structure of the environment',
    Psychological Review, 63:2 (1956), pp.129-38.

2   'OTC derivatives statistics at end, December 2022', Bank for International
    Settlements (17 May 2023). See also https://www.bis.org/publ/otc_hy2305.
    htm

3   Sandbu, op. cit. p.155.

4   'Outstanding derivatives assets held by UK banks 2011-2020', Statista
    (11 Dec. 2023). See also https://www.statista.com/statistics/1214272/
    outstanding-derivatives-assets-banks-uk/

5   Kakkad, Jeegar, Madsen, Martin and Tory, Michael, 'Investing in the

Future: Boosting Savings and Prosperity for the UK' (Tony Blair Institute for Global Change, London, May 2023), p.2.

6   Shiller, Robert, 'Engineering Financial Stability', Project Syndicate (18 Jan. 2010). See also https://www.project-syndicate.org/commentary/engineering-financial-stability-2010-01?barrier=accesspaylog

7   Whiffin, Andrew, 'Lex in-depth: why is the UK stock market so cheap?', *Financial Times* (5 Mar. 2023). See also https://www.ft.com/content/2b40824f-69c6-4768-b313-a544fc1a00d7

8   Tory M., *Britain PLC in Liquidation* (Ondra, London, 2023).

9   Kakkad et al., op. cit. p.9.

10 Kakkad, Jeegar, *Transparency, Accountability, Predictability: Protecting National Security Through the UK's Foreign-Takeover Regime* (Tony Blair Institute for Global Change, London, Mar. 2023). See also https://www.institute.global/insights/economic-prosperity/transparency-accountability-predictability-protecting-national-security-through-uks-foreign

11 OECD 'Corporate Governance Factbook', 2021 (OECD, Paris, Jun. 2021).

12 Bell et al., op. cit. Figure 37, p.156.

13 Edmans, Alex, 'Blockholder Trading, Market Efficiency, and Managerial Myopia', *Journal of Finance*, 64:6 (2009), p.2481-513.

14 See The Purposeful Company (2023), op. cit.

15 The Purposeful Company (2023), op. cit. p.74.

16 Haskel, Jonathan and Westlake, Stan, *Restarting the Future: How to Fix the Intangible Economy* (Princeton University Press, Princeton, New Jersey, 2022), pp.21-45.

17 See Purposeful Company (2021) and (2023), op. cit.

18 The Purposeful Company (2023), pp.26-27.

19 Coyle, Diana, 'Does the BBC offer a model for public service digital platforms?', *Bennett Institute for Public Policy, blog* (17 Jan. 2022). See also https://www.bennettinstitute.cam.ac.uk/blog/bbc-licence-fee/

Chapter 11

1   Crenna-Jennings, Whitney, 'Key drivers of the disadvantage gap: literature review', *Education in England: Annual Report 2018* (Education Policy Institute, London, 2018).

2   Brett, Georgia, Wilson, Heidi, and Christogi, Andreas, 'Deaths due

to COVID-19, registered in England and Wales: 2021', Office for National Statistics (1 Jul. 2022). See also https://www.ons.gov.uk/ peoplepopulationandcommunity/birthsdeathsandmarriages/deaths/ articles/deathsregisteredduetocovid19/2021

3   Bell, Alex, Chetty, Raj, Jaravel, Xavier, Petkova, Neviana and Van Reenen, John, 'Who Becomes an Inventor in America? The Importance of Exposure to Innovation', *Quarterly Journal of Economics*, 134:2 (2019), pp.647–713.

4   See Thatcher (1987), op. cit.

5   Bell et al., op. cit. pp.941-5.

6   Christensen, Martin-Brehm, Hallum, Christian, Maitland, Alex, Parrinello, Quentin, and Putaturo, Chiara, *Survival of the Richest: How We Must Tax the Super-Rich Now to Fight Inequality* (Oxfam, London, Jan. 2023).

7   Lansley, Stewart, *The Richer, The Poorer: How Britain Enriched the Few and Failed the Poor* (Bristol University Press, Bristol, 2022).

8   Cerra, Valerie, Luma, Lama, and Loazya, Norman, 'Links Between Growth, Inequality, and Poverty: A Survey', *IMF* Working Paper No. 2021:068 (12 Mar. 2021). See also https://www.imf.org/en/Publications/ WP/Issues/2021/03/12/Links-Between-Growth-Inequality-and-Poverty-A-Survey-50161

9   Fairness Foundation, 'National Wealth Surplus: Seven Routes to Revenue', Fairness Foundation (May 2023). See also https://fairnessfoundation.com/ national-wealth-surplus/seven-routes-to-revenue

10   Starmans, Christina, Sheskin, Mark and Bloom, Paul, 'Why people prefer unequal societies', *Nature Human Behaviour*, 1(4):0082 (2017).

11   Acemoglu and Johnson, op. cit. p.90.

12   Fetzer, op. cit.

13   *Bloomberg News* (2023) op. cit.

14   'Unemployment', Census 2021 data, Office for National Statistics website. See also https://www.ons.gov.uk/employmentandlabourmarket/ peoplenotinwork/unemployment

15   See Bell et al., op. cit.

16   Judge, Lindsay and Slaughter, Hannah, 'Enforce for good: Effectively enforcing labour market rights in the 2020s and beyond', Resolution Foundation (Apr. 2023). See also https://www.resolutionfoundation.org/

publications/enforce-for-good/

17   Esler, G., *Britain Is Better Than This: Why a Great Country Is Failing Us All* (Apollo, London, 2023), p.288.

18   'Insecure work: Why employment rights need an overhaul', Trade Union Congress website (Jul. 2022). See also https://www.tuc.org.uk/research-analysis/reports/insecure-work-why-employment-rights-need-overhaul

19   Judge and Slaughter, op. cit.

20   See Cebula, Cela, Collingwood, Aleks, Earwaker, Rachelle, Elliott, Joseph, Matejic, Peter, Taylor, Isabel, and Wenham, Andrew, *UK Poverty 2023: The Essential Guide to Understanding Poverty in the UK* (Joseph Rowntree Foundation, York, 2023).

21   Paterson, Ben, *Addressing In-Work Poverty: The EU Minimum Wage Directive and Collective Bargaining* (European Futures, Edinburgh, 2021).

22   'Proportion of employees whose pay and conditions were agreed in negotiations between the employer and a trade union in the United Kingdom from 1996 to 2022, by sector', Statista (11 Oct. 2023). See also https://www.statista.com/statistics/287297/uk-collective-agreement-coverage/

23   Gallie, Duncan, Felstead, Alan, Green, Francis, and Henseke, Golo, *Participation at work in Britain. First findings from the Skills and Employment Survey 2017* (Centre for Learning and Life Chances in Knowledge Economies and Societies, London, 2018).

24   House of Commons Research Briefing, *Trade Unions and Industrial Relations*, p.32, Largest Trade Unions in UK and Statista, *Number of Trade Unions in the UK*, July 2023. Between 1999 and 2023 the number of trade unions had fallen by 113.

25   The Purposeful Company (2023), op. cit.

26   The Purposeful Company, op. cit. p.18.

27   Bogg, Alan, 'Building worker power: Essays on collective rights 20 years after the Wilson and Palmer case established the right to be represented by a trade union', Trade Union Congress website (Jul. 2022). See also https://www.tuc.org.uk/research-analysis/reports/building-worker-power?page=4

28   Johnson, P., *Follow the Money: How Much Does Britain Cost?* (Abacus, London, 2023).

29   'Universal Declaration of Human Rights at 70: 30 Articles on 30

Articles - Article 2', Office of the High Commissioner for Human Rights. See also https://www.ohchr.org/en/press-releases/2018/11/universal-declaration-human-rights-70-30-articles-30-articles-article-2?LangID=E&NewsID=23858

30 Brewer, Mike, Fry, Emily and Try, Lalitha, *The Living Standards Outlook 2023* (Resolution Foundation, London, 2023).

31 Layard, Richard and De Neve, Jan-Emmanuel, 'A new science of well-being will change policy and decision making', LSE CEP blog (27 Mar. 2023). See also https://blogs.lse.ac.uk/impactofsocialsciences/2023/03/27/a-new-science-of-wellbeing-will-change-policy-and-decision-making/

32 Rodrik, Dani and Sabel, Charles, 'Building a good jobs economy', Columbia Law School Working Paper (2019). See also https://scholarship.law.columbia.edu/faculty_scholarship/2608/

33 For the evaluation, see Maximillian and Lehner, Lucas, 'Employing the unemployed of Marienthal: Evaluation of a guaranteed job program', mimeo (2023). See also https://maxkasy.github.io/home/files/papers/Jobguarantee_marienthal.pdf

Chapter 12

1 IFS, 'Early childhood', IFS Deaton Review. See also https://ifs.org.uk/inequality/themes/early-childhood-development/

2 Cattan, Sarah and Farquharson, Christine, 'At their peak, Sure Start centres prevented 13,000 hospitalisations a year among 11- to 15-year-olds', IFS Press Release (16 Aug. 2021). See also https://ifs.org.uk/news/their-peak-sure-start-centres-prevented-13000-hospitalisations-year-among-11-15-year-olds

3 Bhutoria, Aditi, *Economic Returns to Education in the United Kingdom, Government Office for Science* (Foresight – Government Office for Science, London, September 2016).

4 Dearden, Lorraine, Reed, Howard and Van Reenen, John, 'Training and corporate productivity: evidence from a panel of industries', *Oxford Bulletin of Economics and Statistics*, 68:4 (2006), pp.397-421.

5 Tawney, op. cit. p.73.

6 Verkaik, Robert, *Posh Boys: How English Public Schools Ruin Britain* (Oneworld, London, 2019), p.4.

7 Lough, Catherine, 'Private schools see bigger fall in top A-level grades

than state sector', *Telegraph* (18 Aug. 2022).

8 Johnson, op. cit. p.209.

9 Farquharson, Christine, Sibieta, Luke, Tahir, Imran and Waltmann, Ben, *IFS fourth annual report on education spending, 2021*, IFS Report R204, (Institute for Fiscal Studies, London, Nov. 2021).

10 Mortimer-Lee, Paul and Pabst, Adrian (eds), *Covid-19 and Productivity Impact and Implications: NIESR Occasional Paper LXII* (National Institute of Economic and Social Research, London, 2022).

11 Tuckett, Sam, Hunt, Emily, Robinson, David and Cruikshanks, Robbie, *Covid-19 and disadvantage gaps in England 2021* (Education Policy Institute, London, Dec. 2022).

12 Drayton, Elaine, Farquharson, Christine, Ogden, Kate, Sibieta, Luke, Tahir, Imran and Waltmann, Ben, *Annual Report on Education Spending in England: 2022* (Institute for Fiscal Studies, London, 12 December 2022).

13 Tolland, Aidan, Garbutt, Olivia and Stafford, Mathieu, 'Workforce qualification levels across England and Wales data: Census 2021', Office for National Statistics website (17 Feb. 2023). See also https://www.ons.gov.uk/peoplepopulationandcommunity/educationandchildcare/datasets/workforcequalificationlevelsacrossenglandandwalesdatacensus2021

14 Bell et al., op. cit., p.39.

15 Gross, Anna, Borrett, Amy and Foster, Peter, 'Britons squeezed out of top universities by lucrative overseas students', *Financial Times* (21 Jul. 2023).

16 Bell et al., op. cit., p.39.

17 'Over £3 billion in unspent apprenticeship levy lost to Treasury "black hole" new data reveal', IPPR press release (27 Jul. 2022). See also https://www.ippr.org/news-and-media/press-releases/over-3-billion-in-unspent-apprenticeship-levy-lost-to-treasury-black-hole-new-data-reveal

18 Goettler, Andrea, Grosse, Anna and Sonntag, Diana, 'Productivity loss due to overweight and obesity: a systematic review of indirect costs', *British Medical Journal Open*, 7:10 (2017). See also https://www.ncbi.nlm.nih.gov/pmc/articles/PMC5640019/

19 HM Government, *Levelling up the United Kingdom: Department for Levelling Up, Housing and Communities White Paper* (HMSO, London, Feb. 2022), p.63.

20 'Health inequalities: our position' (King's Fund, London, 29 Sep. 2021). See also https://www.kingsfund.org.uk/projects/positions/health-

inequalities

21 Burn-Murdoch, John, 'How to Fix Britain's chronically ill healthcare system', *Financial Times*, 3 June 2022.

22 PA Media, 'A&E delays causing up to 500 deaths a week, says senior medic', *Guardian* (1 Jan. 2023).

23 'A quarter of GP and general practice nursing posts could be vacant in 10 years', press release, Health Foundation website (25 Jul. 2022). See also https://www.health.org.uk/news-and-comment/news/a-quarter-of-gp-and-general-practice-nursing-posts-could-be-vacant-in-10-years

24 'At least 271,000 people are homeless in England today', press release, Shelter website (11 Jan. 2023). See also https://england.shelter.org.uk/media/press_release/at_least_271000_people_are_homeless_in_england_today

25 Romei, Valentina, 'UK renters five times more likely to struggle financially than homeowners', *Financial Times* (14 July 2023).

26 Kanabar, Ricky and Gregg, Paul, 'Intergenerational wealth transmission and mobility in Great Britain: what components of wealth matter?', *UCL Working Paper No.22-01* (UCL Centre for Education Policy and Equalising Opportunities, London, 2022).

27 Kanabar and Gregg, op. cit.

28 'Share of owner occupied households in England from 2000 to 2022', Statista (11 Oct. 2023). See also https://www.statista.com/statistics/286503/england-propportion-of-owner-occupied-households/

29 Bannister, Lucy, Matejic, Peter, Porter, Iain, Sands, Daisy, Schmuecker, Katie, Wenham, Andrew, Bull, Rachel, Ferrer, Ieuan, and Hughes, *An Essentials Guarantee: Reforming Universal Credit to ensure we can all afford the essentials in hard times* (Joseph Rowntree Foundation, London, Feb. 2023).

30 Watling, Samuel and Breach, Anthony, *The Housebuilding Crisis: The UK's 4 million missing homes* (Centre for Cities, London, 23 Feb. 2023).

31 Piddington, Justine, Nicol, Simon, Garrett, Helen, and Custard, Matthew, *The Housing Stock of The United Kingdom* (BRE Trust, London, 2021).

32 Blanchard, Jack, 'David Cameron and George Osborne would not build council houses because it would "create Labour voters"', *Daily Mirror* (2 Sep. 2016).

33 National Institute of Economic and Social Research, 'UK Economy

Beset by Sluggish Growth and High Inflation, NIESR Economic Outlook', NIESR website (11 May 2023). See also https://www.niesr.ac.uk/publications/uk-economy-sluggish-growth-high-inflation?type=uk-economic-outlook

34 Muellbauer, John, 'Why we need a green land value tax and how to design it', INET Oxford Working Paper No. 2023-12 (2023).

35 Organisation for Economic Cooperation and Development, 'Global Compendium of Land Value Capture Policies' (OECD Paris, June 2022); OECD, 'Brick by Brick: Building Better Housing Policies' (OECD Paris, 2021). See also https://www.oecd-ilibrary.org/sites/b453b043-en/index.html?itemId=/content/publication/b453b043-en

36 The Secret Barrister, *Nothing but the Truth* (Picador, London, 2022), p.285.

37 Ministry of Justice, 'Criminal court statistics quarterly: January to March 2023, National Statistics', UK government website (29 June 2023). See also https://www.gov.uk/government/statistics/criminal-court-statistics-quarterly-january-to-march-2023/criminal-court-statistics-quarterly-january-to-march-2023

38 Law Society, 'A decade of cuts: Legal aid in tatters', Law Society press release (31 Mar. 2023). See also https://www.lawsociety.org.uk/contact-or-visit-us/press-office/press-releases/a-decade-of-cuts-legal-aid-in-tatters

39 British Red Cross and Co-op, *Trapped in a Bubble: An Investigation into Triggers for Loneliness in the UK* (Kantar Public, London, Dec. 2016).

40 Chetty, Raj, Jackson, Matthew O., Kuchler, Theresa, Stroebel, Johannes, Hiller, Abigail, Oppenheimer, Sarah, and the Opportunity Insights Team, *Social Capital and Economic Mobility* (Opportunity Insights, London, Aug. 2022). See also https://opportunityinsights.org/wp-content/uploads/2022/07/socialcapital_nontech.pdf.

41 Baroness Minouche Shafik, 'What we owe each other: a new social contract', IFS Annual Lecture (16 Nov. 2022).

42 For a discussion of this policy idea, see the work of the National Youth Corps. See also https://www.uknationalyouthcorps.co.uk/

43 'The Social Capital Index, Solability website. See also https://solability.com/the-global-sustainable-competitiveness-index/the-index/social-capital

Chapter 13

1   McIness, Roderick, 'General Election 2019: Turning votes into seats', House of Commons Library (Jan. 2020). See also https://commonslibrary. parliament.uk/general-election-2019-turning-votes-into-seats/

2   Dunt, Ian, *How Westminster Works... and Why It Doesn't* (Weidenfeld & Nicolson, London, 2023), pp.88-9.

3   Electoral Commission, 'Report on the May 2023 local elections in England', Electoral Commission website (Sep. 2023), See also https://www. electoralcommission.org.uk/research-reports-and-data/our-reports-and-data-past-elections-and-referendums/report-may-2023-local-elections-england

4   Esler, op. cit. Lord Carloway quoted on p.252.

5   Autumn Statement 2023: LGA Submission, Local Government Association 24th October 2023.

6   Breach, Anthony and Bridgett, Stuart, *Centralisation Nation: Britain's system of local government and its impact on the national economy* (Centre for Cities Report, London, Sep. 2022).

7   Newman, Jack, Richards, David, Westwood, Andy, and Diamond, Patrick, 'Local democracy is essential for effective decentralisation in England', *LSE Policy and Politics blog* (9 May 2023). See also https://blogs. lse.ac.uk/politicsandpolicy/local-democracy-is-essential-for-effective-decentralisation-in-england/

8   Forthcoming article by Ivor Crewe, supplied to the author.

9   Timmins, Nicholas, and Baird, Becky, *The Covid-19 Vaccination Programme: Trials, Tribulations and Successes* (King's Fund, London, Jan. 2022).

10   Dunt, Ian, *How Westminster Works... (and Why it Doesn't)* (Weidenfeld and Nicolson, London, 2023), p.331.

11   See British Social Attitudes: the 39th Annual Report (National Centre for Social Research, London, 22 Sep. 2022); 'Half of Britain wants voting system to change, with clear majority among Labour supporters', press release, NCSR website (22 Sep. 2022). See also https://natcen.ac.uk/news/half-britain-wants-voting-system-change-clear-majority-among-labour-supporters

12   Thévoz, Seth, 'Want a seat in the House of Lords? Be Tory treasurer and donate £3m', openDemocracy (6 Nov. 2021). See also https://www.

opendemocracy.net/en/dark-money-investigations/want-a-seat-in-the-house-of-lords-be-tory-treasurer-and-donate-3m/

13   Joint Report by the IFS, Chartered Institute of Taxation and the Institute for Government, Dunt, op. cit. pp.188-9 Joint Report by the IFS, Chartered Institute of Taxation and the Institute of Government.

14   Hutton, op. cit. p.124.

15   Dunt, op. cit. p.182.

16   Johnstone, Richard, 'Civil service "infantilised" by use of consultants, Cabinet Office minister says', *Civil Service World* (30 Sept. 2020). See also https://www.civilserviceworld.com/professions/article/civil-service-infantilised-by-use-of-consultants-says-cabinet-office-minister

17   See Mazzucato, Mariana and Collington, Rosie, *The Big Con: How the Consulting Industry Weakens our Businesses, Infantilizes our Governments and Warps our Economies* (Allen Lane, London, 2023).

18   See Bogdanich, Walt and Forsythe, Michael, *When McKinsey Comes to Town: The Hidden Influence of the World's Most Powerful Consulting Firm* (Vintage, London, 2023).

19   Author's calculations, based on House of Commons Library briefing.

20   Itti, Laurent and Baldi, Pierre, 'Bayesian surprise attracts human attention', *Vision Research*, 49:10 (2009), pp.1295-1306.

21   Vosoughi, Soroush, Roy, Deb and Aral, Sinan, 'The spread of true and false news online', *Science* (2018), 359:6380, pp.1146-51.

22   Shao, Chengcheng, Ciampaglia, Giovanni, Varol, Onur, Yang, Kai-Cheng, Flammini, Alessandro, and Menczer, Filippo, 'The spread of low-credibility content by social bots', *Nature Communications* 9:4, 478 (Nov. 2018).

23   Clegg, Nick, 'Facebook, Elections and Political Speech' (speech given to the Atlantic Festival, Washington DC, September 2019).

24   Broome, Molly, Mulheirn, Ian and Pittaway, Simon, 'Peaked interest?: What higher interest rates mean for the size and distribution of Britain's household wealth (Resolution Foundation, London, Jul. 2023).

25   Bullough, Oliver, *Butler to the World: The Book the Oligarchs Don't Want You to Read - How Britain Became the Servant of Tycoons, Tax Dodgers, Kleptocrats and Criminals* (Profile Books, London, 2022), p.245.

26   Bowers, John, *Downward Spiral: Collapsing Public Standards and How to Restore Them* (Manchester University Press, Manchester, 2024), p.390.

27 Dunt, op. cit. p.339.
28 Evan Harris and Steve Barnett of the 'Hacked Off' campaign provided important material to inform this analysis.

Conclusion

1   Harris, K., op. cit. p.524.

Bibliography

Primary sources – archival documents

'In Place of Strife' (Cmnd 3888), CAB 129/144 – Papers: 101(69)-125(6) (1969), National Archives, Kew.

'Royal Commission on Trade Unions and Employers' Associations', aka 'Donavan Report' (Cmnd 3623) (1968).

Books – primary sources

Hannah Arendt, *The Human Condition* (Chicago: Chicago University Press, 1958).

Aneurin Bevan, *In Place of Fear* (London: William Heinemann, 1952).

William Beveridge, *Social Insurance and Allied Services* (London: HMSO, 1942).

Charles Booth (ed.), *Life and Labour of the People in London*, 17 vols (London: Macmillan, 1902-3).

Robert Bork, *The Antitrust Paradox* (New York: Free Press, 1978).

Chris Bryant, *Code of Conduct: Why We Need to Fix Parliament – and How to Do It* (London: Bloomsbury, 2023).

Anthony Crosland, *The Future of Socialism* (London: Jonathan Cape, 1956).

Friedrich Engels, *The Condition of the Working Class in England* (New York: John W. Lovell, 1887). [First pub. in German, 1845.]

Milton Friedman, *Capitalism and Freedom* (Chicago: University of Chicago Press, 1962).

Milton Friedman and Rose Friedman, *Free to Choose: A Personal Statement* (New York: Harcourt, 1980).

J. K. Galbraith, *American Capitalism: The Concept of Countervailing Power* (New York: Houghton Mifflin, 1952).

George Gilder, *Wealth and Poverty* (New York: Basic Books, 1981).

T. H. Green, *Lectures on the Principles of Political Obligation* (London: Macmillan, 1883).

Friedrich A. Hayek, *The Road to Serfdom* (London: Routledge, 1944).

L. T. Hobhouse, *Liberalism* (London: Williams and Norgate, 1911).

J. A. Hobson, *The Evolution of Modern Capitalism: A Study of Machine Production* (London: Walter Scott, 1894). *Imperialism: A Study* (London: Unwin Hyman, 1902).

John Maynard Keynes, *The Economic Consequences of the Peace* (London: Macmillan, 1919). *A Treatise on Money* (London: Macmillan, 1930). *The General Theory of Employment, Interest and Money* (London: Macmillan, 1936).

Axel Leijonhufvud, *On Keynesian Economics and the Economics of Keynes* (Oxford: Oxford University Press, 1968).

Paul Krugman, *The Great Unravelling: Losing Our Way in the New Century* (New York: W. W. Norton 2023).

Kwasi Kwarteng, Priti Patel, Dominic Raab, Chris Skidmore and Liz Truss, *After the Coalition: A Conservative Agenda for Britain* (London: Biteback, 2011).

————, *Britannia Unchained: Global Lessons for Growth and Prosperity* (London: Palgrave Macmillan, 2012).

Harold Macmillan, *The Middle Way: A Study of the Problems of Economic and Social Progress in a Free and Democratic Society* (London: Macmillan, 1938).

Peter Mandelson and Rod Liddle, *The Blair Revolution* (London: Faber & Faber, 1996).

Ralph Nader, Joel Seligman and Mark J. Green, *Taking the Giant Corporation* (New York: W. W. Norton, 1977).

Karl Polanyi, *The Great Transformation* (New York: Farrar & Rinehart, 1944).

Karl Popper, *The Open Society and Its Enemies* (London: Routledge, 1945).

John Rawls, *A Theory of Justice: Revised Edition* (Cambridge, Massachusetts: Harvard University Press, 1971, rev. 1999).

Karl Rove, *Courage and Consequence: My Life as a Conservative in the Fight* (New York: Threshold Editions, 2010).

Jonathan Sacks, *The Home We Build Together: Recreating Society* (London: Bloomsbury, 2007).

Amartya Sen, *Identity and Violence: The Illusion of Destiny* (New York: W. W. Norton, 2006).

_____, *The Idea of Justice* (Cambridge, Massachusetts: Allen Lane/ Harvard University Press, 2009).

Adam Smith, *The Wealth of Nations* (London: Wordsworth, 2012 [first pub. 1776]).

Joseph E. Stiglitz, *The Price of Inequality: How Today's Divided Society Endangers Our Future* (New York: W. W Norton, 2003). *People, Power and Profits: Progressive Capitalism for an Age of Discontent* (London: Allen Lane, 2010).

Leo Strauss, *Natural Right and History* (Chicago: University of Chicago Press, 1953).

R. H. Tawney, *The Acquisitive Society* (London: G. Bell, 1920).

_____, *Equality* (London: William Pickering, 1931).

Books – secondary sources

Daron Acemoglu and Simon Johnson, *Power and Progress: Our Thousand-Year Struggle Over Technology and Prosperity* (New York: Basic Books, 2023).

Robert C. Allen, *The British Industrial Revolution in Global Perspective* (Cambridge: Cambridge University Press, 2009).

John B. Bader, *Taking the Initiative: Leadership Agendas in Congress and the 'Contract with America'* (Washington D.C.: Georgetown University Press, 1996).

Anthony J. Badger, *FDR: The First Hundred Days* (New York: Hill and Wang, 2008).

Maxine Berg and Pat Hudson, *Slavery, Capitalism and the Industrial Revolution* (London: Polity Press, 2023).

Sidney Blumenthal, *The Rise of the Counter-Establishment: The Conservative Ascent to Political Power*, rev. ed. (New York: Union Square Press, 2008).

David Boaz, *The Libertarian Mind* (New York: Simon & Schuster, 2015).

Walt Bogdanich and Michael Forsythe, *When McKinsey Comes to Town:*

The Hidden Influence of the World's Most Powerful Consulting Firm (London: Penguin, 2022).

Vernon Bogdanor, *The Strange Survival of Liberal Britain* (London: Biteback, 2022).

Oliver Bullough, *Butler to the World: How Britain Became the Servant of Tycoons, Tax Dodgers, Kleptocrats and Criminals* (London: Profile Books, 2022).

Tom Burgis, *Kleptopia: How Dirty Money is Conquering the World* (London: William Collins, 2020).

David Butler and Donald Stokes, *Political Change in Britain: Forces Shaping Electoral Choice* (London: Macmillan, 1969).

Daniel Chandler, *Free and Equal: What Would a Fair Society Look Like?* (London: Penguin, 2023).

Paul Collier and John Kaye, *Greed is Dead: Politics After Individualism* (London: Allen Lane, 2020).

Chris Cook, *Age of Alignment: Electoral Politics in Britain, 1922-1929* (London: Macmillan, 1975).

Nicholas Crafts, *Forging Ahead, Falling Behind, Fighting Back: British Economic Growth from the Industrial Revolution to the Financial Crisis* (Cambridge: Cambridge University Press, 2018).

Ivor Crewe and Anthony King, *SDP: The Birth, Life and Death of the Social Democratic Party* (Oxford: Oxford University Press, 1995).

George Dangerfield, *The Strange Death of Liberal England* (New York: Smith and Haas, 1935).

Patrick Diamond, *The Crosland Legacy: The Future of British Social Democracy* (London: Policy Press, 2016).

Ian Dunt, *How Westminster Works... and Why It Doesn't* (London: Weidenfeld & Nicholson, 2023).

Roger Eatwell and Matthew Goodwin, *National Populism: The Revolt Against Liberal Democracy* (London: Pelican, 2018).

Gavin Esler, *Britain is Better Than This: Why a Great Country is Failing Us All* (London: Apollo, 2023).

Robert Ford and Matthew Goodwin, *Revolt on the Right: Explaining Support for the Radical Right in Britain* (London: Routledge, 2014).

Francis Fukuyama, *The End of History and the Last Man* (New York: Free Press, 1992).

Andrew Gamble, *Hayek: The Iron Cage of Liberty* (London: Polity Press, 1996).

Peter Geoghegan, *Democracy for Sale: Dark Money and Dirty Politics* (London: Apollo, 2020).

Gary Gerstle, *The Rise and Fall of the Neoliberal Order: America and the World in the Free Market Era* (Oxford: Oxford University Press, 2022).

Alison Goldsworthy, Laura Osborne and Alexandra Chesterfield, *Poles Apart: Why People Turn Against Each Other, and How to Bring Them Together* (New York: Random House, 2021).

Maggie Haberman, *Confidence Man: The Making of Donald Trump and the Breaking of America* (New York: Penguin, 2022).

Jacob S. Hacker and Paul Pierson, *Let Them Eat Tweets: How the Right Rules in an Age of Extreme Inequality* (New York: Liveright, 2020).

Jonathan Haidt, *The Righteous Mind: Why Good People are Divided by Politics and Religion* (New York: Pantheon Books, 2012).

Kenneth Harris, *Attlee* (London: Weidenfeld & Nicholson, 1982).

Jonathan Haskel and Stan Westlake, *Restarting the Future: How to Fix the Intangible Economy* (Princeton: Princeton University Press, 2022).

Steven F. Hayward, *The Age of Reagan: The Fall of the Old Liberal Order, 1964-1980* (New York: Crown Forum, 2001).

_____, *The Age of Reagan: The Conservative Counter-Revolution, 1980-1989* (New York: Crown Forum, 2010).

Samuel P. Huntington, *The Clash of Civilizations and the Remaking of World Order* (New York: Simon & Schuster, 1996).

Will Hutton, *The Revolution That Never Was: An Assessment of Keynesian Economics* (London: Longman, 1986).

_____, *The State We're In* (London: Jonathan Cape, 1996).

_____, *The State to Come* (London: Vintage, 1997).

_____, *The World We're In* (London: Little, Brown, 2002).

_____, *Them and Us: Changing Britain – Why We Need a Fair Society* (London: Little, Brown, 2010).

_____, *How Good Can We Be: Ending the Mercenary Society and Building a Great Country* (London: Little, Brown, 2015).

Will Hutton and Andrew Adonis, *Saving Britain: How We Must Change to Prosper in Europe* (London: Abacus, 2018).

Kevin Jefferys, *Leading Labour: From Keir Hardie to Tony Blair* (London: I. B. Tauris, 1999).

Owen Jones, *This Land, The Struggle for the Left* (Allen Lane, London, 2020).

Jones, R., *The Tyranny of Nostalgia: Half a Century of British Economic Decline* (London Publishing Partnership, London 2023).

Eric Kaufmann, *Whiteshift: Populism, Immigration and the Future of White Majorities* (New York: Allen Lane, 2018).

Dacher Keltner, Jason Marsh and Jeremy Adam Smith, *The Compassionate Instinct: The Science of Human Goodness* (New York: W. W. Norton, 2010).

Caroline Knowles, *Serious Money: Walking Plutocratic London* (London: Allen Lane, 2022).

Douglas L. Koopman, *Hostile Takeover: The House Republican Party, 1980-1995* (Lanham, Maryland: Rowman & Littlefield, 1996).

Robert Kuttner, *Going Big: FDR's Legacy, Biden's New Deal, and the Struggle to Save Democracy* (New York: New Press, 2022).

Stewart Lansley, *The Richer, The Poorer: How Britain Enriched the Few and Failed the Poor* (Bristol: Bristol University Press, 2022).

Richard Layard and Jan-Emmanuel De Neve, *Wellbeing: Science and Policy* (Cambridge: Cambridge University Press, 2023).

Sebastian Mallaby, *The Man Who Knew: The Life and Times of Alan Greenspan* (New York: Penguin Press, 2016).

David Marquand, *Ramsay MacDonald* (London: Jonathan Cape, 1977).

_____, *The Progressive Dilemma: From Lloyd George to Blair*, 2nd ed. (London: Phoenix, 1991, rev. 1999).

Mariana Mazzucato and Rosie Collington, *The Big Con: How the Consulting Industry Weakens our Businesses, Infantilizes our Governments and Warps our Economies* (London: Penguin Bodley Head, 2023).

John Micklethwaite and Adrian Woolridge, *The Right Nation: Conservative Power in America* (New York: Penguin, 2004).

Moisés Naím, *The Revenge of Power: How Autocrats Are Reinventing Politics for the 21st Century* (New York: St. Martin's Press, 2022).

James O'Brien, *How They Broke Britain* (London: WH Allen 2023).

Francis O'Gorman, *John Ruskin* (London: Sutton Publishing, 1999).

Margaret O'Mara, *The Code: Silicon Valley and the Remaking of America* (New York: Penguin Press, 2019).

Henry Pelling, *The Labour Governments, 1945-51* (London: Macmillan, 1984).

James Plunkett, *End State: 9 Ways Society Is Broken & How We Fix It* (London: Trapeze, 2021).

Martin Pugh, *Electoral Reform in Peace and War, 1906-18* (London: Routledge Kegan Paul, 1978).

Charles Raw, *Slater Walker: An Investigation of a Financial Phenomenon* (London: Andre Deutsch, 1977).

Chris Renwick, *Bread for All: The Origins of the Welfare State* (London: Allen Lane, 2018).

Emma Rothschild, *Economic Sentiments: Adam Smith, Condorcet, and the Enlightenment* (Cambridge, Massachusetts: Harvard University Press, 2002).

Charles F. Sabel and David G. Victor, *Fixing the Climate: Strategies for an Uncertain World* (Princeton: Princeton University Press, 2022).

Martin Sandbu, *The Economics of Belonging: A Radical Plan to Win Back the Left Behind and Achieve Prosperity for All* (Princeton: Princeton University Press, 2020).

Donald Sassoon, *One Hundred Years of Socialism: The West European Left in the Twentieth Century* (London: I. B. Tauris, 1997).

G. R. Searle, *The Quest for National Efficiency: A Study in British Politics and British Political Thought, 1899-1914* (Oxford: Blackwell, 1971).

Andrew Shonefield, *Modern Capitalism: The Changing Behaviour of Public & Private Power* (Oxford: Oxford University Press, 1965).

Robert Skidelsky, *John Maynard Keynes: Hopes Betrayed, 1883-1920* (London: Macmillan, 1983).

_____, *John Maynard Keynes: The Economist as Saviour, 1920-1937* (London: Macmillan, 1992).

_____, *John Maynard Keynes: Fighting for Britain, 1937-1946* (London: Macmillan, 2000).

Quin Slobodian, *Crack-Up Capitalism: Market Radicals, and the Dream of a World without Democracy* (London: Allen Lane, 2023).

Daniel Susskind, *A World Without Work: Technology, Automation and How We Should Respond* (London: Allen Lane, 2020).

A. J. P. Taylor, *English History, 1914-1945* (Oxford: Oxford University Press, 1965).

Nick Thomas-Symonds, *Harold Wilson: The Winner* (London: Weidenfeld & Nicholson, 2022).

Polly Toynbee, *An Uneasy Inheritance: My Family and Other Radicals* (London: Atlantic Books, 2023).

Mary L. Trump, *Too Much and Never Enough: How My Family Created the World's Most Dangerous Man* (New York: Simon & Schuster, 2021).

Robert Verkaik, *Posh Boys: How the English Public Schools Ruin Britain* (London: Oneworld, 2022).

John Vincent, *The Formation of the Liberal Party, 1857-1868* (London: Constable, 1966).

Duncan Weldon, *Two Hundred Years of Muddling Through* (London: Abacus, 2021).

Chris Williams, *Democratic Rhondda, Politics and Society 1885-1951* (Cardiff: University of Wales Press, 1996).

Martin Wolf, *The Crisis of Democratic Capitalism* (London: Penguin, 2023).

Bob Woodward, *Fear: Trump in the White House* (New York: Simon & Schuster, 2018).

_____, *Rage* (New York: Simon & Schuster, 2020).

Novels

Wilfred Fienburgh, *No Love for Johnnie* (London: Hutchinson, 1959).

William Morris, *A Dream of John Ball* (London: Reeves & Turner, 1888).

Ayn Rand, *The Fountainhead* (Indianapolis: Bobbs Merrill, 1943).

_____, *Atlas Shrugged* (New York: Random House, 1957).

Robert Tressell, *The Ragged-Trousered Philanthropists* (London: Grant Richards, 1914).

Reference works

D. E. Butler, *The British General Election of 1951* (London: Macmillan, 1952).

_____, *The British General Election of 1955* (London: Macmillan, 1955).

D. E. Butler and Richard Rose, *The British General Election of 1959* (London: Macmillan, 1960).

D. E. Butler and Anthony King, *The British General Election of 1964* (London: Macmillan, 1965).

——————————————————————, *The British General Election of 1966* (London: Macmillan, 1966).

D. E. Butler and Michael Pinto-Duschinsky, *The British General Election of 1970* (London: Macmillan, 1971).

D. E. Butler and Dennis Kavanagh, *The British General Election of February, 1974* (London: Macmillan, 1974).

——————————————————————, *The British General Election of October, 1974* (London: Macmillan, 1975).

——————————————————————, *The British General Election of 1979* (London: Macmillan, 1979).

——————————————————————, *The British General Election of 1983* (London: Macmillan, 1984).

——————————————————————, *The British General Election of 1987* (London: Macmillan, 1988).

——————————————————————, *The British General Election of 1992* (London: Macmillan, 1992).

——————————————————————, *The British General Election of 1997* (London: Macmillan, 1997).

——————————————————————, *The British General Election of 2001* (London: Macmillan, 2001).

——————————————————————, *The British General Election of 2005* (London: Palgrave Macmillan, 2005).

Robert Ford, Tim Bale, Will Jennings and Paula Surridge, *The British General Election of 2019* (London: Palgrave Macmillan, 2020).

Dennis Kavanagh and Phil Cowley, *The British General Election of 2010* (London: Palgrave Macmillan, 2010).

——————————————————————, *The British General Election of 2015* (London: Palgrave Macmillan, 2015).

——————————————————————, *The British General Election of 2017* (London: Palgrave Macmillan, 2018).

R. B. McCallum and Alison Readman, *The British General Election of 1945* (Oxford: Oxford University Press, 1947).

Herbert Nicholas, *The British General Election of 1950* (London: Macmillan, 1951).

OECD Corporate Governance Factbook 2021 (Paris: OECD, 2021).

Who's Who, and Who Was Who (London: A. & C. Black, 2023).

Robert Ford, Tim Bale, Will Jennings and Paula Surridge, *The British General Election of 2019* (London: Palgrave Macmillan, 2020).

R. B. McCallum and Alison Readman, *The British General Election of 1945* (Oxford: Oxford University Press, 1947).

Herbert Nicholas, *The British General Election of 1950* (London: Macmillan, 1951).

OECD Corporate Governance Factbook 2021 (Paris: OECD, 2021).

Who's Who, and Who Was Who (London: A. & C. Black, 2023).

Pamphlets and papers

The Story of Robert Owen, 1771-1858: A Brief Guide to His Life and Work (Lanark: New Lanark Conservation Trust, 1997).

Torsten Bell, Tom Clark, Emily Fry, Gavin Kelly and Greg Thwaites, *Ending Stagnation – A New Economic Strategy for Britain*, The Economy 2030 Inquiry (Resolution Foundation/Centre for Economic Performance, London, 2023).

Aditi Bhutoria, *Economic Returns to Education in the United Kingdom* (London: Foresight – Government Office for Science, 2016).

Tony Blair, *Let us Face the Future*, Fabian Pamphlet No. 571 (London: Fabian Society, 1995).

Derek Bosworth, Luke Bosworth, Ha Bui, Jeisson Cardenas-Rubio, Rosie Day, Jude Hillary, Xinru Lin, Shyamoli Patel, Daniel Seymour, Chris Thoung and Rob Wilson, *The Skills Imperative 2035: Occupational Outlook – Long-Run Employment Prospects for the UK* (Slough: National Foundation for Educational Research, 2023).

Anthony Breach and Stuart Bridgett, *Centralisation Nation: Britain's System of Local Government and its Impact on the National Economy* (London: Centre for Cities, 2022).

Molly Broome, Ian Mulheirn and Simon Pittaway, *Peaked Interest? What Higher Interest Rates Mean for the Size and Distribution of Britain's Household Wealth* (London: Resolution Foundation, 2023).

Valerie Cerra, Ruy Lama and Norman Loayza, *Links Between Growth,*

Inequality, and Poverty: A Survey (Washington D.C.: International Monetary Fund, 2021).

Martin-Brehm Christensen, Christian Hallum, Alex Maitland, Quentin Parrinello and Chiara Putaturo, *Survival of the Richest: How We Must Tax the Super-Rich Now to Fight Inequality* (London: Oxfam, 2023).

Mike Brewer, Emily Fry and Lalitha Try, *The Living Standards Outlook 2023* (London: Resolution Foundation, 2023).

Cela Cebula, Aleks Collingwood, Rachelle Earwaker, Joseph Elliott, Peter Matejic, Isabel Taylor and Andrew Wenham, *UK Poverty 2023: The Essential Guide to Understanding Poverty in the UK* (York: Joseph Rowntree Foundation, 2023).

Patrick Diamond, Ed Miliband, Will Hutton et al., *The Challenge Ahead for Starmer's Labour: How to Understand the 1997 'Project'* (London: Mile End Institute, 2022).

Duncan Gallie, Alan Felstead, Francis Green and Golo Henseke, *Participation at work in Britain. First findings from the Skills and Employment Survey 2017* (London: Centre for Learning and Life Chances in Knowledge Economies and Societies, 2018).

Lindsay Judge and Hannah Slaughter, *Enforce for good: Effectively enforcing labour market rights in the 2020s and beyond* (London: Resolution Foundation, April 2023).

Jeegar Kakkad, *Transparency, Accountability, Predictability: Protecting National Security Through the UK's Foreign-Takeover Regime* (London: Tony Blair Institute for Global Change, 2023).

Jeegar Kakkad, Martin Madsen and Michael Tory, *Investing in the Future: Boosting Savings and Prosperity in the UK* (London: Tony Blair Institute for Global Change, 2023).

Roderick McInnes, *General Election 2019: Turning Votes into Seats* (London: House of Commons, 2020).

Julianna Oliveira-Cunha, Jesse Kozler, Pablo Shah, Gregory Thwaites and Anna Valero, *Business time: How ready are UK firms for the decisive decade?*, The Economy 2030 Inquiry (London: Resolution Foundation/ Centre for Economic Performance, November 2021).

Ben Paterson, *Addressing In-Work Poverty: The EU Minimum Wage*

Directive and Collective Bargaining (Edinburgh: European Futures, 2021).

Jill Rutter, Bill Dodwell, Paul Johnson, George Crozier, John Cullinane, Alice Lilly and Euan McCarthy, *Better Budgets: Making Tax Policy Better* (London: Chartered Institute of Taxation/Institute for Fiscal Studies/ Institute for Government, 2017).

Tom Sasse and Sophie Metcalfe, *Tackling Obesity: Improving Policy Making on Food and Health* (London: Institute for Government, 2023).

Stuart White and Niki Seth-Smith, *Democratic Wealth: Building a Citizens' Economy* (London: openDemocracy, 2014).

Greg Thwaites and Daniel Tomlinson, *Stagnation Nation: Navigating a Route to a Fairer and More Prosperous Britain – Interim Report of the Economy 2030 Enquiry* (London: Resolution Foundation, 2022).

Nicholas Timmins and Beccy Baird, *The Covid-19 Vaccination Programme: Trials, Tribulations and Successes* (London: King's Fund, 2022).

Giles Wilkes, *Business Investment: Not Just One Big Problem* (London: The Institute for Government, 2022).

Chapters

John Maynard Keynes, 'The End of Laissez-faire', in John Manard Keynes, *Collected Writings Vol IX*, (Cambridge: Cambridge University Press, 1976); originally published by the Hogarth Press in July 1926.

A. J. P. Taylor, 'The War Aims of the Allies in the First World War', in Richard Pares and A. J. P. Taylor (eds), *Essays Presented to Sir Lewis Namier* (London: Macmillan, 1956), pp. 475-505.

Articles (also see Notes)

'Full text: Theresa May's conference speech', *Guardian*, 7 October 2002, https://www.theguardian.com/politics/2002/oct/07/conservatives2002. conservatives1.

'Margaret Thatcher: A Life in Quotes', *Guardian*, 8 April 2013, https://www. theguardian.com/politics/2013/apr/08/margaret-thatcher-quotes.

'Over £3 billion in unspent apprenticeship levy lost to Treasury "black hole" new data reveal', *IPPR*, 27 July 2022, https://www.ippr.org/news-and-media/press-releases/over-3-billion-in-unspent-apprenticeship-levy-lost-to-treasury-black-hole-new-data-reveal.

'The Scale of Economic Equality in the UK', *The Equality Trust*, [n.d. 2022] https://equalitytrust.org.uk/scale-economic-inequality-uk.

Tim Adams, 'When McKinsey Comes to Town: The Hidden Influence of the World's Most Powerful Consulting Firm', *Guardian*, 31 October 2022.

Nur Ahmed, Muntasir Wahed and Neil Thompson, 'The growing influence of industry in AI research', *Science*, 379/6635 (March 2023), pp. 884-886.

Alex Bell, Raj Chetty, Xavier Jaravel, Neviana Petkova and John Van Reenen, 'Who Becomes an Inventor in America? The Importance of Exposure to Innovation', *Quarterly Journal of Economics*, 134:2 (2019), pp. 647–713.

Mark Bevir, 'New Labour: A Study in Ideology', *British Journal of Politics and International Relations*, 2/3 (2000), pp. 277-301.

Jack Blanchard, 'David Cameron and George Osborne would not build council houses because it would create Labour voters', *Daily Mirror*, 2 September 2016.

Craig Brown, 'Loyal to several faults: "Two Lives: The Political and Business Career of Edward du Cann"', *Spectator*, 23 September 1995.

Alexander Burns, 'Liz Truss Crashes the (Republican) Party', *Politico*, 30 January 2023, https://www.politico.com/news/magazine/2023/01/30/liz-truss-republican-party-00080280.

Mattha Busby, 'Labour calls for investigation over funding for Robert Jenrick's constituency', *Guardian*, 10 October 2020.

Nicholas Capaldi, 'Mill and Socialism', *The Tocqueville Review/La revue Tocqueville,* Vol 33, No 1 (2012), pp. 125-144.

Diane Coyle, 'Does the BBC Offer a Model for Public Service Digital Platforms?', *Bennett Institute for Public Services*, 17 January 2022, https://www.bennettinstitute.cam.ac.uk/blog/bbc-licence-fee/.

Michael Deacon, 'In a world of post-truth politics, Andrea Leadsom will make the perfect PM', *Daily Telegraph*, 6 July 2016, https://www.telegraph.co.uk/news/2016/07/09/in-a-world-of-post-truth-politics-andrea-leadsom-will-make-the-p.

Alex Edmans, 'Blockholder Trading, Market Efficiency, and Managerial Myopia', *Journal of Finance*, 64:6 (December 2009), pp. 2481-2513.

Thiemo Fetzer, 'Did Austerity cause Brexit?', *American Economic Review*, 109:11 (November 2019), pp. 3849-3886.

Francis Fukuyama, 'The End of History?', *The National Interest*, 16 (Summer 1989), pp. 3-18.

Anna Gross, Amy Borrett and Peter Foster, 'Britons squeezed out of top universities by lucrative overseas students', *Financial Times*, 21 July 2023.

Andrea Goettler, Anna Grosse and Diana Sonntag, 'Productivity Loss Due to Overweight and Obesity: A Systematic Review of Indirect Costs' *BMJ Open*, 7:10 (2017), https://www.ncbi.nlm.nih.gov/pmc/articles/PMC5640019/.

Christian Hilber, 'In the United Kingdom, homeownership has fallen while renting is on the rise', *Brookings Institution*, 20 April 2021, https://www.brookings.edu/essay/uk-rental-housing-markets/.

Andy Haldane, 'The case for rethinking fiscal rules is overwhelming', *Financial Times*, 16 May 2023.

Laurent Itti and Pierre Baldi, 'Bayesian Surprise Attracts Human Attention', *Vision Research*, 49:10 (June 2009), pp. 1295-1306.

Michael C. Jensen, 'Value Maximization, Stakeholder Theory, and the Corporate Objective Function', *Business Ethics Quarterly*, 12:2 (April 2002), pp. 235-256.

Richard Johnstone, 'Civil Service "Infantilised" by Use of Consultants, Cabinet Office Minister Says', *Civil Service World*, 30 September 2020, https://www.civilserviceworld.com/professions/article/civil-service-infantilised-by-use-of-consultants-says-cabinet-office-minister.

Geoffrey Kabaservice and Sam Tanenhaus, 'The Man Behind the Modern Conservative Movement, with Sam Tanenhaus', *Niskan Center*, 17 March 2021.

Eric Kaufmann, 'It's NOT the economy, stupid: Brexit as a story of personal values', *LSE Politics and Policy blog*, 7 July 2016, https://blogs.lse.ac.uk/politicsandpolicy/personal-values-brexit-vote/.

Douglas Key, 'Interview: Margaret Thatcher – "No Such thing as Society"', *Woman's Own*, 23 September 1987.

Catherine Lough, 'Private schools see bigger fall in top A-level grades than state sector', *Telegraph*, 18 August 2022.

Jack Newman, David Richards, Andy Westwood and Patrick Diamond, 'Local Democracy is Essential for Effective Decentralisation in England', *LSE Politics and Policy blog*,

9 May 2023, https://blogs.lse.ac.uk/politicsandpolicy/
local-democracy-is-essential-for-effective-decentralisation-in-england/.

Michael Pinto-Duschinsky, 'From Fear of Democracy to Political
Expediency: Lord Salisbury and the Second and Third Reform Acts',
Revue Française de Civilisation Britannique, 8:3 (1967), pp. 65-75.

Susan Schmidt and James V. Grimaldi, 'Nonprofit Groups Funneled Money
for Abramoff', *Washington Post*, 25 June 2006.

Rachel Millard, Rachel and Matt Oliver, 'Inside the "crazy" decisions that
left Britain with no gas storage and vulnerable to Putin', *Daily Telegraph*,
14 August 2022.

Chengcheng Shao, Giovanni Luca Ciampaglia, Onur Varol, Kai-Cheng
Yang, Alessandro Flammini and Filippo Menczer, 'The Spread of Low-
Credibility Content by Social Bots', *Nature Communication*, 9:4787
(November 2018), https://www.nature.com/articles/s41467-018-06930-7.

PA Media, 'A&E delays causing up to 500 deaths a week, says senior medic',
Guardian (1 Jan. 2023).

Richard Partington, 'UK economy in growth 'doom loop' after decades of
underinvestment', *Guardian*, 20 June 2023.

Thomas Pope, Gemma Tetlow, Stuart Hoddinott, Olly Bartrum
and Jeremy Pattison, 'Six Things We Learned from the Autumn
Statement', Institute for Government website, 22 November
2023, https://www.instituteforgovernment.org.uk/comment/
six-things-look-out-2023-autumn-statement.

Valentina Romei, 'UK renters five times more likely to struggle financially
than homeowners', *Financial Times*, 14 July 2023.

Robert J. Shiller, 'Engineering Financial Stability', *Project Syndicate*,
18 January 2010, https://www.project-syndicate.org/commentary/
engineering-financial-stability-2010-01?barrier=accesspaylog.

Carl Shoben, 'New poll: public strongly backing public ownership of energy
and key utilities', *Survation*, 15 August 2022, https://www.survation.com/
new-poll-public-strongly-backing-public-ownership-of-energy-and-key-
utilities/.

H. A. Simon, 'Rational choice and the structure of the environment',
Psychological Review, 63:2 (1956), pp. 129-138.

Joe Simpson, 'The Power of "Usness"', in Fiona Spotswood (ed.), 'Special Issue:
Beyond Behaviour Change', *Social Business*, 7 (3-4), (2017), pp. 293-312.

Anna Stansbury, Dan Turner, Dan and Ed Balls, 'Tackling the UKs regional inequality: binding constraints and areas for policy intervention', *Contemporary Social Science* (August 2023), pp. 318-356.

Christina Starmans, Mark Sheskin and Paul Bloom, 'Why People Prefer Unequal Societies', *Nature Human Behaviour*, 1 (April 2017).

Seth Thévoz, 'Want a Seat in the House of Lords? Be Tory Treasurer and Donate £3 Million', *openDemocracy*, 6 November 2021, https://www.opendemocracy.net/en/dark-money-investigations/ want-a-seat-in-the-house-of-lords-be-tory-treasurer-and-donate-3m/.

Richard John Tyler, 'Victim of our history', *Contemporary British History*, 20:3 (2006), pp. 461-476.

John Van Reenen, Howard Reed, and Lorraine Dearden, 'The Impact of Training on Productivity and Wages: Evidence from British Panel Data', *Oxford Bulletin of Economics and Statistics*, 68:4 (2006), pp. 397-421.

Soroush Vosoughi, Deb Roy and Sinan Aral, 'The Spread of True and False News Online', *Science*, 359:6380 (March 2018), pp. 1146-1151.

Dan Welsby, James Price, Steve Pye and Paul Ekins, 'Unextractable Fossil Fuels in a 1.5°C World', *Nature*, 597 (September 2021), pp. 230-4.

Andrew Whiffin, 'Lex In-Depth: Why is the UK Stock Market So Cheap?', *Financial Times*, 5 March 2022.

John Williamson, 'Development and the "Washington Consensus"', *World Development*, 21 (1993), pp. 1329-1336.

Martin Wolf, 'British politicians owe voters some candour on tax', *Financial Times*, 17 September 2023.

Stewart Wood, 'Why "Indicative Planning" Failed: British Industry and the Formation of the National Economic Development Council', *Twentieth Century British History*, 11:4 (2000), pp. 431–459.

Film and television
Best of Enemies, dir. Morgan Neville (2015).
Firing Line with William F. Buckley, dir. various (1966-1999).
The Mayfair Set, dir. Adam Curtis (1998).
Wall Street, dir. Oliver Stone (1987).

Manuscript
John Bowers, draft manuscript of forthcoming book 'Downward Spiral:

Collapsing Public Standards and How to Restore Them', due from Manchester University Press, 2024.

Theses
Richard John Tyler, '"Victims of Our History": The Labour Party and *In Place of Strife*, 1968 to 1969', PhD thesis, Queen Mary College, University of London (2004).

Talks
David Miliband, speech to the Hay Book Festival, 27 May 2023.
Baroness Minouche Shafik, 'What we owe each other: a new social contract', IFS Annual Lecture, 16 November 2022.

Working papers and resources
'International Journey Time Benchmarking: Strategic Road Networks', Office of Rail and Road, 23 November 2017, https://www.orr.gov.uk/sites/default/files/om/international-journey-time-benchmarking-analysis-report-2017-11-23.pdf.

'Levelling Up the United Kingdom: White Paper' (London: HMSO, 2022).

'The Purpose Tapes: Purpose Driven Leaders in Their Own Words' (London: Purposeful Company, 2021).

Lucy Bannister, Peter Matejic, Iain Porter, Daisy Sands, Katie Schmuecker, Andrew Wenham, Rachel Bull, Ieuan Ferrer and Anna Hughes, *An Essentials Guarantee: Reforming Universal Credit to ensure we can all afford the essentials in hard times* (Joseph Rowntree Foundation, London, February 2023).

Beauhurst, 'UK Unicorn Companies', September 2022, https://www.beauhurst.com/research/unicorn-companies/

British Red Cross and Co-op, *Trapped in a Bubble: An Investigation into Triggers for Loneliness in the UK* (Kantar Public, London, December 2016).

Jagit S. Chadha and Issam Samiri, 'Macroeconomic Perspectives on Productivity', The Productivity Institute working paper no. 030, 2022, https://www.productivity.ac.uk/wp- content/uploads/2022/12/WP030-Macroeconomic-Perspectives-FINAL-131222.pdf.

Raj Chetty, Matthew O. Jackson, Theresa Kuchler, Johannes Stroebel,

Abigail Hiller, Sarah Oppenheimer and the Opportunity Insights Team, *Social Capital and Economic Mobility* (Opportunity Insights, London, August 2022), https://opportunityinsights.org/wp-content/uploads/2022/07/socialcapital_nontech.pdf.

Climate Change Committee, *Progress in Reducing Emissions: 2023 Progress Report to Parliament* (28 June 2023), https://www.theccc.org.uk/publication/2023-progress-report-to-parliament/.

Whitney Crenna-Jennings, *Key drivers of the disadvantage gap: literature review. Education in England: Annual Report 2018,* (London: Education Policy Institute, 2018).

Pat Dade and Les Higgins, 'Values Modes' (1973).

Elaine Drayton, Christine Farquharson, Kate Ogden, Luke Sibieta, Imran Tahir and Ben Waltmann, *Annual Report on Education Spending in England: 2022* (London: Institute for Fiscal Studies, 12 December 2022).

Raphael Espinoza, Julian Gambola-Arbelaez and Mouhamamadou Syl, 'The Fiscal Multiplier of Public Investment: The Role of Corporate Balance Sheet', IMF Working Paper: Fiscal Affairs Department (September 2020).

Fairness Foundation, 'Fairly United: What Britons Think about Inequality and Fairness' Fairness Foundation website, 3 July 2023, https://fairnessfoundation.com/fairly-united.

European Parliament, 'Artificial intelligence: How does it work, why does it matter, and what can we do about it?', Panel for the Future of Science and Technology, June 2020.

Christine Farquharson, Luke Sibieta, Imran Tahir and Ben Waltmann *IFS fourth annual report on education spending, 2021, IFS Report R204,* (London: Institute for Fiscal Studies, London, November 2021).

Marshall Ganz, 'What Is Public Narrative?: Self, Us & Now' (Public Narrative Worksheet, Harvard Library Office for Scholarly Communication, 2009).

Simon Griffiths, 'The Future of Socialism Sixty Years On', paper delivered to 'The Crosland Legacy: The Future of British Social Democracy' conference at Queen Mary University of London, 7 December 2016.

Ricky Kanabar and Paul Gregg, *Intergenerational wealth transmission and mobility in Great Britain: what components of wealth matter? UCL Working Paper No.22-01* (UCL Centre for Education Policy and Equalising Opportunities, London, 2022).

Kieran Larkin, 'Regional Development Agencies: the facts', Centre for Cities, (December 2009).

Josh Martin, 'Experimental comparisons of infrastructure across Europe: May 2019', Office for National Statistics (May 2019), https://www.ons.gov.uk/economy/economicoutputandproductivity/productivitymeasures/articles/experimentalcomparisonsofinfrastructureacrosseurope/may2019.

Roderick McIness,'General Election 2019: Turning votes into seats', House of Commons Library, January 2020, https://commonslibrary.parliament.uk/general-election-2019-turning-votes-into-seats/.

Paul Mortimer-Lee and Adrian Pabst (eds), *Covid-19 and Productivity Impact and Implications: NIESR Occasional Paper LXII* (National Institute of Economic and Social Research, London, 2022).

John Muellbauer, 'Why we need a green land value tax and how to design it', INET Oxford Working Paper No. 2023-12 (2023).

National Institute of Economic and Social Research, 'UK Economy Beset By Sluggish Growth and High Inflation, NIESR Economic Outlook', NIESR website, 11 May 2023, https://www.niesr.ac.uk/publications/uk-economy-sluggish-growth-high-inflation?type=ukeconomic-outlook.

'UK Heading Towards Five Years of Lost Economic Growth', NIESR website, August 2023, https://www.niesr.ac.uk/publications/uk-heading-towards-five-years-lost-economic-growth.

Justine Piddington, Simon Nicol, Helen Garrett and Matthew Custard, *The Housing Stock of The United Kingdom*, (BRE Trust, London, 2021).

The Purposeful Company, *The Purpose Tapes: purpose driven leaders in their own words*, Purposeful Company website, 9 May 2021, https://thepurposefulcompany.org/wp-content/uploads/2021/05/TPC_The-Purpose-Tapes_May21.pdf.

The Purposeful Company, *Advancing Purpose: How purposeful companies and investors can make better common cause*, Purposeful company website, 23 February 2023, https://thepurposefulcompany.org/wp-content/uploads/2023/02/TPC_Report-Advancing-Purpose_23FEB2023.pdf.

Dani Rodrik and Charles Sabel, 'Building a Good Jobs Economy', draft working paper, April 2019, https://drodrik.scholar.harvard.edu/files/dani-rodrik/files/building_a_good_jobs_economy_april_2019_rev.pdf.

Stéphane Sorbe, Peter Gal, Giuseppe Nicoletti and Christina Timiliotis
'Digital Dividend: Policies to Harness the Productivity Potential of
Digital Technologies', *OECD Economic Policy Papers,* no. 26 (OECD
Publishing, Paris, February 2019).

Sam Tuckett, Emily Hunt, David Robinson and Robbie Cruikshanks,
Covid-19 and disadvantage gaps in England 2021 (London: Education
Policy Institute, December 2022).

Samuel Watling and Anthony Breach, *The Housebuilding Crisis: The UK's 4
million missing homes'* (Centre for Cities, London, 23 February 2023).

Online sources consulted
'A decade of cuts: Legal aid in tatters', Law Society press release, 31 March
2023, https://www.lawsociety.org.uk/contact-or-visit-us/pressoffice/
press-releases/a-decade-of-cuts-legal-aid-in-tatters.

'A quarter of GP and general practice nursing posts could be vacant in 10
years', press release, Health Foundation website, 25 July 2022, https://
www.health.org.uk/news-and-comment/news/a-quarter-of-gp-and-
general-practicenursing-posts-could-be-vacant-in-10-years.

British Social Attitudes survey, National Centre for Social Research, https://
bsa.natcen.ac.uk/.

Alan Bogg, 'Building worker power: Essays on collective rights 20
years after the Wilson and Palmer case established the right to
be represented by a trade union', Trade Union Congress website,
July 2022, https://www.tuc.org.uk/research-analysis/reports/
building-worker-power?page=4.

Georgia Brett, Heidi Wilson and Andreas Christogi, 'Deaths due to
COVID-19, registered in England and Wales: 2021, Data and analysis
from Census 2021', Office for National Statistics, 1 July 2022.

Sarah Cattan and Christine Farquharson, 'At their peak, Sure Start centres
prevented 13,000 hospitalisations a year among 11- to 15-year-olds', IFS
Press Release, 16 August 2021. See also https://ifs.org.uk/news/their-
peaksure-start-centres-prevented-13000-hospitalisations-year-among-11-
15-year-olds.

'Deaths Due to Covid-19, Registered in England and Wales:
2021', Office for National Statistics, https://www.ons.gov.uk/

peoplepopulationandcommunity/birthsdeathsandmarriages/deaths/
articles/deathsregisteredduetocovid19/2021.

Electoral Calculus, 'Three-D Politics 2021', March 2021, https://www.
electoralcalculus.co.uk/pol3d_2021.html.

Electoral Commission, 'Report on the May 2023 local elections
in England', Electoral Commission website, September 2023,
https://www.electoralcommission.org.uk/research-reports-and-
data/our-reports-and-data-past-elections-and-referendums/
report-may-2023-local-elections-england.

'Forum: How to Fix the Climate', *Boston Review*, https://www.bostonreview.
net/forum/charles-sabel-david-g-victor-how-fix-climate/.

'Growth Strategy & Innovation', McKinsey website, https://www.mckinsey.
com/capabilities/strategy-and-corporate-finance/how-we-help-clients/
growth-strategy-and-innovation.

Chris Hanretty, 'The Pork Barrel Politics of the Towns Fund', *Political
Quarterly* blog, 6 May 2021, https://politicalquarterly.org.uk/blog/
the-pork-barrel-politics-of-the-towns-fund.

'Health inequalities: our position', King's Fund website, 29 September 2021,
https://www.kingsfund.org.uk/projects/positions/health-inequalities.

'Insecure Work: Why Employment Rights Need an Overhaul', TUC, https://
www.tuc.org.uk/sites/default/files/2022-07/InsecureWork.pdf.

'Investment in Intangible Assets in the UK by Industry: 2019',
Office for National Statistics, https://www.ons.gov.uk/
economy/economicoutputandproductivity/output/bulletins/
investmentinintangibleassetsintheukbyindustry/2019.

Ministry of Justice, 'Criminal court statistics quarterly: January
to March 2023, National Statistics' UK government website (29
June 2023). See also https://www.gov.uk/government/statistics/
criminal-court-statistics-quarterly-january-to-march-2023.

National Youth Corps website, https://www.uknationalyouthcorps.co.uk/.

Richard Murphy, 'The Taxing Wealth Report 2024', Tax Research, 6
September 2023, https://www.taxresearch.org.uk/Blog/2023/09/06/
launching-thetaxing-wealth-report-2024/.

'National Wealth Surplus: Seven Routes to Revenue', Fairness
Foundation (May 2023). See also https://fairnessfoundation.com/
nationalwealthsurplus/seven-routes-to-revenue.

'OTC Derivatives Statistics at End – December 2022', Bank for International Settlements, https://www.bis.org/publ/otc_hy2305.htm.

'Proportion of Employees Whose Pay and Conditions Were Agreed in Negotiations Between the Employer and a Trade Union in the United Kingdom from 1996 to 2022, by Sector', Statista, https://www.statista.com/statistics/287297/uk-collective-agreement-coverage/.

The Purposeful Company, www.thepurposefulcompany.org/.

'Share of owner occupied households in England from 2000 to 2022', Statista, 11 October 2023, https://www.statista.com/statistics/286503/englandpropportion-of-owner-occupied-households/.

'Social Capital Index: World Map 2022', Solability, https://solability.com/the-global-sustainable-competitiveness-index/the-index/social-capital.

'Tolpuddle Martyrs' website, https://www.tolpuddlemartyrs.org.uk/story.

'Total Derivatives Assets Held by Banks in the United Kingdom from the First Quarter of 2011 to the Fourth Quarter of 2020', Statista, 11 December 2023, https://www.statista.com/statistics/1214272/outstanding-derivatives-assets-banks-uk/.

'UK Unemployment Figures', Office for National Statistics, https://www.ons.gov.uk/employmentandlabourmarket/peoplenotinwork/unemployment.

'Universal Declaration of Human Rights at 70: 30 Articles on 30 Articles - Article 2', Office of the High Commissioner for Human Rights, https://www.ohchr.org/en/press-releases/2018/11/universal-declaration-human-rights-70-30-articles-30-articles-article-2?LangID=E&NewsID=23858.

Aidan Tolland, Olivia Garbutt and Mathieu Stafford, 'Workforce qualification levels across England and Wales data: Census 2021', Office for National Statistics website, 17 February 2023, https://www.ons.gov.uk/peoplepopulationandcommunity/educationandchildcare/datasets/workforcequalificationlevelsacrossenglandandwalesdatacensus2021.

'Workforce qualification levels across England and Wales data: Census 2021', Office for National Statistics, https://www.ons.gov.uk/peoplepopulationandcommunity/educationandchildcare/datasets/workforcequalificationlevelsacrossenglandandwalesdatacensus2021.

Index

Financial Times (newspaper) 4, 263, 283, 313
financialisation 256–8
Follow the Money (book) 306
Foot, Michael 73, 99, 193
Forging Ahead, Falling Behind and Fighting Back (book) 73
Fox News 49
Fractured (book) 325
Freddie Mac 33
Free Enterprise Group 87
Friedman, Milton 37, 42, 45, 47, 64, 66, 67, 70, 103, 103
Fukuyama, Francis 50
Full Employment in a Free Society (book) 174
future inequality and prosperity 217
Future Jobs Fund 2009 299
future mission 244–9
The Future of Socialism (book) 180

G

Gaitskell, Hugh 167, 178, 184, 186–7
Galbraith, J. K. 161
GB News 345, 346
Geddes, Eric 148
Geidt, Lord 15
General Electric Company (GEC) 189
General Theory of Employment, Interest and Money (book) 154, 164, 170
geopolitics 16–20
George VI, King 4
Gerstle, Gary 60
Gilda, George 45
Gingrich, Newt 42, 51, 55, 86
Gladstone, Herbert 138
Gladstone, William 18, 118, 134, 138

Gladstone–MacDonald Pact 1903 25, 138, 370
Glass-Steagall legislation 32, 52, 78
globalisation 16, 53, 79, 81
Going Big (book) 34
gold standard 26, 70, 78, 104, 110, 111, 119, 148, 151, 152, 156, 159, 160, 239, 242, 255, 341
Goldsmith, James 69
Goldwater, Barry 40, 41
Good Friday Agreement 5–6
The Good Jobs Strategy (book) 298
Gove, Michael 88, 89, 307, 342
Great Depression 31
The Great Transformation (book) 110
Greed Is Dead (book) 224
Green, Thomas Hill 129–31, 133, 142, 143, 145, 369
Green Party 370
Greenspan, Alan 40, 52
Greenwood, Arthur 172, 175
Grenfell Tower 14
The Guardian (newspaper) 132

H

Hacker, Jacob 53
Hague, William 81, 82
Haldane, Andy 222, 250
Halifax, Lord 172
Halpern, David 277
Hancock, Matt 337
Hands, Greg 340
Hannan, Daniel 86
Hanretty, Chris 248
Hanson, Lord 69
Hardie, Keith 134, 136, 137, 138, 139, 142, 150
Harding, Dido 342
Harris, Kenneth 184

Tory governments
  and industrial relations 192–3
  policy reforms 181
  and post-war dominance 147
Tory Party 6, 81
  see also Conservative Party
Toynbee, Arnold 131
Toynbee, Polly 136
Trade Disputes Act 1906 139, 149, 190
The Trade Union Question 190–3
trade unions 28, 45, 48, 57, 64, 66, 67, 73–4, 126, 128, 137–8, 145, 157–8
  and capitalism 292
  collective bargaining 291–4
  and the Labour Party 137
  and the Liberal Party 137
Trades Union Congress (TUC) 138, 191
Treasury 340–1, 343, 353
Treatise on Money (book) 154
Tressell, Robert 140
Trump, Donald 19, 40, 49, 56–61, 348–9, 368
Truss, Liz 2–3, 6, 29, 40, 87, 92–3, 94, 218–19, 245, 362
Trussell Trust 316
Turner, Adair 257
The Tyranny of Nostalgia (book) 76

U

UK Independence Party (UKIP) 13, 20, 83, 88, 90, 91
UK Infrastructure Bank (UKIB) 249–50, 255, 261–2
UK Office for Science 304
Ukraine 345
  Russian invasion of 18, 19, 20, 22, 53, 225, 247, 296, 318

UN Security Council 4, 369
UN Sustainable Development Goals 272
United Nations 176
Universal Credit 294–6, 317
Universal Declaration of Human Rights 37
University of Chicago 39
Unto This Last (book) 119
USA
  capitalism, alternatives to 46
  capitalism, benefits and expectations of 30–2, 34, 36, 45, 57
  and communism 35–6
  free-market economics 29
  geopolitical shift 16–18
  neoliberalism 42–4, 55, 59–60, 61
  New Deal 16, 24, 26, 29–30, 31–4, 35, 36, 40, 41, 42, 44–7, 52, 52–3, 53, 54–5, 57, 59–61, 62, 78
    and capitalism 61
  Progressive Era 31
  racial discrimination 36–7
  Social Security Administration 33
  US Banking Act 1933 32
  Wall Street Crash 30, 78
    Britain's reaction to 157–61
  World War I, war declaration 146
Uxbridge by-election 348

V

Veblen, Thorsten 283
Verkaik, Robert 305
Victor, David 227
Vietnam war 43, 44
Voltaire 100
voluntarism 118, 127
Vote Leave 86, 88, 347